This book is simply essential reading for corporate executive leaders of all kinds—in the digital age. Responsible and resp stewardship of data and digital assets is the new corporate social responsibility. Through this book, Jeffrey Ritter continues to guide us through this amazing age of transition and opportunity, to better outcomes for companies, institutions, and, most importantly, individuals.

NUALA O'CONNOR,
President & CEO,
Center for Democracy & Technology

I don't know why Jeffrey came back from the future to teach us how to adapt to what's coming, but he did, and I am grateful. Thank you, Jeffrey.

PETER E. SAND, ESQ.,
Executive Director of Privacy,
MGM Resorts International

Jeffrey's ability to explain novel concepts is nothing short of extraordinary. In one two-hour lecture on payment systems, he not only expanded my understanding of digital trust and systems, but favorably altered the course of my future as a lawyer in a new direction. His thought-leadership in this space will transform the dialogue about governance in a digital world.

JULI GREENBERG,
Senior Vice President and Assistant General Counsel,
Citi Retail Services

Jeffrey has been, and continues to be, at the vanguard of connecting technology and the rule of law, always passionate and thinking globally. His book is a valued contribution toward our collective efforts to achieve digital trust across the cloud.

JIM REAVIS,
CEO, Cloud Security Alliance

Achieving Digital Trust should be the dog-eared companion for any intrepid entrepreneur or innovator who wishes to achieve the ever elusive key ingredient in their business or personal life—trust. The methodologies and strategies in this book build upon the human and emotional aspects of trust and create the path toward the possibility of actually achieving a sustainable digital infrastructure. If trust, as Jeffrey presents, can be viewed as a "chain of decisions," the first decision should be clear-acquire and consume this book!

MICHELLE FINNERAN DENNEDY,
Vice President, Cisco Systems,
Founder of The iDennedy Project,
and co-author of *The Privacy Engineer's Manifesto*

Trust, accuracy, and context are everything when it comes to Verifeed's success in translating insights from millions of social conversations into profitable and powerful outcomes. Jeffrey has created tools and insights that I know are game-changers for those companies and causes who know that building digital trust will spell the difference between profit and loss, fame or shame.

MELINDA WITTSTOCK,
Founder and CEO, Verifeed.com

Jeffrey's ground-breaking ideas fundamentally challenge the assumptions that underpin risk management and open the doors to a radically new way of looking at security—built on analysis and quantification of trust. This is a must-read for any security professional wanting to engage in shaping the future of the digital world.

DR. DAVID J. KING,
Visiting Fellow, Kellogg College,
University of Oxford

Jeffrey's treatise (and I don't call it that lightly) is a fascinating new view on trust and risk. This book matters not just to information security professionals or any other branch of IT, but for any professional where decision-making on less than complete information is required—in other words, all of us!

DAVID MORTMAN,
Chief Security Architect
and Distinguished Engineer, Dell

For the 25 years I have known him, Jeffrey has been a visionary, always staking out new approaches on the law and technology. This new book continues his quest to bring lawyers, corporate executives, risk managers and board members into the brave new world of digital trust. His unique paradigm breaks new ground and provides us with the opportunity to view our existing and future landscapes with new eyes. With *Achieving Digital Trust*, Jeffrey has cemented his legacy as a brave and revolutionary thinker in this amazing new world.

LAWRENCE J. CENTER,
Assistant Dean,
Georgetown University Law Center

From the Board Room to our modern day asymmetric battlefield, Jeffrey Ritter's *Achieving Digital Trust* will open eyes. It provides us with a reference model that management and software architects have been seeking. The survival of the Internet as we know it is currently at stake. This book provides a look into the transparency of 'Trust Decisions' and how ensuring digital truth will shape our global governance for decades to come.

PETER L. HIGGINS,
Managing Director & Chief Risk Officer,
1SecureAudit

Those things that no one wants to face are those most in need of attention. Trust is one of those things. Jeffrey provides a unique perspective on trust as a human value that has the potential to rock the structures of all our relationships in a humbling way that is overdue. This book is about digital trust, but so much more!

TRISH WHYNOT, D.C.ED.,
Author, Counselor

Jeffrey is a global authority on digital trust. He is one of the few people that understands where information security, risk and law converge, where they are headed and how they relate. This book breaks new ground and is a must-read for boards of directors and executive teams.

BOB WEST,
Managing Director, Careworks Tech

Ten pages into this book, you'll understand why author Jeffrey Ritter is described as "passionate," "inspiring," and "visionary" by his students at Oxford, Johns Hopkins and Georgetown. He embraces this topic of digital trust in all of his work and eloquently gets across why we should care about it. His book empowers us to know what we can do to keep ourselves and our organizations safe in cyberspace. Read it and reap.

SAM HORN, CEO of Intrigue Agency
and author of *Tongue Fu!* and *Got Your Attention?*

Civility begins with trust. In this digital world, Jeffrey Ritter has taken on the challenges of building and achieving trust with remarkable insight. His tools enable all of us, regardless of our roles, to collaborate, communicate and work together more effectively. *Achieving Digital Trust* empowers you to work, live, and thrive with greater civility and an enhanced level of professionalism.

SUE JACQUES,
The Civility CEO® and author of *What The Fork?*

As a landscape architect, I know the challenges of identifying, synthesizing, and navigating all of the rules required to create something functional, aesthetic, and valued. In this book, Jeffrey Ritter is giving all of us new tools with which to design, build, and use digital assets within the vast complexity of cyberspace. This is an exciting contribution to the architecture of our world.

BIBI GASTON, Landscape Architect
and author of *The Loveliest Woman in America: A Tragic Actress,
Her Lost Diaries, and Her Granddaughter's Search for Home*

ACHIEVING
DIGITAL TRUST

ACHIEVING DIGITAL TRUST

THE NEW RULES FOR BUSINESS AT THE SPEED OF LIGHT

To Matt:
Welcome to the digital trust revolution!
Toward the Future!

8/9/2016

JEFFREY RITTER

Achieving Digital Trust:
The New Rules for Business at the Speed of Light

©2015 by Jeffrey Ritter

Library of Congress Cataloging-in-Publication Data
Ritter, Jeffrey
     Achieving Digital Trust: The New Rules for Business at the Speed of Light / Jeffrey Ritter
p. cm.

ISBN: 978-0-9965990-0-9

Printed in the United States of America
22 21 20 19 18 17 16 15 |CS| 10 9 8 7 6 5 4 3 2 1

Editorial development and creative design support by Ascent:
www.itsyourlifebethere.com

Design by Peter Gloege | LOOK Design Studio

Graphic illustrations by Paul McTaggart

Content editing by Jane Kuhar and Lee McIntyre

Follow Jeffrey Ritter:
www.JeffreyRitter.com   jeffrey.ritter52   @Jeffrey_Ritter

This book is dedicated to my daughters,
Jordan Michelle and Chelsea Marie,
and their inspiring passion to make this a better world.

TABLE OF CONTENTS

PREFACE: The War on Trust 13

THE TRUST DECISION MODEL—PART I

1: The Global Demise of Risk Management 31

2: The Power of Trust 45

3: The Trust Decision Model from 40,000 Feet 59

4: Context Is Everything! 79

5: Describing the Circumstances and Resources 103

6: Classifying Resources 127

7: Drawing the Lines 161

8: Defining Work 179

9: Time, Money and the TDT 217

10: Dancing the Tango of Wealth and Trust 251

11: T Minus and Holding 275

DESIGNING DIGITAL TRUST—PART II

12: Introduction 289

13: Facing the Challenge of Digital Trust 293

14: The Velocity Principle 303

15: Bridging the Chasm of SIAM 333

16: The Rules for Composing Rules 357

17: The Digital Trust Design Principles 379

18: The Unified Rules Model 393

19: The Unified Information Model............................... 441

20: Creating Wealth with Digital Trust........................... 465

MANAGING & GOVERNING DIGITAL TRUST—PART III

21: Achieving and Sustaining Digital Trust 487

22: Achieving the Outcomes 491

23: The Trust Prism 501

24: Using the Trust Prism 527

25: Entering the War and Winning the Revolution 537

APPENDIX: Trust Decision Tools......................................549

GLOSSARY: Trust Vocabulary Terms 555

References and Additional Sources 565

Acknowledgements 571

Author Biography... 576

THE WAR ON TRUST

ACROSS THE WORLD, daily headlines confirm there is a global war for control of digital information. The targets are immense—Sony, Target, Boeing, JP Morgan, Chase, Home Depot, AT&T, eBay, Google, power utilities, airlines, and virtually every governmental agency in any nation. The targets are small—your credit card, your browsing history, your calls for taxi services, your health data, and your preferences for beer.

This war is being shaped by weapons of attack we have heard about—Stuxnet, Backoff, DDoS, Gauss, malware, sniffers, and eyeglasses that film you punching in ATM passwords. This war is being shaped by weapons of attack that have yet to be created, designed to exploit the weaknesses and vulnerabilities of new technologies that, themselves, have yet to be invented.

The objective in this war is simple—to gain control of the digital knowledge assets each of us seeks to use in the decisions we make every day:

Important decisions like picking the best schools for our children or choosing the doctor to perform life-altering surgery.

Small decisions like finding the gas station with the best prices.

"Bet it all" decisions that place a nation, a company, a division, an employee team, or the wealth saved across generations at risk—the decisions that leave you sweating bullets and not sleeping.

When the information you need to make decisions is controlled, the quality of your decision is controlled and the possible outcomes from which you can choose slip from your control. Where there is less information, your decisions become vulnerable. As an executive, an IT architect, an investment manager, an educational director, or even a parent, your job is to lead with good decisions. You want your decisions to be ones that others will follow. But those ambitions erode when those fighting the war to control digital information are winning.

In reading this book, you will explore and acquire an entirely new portfolio of tools and strategies to help shift the momentum of that war. As in any combat or battle, to succeed, it is essential for you to understand what is at stake. What we are facing is more than a war to control information. It is a war on our ability to trust information. Yes, a war on trust.

At every turn, you can sense that, somehow, the critical fabrics of trust that have been woven together for thousands of years and that allow us to live in social systems are unsteady, trembling, and fragile. It is as true in our national governments, corporate boardrooms, and compliance programs as it is in our interactions with sales clerks and neighbors. Decisions you take as a leader are questioned more intensely. As a team member, business analyst, armchair investor, or family financial officer, you have become more reluctant to accept the decisions of others. Blind faith is no longer an acceptable justification to lead others in a charge over the hill, or a basis on which you choose to follow others. Why is trust under attack at so many levels, across so many economies, and in so many routine, ordinary decisions through which we live our lives?

THE CURRENT PLAYING FIELD

The Internet, the embrace of cyberspace, and the ubiquitous presence of digital information in human society are making immense, positive contributions. In the simplest actions of our daily lives and in the most important decisions we make in business, in government, in education, and in choosing between war and peace, we have become reliant upon the availability and presence of digital information. As our reliance speeds into dependency and, in turn, addiction, there are two profound shifts occurring that are shaping the direction of this war on trust.

First, technology is compressing the time we have to make good decisions. The immediacy with which information can be accessed, the speed of communications, and the competitive pressures to make decisions NOW are carving tighter decision-making deadlines into everything we do. Automation is requiring you to make decisions faster. Global competition makes each decision you execute more consequential. The pressure to get to the next decision is exacerbated by the ease with which technology places information for the current decision at your fingertips.

There are two profound shifts occurring that are shaping the direction of this war on trust.

As a result, to act within the time constraints of deadlines, the presence of fiercer competition, and the looming threat of higher lost-opportunity costs, you have no choice—you must *presume* the trustworthiness of the information you acquire to make decisions. Deciding now requires you to acquire the information you need from the most accessible source, with zero time to ask the important questions: "Where did this information come from? Who put this report together? Has the data been confirmed to be accurate? Who actually authored the analysis? Is the history you are teaching my children objective? Does this bank statement reflect all of our deposits?"

Answering these types of questions is inherent to how we make good decisions. You seek information that serves as fuel for your decision. You work hard to validate that the information can be trusted. You calculate toward your decision, constantly evaluating whether the information holds up its reliability. But in today's 24/7/365, wired decision-making landscape, there is no time to ask those questions. Those controlling the information you need understand that pressure and require you to presume their digital information is trustworthy and reliable for making your decisions. Thus, to gain control of digital information is to succeed in imposing an enormous handicap—removing your ability to challenge its trustworthiness by asking the right questions.

Second, information technology has rapidly created a different kind of infrastructure through which information and knowledge can be stored. The Net is a global facility that never was designed for how we now use it—as a primary and essential repository for the knowledge of human experience. Cloud-based services, distributed storage systems, and server farms on every continent—all are locations in which the information you need for your decisions

Those controlling the information you need . . . require you to presume their digital information is trustworthy.

may be found. Yet, the custodians who operate these facilities are not the public library or local university; instead, a mind-boggling inventory of multiple, connected networks of service providers, application providers, contractors, sub-contractors, and agents—both human and automated—interconnect to support the global appetite for information through agreements, contracts, terms of service, and other rules of play into which you have had no input and the details of which you may never have knowledge.

In the 20th Century, companies kept their information assets under lock and key. In science, libraries curated and archived information and validated the authors and the bases of their research. Governments were trusted to preserve and keep accessible the vital records of those they governed. When you sought out information, you could trust the source. Today, that is the second shift—you no longer can presume the trustworthiness of the information sources. Indeed, you not only are asked to presume their reliability as sources of information; you also must presume their security as custodians engaged in collecting the surveillance, monitoring, and behavioral data about you, your family, and your company.

These two shifts are inexorable and serve as the best evidence of the momentum of the war. As the headlines now report on a daily basis, neither trust in digital information nor trust in the sources and custodians of digital information can be presumed.

For those of us who are decision makers, these are huge problems. With growing velocity, we are losing our ability to trust digital information to be factual, accurate, reliable, and authentic. But we also are losing something far more important—trust in the quality of our own decisions and our confidence in those we trust to make good decisions.

You no longer can presume the trustworthiness of the information sources.

THE BREAKDOWN OF TRUST

Whether in government, in business, in classrooms, or at the dinner table, the ubiquitous presence of digital assets and devices enables us to do something radical—immediately seek out information that allows us to challenge and evaluate our trust in the decisions of others we are expected to follow. So, in addition to your own decision process being shaken, so too are the evaluations others make to trust your decisions. If you are a business leader, IT executive, information security manager, systems architect, elected public official, educator or stay-at-home parent, you have surely felt the discomfort.

As soon as you announce a decision, someone is thumb-typing on a device to find information to validate or contradict you. A few clicks and your questioner has acquired data that enables that person to challenge your decision process, view it differently, or weigh it with less confidence. Admit it, you surely have done the same when you are on the other side of the table, hearing the decisions, opinions, or guidance of others—a superior officer, a corporate manager, a business partner, a teacher, or even a spouse.

Technology is empowering us with accessibility to information but undermining our effectiveness in how we use information to make decisions. The Net is delivering unprecedented immediacy in how we communicate decisions to our teams, yet empowering them to question the qualities of our decisions and, in turn, hold back their trust until they do so. We are at a tipping point that is very different than previously imagined. Rather than tipping forward in mass market adoption, we are somehow struggling, wavering, and uncertain about the directions in which to move.

As soon as you announce a decision, someone is thumb-typing on a device to find information to validate or contradict you.

It is really very simple. In the foreseeable future, we will not function as a global society without the Net and the immense digital resources and information assets of our society. The addiction is established—commerce, government, education, and our neighbors offer no option other than to require that we rely upon digital information in making decisions. But we will not function successfully if the war for control of those assets is lost. The battlefield, however, is the one on which trust is to be gained or lost—trust in the information we use, trust in the infrastructures that support us, and trust in the decisions we make in a digital world.

If we are to turn the tide in the war for control, and prevail in maintaining a digital infrastructure through which we can sustain societies and a functional, global economy, we must design and achieve trust in the digital information we use, trust in the infrastructure of the Net through which we live, and trust in the decisions we make in a digital world—we must build what I call *digital trust*.

WHAT IS DIGITAL TRUST?

Some years ago I began to study how we place our trust in digital things—networks, computers, systems, applications, and, of course, the information that is both the fuel and the output of their operation. In pursuing an understanding of digital trust, I learned that two far more difficult challenges first had to be conquered—I needed to figure out how we, as human beings, *decide* to trust, and I had to figure out how any of us makes decisions that *can* be trusted.

The questions rose up and multiplied:

Is trust just an emotion, a feeling that we sense and use like a crude compass to find our way from here to there?

How do we decide to trust the people in our lives, the tools we choose to perform our work, and the information we consume, whether in business, education, or entertainment?

How do we choose our employers or employees, supporting financial institutions, board members, or our governments?

How do we calculate the value we will pay for the products, services, and resources in which we place our trust every day in order to live our lives?

How do we lose trust in something or someone?

How does a leader gain the trust of those following, and how can that trust be lost?

Is trust merely the condition in which we live when we are not in fear of known risks, a default setting that is hard-wired into how we think?

Uncovering the answers to those questions about how we decide to trust, and how we make decisions that can be trusted, came first. Only then could I proceed to ask and try to answer the additional, increasingly complex questions about how we might build and achieve *digital trust*.

What changes when you are deciding to trust a machine, a mobile device, a game, or a business application?

How do you decide to trust digital information that is intangible and cannot be lifted, opened, or flipped through?

What questions do you need to ask to conclude that trust is justified in both digital information and the sources from which you acquire the information?

How do you make trust decisions about people, associations, tools, or their value when the information upon which you will rely is increasingly digital and intangible?

In a global culture in which digital trust is under attack and degrading, how can you build and engender old-fashioned human trust with your customers, business partners, associates, and employees?

Flooded with digital information, devices, and the capacity for others to question decisions, how can you make better decisions, choose the superior alternatives, and reduce the number of decisions that "just take the risk" because of data that is missing or not proven to be reliable?

Can achieving digital trust be proven to be good business and create new wealth in a global, 24/7/365 marketplace that demands increasing velocity while also increasing the risks of living digitally?

This book present the answers—the right answers—to those questions. In doing so, these pages help you understand how to demand and build authentic trust in the digital information and the devices, systems, and networks of the Net you access to do your job. Certainly this book will empower you to be more successful at building and delivering digital information devices, applications, and data assets that gain the trust of all of the stakeholders with greater velocity and increased value. But this book also will help you to craft and execute your decisions differently and more effectively in a digital world.

Whether in business, science, education, finance, or at the family kitchen table, each of us is a leader to whom others look for guidance and support. If you are prepared to invest your time to learn the insights, principles, tools, and strategies assembled in these pages, you and your decisions will be more trusted.

> To read on is to admit that what seems to work today is . . . crumbling from the effects of war.

Doing so will require a bit of courage on your part; after all, to read on is to admit that what seems to work today is, in fact, crumbling from the effects of war. Yet to deny that the war is underway is not a viable option.

WHAT IS IN THIS BOOK FOR YOU?

In *The Trust Decision Model—Part I*, you will acquire a new way of thinking about how trust decisions are made. You will learn about all of the moving parts in trust decisions and how to view them differently. You will be introduced to new tools that allow you to better navigate the interaction of those parts and, in doing so, to improve your control of how your decisions earn the trust of others.

If you lead a team, these new tools will strengthen how you structure and execute the tough decisions on which your company, and your ability to lead, are on the line.

If you take responsibility for auditing or testing how well decisions are being made, these new tools will enrich the questions you ask and the answers you deliver to those who are counting on you to watch their backs.

If you want to elevate the trust with which your decisions are accepted, these new tools will improve your ability to communicate how you reach your decisions and how you collect and process the information required.

In *Designing Digital Trust—Part II*, you will learn how to design and build *digital trust*. You will have the opportunity to expand on your knowledge of trust decisions and be introduced to additional new tools to build, select, and create wealth from trusted digital assets.

In *Managing and Governing Digital Trust—Part III*, you will discover that building digital trust is not enough; to survive and prosper, you must sustain and improve digital trust. The strategies and tools to do so are uncovered, together with recommendations for the next steps to be taken.

If you design technology or digital solutions, this book will transform how you build those solutions and achieve greater effectiveness in the design, development, and operation of your work product.

If you manage a business, whether at the family kitchen table or in a corner suite in one of the world's tallest buildings, this book will change how you define and shape your strategies to create new wealth, compete, and survive in a world that soon will be only one digital marketplace.

If you select and use digital assets (and, among us, who does not?), this book will give you new mechanisms for making better decisions when selecting among your options, taking into account the trade-offs among trust and risk, and the wealth to be created (or lost) with each.

If you are reading this book as a regulator, lawyer, or policy geek, this book will alter how you will perform the responsibilities of authoring and administering the rule of law in the Digital Age.

Despite decades of research on organizational trust, behavioral sociology, marketing, artificial intelligence, user interfaces, and human relationships, the vocabulary and tools needed to build digital trust simply do not exist. So, within these pages, I share with you a new portfolio of tools and resources:

PART I

A *Trust Vocabulary*, composed of new phrases and terms and new meanings for existing words (with appropriate acronyms and symbolic notations), which enables us to discuss trust decisions and digital trust differently and with greater effectiveness.

A *Trust Decision Model*, an integrated view of the sequential decisions and information layers that link together the steps we take in deciding to trust and enable us to connect the dots between human trust and computational trust.

PART II

The *Rules for Composing Rules*, a set of eight simple principles for authoring rules that are effective when crossing the chasm between the ambiguity of broad, governing rules (such as statutes or regulations) and the binary precision required by the executable code of software applications.

A *Unified Rules Model*, a new architecture that enables us to organize all of the complexity of business, technology, and legal rules into unified, functional structures that support the design and execution of digital systems that truly deliver compliance and earn our trust.

A *Unified Information Model*, a new framework for organizing and designing digital information assets in order to execute more effective trust decisions and perform more effective governance.

PART III

The *Trust Prism*, an entirely new, 3-D, visual tool for evaluating, improving, and governing complex information systems and information assets. The Trust Prism unleashes our potential to build and sustain digital trust in those systems and information assets for enduring generations.

Ultimately, I hope this book will contribute to global dialogues about how we will govern ourselves. In these opening decades of the Digital Age, the world is one. Very shortly, there will be no further emerging markets. The boundaries of our political states already have become secondary to the boundaries of our networks and our systems, and the economic wealth we hold in our wallets and bank accounts is becoming secondary to the value of the digital information we can access and control.

Only the digital information that we truly can trust will have such an impact. If we cannot resolve how to tell the difference among digital assets we can trust and all of the rest, and if we cannot author rules that can be enforced globally by both nations and systems, the global dimensions of the Internet will collapse, national boundaries will become new Berlin Walls, sponsored acts of digital terrorism will become routine headlines, and the potential of these amazing technologies to bridge the chasm between man and machine will not be realized.

In early 2015, during the final development stages of this book, senior executives from Microsoft, Cisco, and Salesforce.com were speaking at global forums about the need to build digital trust and the economic costs of recovering from a loss of trust. The EU is committing vast resources toward building competitive digital markets. Yet the digital infrastructure that now runs our world—despite all of its capabilities and services—is broken. History has always confirmed there is a time when existing infrastructures can no longer merely be patched and kept in service. I believe any further patching of what now exists will fail; instead, something new must be designed.

WE *CAN* WIN

If we are to prevail as a *civil, global* society, designing and achieving digital trust is now a necessity. We must find the courage to move beyond what seems to work today but actually is crumbling.

We must move beyond merely shoring up our defenses with stronger, more robust spending. Instead, we must begin anew, replacing what *is* with what *needs to be*—a robust, dynamic, interconnected, digital space through which we can communicate and live as a global society. In doing so, we can improve our confidence in our decisions and the decisions of our leaders.

Now is the time to accept the tremendous opportunity we have to truly build and achieve new systems and new information assets that can deliver and sustain digital trust. Welcome to taking the first steps to shifting the tide and winning the war.

PART ONE

THE TRUST DECISION MODEL

CHAPTER 1

THE GLOBAL DEMISE OF RISK MANAGEMENT

I COMMITTED A LONG TIME AGO that any book I would write on digital trust was not going to begin with an endless tirade of how bad things are in cyberspace. There is simply no need; the daily headlines from the digital battlefield are enough. Google (or your search engine of choice) can provide you with abundant stories of the continuing sophistication with which malicious actors are achieving victories in the war to degrade our security protections on information and gain access to the digital knowledge, records, and controls that we most value. There are detailed reports, surely more than your appetite can sustain, explaining the economic and operational impacts of hacks, criminal syndicates, espionage, and state-sponsored take-downs of entire networks and systems. All seem to be compelling evidence of the fact that digital trust is under attack.

Yet, before we journey on, you deserve to know that not a single commercial publisher presented the opportunity to publish this book elected to do so. The reasons, remarkably consistent across nearly a dozen discussions, included:

> "We don't sense there is a 'felt need' to which your book responds."

> "Building and sustaining digital trust does not seem like a hot button topic; no one else is writing about it."

> "Your book is too broad; none of our subject editors (Technology, Security, Public Policy, Sociology, Law) saw a good fit."

Somehow all of the headlines did not have any impact. Indeed, one anecdote gave ironic support to their failure to be persuaded. In late 2014, after more than 10 years of existence, the Trustworthy Computing Initiative within Microsoft Corporation was closed, with its team members distributed across other divisions or laid off.

As mentioned in the Preface, however, in early 2015 (and after the publisher rejection notices had accumulated), things seemed to be changing.

> ⟫ At the 2015 World Economic Forum in Davos, Marc Benioff, the CEO of Salesforce.com observed:

> > "The digital revolution needs a trust revolution. There has been an incredible shift in the technology industry. . . . We've gone from systems of record to systems of engagement and now we are about to move into a world

of systems of intelligence. But none of these will retain form or have referential integrity unless the customers trust them.

Trust is a serious problem. The reality is that we all have to step up and get to another level of openness and transparency."*

*http://bit.ly/1eQ23BK

≥ The White House organized a Summit on Cybersecurity and Consumer Protection in February 2015, which the President personally attended.

≥ The European Union has recognized digital trust as an essential pillar in their overall Strategy for a Single Digital Market.

≥ Global, rising technology companies are establishing the new executive role of Chief Trust Officer.

≥ The Cloud Security Alliance, a new professional association with thousands of technology professionals and hundreds of corporate sponsors, is authoring and publishing new protocols for achieving trust across the global complexity of Cloud services (and a portfolio of acronym-defined services: PaaS, IaaS, and SaaS).

≥ At the University of Oxford, the Department of Computer Science includes professors and students focusing on trusted computing and trusted infrastructure, with an emphasis on Cloud-based distributed computing systems.

> In China, in September 2014, the 13th Annual Conference on Trust, Security, and Privacy in Computing and Communications was convened, with over 100 papers presented. Held under the auspices of the prestigious IEEE, what is intriguing is the frequency with which an international conference of this calibre is so frequently held in China and the strong, diverse contributions from Chinese and Asian researchers (as opposed to U.S.- or European-dominated programs).

Let me emphasize the last example—13th annual! Yet another is scheduled in 2015. There is an obvious passion in China toward building digital trust, one that seems reaffirmed with each new conference. Given the level of investments in research reflected by the papers and attending organizations, authentic momentum and progress are being achieved. Each year the volume of contributions, the sophistication of research, the diversity of topics, and the structural complexity of the Conference are richer. Here are just four recent examples: "Public-Key Encryption Resilient against Linear Related-Key Attacks Revisited"; "A Robust Authentication Scheme for Observing Resources in the Internet of Things Environment"; "To-Auth: Towards Automatic Near Field Authentication for Smartphones"; and "Proofs of Ownership and Retrievability in Cloud Storage."

Citations and links to materials appear in References and Additional Resources at the back of this book.

CHINA TAKES THE LEAD

This event is more than just another throwaway "angels dancing on heads of pins" conference, and the strong, continuing contributions from Asia are not merely coincidence. China, as an economy, research center, and population mass, clearly recognizes value in pursuing and advancing digital trust. The annual event has another benefit—vacuuming into one collection point the scientific papers, emerging corporate best practices, and published innovations of researchers and entrepreneurs from the world's most recognized universities and companies, as well as those across that nation's own vast resources.

Five compelling principles explain this Chinese momentum on trust. Yet there is nothing *digital* about them. Each is proven to influence economics, social organizations, governance, and human behavior. Each has guided the destiny of commerce for centuries, determining the outcomes of countless battles for investor capital, product innovation, consumer choice, and, ultimately, control of market share.

Shaped long before Alan Turing, the first research grant that funded the Internet, the first protocols of the World Wide Web, or the birth of an Internet of Things, these principles have consistently marked the winners in human society. Yet we are only now realizing what the Chinese understood in hosting the earliest conferences on digital trust, security, and privacy at the beginning of this century—in the next generation of the Digital Age, the winners will be distinguished from the losers by these principles.

> *Every transaction creating wealth first requires an affirmative decision to trust.*

Building trust creates new wealth.

Sustaining trust creates recurring wealth.

Achieving trust superior to your competition achieves market dominance.

Leadership rises (or falls) based on trust (or the absence of trust).

Take a moment and think about each of these with respect to what you do in your business or in your job. How does the organization acquire wealth? Where does new wealth originate? How are customers retained? What provokes them to keep coming back and paying for your goods or services? Why does the leader in your market succeed? If you are not the market leader, why not? How is the loyalty of your team maintained?

If you lead a non-profit, a government agency, or even a community association, your focus is only slightly different but the trust is often harder to earn. You still require sponsors, funding sources, and need those you serve to place their trust in your organization and your leadership. But the direct exchange of value between a buyer and seller is not present. What must be done to secure the trust of your funding sponsors? How is your success measured when renewed funding is requested? How are you effective at leading change when, quite simply, you are not able to pay the same as the private sector? If there are options—whether for funders, those you serve, or both—how do you compete against those options? What is required to secure their trust?

For both profit and non-profit, whatever provokes funding sources to trust seems to drive everything. Trust surely will have the same determinative force within the broad expanse of the Net and its networks, systems, devices, and the full portfolio of the digital information assets of humanity. Yet, why did the publishers not see the critical importance of *digital trust*? Why have the technology leaders from North America taken over a decade to catch up (if only in their rhetoric) to the investment China has been making in figuring out the building blocks needed to achieve digital trust?

I suggest they are caught in a *Twilight Zone*-like episode called "The Dilemma of Dead Man's Curve."

THE DILEMMA OF DEAD MAN'S CURVE

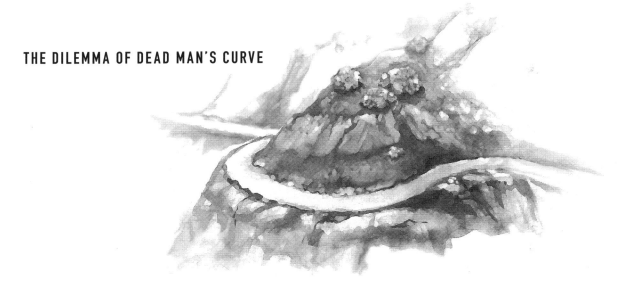

In the early 1960s, "Dead Man's Curve" was a catchy pop song by Jan and Dean in the United States. The lyrics of the song tell the story of a dare, a green light, a race to Dead Man's Curve, and a hideous crash. There actually was a real Dead Man's Curve, part of the Old Timber Road in California, a tight, 270-degree curve and switchback with no berms and steep, unguarded drop-offs. It demanded slow and careful navigation . . . or else. But it was a road, a superior means of transit to get from here to there than what had existed before.

The road itself was just that, nothing more. It worked in earlier years when the number and speed of cars and trucks were both few and slow. But as the velocity of cars increased and more drivers of younger age took the wheel, there really were multiple crashes and deaths—wheels slipping off the edge as the laws of physics overcame foolhardy bravery (often fueled by fermented fluids), or head-on collisions between cars driving blind to approaching vehicles on the other side of the curve.

Yet, despite the losses of life, rather than replace the infrastructure the road represented, the government continued to take the risks. The road remained in use. While there is no historical record I could find, we can only imagine the budget meetings and improvements discussions over time.

> "Perhaps we can put up wooden guard rails."

> "No, it will be cheaper just to post a warning sign on both sides of the curve."

More kids died.

> "Perhaps we need to put up metal guard rails; I saw them being used in Chicago on a new bridge."

> "No, too expensive. But let's put in the wooden guard rails we talked about last year."

But the cars were even bigger, the motors stronger, and the drivers a bit more reckless, crashing through the wooden guard rails. More kids died.

> "We have so many cars and trucks now using the

Curve, perhaps we should just blow that rock out of there and straighten the road."

"Our road budget is fairly tight; perhaps we can replace the wooden guard rails with the metal fencing you saw in Chicago."

Still more kids died.

The Dilemma of Dead Man's Curve is this: when the existing infrastructure no longer supports the demands placed upon it—causing injuries, loss of life, disruptions of operations, etc.—the operators of that infrastructure always will try to mitigate the related risks by installing patches at the lowest possible cost. Their goal is to extend the useful life of the investment in the infrastructure, despite the expenses of losses that may result. Patching Dead Man's Curve is always lower in cost than investing in building a new, functional infrastructure. But the patches merely delay the issue—when should we decide to abandon what exists and invest in building something new that will work?

THE INTERNET IS A DEAD MAN'S CURVE

The Internet, for all of its power and unexpected capabilities, is merely a digital version of the Old Timber Road. It originally was envisioned as a military communications infrastructure to move messages, resembling an electronic interstate highway system. The Internet was never designed to support the full demands of the global human population for commerce, government, warfare, entertainment, intelligence, knowledge, education, online dating, and homeowner association newsletters.

In the headlines and in our daily interactions with the Net, more

Patching Dead Man's Curve is always lower in cost than investing in building a new, functional infrastructure.

and more we see the debates over what spending is needed and how the Net is outgrowing our ability to govern it. Yet, in corporate board rooms, IT spending plans are no different than the budgets presented to the county supervisors overseeing Dead Man's Curve—asking for money to patch, rather than to build new.

We hear the sounds of alarm; we become direct victims of identity theft, credit card fraud, and the unauthorized publication of personal photographs. Our corporate websites are compromised, financial accounts hijacked, and trade secrets and intellectual property digitally stolen. And yet, rather than invest in building something truly new and functional, we continue to justify spending on patching. Time and time again, the prevailing votes are cast based on the perception that spending on patching will best protect the wealth of the organization.

In contemporary consultant-speak, there is another term used to describe the continuous patching of existing infrastructure: "risk management." The sad truth is, of course, that risk management is not delivering any true improvements. The infrastructure is merely being patched. While the demands for service and the pace of commerce gain velocity, so fast as to be measured in nanoseconds, there are still disrupted transits of data, dropped packets, and recurring major system breaches.

The reason risk management fails is simple and fundamental. There is only one source of funds for risk management—the net profits of the organization after all of the other production and management costs have been paid. Spending for reducing risk is never connected to how customers make their trust decisions to buy the goods or use the services of a business. It is always viewed

The sad truth is . . . that risk management is not delivering any true improvements.

as a deduction against profits, spending to be minimized or avoided altogether by decisions to "take the risk."

For decades, the champions of information security, records management, and compliance have battled for adequate funding. They usually lose, receiving nothing or only a small portion of the requested budgets. Why? Because the only source of funds that could be tapped were the profits, wealth otherwise traveling into the pockets of the shareholders. The battles already were lost before they began. "Risk management" is, in its essence, a simple way of saying, "What's the lowest possible amount to be spent from our profits to reduce the risks of the existing infrastructure failing to deliver wealth to our pockets?"

In advocating a different path, I submit that risk management is failing as a business discipline; in fact, the increased rhetoric and activity for digital trust already may be the first nails sealing the coffin in which risk management will be buried.

If I am right, the publishers are going to resist. They make their money by selling lots of books, webcasts, and software products that are "patches" to manage risk. So too will the consultants, venture-funded start-ups, lawyers, and policy regulators who have great job security delivering patches. Bluntly, managing risk is very lucrative, particularly after a successful attack or theft has placed your client or customer's management team under scrutiny.

You identify the risk, you build a defense, and you install the defense, hoping the adverse incidents go down in their volume or severity or disappear entirely. It is really no different than install-ing guard rails on a main road that needs to be abandoned, not patched. The current infrastructure is being preserved, even when the demands are clear that *something new is needed.*

China understands the difference. The EU, at the highest levels of strategic planning, understands the difference. Those investing today in digital trust standards and protocols that work across the full, broad dimensions of the global society get it. Each recognizes and values the potential rewards that can be achieved if something new emerges that is superior to the status quo. New investments in new infrastructure—networks, systems, devices, applications, and information assets—that are designed to be trusted will prevail, in accordance with the 21st Century versions of the time-honored trust principles highlighted at the beginning of this chapter:

> *Affirmative decisions to trust made by the market will create wealth.*
>
> *Building and expanding trust across more services will create new wealth.*
>
> *Sustaining trust will create recurring wealth.*
>
> *Achieving trust superior to the competition will achieve market dominance.*
>
> *Leadership will be awarded to those who rise to be trusted.*

There is one more reason why risk management is failing. The managers and champions for the spending have never been able to connect the proposed investments to how their companies can create wealth. By focusing with a digital perspective on the five principles of trust that drive economies, companies, and leadership, the dialogue changes. Now the same spending has a different connection point—improving how companies can create and sustain new wealth. So, when China, the EU, and others begin shifting the public conversation toward digital trust, know they already made the shift internally a long time ago.

DESIGNING, ACHIEVING, AND SUSTAINING *DIGITAL* TRUST

Building digital trust means investing in the architecture, design, and production of something new. The building process is one that must be continual.

Designing digital trust means researching the rules used by others to determine what products or services they will trust enough to pay value. You need to know *their rules* in order to create something new that will earn the trust of your customer, business partner, colleagues, team, or classroom. That may seem simple, but the challenge in the Digital Age is that none of us knows what those rules need to be.

Achieving digital trust means building and executing your products and services in alignment with those rules and with a transparency that enables the trust decisions of others to be made with greater speed and certainty. You must leverage the capabilities of technology to deliver to them the information they need to make their trust decisions rather than control or restrict their access to that information.

Sustaining digital trust means designing your products and solutions to be adaptive and responsive to changes in the rules. Nothing will be more important in the 21st Century than building into the design of the Net and all things digital the agility and flexibility to react quickly. Regardless of the geography, the market, or the system that defines the playing field, it is certain in the Digital Age that *the rules will change.* The winners who survive and prosper will be those who build a flexible infrastructure and solutions that enable adaptation and responsiveness to changes in the rules. Those who continue to focus on managing risk and patching the current infrastructure will not.

It is inevitable that the existing infrastructure of the Net will end in the same fate as Dead Man's Curve. Now, it is an abandoned, overgrown stretch of crumbling blacktop that can be seen in the distance from the superhighway that replaced it. The patching ultimately stopped. New rules were built to sustain and support commerce and the higher volumes and velocities that were possible. New investments were made, transit moved more quickly, sales occurred with greater velocity, and the communities served thrived.

In the next few years, those who are first and best in achieving digital trust will become the new superhighways for a unified, single economy firing across a globally connected world. Using the resources and strategies delivered in this book, you can catch up with those who already have figured it out, and then accelerate past them. The first step is to acquire a new way of thinking about trust itself. In the next chapter, that process begins.

CHAPTER 2

THE POWER OF TRUST

TRUST CONTROLS VIRTUALLY all human behavior. At each level of interaction among people and the objects and things around us, trust is the foundation of our decisions. At some point just beyond behaviors that are purely instinctive (such as the beating of your heart or the synapses firing within your brain), each and every action with which you live your life is informed by the strength and quality of trust.

Trust is also the essential quality of leadership. Effective leaders succeed because they make decisions that will be trusted. Nothing is more powerful. Trust is achieved by making decisions that produce favorable outcomes. What matters to leadership is that those outcomes are measured against the criteria of those who are to be led. Yet trust also is incredibly fragile; a single decision with catastrophic consequences can destroy one's ability to ever again earn the trust of others. In nearly every decision we make, the most cherished asset at stake is the trust others place in our decisions:

≥ After 17 years of growth, the company was losing market share. Imports, shipped directly to consumers from overseas, were corroding revenues. The CEO faced a decision—to fund a new automated production line, does the company lay off 20% of their employees or merge with an overseas competitor with a new facility but no current market volume?

≥ Challenged to use Cloud-based services to reduce operating costs, a CIO must select between three competing vendor proposals, none of which delivered the performance reports required to evaluate their remediation response times. Will the CIO's decision to not select any of the vendors be trusted by the Board members?

≥ Employees were clamoring for the right to use their own mobile devices in the field for building bid estimates and securing sub-contractor quotes. The information security team had to decide which security configuration to adopt and where to lay the blame if the selected option proved inadequate against new attack vectors being used against mobile devices.

In each of the preceding instances, the leader must make a decision on which option to trust. Yet each decision is itself being evaluated as to whether the decision will earn the continued trust of others.

Deciding to trust is something you do every day. Frequently. Constantly. In business, your success or failure is measured by the decisions you make to trust your business partners, suppliers, customers, market data, sales analyses, lab reports, and new-hire prospects. In daily life, you make decisions to trust people, objects, tools, systems, vehicles, computers, information, clothing, highways, stoplights, aircraft, entertainment media—even the water you drink and use to wash yourself.

Making trust decisions is how you select and navigate your path through each day. When you are more than one, acting as a part of a company, a community, a trading network, a social club, or a neighborhood gang, your trust decisions are even more critical. Your decisions have an influence on the collective; your success and failure often ride on whether the members of that collective place their trust in you and your decisions.

Will the Board vote to support your five year strategic plan? Will your team work overtime under your leadership to finish a new product ahead of schedule? Should we take your advice and buy added raw inventory? Have you double-checked all the financials for the proposed acquisition? Will they follow you over the bridge into enemy fire? These are all moments when you are being measured and evaluated on whether you—and your decisions—can be trusted.

What is trust? When does trust engage with our behaviors and our actions? How does trust govern our conduct in the many roles we perform? How do we decide to trust—as individuals, family members, employees, town citizens, consumers, corporate presidents and investors, bankers and borrowers, artists and concert goers, care givers and patients? How can you, individually and as part of the communities to which you belong, make better trust decisions? How can you become more trusted as a leader, manager, innovator, and advocate?

> Making trust decisions is how you select and navigate your path through each day.

How can you better avoid placing your trust in people, objects, or things that are, in fact, untrustworthy? How can we design products and services that earn the trust of customers and others more rapidly, and sustain and increase their trust? How do we govern ourselves to protect against those people, objects, or things that exploit and abuse our trust, causing pain, losses, damages, and harm?

Your decisions guide how you interact with the objects, people, and information that you touch, select, use, share, and interact. Your decisions also direct you around, away from, and in avoidance of those objects, people, and information that you determine cannot be trusted. Trust is fundamental to how we interact with the world. Yet there are two prevailing characterizations of trust that must be dismissed—they are both fundamentally inaccurate.

WHAT TRUST IS

Trust is *not* an instinct.
First, trust is *not* an instinct. Sure, most trust decisions in daily life occur within an instant, so fast that the decision may be functionally inseparable from the actions taken in reliance on the trust decision itself. You decide to trust the red stop light facing opposing traffic only as you continue into the intersection without braking. You evaluate an online website's security only as you are entering your credit card information to complete a last-minute gift purchase. You consider the safety of entering a dark room only as you take your first step across the threshold. You decide whether to trust the directions being given by the service station attendant only as you are asking for the directions themselves.

Trust is *not*
an instinct.

Other trust decisions, especially in business, can be far more time-intensive and deliberative. They can extend over minutes, hours, days, weeks, or even longer. The slower pace at which these decisions unfold expose careful, complex balancings and weightings of variable facts and figures, as well as aggressive dissections of our "gut instincts." When more assets are at stake, when more lives are in play, when there are potentials for greater wealth and greater loss, the decisions are more deliberative.

Complexity makes trust decisions more visible. We can see with greater transparency the variables of rules, information, outcomes, and costs involved in our decisions. Creating and entering a joint venture, committing to a new production plant, hiring a key management team member, accepting a proposal to sell your business—these are all trust decisions and often incredibly challenging to align all the moving parts. No instincts are welcomed.

Trust is *not* an emotion.
Second, trust is *not* an emotion. Trust is not an amorphous, vaporous variable within the quality of the human heart impossible of more precise expression. While we often express our trust in the vocabulary of emotions and metaphors, something far more analytical occurs when trust is achieved or lost. We retreat to emotional expressions of the presence or absence of trust because it is so hard to express the authentic attributes of trust.

So, what *is* trust?
Trust is the affirmative output of a disciplined, analytical decision process that measures and scores the suitability of the next actions taken by you, your team, your business, or your community. Trust is the calculation of the probability of outcomes. In every

Trust is *not* an emotion.

interaction with the world, you are identifying, measuring, and figuring out the likelihoods. When the results are positive, you move ahead, from here to there. When the results are negative, you rarely move ahead; you stay put or you find an alternate path.

In making personal trust decisions, you are choosing to rely upon some one, some thing, or some *information* with which to live the next experience of your life, to finish the tasks that await completion—illuminate the room at dawn, provide music in the shower, nourish your child, transport yourself to work, read electronic mail, reply to electronic mail, attend a lecture, or select a teammate for a pick-up game of football. In every interaction, you make a trust decision that precedes what is next. You even ask if you can trust yourself! Am I strong enough, smart enough, or capable of doing what lays ahead? It is what we do as human beings—it is what most sentient species do as they engage with the world around them.

In making trust decisions within companies, networks, organizations, or communities, whether acting alone or as a collective, the process tracks to how you act individually. Tasks or objectives are defined, the available resources are evaluated, the possible results and risks are evaluated, and trust decisions are made as to how to proceed. Which option can be most trusted to achieve the intended outcomes? Which options present risks to our assets, our operations, or ourselves? Which information gives us the best analysis on which to make our decisions? Which tools can be most trusted to enable us to create new wealth?

Trust decisions are the most complex computations possible. Yet trust decisions have consistency, design, and structure that are possible to visualize and express with remarkable congruity, regardless of the complexity of the variables or the time during which a trust decision must be completed. Trust decisions, properly executed, take account of the circumstances in which you are about to act; the qualities of the person, thing, or information on which you intend to rely; and the value you intend to invest, and realize, from giving your trust.

THREE ESSENTIAL QUALITIES OF TRUST

Trust, and the trust decision process, are governed by three qualities central to the analysis presented in this book. First, trust is a rules-based exercise. To complete trust decisions, you assemble and organize the rules that will direct your choices. As the trust decision process proceeds, you may discard some rules, determine that other rules cannot be met, or call up new rules that will be the foundation on which you move forward. But the fact remains—trust decisions are grounded upon, and executed against, a structured set of rules that define the boundaries and the outcome of each trust decision.

Second, trust decisions are fueled by information. As your rules are assembled, you seek information that allows you to calculate if the target of your decision (that is, the thing you are deciding whether or not you can trust) meets those rules. You sweep up information from your own memory, surrounding circumstances, records and reports, and reliable sources. You align the information against the rules and you calculate the results. Does the information about the target conform to your rules? If the information does not conform, or information required by the rules is not considered, then there can be no affirmative trust.

Third, trust decisions are mathematical. In order to align the information we gather with the rules we have assembled, we deconstruct the rules and the information down to essential elements that enable simple calculations. For each rule, we ask: "Does the information meet the rule?" The deconstruction continues until the answer becomes a simple "Yes" or "No." In order to trust some one or some thing, you add things up to determine if all of the elements are present under your rules. You make deductions that subtract from your analysis. Sometimes the deductions can outweigh everything else and you elect to not give your trust. At times, a single deduction (such as how you calculate the risk of death resulting from your decision) can be determinative.

In calculating trust, each of us also makes mistakes. Sometimes you will fire your engines and make decisions without enough information, or with information that later proves itself to be untrustworthy. You may rely on someone to help you make your decisions or rely on their opinion, only to discover that person was not a good choice. Through our mistakes, we refine how we calculate trust and update and revise our trust decision process, make new rules, and change what elements to take into account and how to measure them.

The results are remarkably binary—either there is an affirmative outcome or not, "yes" or "no"; "1" or "0." "Maybe" is not allowed. Of course, as variables increase in number, the rules become more complex, the information greater in volume, the amounts at stake more valued, and the calculations are more difficult to execute. But, in all trust decisions, what is occurring is nothing more than a mathematical calculation. Do the results add up to trust?

These three qualities of trust decisions—rules-based; fueled by information; mathematical—allow us to embrace an understanding of trust that rejects both instincts and emotions. Instead, trust (or the absence of trust) is and always has been the resulting sum of a rules-based, information-fueled calculation.

In a digital world where we are struggling to sustain and build trust across a global, wired landscape of human affairs characterized by reports and allegations of cyberwars, digital theft, electronic espionage, and the loss of human dignity through ubiquitous surveillance, this essential truth changes everything.

FINDING YOUR WAY TO TRUST

Like any calculation, trust decisions have structure, sequence, and process. There is a beginning, a middle, and an end. At any level of society or commerce, there is remarkable consistency in how good trust decisions are made. Indeed, regardless of the complexity confronted in making trust decisions, for trust to exist, and for trust to be strong, the process must be executed rigorously. The rules must be followed; the required information must be collected; and the calculations must be completed. There are no shortcuts.

To succeed, a good map is needed, one that shows how the trust decision process unfolds from beginning to end. In the next chapter, you will be introduced to a new map for trust decisions. Unlike the old, paper maps in your car (or your parents' car), this one has layers that build one upon another until we can see the full picture of the trust decision process. At the same time, trust decisions are occurring in a sequence, moving from beginning to end. So, to explore this map, we will look down through the layers while also moving from a starting point to the end. It is a lot like watching a film and the process aligns well to how animated films once were created.

Trust (or the absence of trust) is and always has been the resulting sum of a rules-based, information-fueled calculation.

Films are, of course, a series of photographs presented at a high rate of speed that convinces the human eye of continuous action. In 2015, films are created and displayed at variable rates, 24 to 300 frames per second. The film technology controls how many frames are exposed during each second of action occurring before the camera. When we slow a film down, the differences between each frame become visible. When we focus on a particular element, such as the placement of a receiver's toes on a sideline pass, the changes between two or more frames are isolated. We can see the movement by seeing the differences between the images that become visible at each point in time. We can see what changes.

A trust decision is no different—*except that it is invisible. It happens in our minds*. The process is a continuing blur of dynamic, volatile calculations that often occur with impressive velocity and always involve complexity. A single trust decision is actually a series of decisions linked together, in which the shifting activity of all of the moving elements, actors, and variables becomes difficult to navigate. Your ability to stay focused on just one motion is challenged by the surrounding dependencies, interactions, counteractions, and entrances and exits from the boundaries of the images. But when we slow down the speed to freeze each moment as an individual frame for review, the trust decision process becomes more visible. Each element can be isolated better and, between two or more images, we can see what changes.

Of course, even if each frame of just one second of film represented one point in a trust decision, we would not have enough frames in that one second to display the full trust decision making process. To do so would require even more than 300 frames per second. Indeed, with automated trading systems and banner ad auctions now measuring their velocity toward completion in nanoseconds (one billionth of one second), we would need quite a few more frames per second to devote one frame to each movement of change among all of the elements. But I believe the metaphor works—by using a freeze-frame analysis, we can stop the action and look more carefully at what occurs when you, your business colleague, your leader, or your team make trust decisions. We also need to see the layers of action within each frame.

Before computer animation, artists would paint and color individual illustrations on sheets of transparent celluloid (known as "cels"), with each character and each part of the scenery separately painted on those individual sheets. Then the cels would be stacked together and the camera would photograph the entire pile. The result would be a single, unified image of all of the individual sheets, creating one frame of film.

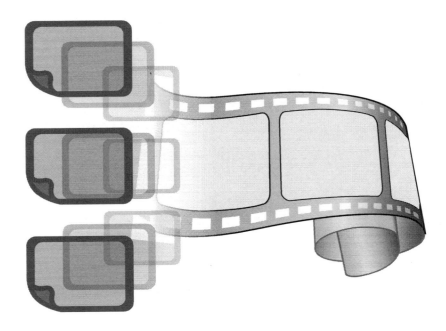

In the same manner, over the next several chapters, each layer of the trust decision process will be presented and explored in detail. As we begin to stack the layers one upon the other, and one frame proceeds to the next, you will be able to visualize the fascinating interactions that occur within and among the layers.

In every trust decision, there is always a controlling actor, the one making the final decision whether or not to trust. As our map unfolds toward the final destination, you will come to understand how the person deciding to trust interacts with the different layers and elements. You also will learn how those interactions are viewed by those who are evaluating the quality of the decision. When you are the person controlling that decision, improving your navigation skills across those interactions will help increase others' trust in your decisions.

So, let us take a look at our map, the Trust Decision Model.

THE TRUST VOCABULARY

In this chapter, you will learn the following words:

Chaining

Decision Maker (DM)

Information

Resources

Rewind and Recalculate (R & R)

Rules

Trust Decision Model

Trust Decision Target (TDT)

Work

CHAPTER 3

THE TRUST DECISION MODEL FROM 40,000 FEET

FOR EVERYONE ELSE in Wise Industries, a normal long, holiday weekend unfolded. But the CIO had a different few days. Restless nights, pre-dawn reviews of the strategic plans on her laptop, 17 phone calls to her team leads to double-check their field audits on the data centers and service providers, and three text messages from the chair of the Audit Committee: "What is your decision? Can we achieve $47.5 million in savings by moving IT to the Cloud?" No matter that it was the weekend; at 09:00 AM tomorrow, she would be standing before the Committee.

Regardless of the size of your business, you likely have had one of those weekends sweating bullets with a deadline ticking toward you. A decision is required. It is a big one. The stakeholders above you will be ready to pounce on your decision, protecting their backsides by testing whether they can trust your analysis. Your team members are waiting to trust you, their leader, to make the decision that justifies the weekend's phone calls and months of advance field work. The bidding contractors and service providers are waiting for you to trust one of them and write a check that will make the winner a bit wealthier.

As you stand on the ledge, every aspect of your decision is reviewed again. And then, ignoring the fourth insistent text message, you pull up the five-year, return-on-investment projection on your laptop. Something catches your eye and your stomach turns. A cell is just not computing properly. A click reveals a key formula is missing a variable. You suddenly realize you never received the second audit to confirm the projected direct costs on which all the calculations depend.

In this scene, I tricked you—*you* are the CIO! How do you make the decision? Do you freeze the process until you get the validation audit? Do you hope no one stands up and points out that the second audit was never initiated because the required funds had not been allocated? Who can you trust? What information can you trust to be real? Can *you* be trusted? What do your decisions look like? For each decision, what are you deciding to trust? If you have multiple options, how will your decisions influence how the final recommendation will be selected?

Navigating the answers to these questions is what makes decisions so challenging! Despite the apparent complexity, the good news is that trust decisions inherently follow a consistent, dynamic process which enables the decision to manage multiple, moving, and interactive parts. That process is the *Trust Decision Model*.

THE TRUST DECISION MODEL

This chapter introduces you to the Trust Decision Model from high above, as if you were flying 40,000 feet above the Earth. At that

Despite the apparent complexity, the good news is that trust decisions inherently follow a consistent, dynamic process. That process is the *Trust Decision Model.*

altitude you can nearly see to the horizons of entire continents, but you cannot see the chaos and collisions of commerce and life below. This chapter is similar, providing you the full picture of the trust decision process. As the book proceeds, we will zoom in to see up close the complexity and remarkable structure of trust decisions and all of its variables and dynamics.

Professional cartographers emphasize that one of the hardest tasks in creating a map is determining what details to leave out. The same axiom plays out in this chapter. Not all of the moving parts of the trust decision, and not every variable in every calculation, can be displayed here. The Model displays trust decisions as a connected set of five layers; it is a visual map of the process. We will look at each layer and then end this chapter considering the full Model. In the following chapters of Part I, we will dismantle the layers in detail, much as an automotive racing team takes apart a race car piece by piece before rebuilding it in order to find greater speed.

TRUST DECISION CHAINING

As illustrated by our CIO's decision crisis, deciding to trust is not a single action but multiple decisions occurring in sequence. They connect, with each new decision leveraging the outcomes of prior decisions and then inputting and processing new variables that influence how the trust decision process progresses. The outcome of each decision links to the next, delivering information that the next decision requires. These multiple decisions within the trust decision process are visually expressed in the Trust Decision Model in this manner:

Moving from the left, each decision builds upon the previous one, overlapping much as the links of a chain. This introduces us to the Trust Vocabulary. In that vocabulary, these trust decisions are *chaining* together. No single decision is autonomous; each decision, if improperly executed, can dramatically change the direction of what follows. Indeed, some single decisions carry so much momentum across the process that an improper calculation can abort everything that follows, much like a space launch that is stopped even before it begins.

Chaining begins immediately, in the very first frame of the film of any trust decision. But the act of chaining is not entirely linear. In fact, if you were to slide the circles above into a stack, like the cels of an animated film, you would have a better sense of what is happening in every frame, with multiple decisions occurring concurrently in different layers of each frame. Decisions can also chain to multiple other decisions, whether within other layers in the same frame or in succeeding frames. Finally, as trust calculations progress, the results of later calculations often direct the decision process to rewind, refine the input to previous linked decisions, recalculate the decision, and then move forward again ("Three links back, now one link forward again, and the next . . . "). In our trust vocabulary, this is called *Rewind and Recalculate (R & R)*.

The result is similar to an athletic coach watching film of a game, rewinding and stopping the action to identify all the variables required for better decisions in future games. That is likely no different from just about any analysis you are asked to make in business (or in life)—moving in one direction, making sequential decisions, learning new data, and going back to reevaluate earlier calls, ideally before any harm comes from making decisions without the new data. There is one important difference between coaches in the film room and trust decisions in business and in life—you must make your trust decisions in real time, with a clock always ticking.

SPECIFYING THE WORK

Every trust decision is a determination to trust an object, person, group, system, device, or information asset to be used to accomplish a specific task:

> ≥ What do you wish to accomplish?

> ≥ What must your team do in order to succeed?

> ≥ How many widgets per hour need to be constructed?

> ≥ What information must be acquired or produced?

> ≥ How will performance of these tasks be measured?

> ≥ How will success be defined? What will represent failure?

In asking these types of questions, you are building a specification. In our trust vocabulary, this specification is called *Work*. It can be very simple, such as hammering a nail into a wall or composing a quick email to your supervisor to report on the day's events. Work also can be amazingly complex, such as deciding to move the IT operations to the Cloud. In later chapters, we will explore the full complexity of how to develop the specification for Work. For now, to understand the Model, it is sufficient to think of Work as the job that needs to get done. In many ways, Work is no more difficult to understand than that.

FINDING THE TARGET

Each trust decision, informed by a specification of Work, is focusing on and evaluating a target—a tool, system, device, information, or other resources—to determine whether or not it can be trusted to complete the Work. The target is the end point of each trust decision; in our trust vocabulary, it is a *Trust Decision Target* (or *TDT*). Each decision is being made by the CIO, a Board, your team, or you; in our trust vocabulary, the entity making the trust decision is called the *Decision Maker* (*DM*).

A TDT is always a resource that the DM evaluates to use in performing the Work. In our trust vocabulary, the overall universe of assets from which TDTs may be selected or assembled is called *Resources*. A TDT can take many forms. It can be:

> ≥ a strategic business partner or team member, selected to complement your company's strengths to create greater market share and revenue.

> ≥ a person, such as a teacher to be trusted as a source of knowledge and training skills for your child.

> ≥ a group, such as the members of a pick-up game of football in the schoolyard.

> ≥ a tool, whether it is a hammer, a computer program, or a residential home.

> ≥ a system, such as a retail clothing warehouse storage and conveyor system, a distributed, connected system of data centers, or a Cloud-connected wristwatch.

> ⩾ a book, a magazine, a poem, a database, a purchase order, or a web page of digital content.

> ⩾ yourself.

>> ⩾ Can you trust your own strength to lift a heavy box of books, your ability to calculate in your head the estimated harvest yield for the season, or your judgment in making a decision to spend $47.5 million one way or another without any due diligence or consultations with others?

>> ⩾ Can others trust you to make effective decisions about the direction of the company's marketing campaign? Do you make good choices in hiring new members of the team? Have you properly analyzed the capabilities of a proposed joint venture to create new wealth for the company's shareholders?

Not every trust decision for a specific TDT has a favorable result. On any day in your ordinary life, you make decisions that a TDT is not trustworthy. The summary sales report for the Southeast region does not have enough detail to produce a new quarterly revenue projection for each store location. A potential team member seems not to have the "right" answers to questions you ask regarding career ambitions and dreams. Your partner's three-inch dress shoe heel was a possible hammer for nailing up that one picture, until you remember the drywall was mounted on concrete. In each case, you completed the trust decision process and determined the TDT was not to be trusted to perform the Work.

The same structural process unfolds when evaluating the utility of digital assets as TDTs. Networks, systems, devices, applications, information assets—their digital quality does not alter how any of us is wired to calculate whether to trust. With each possible use of a digital asset, an affirmative determination must be calculated that a specific TDT can be useful in completing the Work.

THREE OPTIONS IN EVERY TRUST DECISION

If every trust decision focuses on a specific TDT, how does the DM locate and select the target itself? As the CIO, how would you define the boundaries around the various contractors, systems, devices, applications, and data sources in order to construct what the TDT looks like? What are your options?

At every level, and in each frame, a DM is constantly evaluating and comparing among three options for completing the Work:

> ⩾ Do nothing.

> ⩾ Undertake the Work using entirely one's own personal capabilities: physical strength, agility, counting on your fingers and toes—whatever it takes without using any other Resources.

> ⩾ Select one or more external Resources to be trusted as a TDT with which to complete the Work.

The process is a dynamic one. Very rarely will the first option make sense—after all, performing Work produces income, creates product, advances knowledge, or delivers entertainment. Nor does the second option frequently stand up as an option—in business,

A DM is constantly evaluating and comparing among three options for completing the Work.

teams, or communities, we maximize our productivity by working with others and using others' Resources, not ignoring them. But exercising the third option to select any Resource or Resources to be a TDT requires a predicate decision—is the selection a viable choice? If not, additional decisions chain together, more information is acquired, and the requirements for what will be suitable Resources refine until, at some point, the process identifies a specific Resource (or combination of Resources) to be worthy of further evaluation. The identified Resource(s) become the TDT, literally the target for the trust decision—can the Resource(s) be trusted to perform the Work?

Making any decision that can be trusted is made more complicated by the reality that the variables to be considered are volatile, constantly changing. Surrounding conditions may shift, Resources may alter in their condition or availability, or a customer's requirements may be revised. The DM must be capable of identifying and responding to the changes if the resulting decisions are going to be trusted. Every trust decision is comparable to how a surgeon once described his work to me, "We do the same thing as an auto mechanic, except the engine is still running at all times."

Chaining as a process enables us to visualize how and where the dynamic changes and complexity can be mapped, and the interactions among all of the moving parts can be recalculated toward measuring the trustworthiness of a TDT. But one constant, from beginning to end, is that Resources are the inventory from which TDTs are selected, evaluated, and used. So the Trust Decision Model shows Resources as the top layer:

Chaining as a process enables us to visualize how and where the dynamic changes and complexity can be mapped.

RESOURCES

Resources have immense diversity—people, objects, systems, information, money, or property. But a Resource (and any TDT) is always an identifiable object, some one or some thing, physical or digital, that you can identify, classify, and ultimately evaluate, individually and as part of a collection or assembly with other Resources, for its trustworthiness.

RULES

Since trust decisions are rules-based, rules are an inherent, continuous presence in the process. Rules do one of three things: they express what is required, what is permitted, or what is prohibited. In our trust vocabulary, all of these are *Rules*. The Model presents them as a foundational layer below the decision chaining:

Rules drive every aspect of every trust decision. Our Rules shape the selection of possible Resources to consider or reject, the structure and mathematics of our calculations, and the probabilities the DM requires for a final trust decision to result. Decisions at each layer of each frame test the adequacy of Rules, mandate the Rules to be selected, and instruct the authorship of new Rules upon which you may rely in making future trust decisions.

There are many sources of Rules—formal laws and regulations, guidances and interpretations, corporate policies and procedures, contractual obligations and informal rules of engagement, best practices, technology standards, and code-specific architectural requirements, to name just a few! For IT architects, business executives, compliance officers, venture capitalists, or Scouting leaders, the daily challenge in decision making is to identify and properly navigate the Rules. Once the Rules are known, everything else follows. Later chapters introduce new ways of thinking about those processes and how to identify, filter, rank, author, revise, and execute with greater precision the Rules that matter. For now, at 40,000 feet, it is enough to know they are the foundation for the entirety of the trust decision process.

INFORMATION

To execute, follow, author, apply, or make trust decisions based on Rules requires information (*Information*, in our trust vocabulary). As introduced in Chapter 2, Information is the fuel on which trust decisions proceed. The interactions among Rules and Information are continual and complex. Information is required about the Resources, the Work, and how success in performing the Work will be measured. Information about the surrounding circumstances, the intended results, the possible risks, and the potential rewards

> Information is the essential fuel—it feeds into the Rules to power the decisions evaluating the Resources.

and losses—all of this knowledge is required to execute and chain together the layers and the frames into a complete trust decision. The interdependence among Information, Resources, Rules, and chained decisions is inherent. Information is the essential fuel—it feeds into the Rules to power the decisions evaluating the Resources. In reverse, evaluation of the Resources drives adjustments in the Rules, and new Rules require new Information. The Model shows the presence of Information in this manner:

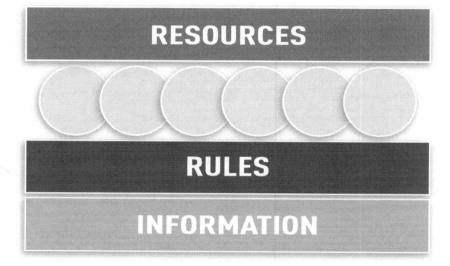

TIME

In making decisions, time is the one most overlooked asset, yet it is the most valuable asset in play within every trust decision. You surely have felt the pressure to make a decision by a defined deadline. Whether it is a large or small one, the imposition of deadlines changes how a decision unfolds, compressing the time to make it into a confined space. In business, government, transit, education, home repairs—time often emerges as the variable that can most alter the decision process and the outcomes.

When time is compressed, we tend to make different choices

in identifying Resources, describing the Work, selecting Rules, acquiring Information, and Rewinding and Recalculating earlier chained decisions. While the chaining architecture of trust decisions works best when decisions chain vertically between layers and then across frames, the compression of time imposes a linear structure, forcing progress toward making a final decision. Deadlines reduce and quickly eliminate the ability to perform look-backs and revisions, making each decision downstream more reliant on the accuracy and effectiveness of those preceding it. Returning to this chapter's opening scenario, realizing the five-year, return-on-investment projection is defective, you, as CIO, no longer have the time to go back. The deadline is now. You are going to make your decision based on the weeks of preceding analysis. You feel the pressure to send the Audit Committee chair a text response, even though you have one more night to process the decision. It is Sunday night at 09:15 PM. What are the implications of the choice to be made?

TIME *IS* MONEY—AND MAYBE A LOT OF MONEY

In the Trust Decision Model, two measures of time are initially important. The first measure is the time consumed by the trust decision process to reach a final decision. As mentioned in Chapter 2, while many trust decisions are nearly instantaneous, that is not always the case. When the decision is a "bet the company" decision, a significant amount of time may be consumed. In our daily affairs and in planning the big decisions, we rarely focus on that time metric or the accumulating cost of taking the time to make decisions that must be trusted. Executives, advisors, lawyers, department managers, compliance executives, consultants, accountants, line employees, service providers, contractors—in a major corporate deal, all are consuming time to work toward the ultimate decisions of a complex deal.

Despite this fact, in nearly 30 years of participating in corporate deals, I rarely saw a calculated estimate of the all-in time required to move through the trust decision process to reach a final determination. The estimates I did see were rough guesses, more focused on the out-of-pocket costs of doing the deal. Never did I see alternative process models that compared alternative strategies for how to complete the contributions of each stakeholder in less time. What tools would enable the work to be done more quickly? What process rules will better minimize the risk of overlooked validation studies? How can we leverage technology to enable faster analysis? At best, during those years there was an occasional comparison of raw costs, such as the rates charged for using outside versus inside counsel, or sending contract due diligence to India rather than Des Moines. Even now, we are just beginning to see project design tools that allow resource planning to consider alternative scenarios. The focus continues to be on financial costs, not on time.

The second measure of time important to trust is the time that is on the other side of the trust decision process—the lost opportunity cost of a decision delayed by the process. When you are making decisions in business, you are driven by the appetite to create new wealth or preserve existing wealth. When trust decisions consume time, they are also consuming the time on the other side of the transaction when wealth could be created or lost. As CIO, the projections show the company would save $1.2 million in operating costs each month; if you decide to defer the decision for two more weeks while the second audit is performed, the delay in making the decision has a $600,000 direct impact. Even in making personal decisions (when to have dinner, what movie to watch, or which lawn mower to purchase), time is the ultimate currency in play when making trust decisions.

Both of these measures of time—the time consumed and the lost opportunity time—are important and can be incorporated into the Model in parallel:

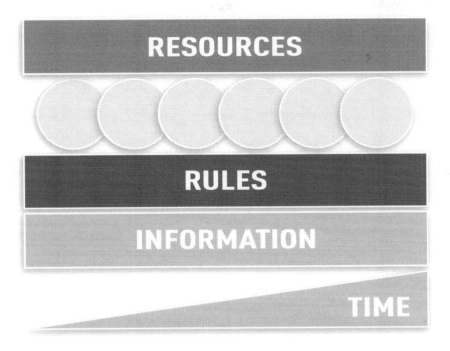

As time advances from left to right, the time consumed by the decision (and the related costs) grows in volume. The opportunity value of time lost awaiting a decision (and the related wealth to be created or preserved) grows as well. Both measures are proportional; and the more time consumed making a decision, the more the pressure increases to produce a decision that will be trusted.

A FINAL GLANCE FROM 40,000 FEET

When a deadline is imposed, forcing linear structure onto the trust decision process, we must start making choices for which no further R & R will be possible: some Resources are not viable to further evaluate; some Rules will be ignored; or some Information will not

The more time consumed making a decision, the more the pressure increases to produce a decision that will be trusted.

be gathered or, if collected, may not be properly vetted. You surely have been there when the deadline is forcing a decision and you have to make choices. You know a Resource, a Rule, or Information may be relevant but, driven by the deadline, you knowingly exclude it from further consideration. Time has run out.

In contrast, when there are enormous assets on the line—a major sale, a joint venture, imposing a new regulation, filing a major lawsuit, expanding a division, reducing the workforce—you also want to make the best possible decisions. You want your decision to be trusted; you want to be trusted as contributing well to the decision. If there is no deadline, then the decision process expands, allowing the circling back and recalculations that are part of its architecture. More Resources are considered; more combinations of Resources are modeled; the outcomes under more Rules may be evaluated; new Information is sought against which to align the Rules; and existing Information is vetted more closely. You choose to be more thorough even while time ticks away.

PERSPECTIVE MAKES A VAST DIFFERENCE—DOESN'T IT?

By looking at the Trust Decision Model, even from a "higher elevation," you can see what happens when those choices are occurring. Under deadlines, with big stakes on the line, or in ordinary decisions, you can tag each one of the choices you make in moving forward as a decision to leave out or add a Resource, a Rule, or Information. It is how you or any DM proceed in every decision. Exclusions are intended to save time (to make the deadline) in order to gain time (reducing the lost opportunity cost); additions consume more time (for a more thorough analysis) and potentially cost time (deferred opportunity) on the other side of the pending decision.

Yet, at 40,000 feet, we can observe what happens when elements are included or excluded. To make those decisions, the constituents within the layers must be ranked. Rules must be mathematically scored and stacked; Information must be scored and stacked; and Resources must be scored and stacked. How else do we express the importance or disposability of any specific element? The process is entirely mathematical. The Rules, Information, or Resources included or excluded from the later frames of the decision process result from a ranking of their values—the process is not emotional, it is arithmetic. Once the rankings are in place, we can draw lines and boundaries.

A more complete trust decision, however, has one additional critical measure to be introduced in this chapter: wealth. Decisions that are thorough—decisions that are to be trusted—create more wealth. When, within the trust decision, there is greater, more complete balancing among Resources, Rules, and Information, and the chaining of decisions is not forced by deadlines into a linear structure, the outcome will always be a decision that is more successful. Fewer elements are excluded—more Resources are considered; more Information is collected; and more Rules are evaluated—creating better measurements of the probabilities of achieving success in performing the Work. That is the ultimate measure of trust—achieving success consistent with the calculated probabilities.

Yes, more time is consumed and, in theory, that can mean a growth in lost opportunity cost. But imagine if a more thorough decision can be generated *and* given velocity, producing outcomes that are more trusted and require less time, thereby not incurring the greater lost opportunity cost. Imagine a more comprehensive consideration of the full portfolio of what the Trust Decision Model embraces, with fewer exclusions of Rules, Information, and Resources that deadlines or competitive pressures would otherwise require.

A MODEL THAT MAKES YOU A BETTER LEADER

As someone whose decisions are to be trusted, is that not what you would like to report? As someone who evaluates the decisions of others (and we all do), would you not value greater thoroughness and velocity in the decisions you review? Of course. Had you, as CIO, previously built a Rule that did not allow projected direct costs to be input without your sign-off on the second audit report, there would be no stomach churning. Had your decision model forecasted the opportunity cost of delayed decisions, spending an extra $50,000 to accelerate the second audit would have been viewed as a small added expense to achieve a faster, more trusted decision.

In its basic layout, the Trust Decision Model enables us to begin seeing our decisions structurally, as a dynamic of known, identifiable moving parts within a chaining of decisions. We begin to understand, against the measure and value of time, how our decisions to exclude or include any of the moving parts, arithmetically calculated and marked by drawn lines, affect the trustworthiness of our decisions. As the Trust Decision Model further unfolds, and we look ever closer at further layers and frames, the importance of connecting trust and time becomes essential, determining who will win or lose in the next generations of the Digital Age.

ZOOMING IN FOR A CLOSER LOOK

In the next chapter, we will zoom in to look closely at the first layers of the first frame and how we conceive and stack those layers. Indeed, since so much is going on in the first moments of a trust decision, imagine we are increasing our film speed from 24 to 1,000 frames per second. By increasing the number of frames, we are creating 1,000 pictures of what occurs within one second. Now comparisons between the frames will expose the very small, but important, shifts at each layer and the interactions among the moving parts will become more visible.

One more thing: remember how trust decisions are occurring inside our minds? As we move ahead, we are going to be looking inside, as if the exterior of our trust decisions became transparent. As that level of detail comes into focus, moving slowly frame by frame, you soon will discover that many trust decisions are aborted before they truly begin. "Taking the risk" means choosing not to calculate trust and the first opportunity to do so occurs far earlier than you might ever imagine.

THE TRUST VOCABULARY

In this chapter, you will learn the following words:

Anticipated Causality

Circumstances

Context

Known Causality

Principle of Indifference

Rhett Butler Rule

Trust Decision Context (TDC)

CHAPTER 4

CONTEXT IS EVERYTHING!

THE TRUST DECISION PROCESS rarely begins with a clear sense of the destination. Instead, every trust decision begins at a moment in time, in a specific context. That is where everything begins, with the DM preparing to perform Work:

> ≥ You are standing in a Board room, before all of the Directors, poised to make a decision on the Cloud-based services proposal.

> ≥ You are sitting before your keyboard about to begin building the monthly sales report for your division.

> ≥ You have input all of the division's performance data into the software and are about to push the "Calculate" button to determine whether the division should be preserved or closed.

Surrounding you may be an office, the industrial conveyor and trolley system used in distribution centers, desktop computers and paper files, the full diversity of your company's competitors battling for market share, or the comfortable and familiar contents of your home kitchen. In every situation, a trust decision begins as the DM starts to construct an awareness of the surrounding context.

Yet more than mere awareness is required. The strength and integrity of a trust decision (and the power to defend it) hinge on having an accurate, objective, and descriptive understanding of the surrounding elements that will influence what follows. In our trust vocabulary, *Context* is the totality of information describing the surrounding environment that you can collect (think of the limits of the Universe, if there are any, as the outer reaches of the Context!). The *Trust Decision Context* (or *TDC*) is a subset defining the boundaries of the environment within which a trust decision proceeds. The TDC serves as the edge of our map, defining the limits of what will be considered. Outside its boundaries are the variables that will not be considered.

MAKING THE WRONG CHOICES

Every one of us can make wrong choices if we exclude environmental factors that turn out to adversely influence the outcomes of our specific decision to use a particular TDT. Often it is only in hindsight that we can see the wrong choice that made all the difference, realizing then what was excluded. For example:

> an audit firm that specializes in calculating the all-in operating costs for outsourcing to the Cloud is not employed;

≽ long-distance weather data is not considered on a rocket launch;

≽ anomalous performance data from a network sensor is not evaluated by the triggers that immediately can halt operations; or

≽ one broker, employed for 12 years with complete trust, is not monitored when he options 100,000 shares of a company at which his roommate is employed.

In each instance, excluded data, if it had been considered, would have triggered better outcomes (a more reliable projection, delay of the rocket launch, a diversion of traffic to an alternative network, or a suspension of the broker's trading before the SEC investigation and resulting sanctions). But the Information, and the environmental elements that were described, were excluded from how the decisions were being made.

Isolating Context and TDC illustrates that the wrong choices were not defects in the overall controls occurring within the larger decision process. Instead, the decisions in error were the result of exclusions in our knowledge base. Those exclusions improperly set the stage for everything that followed. By freeze-framing on the very first layer of the first frame, much like the animation artist drawing in details on the cels that will illustrate the background, we can see where the errors occurred.

For every decision, there is a continuum on which the decision can be placed. On one extreme, there is the decision made with too little Information gathered about the Context. On the other extreme, there is the decision that is never made because the DM is always seeking more Information and is unwilling to move forward. The challenge, of course, is to know the right place on that continuum for each decision.

What Information must be observed and recorded about the full Context to properly develop the TDC? What Information goes inside the boundaries? What Information is left outside? Why is the process of building the TDC so often the moment where the trust decision process itself aborts? In this chapter you will find the answers to those questions.

THE FIRST FRAME / THE FIRST LAYER

Every TDC is complex, framing Resources, Rules, Information, and calculations toward a final outcome. But, in many ways, a TDC begins simply—it describes "where" you are at the moment a trust decision begins. Much as the first moment of a film illuminates and brings into focus the initial scene, as you begin to gather Information about the environment around you, you describe the TDC and set the stage.

The TDC description begins within the first frame. On one layer the TDC is being sketched. Within other layers for the same frame, as hinted in the prior chapter, the definitions of the TDT and Work also begin. The work is concurrent, but at slow speed we can see how each layer evolves.

Imagine three different artists working at their drawing tables, side by side. While holding separate pencils, they often are collaborating and comparing notes, sharing and displaying their images on the cels to assure the eventual integrity. Every frame of the trust decision process is similar, with more and more artists working on more and more layers as the inventory of moving parts becomes more complex. However, in the initial frames, as we watch the process begin, we will see that the TDC artist is the first to complete his work, putting in place the boundaries within which the others must proceed. The same is true even if there is only one DM acting alone.

SETTING THE TDC BOUNDARIES

To create the boundary we use decision tools to select and organize elements of the Context into a subset that is the TDC. The boundary is not a formal line; rather it is shaped by the elements to be included in the TDC. The DM is choosing from the entire Context two kinds of elements to place into large baskets, called *Circumstances* and Resources. (Resources were briefly introduced in Chapter 3's discussion of the Trust Decision Model; building the TDC is the first "call" upon them.) The TDC is defined initially by the Circumstances and Resources that are selected (see Figure 4-1).

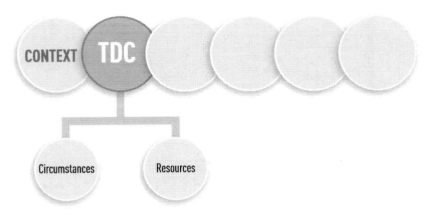

Figure 4-1

> Circumstances are those Context elements that have a *Known Causality* on how the Work will be performed.

CIRCUMSTANCES

Circumstances are those Context elements that have a Known Causality on how the Work will be performed. "Known Causality" means that you possess (and can directly access) Information that the element can cause different outcomes in the success or failure of the Work. The DM derives this information by comparing current sensory information the DM observes around her to direct knowledge that what is being observed has previously affected how Work might proceed. Immediately, two layers are involved—the layer on which the DM is sketching the TDC and the layer on which the DM is developing a description of the Work itself. What is important here is that the DM is, in this first frame, relying solely on knowledge that is immediately accessible. Here are several examples:

> The physical square footage still available in the data center is a Circumstance that affects how the IT architect develops the strategic plan to expand the number of server racks to be installed.

> The 20 year prevailing wind patterns on the Summit Ridge are a Circumstance that affects how a proposed wind turbine farm will be engineered and positioned.

> The absence of any warehouse space within a 25 mile radius of the Free Trade Zone is a Circumstance that affects the overall estimates for rolling equipment usage and replacement costs.

When known causality exists, the DM begins to alter the definition of the Work. It may begin as early as the very next frame (remember, our frames are now at a rate of 1,000 per second). The observed knowledge of Circumstances sketched into the TDC layer moves into the next frame and, like animating the wind blowing a character's hair, causes shifts. The link between observing Circumstances and defining Work can be so close that the DM might be doing both concurrently, almost like a single cartoon artist drawing all of the layers for a frame, flipping to change the drawing of Work that is resting in the same stack as the TDC drawing.

RESOURCES

To be part of the TDC, Resources now require a more robust understanding. Resources are those elements in the Context that could be used to perform the Work. As we zoom in more closely, Resources become more dominant as part of the TDC—they are the tools and other assets that have an *Anticipated Causality* in their use to perform the Work. Every TDT begins as a Resource or assembly of Resources within the TDC, something accessible with functional value toward performing the Work.

Anticipated Causality is very different, of course, from Known Causality. Anticipated causality means the DM possesses (and can directly access) Information that enables her to immediately calculate a probability that the Work can be accomplished through use of or reliance upon the Resource. As with Circumstances, the DM must have current sensory information that the Resource is present and accessible within the Context and direct knowledge that the Resource, alone or in combination, has attributes that will enable the Work to be performed. Once again, multiple layers are involved—the layers on which the DM is sketching the TDC and the Work. But, unlike Circumstances, the DM does not require knowledge that a Resource has previously been used to perform Work successfully.

Here are several examples:

> ≥ A nearby warehouse recently vacated already has

Resources are those elements in the Context that could be used to perform the Work.

40,000 square feet of refrigerator-cooled space (to be easily converted into a data center with a false floor to handle the cabling).

⯈ A wind turbine vendor catalog listed wind tolerance limits for the turbines 200% higher than the highest recorded wind speeds on Summit Ridge.

⯈ The existing parallel computing array supported computational output of 42 gigabytes per hour of new data.

THE FIRST EXCLUSIONS

What is important in this first frame is that the DM is relying solely on immediately accessible knowledge. If the DM has no knowledge that an element of the Context has (or can have) a known or anticipated causality to the Work, that element or variable will *not* be part of the Context. In turn, it will not be part of how the TDC is described. It is literally unknown to the trust decision. The process moves forward to the next frame or frames without any current accounting for those elements.

This concept is important to emphasize. In this first frame, the actual knowledge that you (or any DM) possess drives how both Context and the TDC are determined. You must have sensory awareness of an element, whether it is to be classified as a Circumstance or Resource. In turn, you require an ability to connect the sensory awareness with, and compare it to, knowledge you retain of other elements. In this frame, you are classifying each element, describing what "it" is.

In our memories, each object or environmental condition is itself described by its attributes. So, almost immediately, as a DM you are beginning to align inbound Information about the Context with your known, retained, accessible knowledge. If there is an alignment, and only if there is an alignment, then the next frame of film initiates an inquiry as to causality (e.g., "Will this performance data affect how many staff I assign to the project?"). Do not worry; there are plenty of later frames in which you have the chance to acquire additional Information from outside your memory to supplement your decision analysis!

This two-phased process of aligning inbound sensory Information against known, retained, accessible knowledge is a recurring, disciplined function within the trust decision process. It is how each decision progresses. At each moment, for each Context element, there is a separate decision analysis:

> ⩾ Is this something I recognize? Is it what I believe it to be? If "yes," what do I know about its causality with the Work?

> ⩾ If I do not recognize it, what is it? (Once classified, the process repeats: Is this what I believe it to be? If "yes," what do I know about its causality?)

These sequential decisions, of course, are chaining together. The outcome of each decision of classification and causality then links to the next, creating a sequence of decisions that builds the forward momentum of the decision process. Each frame is a separate link, chaining both to prior decisions and future ones within the larger process.

The outcome of each decision of classification and causality then links to the next, creating a sequence of decisions.

CIRCUMSTANCE OR RESOURCE—
HOW TO TELL THE DIFFERENCE

When looking around you, it can sometimes be hard to distinguish a Circumstance from a Resource. Both have a causality to the Work: Circumstances influence how the Work will need to be performed; Resources enable the Work to be completed. As you will discover over the next several pages, how a Context element is classified can have an enormous difference on the quality of the final decision.

The distinguishing feature of Resources is the capacity of the actor performing the Work to control the use of the Resource and successfully accomplish the Work. A Resource must be capable of being controlled, either by the actor or by other Resources under the actor's control. Circumstances are outside the control of any of the actors—they are *factual* elements of the Context within which Work is performed.

> The wind is a Circumstance; the kite chosen as the best one to fly is a Resource.

> Raw borax availability in People's Mine #237 is a Circumstance; the miners and equipment required to extract the raw borax at a rate of 300 cubic meters a day are Resources.

> Water flowing over Niagara Falls is a Circumstance, but becomes a Resource when channeled into the power company's turbines.

So, to receive further consideration, both Resources and Circumstances must be known to exist and have potential causality (the actual calculations of which occur in later frames). But Resources are capable of being controlled in accomplishing the Work—that is a key difference.

Now that we know the difference, which Resources and Circumstances do you include in the TDC? The answer is calculated mathematically, based on lines drawn by the DM (or others) who set measures of the levels of causality that matter. That sounds far more difficult than drawing cartoons . . . and it is.

Resources are capable of being controlled in accomplishing the Work.

THE PRINCIPLE OF INDIFFERENCE

The most influential force defining the TDC occurs when a DM applies the *Principle of Indifference* to exclude certain Circumstances and Resources from the TDC. In mathematics, this principle allows calculations to exclude variables whose potential impact is so insignificant that, if included, they would generate no measurable consequence within the range. For example, if you were required to calculate a result to the nearest .0001, the existence of a variable that could change the result by .000000000001 becomes something to which you (and your calculation) are indifferent.

Remember that a Circumstance is qualified by its *Known* Causality and a Resource is qualified by its *Anticipated* Causality. Applying the Principle of Indifference, a DM decides the potential impact of a Circumstance or the likely value of a Resource to complete the Work is so low that it deserves no further consideration.

> ≥ The presence on the edge of the field of a tree that can consume a kite did not deter you from the Work of flying a kite.

> While earthquakes are known in California, indifference has been calculated by millions who have chosen to live there.

> With 98% operational uptime over five years supported by two technicians, a third maintenance technician was unwarranted (as a Resource) to perform the Work of maintaining operational functionality.

At this moment, there is a mathematical computation occurring, often no sooner than Context-based Information is sensed and recognized. In our process, the math occurs within one or two subsequent frames. In that computation, the DM is ranking arithmetic expressions of the known causality of potential Circumstances and anticipated causality of potential Resources, ranking them from high to low. Then the DM is drawing a line.

Below the line are the Circumstances and Resources to be excluded; they are being placed outside the boundaries of the TDC almost as if the animator used an eraser to remove them from their respective layers in subsequent frames. Their exclusion mathematically keeps the later decision computationally feasible. Even with the use of computers, there are only so many possible Circumstances and Resources that can be considered inside the boundaries of the maturing TDC description—just like a map, there must be an outer limit. Acting under the Principle of Indifference is the only legitimate mechanism by which a DM can create structure for the TDC. What remains in the TDC and above the line is what matters to how to succeed in the Work.

How does the DM calculate the rankings? What are the underlying mathematics used to draw the line by which other Circumstances

Acting under the Principle of Indifference is the only legitimate mechanism by which a DM can create structure for the TDC.

and Resources are excluded from the TDC? Good questions, to be sure; however, in these first frames, it is too early to calculate the math. Remember, in a properly executed trust decision, the many individual decisions chain together and the process allows Rewinds and Recalculations. It is only in the later frames, as more Rules and Information come into play, that the math we require to more precisely define the boundary of the TDC (and determine the levels of indifference to be imposed) becomes important.

What *is* important in these opening frames is for the DM not to rely on the *Rhett Butler Rule* to exclude any Circumstances or Resources. When that happens, the ensuing trust decision is potentially aborted.

THE RHETT BUTLER RULE

I have named the Rhett Butler Rule after the famous film scene in *Gone with the Wind* in which Rhett Butler proclaims, "Frankly, my dear, I don't give a damn." When invoking this Rule, a DM *knowingly* excludes from the TDC Circumstances or Resources that are otherwise appropriate candidates to be included *above the line.* In other words, even though a Circumstance or Resource has known causality that could impact the Work or its performance, the DM makes an affirmative, conscious decision to exclude it—"I don't give a damn." When that occurs, the TDC definition acquires an entirely different shape and the potential trust decision process is at risk of being entirely aborted before it begins.

> ⪼ A real estate developer is fully aware of the adverse geological projections for the impact of rising tides on the Carolina Outer Banks (Circumstance) but proceeds to purchase the land and commence construction.

≥ A manufacturer places 100% reliance on People's Mine #237 extractions and elects not to consider alternative suppliers operating outside of nation-state control (Resources).

Let us slow our film down and zoom in to look very carefully at each layer within each frame. Is the trust decision process in jeopardy for both Circumstances and Resources excluded by the Rhett Butler Rule?

For Circumstances, the answer is yes. The rules-based, information-fueled, mathematical qualities of the trust decision are fatally compromised when the Rhett Butler Rule is exercised by a DM. Every trust decision requires structure and, if the foundational work of this opening frame in the film is undercut by a knowing, intentional failure to include accurately relevant Circumstances, the process is broken at the outset. A DM simply cannot reach an affirmative calculation to trust a TDT if one or more Circumstances' known causality on the Work are excluded even before there is a ranking.

Expressed mathematically, it is as if the DM is leaving out critical Information—if "X" is a description of the TDC, and "X" is not fully presented, the trust decision cannot be fully calculated. Whatever follows may be a decision, but it is a decision to accept risk, not an affirmative decision to trust.

What about a Rhett Butler exclusion of a Resource? A person with expertise, a database, or a specific tool exists, but the DM knowingly excludes it from further consideration. In this instance, there is *not* an inherent failure of the trust decision. The DM simply is narrowing the inventory of possible Resources to be called upon as a TDT with which to perform the Work. For example:

> The CEO parking space is open but it is not a suitable Resource to use for parking on arrival at work (unless, of course, you are the CEO!).

> The left shoe of your partner's $400 dress heels is not a suitable hammer for driving a nail into the masonry wall of the garage. Yes, it is a potential Resource, but excluding it from consideration does not end the trust decision; you just have to go find a suitable, real hammer.

A DM may knowingly elect to exclude a potential Resource from the TDC for various reasons, often economically driven. Before even ranking the potential suitability of a Resource, the price tags disqualifies it. A new turbo-charged Porsche may be an entirely suitable TDT for driving to California, and it is sitting right in front of you on the dealer's lot as a potential Resource. But that price tag is not within reach, even as a rental!

But look more carefully; slow the film down. You, as the DM, were checking the cash assets recorded in your checkbook to reach the decision to exclude the Porsche. The available cash balance was actually another Resource that you were placing inside the boundary of the TDC and above the line. Because the cash balance is not available, you were not even able to begin considering the Porsche as a Resource. So, while the Porsche was a possible Resource with which to get to California, there was a dependency requiring cash as an additional Resource. A quick check of the Context showed insufficient checking account funds, so the Porsche was then excluded from the TDC.

There were quite a few separate actions:

- The Porsche was observed and classified as a vehicle.

- The attributes of the Porsche were validated as a potential Resource to select and use as a TDT to get to California (a decision).

- A dependency was recognized as part of the Porsche's attributes—the price tag! Still, at this point, the Porsche is a potential Resource and within range as part of the TDC.

- The price tag triggered a further acquisition of knowledge about the Context—to identify the bank account as another Resource.

- Direct knowledge of the inadequate funds fueled the resulting decision to exclude the Porsche.

By slowing things down, we begin to see dependencies in how multiple Resources are identified and evaluated in near-instantaneous sequence as the TDC and Work descriptions are being constructed. To get to California remains the original Work description. However, when one Resource (cash) is not available resulting in the exclusion of the Porsche from the TDC, the description of the Work changed, modified by the Resources that remain within the boundaries of the TDC. Now the Work is described as "To drive to

California spending no more than the cash available in the checking account."

This interaction is happening quickly. As each potential Resource is identified, the definition of Work concurrently begins to gain substance, with each frame gathering additional density. If played out in the animation studio, the artists for each layer are jabbering back and forth, flashing sketches, adding layers, removing layers, revising drawings, and interacting to properly compose how the different layers will be integrated, all of this work merely for the first frame or two of the trust decision process.

Thus, when the Rhett Butler Rule pushes potential Circumstances outside the TDC boundary, the trust decision aborts. But when Resources are pushed outside, the process continues, though the definition of Work immediately may begin to evolve to reflect the impact of the exclusions.

VISUALIZING AND ADDING PRECISION

As the characterizations of the TDC and the Work evolve in response to synergistic changes, we introduce precision into the trust decision process. It can be very, very hard to isolate these interactions in human decision making. The process is there, but hard to visualize. I believe this largely explains why we historically have retreated to characterizing trust as an emotion—the math is just so hard.

Inside computers, however, these calculations are entirely possible and often mandatory requirements. Indeed, today's most advanced computing research is working on how to render the TDC boundary-defining processes more visible, more comprehensive, and more computationally feasible. Their work is quite literally expanding our capabilities to identify and include into the TDC added Circumstances and Resources that were computationally infeasible in prior generations, both for humans and machines. The result is that fewer elements of the TDC are excluded as mathematically below the line of indifference and more Resources (and combinations of Resources) can be considered to define and refine alternatives descriptions of TDTs with which to complete the Work.

And that is precisely the point: as our computers grow in their computational capabilities, you, as a DM, have the potential to dramatically improve the quality of your trust decisions—the very first links in the trust decision process. You can do so by leveraging the capabilities of computers to store and analyze more Information about the Circumstances and Resources than you can process internally.

Recall that you build the TDC based on direct sensory information *or* on knowledge you amass, retain, and access. Nothing in the Trust Decision Model requires that knowledge to be internal to your memory. To the contrary, there are very real limits on what humans can recall and process, even in the early stages of any trust decision process. In everyday business and life, we are increasingly transferring to the machines our knowledge of facts that we observe and our descriptive records of them, and we rely on the machines to recall and deliver back to us our knowledge and records. That may seem simple, but the implications for how better, faster trust decisions are made become significant.

So often, the demands of deadlines and pressures to make decisions undercut how we would otherwise devote time to building an understanding of Context, TDC, Circumstances, and Resources. We

As our computers grow in their computational capabilities, you, as a DM, have the potential to dramatically improve the quality of your trust decisions.

rely on the Rhett Butler Rule to make our trust decisions easier. In the very first frames, we reduce the complexity and compress our decisions into what time, money, or our boss permits as the limits within which to act.

By contrast, the technology-enabled DM builds and relies upon information assets within her computers to retain, recall, and help complete the calculations that score the Known Causality and Anticipated Causality for, respectively, potential Circumstances and Resources. In the very first frames, rather than relying solely on sensory-based information about Context, the DM can plug into more data, identify greater numbers of Circumstances and Resources and, in turn, recognize and calculate dependencies and interactions among them as the TDC elements and influences on Work become more precise.

Leveraging digital Information achieves two important outcomes in the trust decisions the DM needs to make. First, the boundary of the TDC is expanded to better incorporate and place above the line Circumstances and Resources that otherwise might be omitted. Variables she might place outside the TDC boundary in reliance upon the Principle of Indifference are brought inside—in effect, the decimal place is moving to the left (from .001 to .0000001) in order to more precisely calculate the quality of the ultimate trust decision.

Second, there is a reduced necessity to consider or apply the Rhett Butler Rule; computers allow the computational feasibility of including Context elements that otherwise would be excluded. As observed earlier, the Rhett Butler Rule often gets called into play just after saying, "Not enough time. Not enough money. No one is around to provide input."

When we leverage our computers to take less time, use less money, or access the people with the required knowledge, better trust decisions result. All of this occurs during the first frames of every trust decision process—and it is where so many trust decisions immediately are compromised. If relevant Circumstances are excluded, the decisions are no longer about trust. If possible Resources are ignored, achieving the Work successfully can become more challenging.

THE CONSEQUENCES FOR LEADERSHIP

Many business executives may view the preceding analysis as an ordinary outcome: "Been there. Done that. Automation 101. Six Sigma with different words." But I believe it focuses on something very important and is very different from merely automating a process. It helps you to take the first step toward becoming more trusted as a leader, a manager, an innovator, a teammate, a parent, or a friend.

As each of us makes decisions, we face two fundamental tests of our efforts. With every decision, someone in our community of connections challenges us by asking: Can the decision maker be trusted to make good decisions? Can the decisions that have been made be trusted by others?

If each trust decision is a film, then the sequel begins immediately afterwards. Each decision comes under immediate scrutiny as others begin to determine whether to trust the DM and to trust the decision that is in play. We are wired as humans to evaluate the trust decisions of others and, in turn, to evaluate the trust we are prepared to place in the DM for each trust decision. By understanding Context, TDC, Circumstances, Resources, and the concepts of boundaries, indifference, and the Rhett Butler Rule presented in this chapter, you are discovering a path to better understanding the human trust decision process and the utility of the Trust Decision Model.

What makes people trust you as a leader, an executive, a teacher, or a parent? Since trust is not an emotion, but rather a rules-based, information-fueled series of calculations, answering that question begins by examining how you first assemble and define the TDC in which you will make your decisions.

When your decisions are to be evaluated, the first set of questions by others probe to determine if you, as the DM, fully accounted for the Context and, in particular, identified and properly calculated the Circumstances and Resources to be above the line and inside the TDC. Hindsight is intensely powerful and the queries are brutal: "Did you see X as a variable?" "Why in the world did you not install safety controls on Y?" "Why did you ignore the dark clouds of rain just at the edge of town?"

Take a moment and change positions; think about a decision someone above you has made and the similar questions you asked about them and their decisions. If those types of questions cannot be answered, if the DM keeps her process hidden and veiled, you know how uncomfortable the feeling in your stomach as you try to calculate whether you will trust her or her decision. Change back to being a DM in our Digital Age and imagine how you can better gain the trust of others by offering the transparency that allows you to anticipate and answer their questions.

When you use the vocabulary of trust both to organize your own trust decisions and to present the outcomes to others who must live with your decision, you create visibility, allowing a dialogue about

With transparency,
others now
are better able
to evaluate
your decision
by visualizing
your process.

your decision process to occur. The questions still may be brutal, but the dialogue shifts. For the others, the dialogue may be entirely internal, evaluating you and your decisions without verbal discussion, but nevertheless processing the information they can gather about your decision. With transparency, others now are better able to evaluate your decision by visualizing your process.

Every day, each of us is determining whether to place our trust in others. The person evaluating you as a DM actually is producing a trust decision about you as a TDT! If you can explain how you constructed the boundary of the TDC, as well as how you considered more Circumstances and Resources with Known or Anticipated Causality, you are expanding access among the stakeholders who rely on you to make good decisions to Information they require to process their trust in you. As you will learn later in this book, the transparency that accompanies that access is becoming fundamental to how we will make trust decisions in the Digital Age.

The availability of Information; the accessibility of computational capabilities; the ease with which seemingly infeasible complex decisions become more feasible; the visibility into complex circumstances and optional choices—all of these features of living and interacting in a wired world are shifting how others evaluate any of your trust decisions. Each of the digital resources with which you are equipped also are shifting how you evaluate the trust decisions of others.

In prior centuries, humans were required to presume the trustworthiness of the king, the company president, the department manager, the public agency, or the sales clerk handling our credit card at the register. Now technology is empowering us to disregard those historic presumptions. Regardless of title, rank of office held, or even official instructions to trust another's decisions, each DM is subject to greater scrutiny, and each decision is more vulnerable to criticism.

FILLING IN THE DETAILS

What more must you learn about Circumstances and Resources to build the TDC? How do we better distinguish Circumstances and Resources to avoid misapplication of the Rhett Butler Rule to Circumstances? What are the next steps to refine a description of the Work and, at the same time, begin to develop the requirements for a TDT? When have we gathered enough Information to move to the next frames of the trust decision process?

To answer those questions, we return to the Trust Decision Model and examine in greater detail what is needed from the layers below: some Rules and some Information.

THE TRUST VOCABULARY

In this chapter, you will learn the following words:

Decisional Information

Descriptive Specification ($_{SP}$)

Functional Specification ($_{FSP}$)

Mandatory Pairing

Trust Decision Context-Circumstances (TDC$_{CIR}$)

Trust Decision Context-Resources (TDC$_{RES}$)

Trust Decision Context-Rules (TDC$_{RUL}$)

CHAPTER 5

DESCRIBING THE CIRCUMSTANCES AND RESOURCES

LONG BEFORE THE WEEKEND of sweating bullets, the CIO had to determine the variables to include in her analysis of whether to trust the proposed Cloud service vendor to deliver the services and produce the promised savings. (In our vocabulary, the Work was the company's IT operations and the Resources were the vendor's managed computing services, offered at a projected lower cost than she could accomplish in-house.) At the earliest stage, she was surveying Context and selecting and narrowing the Circumstances and Resources to be considered. Which elements would she take into account? Which elements would she ignore, including by applying the Rhett Butler Rule? She had to identify what both her company and the vendor could control (a combination of the vendor's Resources and her own management team) and the elements outside anyone's control that would influence how the

Work would be performed (the Circumstances, such as the intensity of Cloud-based attacks on the company's IT systems). What would be the boundaries within which her analysis would proceed?

As highlighted in Chapter 4, for every decision certain Context elements need to be excluded to maintain a computational feasibility. To calculate what will be included and excluded, rankings are needed and, to do the math, more Information is required. To create those rankings and give shape to her decision, the CIO needed to find, select, and organize the relevant Rules, and then find and input the Information required by those Rules. Here is our first awareness that the decision process is shaped by Rules.

Without using our trust vocabulary, what is being described may seem almost elementary or instinctive. In every decision you take, you define the boundaries of what to evaluate and go from there. But once our trust vocabulary is introduced, and the film slowed down, we can see better how the chaining of what follows depends heavily on how the TDC is constructed. Getting the TDC right sets the framework for everything that follows. As the film begins to move forward, deadlines and other constraints will foreclose your chances to do Rewinds and Recalculations.

The CIO might conclude that the physical location of the vendor's data server farm is irrelevant to where the financial performance records of the marketing division are located. So she relies on the Rhett Butler Rule to toss this aspect of Context out of the TDC. Two months after the rollover of everything to the vendor, a long-brewing internal political struggle within the vendor's homeland explodes and the server farm is "nationalized." Oops.

MAKING A BAD CALL

Hindsight can be brutal when later events disclose that Context elements were left out of the decision process. Called onto the carpet, you feel awful, like the soldier ordered to search for a ticking time bomb. He looks everywhere, turns over 100 stones, checks every shed, but does not find the bomb. Then the bomb, tucked into a bridge trellis, blows up, causing death and destruction and the Major asks, "Why did you not look under the bridge?" Once things blow up, there is never a good excuse for having not looked under the bridge. Just imagine the CIO having to try and explain to the Board Committee why she did not contemplate the impact of the political turmoil as a disruptive force in her decision to trust the vendor.

Identifying the Circumstances and Resources to be taken into account matters a great deal. With every decision you make, it is vital that you describe and document the boundaries of the TDC. Doing so is the strongest defense against hindsight's bite. Once again, it works both ways—focusing on the Circumstances and Resources is one of the strongest offensive strategies when navigating a decision under scrutiny.

When you are questioning the decisions of others which you are being asked to trust, where does your attention first go? You rewind to the beginning and start asking questions that focus on the first frames: "What Context elements did the DM take into account? What factors were disregarded? For those elements that were considered, how much weight was assigned to those elements?"

There are a lot of moving parts that begin to come into play in building an effective TDC description. To identify them and to track

Once things blow up, there is never a good excuse for having not looked under the bridge.

their movements, several terms (and their symbolic notations) need to be added to our expanding trust vocabulary.

EXPANDING OUR VOCABULARY

First, from this point forward, TDC_{CIR} or TDC_{RES} will be used to designate, respectively, that a Circumstance or Resource is *within* the boundary of a TDC. These designations are useful to navigating later points in the Trust Decision Model. There is no change in what these terms represent.

Second, for each TDC_{CIR} or TDC_{RES}, there are certain Rules that direct how the Information you gather is to be placed into two baskets. There is a *Descriptive Specification* (designated as $_{SP}$), which is a complete, factual description of the dimensions and characteristics of the TDC_{CIR} or TDC_{RES}. These are represented as TDC_{CIR-SP} and TDC_{RES-SP}. There also is a *Functional Specification* (designated as $_{fSP}$) that details how the TDC_{CIR} or TDC_{RES} performs (e.g., velocity, volume, units per time, watts per kilogram, purity, etc.). These are represented as $TDC_{CIR-fSP}$ and $TDC_{RES-fSP}$.

These notations allow a more granular way of describing what a Context element is (the Descriptive Specification) and forecasting how it impacts or can perform Work (the Functional Specification), as follows:

$$TDC_{CIR} = TDC_{CIR-SP} + TDC_{CIR-fSP}$$

$$TDC_{RES} = TDC_{RES-SP} + TDC_{RES-fSP}$$

For a TDC_{CIR}, the Functional Specification expresses the measurable impact of the TDC_{CIR} on how the Work will be performed. For example:

≥ Supplier trucks delivering just-in-time inventory for the assembly line are slowed to eight mph by a 12-vehicle crash (a Circumstance), requiring production to slow to four units per hour until the inventory arrives.

≥ Fast-moving flood waters (a Circumstance) require installing flood barriers to allow the home construction 100 meters from the river to continue.

≥ Internet transmission speeds are crawling due to multiple DDoS attacks on a major ISP (a Circumstance), and the validation audit is not loading onto the CIO's laptop as she tries, under pressure, to check the numbers in the waiting room outside the Board meeting.

For a TDC_{RES}, the Functional Specification expresses the measurable impact of the Resource toward completing the Work, either alone or in combination with other TDC_{RES}. For example:

≥ New RFID technology (the Resource) will enable 100% digital tracking of container pallets in transit (the f_{SP}), reducing the shrinkage due to in-transit thefts to zero (a second f_{SP}), allowing the transfer of pallets with zero shrinkage loss (the Work).

≥ An in-wall power supply available in the London hotel (a Resource), when combined with the 3-prong, flat-bladed adapter the CIO's assistant tossed into her bag as she left the New York office (another Resource), allow her to power up with the appropriate wattage (the f_{SP}), log in, and succeed in acquiring the validation audit at midnight.

Third, TDC_{CIR} and TDC_{RES} are interactive. Circumstances, alone or in combination, can influence how one or more Resources will contribute to the Work; the selected Resources and their effectiveness can define the Circumstances in which the Work can be performed. These interactions are not random but, rather, both Rules-based (if X, then Y) and reciprocal (if Y, then X). In effect, as the DM takes inventory of the Context, various Circumstances and Resources are being paired among themselves, helping to define the Work.

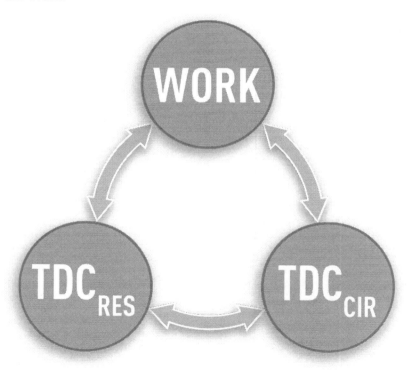

These pairings are a function of applying Rules that the DM identifies and references from direct knowledge. It is not very hard at all. From our experience, we have recollections of the causality among these Context elements (e.g., wind [TDC_{CIR-SP}], wind velocity [$TDC_{CIR-fSP}$], foldable pocket umbrella [TDC_{RES-SP}], resistance to wind before breaking [$TDC_{RES-fSP}$], and staying dry before walking into the Board meeting [Work]), and we have knowledge of the Rules for how to connect the variables in order to describe what exists (which is what the TDC is, after all—a subset of the entire Context). That the sky is so dark the street lights come on may be an observed Circumstance, but it has no known causality to the task of staying dry and therefore is excluded from further consideration as part of the TDC.

THE RULES OF THE TRUST DECISION CONTEXT

As a practical matter, the Rules upon which a DM relies to shape the dimensions of the TDC (i.e., creating the pairings) are themselves part of the TDC. These Rules are notationally represented as TDC_{RUL} and expand the inventory with which the TDC develops. While the Rules may be, in these early frames, internally stored within our memory, other Rules within the Context become relevant as the trust decision process moves forward. Just like TDC_{CIR} and TDC_{RES}, each TDC_{RUL} has a Descriptive Specification (i.e., what does the Rule require?) and a Functional Specification (i.e., how does the Rule affect how Work will be performed or how we will measure success in the Work?). The dimensions of the TDC, therefore, are being shaped now by three types of building blocks— TDC_{CIR}, TDC_{RES}, and TDC_{RUL}.

To illustrate that structure within the film metaphor, imagine that each of the TDC_{CIR}, TDC_{RES}, and TDC_{RUL} is a stack of cels organized in separate layers. As multiple layers are stacked together within each category, and then stacked again across categories, the TDC acquires greater depth and detail, much like a fully illustrated animation with many different characters fitting into the final image.

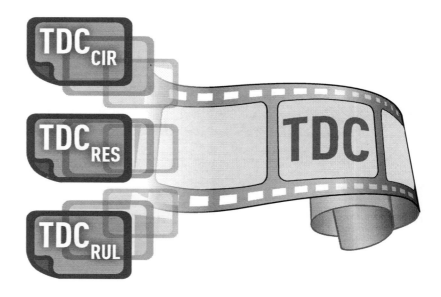

Notationally, the TDC structure can be illustrated in this manner:

$$TDC = TDC_{CIR} + TDC_{RES} + TDC_{RUL}$$

TDC_{RUL} tell us what Information must be collected to develop a full description of each of the TDC_{CIR} and TDC_{RES}, including the Rules associated with each TDC_{CIR} and TDC_{RES}:

$$TDC_{CIR} = TDC_{CIR\text{-}SP} + TDC_{CIR\text{-}fSP} + TDC_{CIR\text{-}RUL}$$

$$TDC_{RES} = TDC_{RES\text{-}SP} + TDC_{RES\text{-}fSP} + TDC_{RES\text{-}RUL}$$

Building architects do the same thing when they are designing a new structure. They first must identify the physical land and surrounding environment. For each characteristic (TDC_{CIR}), the architect must:

> Develop a Descriptive Specification (TDC_{CIR-SP})—such as ground composition (clay, earth, topsoil, granite, limestone).

> Learn the measurable qualities ($TDC_{CIR-fSP}$)—porosity, density, viscosity under differing weight loads.

> Acquire the related Rules for potentially suitable structures ($TDC_{CIR-RUL}$)—shed, home, egg processing facility, skyscraper.

The architect also accounts for the inventory of possible Resources with which the building may be constructed. For each (in our trust vocabulary, a TDC_{RES}), the architect must:

> Develop a Descriptive Specification (TDC_{RES-SP})—bricks, joists, shingles, cinder blocks, mortar, poured cement, floorboards, etc.

> Learn the measurable qualities ($TDC_{RES-fSP}$)—density, porosity, weight limits, stability on different ground conditions.

> Acquire the related Rules for using the Resource in the identified Circumstances ($TDC_{RES-RUL}$)—no wood frame houses built without poured concrete footings on the Eastern ocean shore.

The TDC definitions and structure give the architect, as DM, the tools to now:

> gather Information to build a description of each TDC_{CIR} and TDC_{RES};

⯮ recognize and incorporate the related TDC_{RUL};

⯮ use the TDC_{RUL} to better define the Work; and

⯮ rank the TDC_{CIR}, TDC_{RES} and TDC_{RUL}, deciding those to which she will be indifferent (in order to draw the boundary line) and move ahead.

Almost. As Steve Jobs was famous for saying: "One more thing."

If TDC_{RUL} are part of how we define the TDC, and TDC_{CIR} and TDC_{RES} are to be ranked, should not TDC_{RUL} also be ranked? Are there not certain Rules that are part of the Context that are more important than others? Of course there are! Certain Rules (like the laws of physics) cannot be avoided, and compliance with those Rules in performing Work is not discretionary. Other Rules—including such items as statutes, regulations, corporate policies, and specific procedures an IT Group must perform—can be ranked and placed *below* the line of indifference and, therefore, outside the TDC. Who has not decided to ignore or turn their backs on certain Rules in order to reach a decision? It happens all the time!

Rules have both Known Causality with the Work (defining the parameters of how Work can be performed) and Anticipated Causality (compliance does not always guarantee the Work will be achieved). So what happens if the DM applies the Rhett Butler Rule to knowingly disregard a Rule ("Frankly, I don't give a damn if Idaho does require prior notice to medical patients of a nurse's criminal record. We are not going to build a national hospital system and worry about one state rule!")? Does the trust decision abort? Actually, not always.

The DM still may be able to decide to trust a TDT and proceed to perform the Work even if she does nothing more to rank and evaluate a Rule as part of the TDC. But the possibility of excluding a Rule exposes one further pairing that occurs between layers—certain Work, to be successful, *requires* certain Rules to be satisfied. In other words, the Work cannot be achieved unless the performance complies with one or more Rules. Exclude the Rule(s) and, by default, it is not possible to complete the Work successfully:

> ≳ If Work equals "You are required to select a Cloud vendor that will deliver medical information service support that complies 100% with the laws of every state in which we operate a clinic," then Work would fail because of non-compliance in Idaho.

> ≳ If Work equals "Construct a home that is certified for occupancy by the Building Authority" and the architect knowingly ignores the related mandatory Rules on the number and placement of fire extinguishers, then Work would fail.

In our trust vocabulary, this is an example of *Mandatory Pairing*. This exists when Work cannot be completed properly unless a specific Rule, Resource, or Circumstance is included in the TDC as a basis for how Work will be defined.

When there is not a Mandatory Pairing, then the exclusion of a Rule, whether by applying the Rhett Butler Rule or by drawing a line to calculate indifference, does not abort the trust decision. But excluding a Rule from the TDC (and, in turn, the definitions of how the Work will be measured) always has a consequence. That consequence is the creation of new risks—sanctions, fines, added expenses, greater expenditures of effort, etc.

To emphasize: Chapter 1's declaration of the demise of risk management did not suggest that we should disregard risks. Instead, we must account for them in a more explicit new structure embracing the objective of calculating, not presuming, trust. If a Rule is not included in the TDC, later frames of the film will illuminate how the related risks are taken into account. For now, what matters in the opening frames is that a TDC is shaped by how all three Context variables are identified, paired, ranked, and included or excluded—TDC_{CIR}, TDC_{RES}, and TDC_{RUL}.

DECISIONAL INFORMATION

"That sure seems like a lot of work!" is a justified reaction to what we have covered so far. I agree! Yet, every authentic trust decision requires just that—inputting Information gathered both from the invisible elements of our memory and external sources, processing that Information against a defined set of criteria, and producing a decision.

The CIO's decision to not include geography in the Context cost much more than a disruption of operations. Domestic backup facilities had been turned on quickly, but the foreign servers themselves had only used two-factor authentication controls capable of being hacked by brute force attacks if the primary security layer of the vendor was gone (and it was). News of the political takeover began to leak out, listing the names of corporations found on the server account records. Within days, field managers were reporting customer cancellations, near-final contracts being placed on hold, and a 47% decline in new lead generations. The customers were

We should not disregard risks. . . we must account for them in a more explicit new structure embracing the objective of calculating, not presuming, trust.

behaving just like consumers who had their privacy breached, voting with their checkbooks. The CIO was, of course, the ex-CIO. All of this resulting from a bad call on the information to be gathered to make a decision.

Thus, *Decisional Information* is our next trust vocabulary term (and our last one for this chapter!). Decisional Information is the Information required by the Rules within a TDC to execute a trust decision. In each frame, on each layer, we are seeing new Rules added that require the collection of Decisional Information to calculate trust properly. The Decisional Information fills in the blank for every "X" that the Rules require. It becomes a stockpile of the fuel required to perform the calculations at every frame of the trust decision process. The first use of Decisional Information is to determine which Context-based elements become TDC_{CIR}, TDC_{RES}, and TDC_{RUL}.

Our expanded trust vocabulary now allows a return to where the chapter began, adding layers and moving through the next frames in order to emerge with a functional sense of the TDC within which the trust decision can unfold.

> Decisional Information is the Information required by the Rules within a TDC to execute a trust decision.

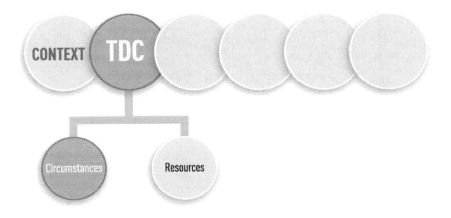

CLASSIFYING CIRCUMSTANCES

As Context elements are recognized, the first classification decision is to determine whether "X" is a TDC_{CIR} or TDC_{RES}. In Chapter 4, we learned that Circumstances and Resources are distinguished by whether there is Known Causality or Anticipated Causality with respect to the Work. We also learned that Resources must be capable of being controlled, therefore allowing us to perform the Work. So the first step proceeds in reverse order—the DM will toss out any Context element that, on first blush, shows no possible causality.

The process occurs quickly. The DM relies on direct knowledge to *exclude* any Context elements that are not possible Resources with some level of Anticipated Causality and among those that remain, have no Known Causality to how the Work will be performed. Remember, absent a deadline or other linear constraint, these decisions can be reviewed later when the DM accesses additional sources of knowledge and can rewind and recalculate by inputting new Decisional Information. But some substantive first decisions keep the process under control.

CLASSIFYING CONTEXT ELEMENTS

To remain a candidate for being a TDC_{RES}, a Context element must be placed into one of three classifications:

> ⩾ The DM must identify single Resources that, if used, can perform the Work (think of a hammer used to drive a nail into a wall).

> ⩾ The DM must identify and evaluate how to combine or assemble more than one Resource to perform

the Work (think of a complex IT system to visualize the potential scope of this exercise or, more simply, using a stepladder and hammer together to drive the nail at a height three feet above your reach).

> The DM must identify Resources that may be used for the Work in ways for which they were never intended (think of using a partner's dress shoe with a three-inch heel as a hammer on a nail to hang a picture).

In the preceding deliberation, the DM's criteria have not changed; one is looking for Anticipated Causality—a means of connecting the potential Resources to completing the Work—and *control*. If a Context element does *not* fit into one of the preceding three classifications, it will not be considered as a potential Resource. For this purpose, the DM is building an initial Descriptive Specification and Functional Specification and making a call. It is worth emphasizing that these exclusions do not involve tossing out any TDC_{CIR}, only potential TDC_{RES} (for which their exclusion has no abortive effect on the trust decision process).

But what happens next? The DM evaluates the remaining Context elements. If there is Known Causality to Work, the elements are classified as TDC_{CIR} and retained above the imaginary line. Remember, TDC_{CIR} are objective facts that describe the TDC and can influence the Work. They may be dynamic or even volatile, changing at any later moment during the trust decision process (such as the changing nature of the wind or the market price for raw components needed to complete the Work). But, for those Circumstances left as part of the TDC, the DM will be required to observe them continually and take into account their causality on how the Work will be performed and the Resources required to do so.

As the trust decision progresses, the number of TDC_{CIR} evolves, with some initial ones later calculated to be irrelevant to the final decision and therefore below the line. This occurs through the gathering of Decisional Information about the TDC_{CIR} that creates greater detail in both the Descriptive Specification and the Functional Specification. It is almost like, for each TDC_{CIR}, there is a separate cel layer on which the Decisional Information is being collected.

As in the earliest frame, the process is interactive. As we gather more Information about TDC_{CIR}, it influences which TDC_{RES} are relevant through pairings and the application of relevant Rules. For example, if the wind is gusting to 25 mph, the pocket umbrella becomes an irrelevant TDC_{RES} for staying dry. If there is no plug adapter in your suitcase (i.e., a Resource), the Functional Specification for the power supply (a Circumstance) becomes irrelevant.

As the DM gathers Decisional Information about the observed TDC_{CIR}, the interactivity then focuses on how the TDC_{CIR} impose selections on the definition of Work. The DM is pairing TDC_{CIR} to the Work layer, building a more robust definition of the tasks to be completed within the boundaries of the relevant Circumstances. Now the Functional Specifications ($_{f}SP$) of each potential TDC_{RES} become relevant. The question shifts to "What Resources are available to complete the Work within those Circumstances?"

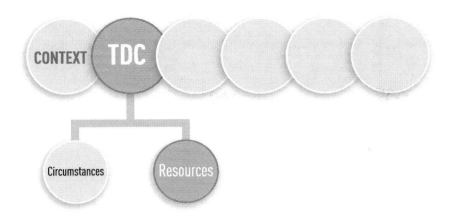

CLASSIFYING AND DEVELOPING RESOURCES

As the nail, hammer, and fancy shoe example illustrates, the evaluation of Resources becomes more complex when alternatives exist, and even more complex when Resources can be combined (such as a stepladder and the hammer) to perform the Work. Once again, we need to slow down the film to look carefully at how Resources are to be added to or removed from the TDC. Imagine our artist responsible for placing the Resources into the TDC has a palette of possibilities from which to choose. How might the Resources be organized on the palette? The first culling of the Context elements with no causality to the Work has occurred. How do we proceed?

Take a moment and think about the last major decision you needed to make on how to execute a big project. For the CIO in our earlier scene, she and her team had been evaluating hardware, software, vendor management team personnel, security controls, policies, procedures, contract language, internal human resources, external supporting vendors, and more. What Resources were possible options?

The CIO's preceding list is just a high-level inventory, merely a checklist of categories that provides neither Descriptive Specifications nor Functional Specifications against which Decisional Information can be collected and evaluated.

How about your decision? How many questions did you ask about each Resource? How did you structure your comparative evaluation? What descriptive Information did you gather? What functional performance data did you require? How did that Information influence your formulation of how you described the Work to be completed based on the Resources that were available? How were you able to compare "apples to apples"?

As a leader and decision maker, you are trusted to organize, structure, analyze, and deliver a decision that navigates those variables. You are expected to demonstrate that you considered all of the possible tools and resources and made the best choices possible for performing the Work. As a follower, you expect your leaders to do the same. Yet, as the Digital Age gains momentum, there are two hard truths that are altering how we identify and classify potential Resources and ultimately make our trust decisions.

First, for so many of the decisions we are asked to make in business, there is greater and greater complexity in the number, combinations, and availability of Resource options. Technology is empowering that complexity, creating both agility and innovation in how different potential TDC_{RES} may be combined to perform the Work. The decisions are so much harder than merely choosing between a hammer and a fancy shoe. Outsourcing, on-demand computing, shared service models (from bicycles to taxi services to rented air mattresses), Cloud-based services—all create incredible pressure in how Resources are identified, described, and ultimately evaluated and ranked during this early part of the decision process.

Omitting a Resource could exclude the one key component for building a better mouse trap. At first glance, that should not be a fatal problem. In the Trust Decision Model, if an initial decision does not seem optimal, there is always the chance to rewind and recalculate which Resources are considered. But that Model is rarely "normal" in today's business world. When deadlines or other constraints foreclose rewinds and recalculations, those early exclusions can lead to sub-optimal outcomes with which you are stuck. The complexity makes it even harder.

Second, as you work to organize the Decisional Information about any potential Resource (as well as alternative configurations of multiple Resources), digital Resources (networks, systems, devices, applications, and digital information) are the hardest to gather and fully understand. You want objective, descriptive, and comparative Specifications about each Resource and each possible combination of Resources (the TDC_{RES-SP}) and objective, measured expressions of how each will contribute to performing the Work ($TDC_{RES-fSP}$). Yet, despite all of the headlines about increased transparency associated with technology innovation, the Decisional Information is harder to identify and even harder to compare when digital assets are the TDC_{RES} being considered.

Imagine the CIO's team's task of evaluating all the submitted proposals before reaching the big decision on the surviving vendor. Her company's $47.5 million is at stake. The CIO's Request for Proposals (RFP) identified over 15 business process systems to be shifted to the winning vendor's platform. Operating under the measured metrics of Six Sigma, the RFP included over 75 performance metrics for which vendor proposals needed to submit conforming performance reports. It also requested systems architectural drawings; device and model numbers for supporting equipment; all third-party software licensing agreements; and information on all data center operating locations, including background checking protocols and security control service records for each location.

When the proposals came back, the proposal evaluation team was more than flummoxed by the responses; they had been virtually stonewalled by all but one vendor. Due diligence is supposed to be a chance to validate the integrity of vendor submissions. But, as with so many RFP exchanges, the vendors submitted pretty pictures but failed to include conforming performance reports or, for two that did include them, the reports only listed less than 40% of the relevant performance metrics. Two of the proposals referenced technologies and acronyms not even included in the RFP, somehow believing the added complexity of the context would be impressive. One vendor refused to list the data center locations they might use, offering, "Our large network of contracted facilities is the strength through which we can offer these prices; on-demand Cloud services require that we retain the flexibility to shift data services among our location facilities at our discretion." Similar defects characterized the other parts of each submission, save for one surviving vendor. The survivor submitted the required data, though the conforming performance reports showed that, in several major categories, the vendor's data transmission speeds, service restoration time metrics, and testing of secure shutdown speeds were far below what the CIO currently accomplished. Indeed, two of the vendor's shutdown test protocols did not include required procedural elements to initiate concurrent backup services.

The CIO was not making trust decisions about any of the other pro-posals. They never made it to the starting gate. Because the other vendors failed to provide disclosures of the complexity or conform-ing performance reports for their component Resources, the CIO was not getting the TDC_{RES-SP} nor the $TDC_{RES-fSP}$ that the RFP spe-cifically requested. Even the surviving vendor was not measuring up, but at least there were metrics!

Complexity and opacity—when combined, these two digitally-driven forces challenge any DM to build a strong, functional description of the TDC and make further decisions. Instead, the endless web of connections among black boxes into which you cannot see are becoming the Resources you are asked to trust. When the Work includes physical tasks (such as selecting the right hammer in the tool aisle), you still scan the QR code to look up consumer reviews and check for pricing specials from online retailers without truly being able to make trust decisions. When the Work is itself digital, executing activities that use digital assets, due diligence becomes more critical and even more difficult, increasing the burden on the DM to presume trust rather than calculate the outcome.

This is where the struggles begin in both the war for control and the war on trust. When a vendor resists providing more details on how they structure and deliver security around their digital ser-vices (as just one example of frequent opacity), they are placing the Descriptive Specification inside a black box. When vendors resist agreeing to defined functional levels of performance in contractual service level agreements, they are disabling the Functional Spec-ification you require to make a trust decision. If you do the same to your customers, you similarly are affecting their trust decisions. Remember, after the bomb explodes, there is never any valid excuse for failing to look under the bridge.

> The endless web of connections among black boxes into which you cannot see are becoming the Resources you are asked to trust.

Those battling for control of digital information win on the battlefield when DMs are deprived of the Decisional Information their trust decisions require. If you cannot calculate the potential value of a TDC_{RES} to complete the Work, later chained decisions in the Trust Decision Model become increasingly speculative. Moreover, when viewed by others in hindsight, your inability to demonstrate the calculations you made about available Resources degrades their trust in your decisions.

So, at this point in the Trust Decision Model, Context matters! TDC_{CIR} are inherent to the decision process and set the initial framing for selecting Resources as TDC_{RES} that, in turn, may be evaluated as possible TDTs to perform the Work. But the weight of any trust decision falls most heavily on the DM's ability (or inability) to gather and process the Decisional Information required to evaluate and select among those Resources.

Today, complexity and opacity have become the attributes of Dead Man's Curve. As decision-makers, the roads we travel are blocked by barriers to the Decisional Information we require to make good decisions. Something different is required. In the next chapter, as part of the Trust Decision Model and in anticipation of the Trust Prism and the tools to be discovered later in this book, you will find a classification scheme for Resources that reconfigures 20th Century business decision models to meet Digital Age requirements. As always, Rules are the driving force.

THE TRUST VOCABULARY

In this chapter, you will learn the following words:

Code

Data

Human Resources

Physical Assets

Process Rules

CHAPTER 6

CLASSIFYING RESOURCES

As the CIO begins sketching out her team's due diligence plan, she knows from many prior projects that she will be required to compare the status quo of her own IT operations to how the systems will perform if she decides to trust one of the vendors' proposals. Balancing how things *are* versus how things *might* be is the constant in deciding whether to trust. Her job is to continuously evaluate the available options and determine how well previous decisions now embedded in the status quo measure up against the metrics used to select them. "Trust" is how we express our calculations of the probabilities for achieving a desired performance level among competing options. Calculating those probabilities includes considering the possible outcomes and the possibilities for adversity.

As a DM, you are always in the same position. You know with some certainty the productivity and limits of the status quo; at stake is whether the options that would bring about change will increase income, reduce costs, grow market share, or eliminate competition. After all, every business decision is driven by the original motive to

> "Trust" is how we express our calculations of the probabilities for achieving a desired performance level among competing options.

127

be in business—to create new wealth. In commerce, the effectiveness of trust decisions is measured against that singular objective.

Each TDT is constructed from the TDC_{RES} located within the TDC. Except for the simplest of tools, such as a rock tossed to knock down a dangling apple, any TDT is an assembly or collection of TDC_{RES}. Homes, planes, trains, automobiles, and information systems are all the same—each is a system constructed from Resources. If the TDC_{RES} are not everything that is required, we acquire or create new Resources that can be added to the existing TDC_{RES} to become the TDT that is required to do the Work.

We have discovered that, to be considered as a TDC_{RES}, each Resource within the Context must be known to the DM, have Anticipated Causality, and be capable of control. In business, that should be pretty simple; any corporate enterprise resource management (ERM) system works well at tracking the Resources within the status quo. Couldn't the CIO rely on her existing ERM system to map the Resources listed within the vendors' proposals? That certainly seemed to work to create the RFP, but the responsive proposals had presented such inconsistent architectures! Somehow the CIO's team was being foreclosed from building the performance comparison she knew the Committee would require.

The growing frustration was painful. After three weeks and plenty of complaining instant messages among the team, the "elimination vote" among the vendors was going to be tough. The CIO looked at the spaghetti drawings. Trying to connect different elements of each of the proposals, the lines drawn in different colors cutting across each other, she sighed, recalling the famous line from the sheriff in *Cool Hand Luke*: "What we have is a failure to communicate."

Much of my career focused on helping people focus on effectively communicating while structuring complex IT transactions. This meant working as part of the teams acquiring or delivering innovations that improved upon the Resources of the status quo. Yet, no matter the maturity of the deal players, creating functional, transparent and useful mappings of the Resources between the old and the new was immensely difficult for the teams and, ultimately, a source of considerable anxiety and risk. Complexity and opacity exacerbated the tensions in every big deal—vendors wanted to protect their "secret sauce"; customers wanted to share only so much about their status quo. Both sides struggled to accomplish what was needed for a win-win.

It took me years to realize what was fundamentally wrong—the parties were not focusing on the true points of differentiation in play. Neither side was asking the right questions to properly develop the TDC and Work definitions. The customer needed those definitions in order to evaluate accurately the TDT the vendor was proposing. The vendor needed those definitions to evaluate the TDC in which the TDT would be operated. What was missing, I realized, was a classification structure that helped the parties coherently take account of all of the Resources.

As the deals became increasingly digital, the accountings were more awkward and ever more difficult to achieve. Today, the pressures to make decisions without a full accounting are even worse. You feel it every day—each decision requires more analysis of the complexities, and deadlines or competition compress the time to do the job even further. In the following pages, we open up the Resource layer of the Trust Decision Model to expose a new classification structure that would have made all the difference in the past deals on which I worked.

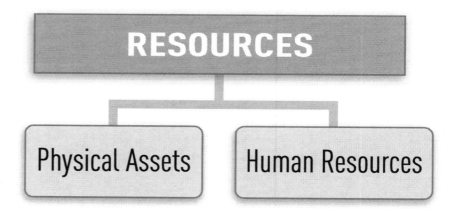

The first two classifications are straight-forward, embracing *Physical Assets* and *Human Resources*. For millennia, Physical Assets and Human Resources were the basis of all transactions in commerce or society—the things and the people used to create products and deliver services. Pretty basic Business 101. In our trust vocabulary, Physical Assets are exactly that—any tangible asset that can be touched.

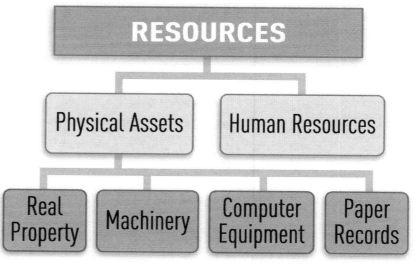

Figure 6-1

Figure 6-1 is just a simple illustration of the diversity and range of Physical Assets that we use as Resources. This Resource class is substantial and includes both natural and manufactured objects. Physical Assets are items that can be used to perform the Work.

Human Resources are equally easy to describe—living, breathing people engaged in actions that perform some or all of the Work. The physical location of a person is irrelevant; what counts is the causality of their actions in achieving the Work. We also soon will explore another dimension of what counts in evaluating Human Resources in trust decisions—the quality of the governance of their conduct according to the relevant Rules.

As time advances, each new generation learns how to use Physical Assets and Human Resources to construct and use products and services with greater complexity. A home builder organized Physical Assets and Human Resources and contracted to build and deliver a house. Railroads used Physical Assets and Human Resources to move goods and people. Automobile companies used Physical Assets and Human Resources to build and deliver cars and trucks to move goods and people faster than railroads. Airlines did the same to improve over the velocity of railroads and vehicles. But the building blocks were the same: If your business needed more space or more inventory, you acquired them. If your company needed extra personnel in the packing stations during the holidays, you hired short-term laborers. Using fairly straightforward math, a company was able to determine when it could improve its status quo—will we create more wealth if we acquire and use more Physical Assets or Human Resources?

But homes, automobiles, trains, and planes exposed a new attribute of Resources. Cars were not merely rolled out of a boxcar but assembled from components manufactured in multiple plants, shipped just-in-time to the warehouse doors of the automobile company, and built with a controlled process. Railroads only worked when miles and miles of rails, switches, and rolling stock synchronized as one. Fashion inventory storage grew from stockrooms behind the counter into retail distribution warehouses built from coordinated assemblies of storage bins, conveyors, trolleys, scanning stations, tilt-trays, and fork lifts working smoothly to move merchandise toward the loading docks and into trucks headed to the retail stores. All of these were manufactured systems operated and used by multiple stakeholders and actors. As systems, they included new Resources that ERM inventories still do not tally effectively.

WHAT IS A SYSTEM?

Such a simple question, yet I know from personal experience that question is never asked, nor answered, in law schools. Students are trained to become experts in the laws governing financial systems, healthcare systems, transportation systems, education systems, trade systems, environmental control systems, banking systems, and information technology systems. In teaching lawyers to understand the rules for these divergent and important systems, no one (to my knowledge) has ever recognized the importance of putting in place a foundational understanding of what systems are in order to author or apply the relevant Rules. Indeed, many Federal regulations use the word "system" without ever defining it.

Kenneth Boulding felt that "General Systems Theory" was the quest to establish a way of organizing into one body of knowledge all of the systematic theoretical constructs for explaining the relationships of the empirical world. The field of *systems theory* is diverse, robust, and complicated, cutting across different disciplines and, of course, indispensable to modern computing, networks, and information systems. Across many disciplines, there are many different definitions of *system*, distinguished by whether the target of discussion is biological, mechanical, computer, or chemical.

Yet these definitions share several common, persistent elements:

> ≥ A system has an objective or goal (in other words, it has defined *Work* to be accomplished).

> ≥ A system contains multiple components (or *Resources*).

> ≥ A system's components work together, each performing defined functions, to enable the objective or goal to be achieved.

What is true in the 21st Century, far more than in the final quarter of the 20th Century, is that nearly every single trust decision we are *required* to make is calculating whether to trust a system or a product of a system which we must separately decide to trust. A simple hammer is constructed of multiple components, created by different suppliers, assembled in one or more locations, shipped in larger inventories to retail stores, then tagged and bar-coded for inventory management. You are not purchasing merely the hammer, but the output of complex manufacturing, distribution, and retail systems. The same is true, of course, for trains, planes, automobiles, medical diagnostic equipment, desktop computers, and eyewear-installed calculators.

What is true
in the 21st
Century . . .
is that nearly
every single
trust decision
we are *required*
to make is
calculating
whether to
trust a system
or a product
of a system.

To decide whether to trust any TDT (which is more than a stone or similar natural object) requires you to decide to trust one or more systems. I submit that, beyond the trust decisions we make in the most intimate of personal relationships, even our decisions to trust other people are grounded in systems analyses. In order to trust an individual, we execute decision chains that require us to decide to trust connected systems.

> An *investment advisor* (the TDT) is someone in whom clients place their trust to advise them on how best to reach their financial goals (the Work). A decision to trust the TDT requires decisions to trust all of the systems with which the professional is connected:

> > Both Federal and state regulators operate regulatory licensing systems that require training, competency, supervision, and continuing education controls to perform advisory services.

> > Brokerage firms operate employment management systems that conduct detailed due diligence, require in-house training in technologies and business controls, and electronically monitor and test all digital communications and activities (including keystroke loggers), to assure an advisor's compliance with both public law requirements and the internal rules of the brokerage houses.

> The advisor connects to multiple knowledge networks, trading platforms, news analyses, and financial planning tools used to acquire information and produce work product that serves clients with greater effectiveness.

> Each network, platform, news feed, and planning tool is itself a product of complex systems that have been built in order to support advisors in their Work.

> A *teacher* is a source of information (a TDT) from which to learn (the Work). But a teacher is not standing alone in a field. Instead, the teacher is part of one or more complex systems.

> There is a national, state, or other regional authority that administers a system for testing and measuring a school system's conformity to published requirements for assuring quality education.

> There is a local school district and building principal operating an administrative system through which the teacher has been recruited, interviewed, trained, and supervised to assure the quality of work performed in the classroom.

- There is a school building (or perhaps a formal campus with many buildings), itself a system, including physical resources for the educational environment to be functional—utilities, food, plumbing, play space, and a nurse's office;

- Within the classroom, there are visual displays, blackboards, whiteboards, and media display screens, as well as books, learning guides, and online assets to which the teacher can refer or invite interaction by the students to support the Work performed to transfer knowledge;

- Each of those books, learning guides, and online assets is itself the output of a more extensive production process involving authors, editors, layout designers, printers, binders (for the tangible stuff), and distributors (and for the online assets, hosting services!).

The same analysis occurs with Information to be relied upon as a TDT, whether digital or any other format. In order to trust the Information as a tool to use in performing Work, we execute decision chains that require us to trust connected systems.

- An investment advisor's recommendation provokes the customer to ask about the presence, reliance upon, and interactions with all of the same systems.

- A teacher's interpretation of historical facts provokes some of us, as parents, to make inquiries as to the sources and systems of information he relied upon in developing that interpretation.

» The CIO's curiosity about the integrity of the audit was itself the output of a decision chain in which she was evaluating the systems and controls with which the financial numbers had been developed; clearly there was concern about their integrity.

In sum, our ability to calculate the trustworthiness of Information relies upon our ability to execute decision chains regarding the sources and systems from which the Information has arrived. Indeed, for any class of Resource, we always have questions that explore the provenance of the systems through which they have passed.

Sometimes the connected systems are visible and easily considered in the decision chains; sometimes there is merely the faintest glimmer of the supporting systems and there will be no visibility at all. Imagine selecting an investment advisor for managing your retirement account solely based on their physical appearance and gracious smile. So, in this book, trust decisions for any TDT involve decision chains to trust systems.

Still, I struggled to discover a unifying explanation of what enables the components of a system to work *together* in order to understand more conspicuously what it is we should trust. What Resources are being added to Physical Assets and Human Resources to enable systems to exist? Was the omission of these Resources in the RFP description of the CIO's systems the origin of the team's problems in evaluating the vendor proposals? The question needs to be restated, "What is a system?"

Trust decisions for any TDT involve decision chains to trust systems.

A CASE STUDY:
THE LESSONS LEARNED IN LADIES' APPAREL

I was introduced to the complexity of answering that simple question in a crowded conference room. The room was filled with engineers who specialized in the design, installation and management of the machinery and computers that make up the internal guts of the warehouses in which retail merchandise is received, stored, and distributed to retail stores and catalog customers. As the "lawyer guy," I had been assigned the responsibility of drafting the contracts and agreements through which my client, The Limited™, would contract for the installation of the largest merchandise distribution system in their history—a single warehouse filled with specialty fashion apparel for women, capable of supporting over 250 retail stores around the United States. The system was not just one system; instead, the finished warehouse would contain a series of systems, all operated by and exchanging information among different connected computer systems—dock loading sensors, conveyor belt systems, tilt-tray systems, rack-and-trolley systems, labeling systems, packing stations and sensors, etc.

The engineers were skeptical of my presence, as was I! After all, I had no training in engineering nor computing. I had no prior experience in developing agreements for a project that involved mechanical engineering, process engineering, computer systems, warehouse management best practices, loading docks, bar code readers, tilt-trays, trolleys, conveyor belts—lots of moving parts for which the contract was expected to be the adhesive through which The Limited™ would govern the process and assure that the final multi-million dollar construction could do the required work.

The engineers began by spreading out some large blueprints to explain the tilt-tray sortation system—a continuous belt of trays that would receive merchandise items from various conveyor belts connected to storage areas within the warehouse. As the belt moved forward, each tray was electronically assigned as a collection point for an individual store's shipment. The tray would collect merchandise items as it passed different conveyor belts. At the proper packing location, the tray would tilt and the items would slide down a chute to the packing station where an individual organized and boxed the merchandise for shipment.

It was an efficient and proven process. As I looked at the overall blueprint and absorbed the oral description being provided, it occurred to me that the entire system was at risk. If a tray did not properly tilt at the designated packing station but continued around, items would remain in the tray, creating confusion at the next conveyor belt loading and bungling at least two different orders—the order for which the merchandise did not tilt the first time and the second order (assuming a tilt occurs) that included unwanted items from the first go-around. It seemed sensible that the system needed a new rule—all trays, whether empty or not, had to be forcibly tilted at a final "clearing" bin before arriving at the next conveyor belt loading station. In that manner, no tray would recirculate with any merchandise. The rejected merchandise then could be recovered from the clearing bin and rerouted. So I made that precise suggestion.

The next moment changed my career, and perhaps was the true beginning of my search for a new way to understand systems more fully. The engineers were stunned that a lawyer, without any prior experience in their disciplined arts, saw the problem and identified an engineering solution by suggesting a new rule against which the system must be designed and perform, a rule that needed to be expressed in the design and the contract. As it turned out, that rule was already in place but it had not yet been explained to me. Nevertheless, the team coalesced at that moment.

We all understood that, in fact, each of us had a role to play in identifying and working with all of the rules by which the sortation system would be built and operated. The engineers realized that they could discuss those rules with me, and the contract no longer served as a legal distraction, but matured into part of the overall solution. Rather than sitting in a dust-covered filing cabinet, the contract became an integrating tool enabling improved management and governance of the full process by all of the stakeholders.

My contribution was to help assure that all of the rules shaping the quality, integrity, and operating effectiveness of the overall system were identified and organized into a coherent structure. Then, the duties and constraints could be assigned to the responsible parties. The terms and conditions of the agreement became the controlling instrument, equal to the engineering blueprints in expressing what was expected of the overall process and resulting systems.

But something else occurred. As we discussed the tilt-tray sortation system, we also discussed how that system, to be trusted, relied upon the performance of other systems contained within the warehouse, including systems independently operated by the company (such as retail store planning and scheduling systems). Both the company and the engineering

Rather than sitting in a dust-covered filing cabinet, the contract became an integrating tool enabling improved management and governance of the full process by all of the stakeholders.

firm, while independent stakeholders, were making a series of connected trust decisions. The company was making one trust decision with respect to all of the new systems to be assembled and installed (as a singular TDT). Both the company and the engineering firm were making trust decisions involving the separate systems connecting to the new systems; both sides had to achieve trust in the ability of the separate systems to connect with the new systems and work as one larger, integrated system to be known as Warehouse #1.

As the team worked through the details, it became clear three additional asset classes needed to be described and addressed by the agreement in order to enable both sides to reach the affirmative decision the new Warehouse #1 could be trusted to work.

The *first asset class* consisted of the rules that defined and governed how the systems (and their components) worked together. These were the specifications for the interoperability of the systems, covering both mechanical operations and the electronic communications and signaling occurring among the devices and systems. More than blueprints, these specifications expressed comprehensive operating rules, even including training requirements for human personnel working at various critical stations or responsible for maintenance and repair of the systems.

The *second asset class* were software applications installed as part of the new systems. The software applications performed three consistent functions across the different systems:

> The applications controlled the operation of each device in each system. Based on input

received, the applications instructed the devices' actions.

⩾ The applications instructed how each device recorded and generated data about its operations, creating real-time performance reporting that would be monitored.

⩾ The applications connected the devices and systems, enabling data to be transmitted and received among them.

The *third asset class* was something never previously considered of any consequence—the digital information that flowed between and among the systems and devices to enable their interactions. The information each system generated through the installed software applications allowed The Limited™ to verify on a continuing basis the consistent performance of individual devices (such as each tilt-tray on the tilt-tray conveyor) as well as the full warehouse system. The digital information was used to measure if the metrics that measured success were being achieved.

Stated in our trust vocabulary, the TDT was the full warehouse system. The TDC_{RES} included:

⩾ the physical machines for moving, storing, and distributing the apparel;

⩾ the warehouse workers required to operate around the machines;

- the computer hardware connected to the machines;

- the software applications installed on those computers;

- the sensors, cameras, scanners, and wiring that recorded bar codes, tilt-trays, conveyor feeds, and packing stations;

- the information records being generated by the preceding equipment; and

- the design and integration specifications against which the multiple systems were engineered, constructed, installed, and operated.

As a result, I crafted a new kind of agreement, one that previously had not been seen by the suppliers nor my client's team. The agreement identified, and bound together, all of the sources of the rules that applied for each component system and for the full system—these sources included corporate policies, database designs, data directories, training manuals, architectural blueprints for the various systems, performance report formats, etc. The contract itself set forth the requirements by which the entire system would be tested, including the types of records to be generated across the operational grid of the warehouse, their function in validating operations, and approval mechanisms for final acceptance and payment.

The vendor was not required to merely deliver systems in "good operating order." Instead, the contract stated clear metrics for the required performance quality—processing rates, error rates, weight loads, packing efficiency, etc. Without these metrics, the system's value to The Limited™ would be impossible to evaluate consistently at each step of the installation, launch, operation, and optimization.

We also developed perhaps the first multimedia performance metric! It became almost impossible to write down all of the interacting rules that identified the full assortment of merchandise to be used with the trays—sweaters, blouses, socks, jewelry, and unmentionables. The Limited™ needed some way to assure the merchandise would be loaded onto a tray without damage or breakage and would slide smoothly from the tray into the packing station. But the manufacturer, located in Nordic Europe, was required to build and test a prototype at their facility before manufacturing the entire system, using each item of merchandise to confirm the tray systems worked properly.

How could The Limited™ be sure that the performance testing was completed fully and that the system would work for all of their merchandise? The parties elected to create a videotape of the entire test. The camera rolled as each inventory item was placed onto the tray and off-loaded correctly. The contract expressly referenced the videotape as the specification for how the system would perform when installed, proving that, indeed, a picture could be worth a thousand (or more!) words.

A SYSTEM IS BUILT WITH RULES

So, what is a system? Inspired by the tilt-tray sortation system experience, I researched various sources of systems theory off and on for several years and concluded no one had expressed the perspective we had gained on that single transaction. As a team, we concluded that the target system exists and functions effectively only if we viewed the full portfolio of Rules governing the behavior of this system of systems as an integrated component of the overall TDT system itself.

A simple illustration of a system that emphasizes the Rules as an essential but distinguishable element of the system can be portrayed like this:

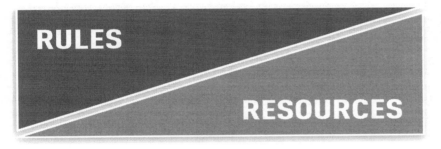

Originally, this sketch was not intended to create a new way of discussing systems. I simply needed a tool to explain to my clients and others how the contracts for which I was responsible fit into the overall design, serving to organize and assemble all of the Rules into a coherent structure and identifying the sources of other controlling Rules (such as the blueprints, prototype designs, field tests, etc.). But the sketch does more—it shows those Rules as part of the system being purchased, licensed, rented, or otherwise used by a customer. The Rules had an importance equal to all of the Resources, whether the Rules were embedded in the software applications or expressed in and incorporated into the agreements.

The sketch evolved to also illustrate the presence of digital information as another asset within a system, serving as the mortar between the Rules and the system components, as shown in Figure 6-2.

Figure 6-2

In each succeeding deal, this small change empowered more comprehensive analyses of both the status quo and the proposed new solutions. The parties focused not just on the mechanical functions of a system and the quality of the manufactured product or services. In addition, both the utility and value of digital information consumed as fuel and produced as output became important to deciding whether a new solution could be trusted.

NEW CLASSES OF RESOURCES

Return back to our CIO and her team. Imagine we are reviewing the RFP and, of course, discovering the schematics and descriptions of the existing systems did not account for all of the internal control procedures that were part of the existing systems, nor present an inventory of all of the data required to enable operational systems to be moved to the Cloud. None of the internally developed applications within Wise Industries had been designed to connect to externally performed services; they lacked the built-in interfaces that would enable a more coherent transition to third-party Cloud services.

But we can do better. By adding three new classifications to the Resource layer in the Trust Decision Model, descriptions of the Resources become more thorough and, in turn, descriptions of systems as TDTs become more comprehensive. This will enable more focused, specific trust decision chains. The three new classes are Process Rules, Code, and Data (as shown in Figure 6-3).

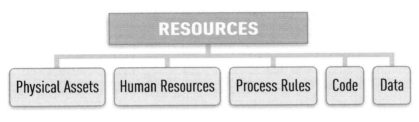

Figure 6-3

PROCESS RULES

Process Rules are architectural; they describe how a system's components work together to accomplish the Work. If a TDT is a system, the Process Rules drive the Descriptive Specification (e.g., "What is this system? What are its components? How do the components work together?"). Process Rules define the connecting points among a system's components and, as well, among a system and other systems.

Process Rules are not inherently part of any TDT. Instead, they exist within the larger Context as a potential subset of TDC_{RUL}. As with any TDC_{RES}, they must be known and have a causal connection to enabling Work. In addition, compliance with Process Rules must be capable of being controlled. Process Rules enable assemblies of Resources to work as systems. When they are selected and used in the design, assembly, and operation of a TDT, they mature into additional TDC_{RUL}.

Notice the small distinction in the final criterion—for Process Rules to be TDC_{RES}, what is controlled is the ability to cause other TDC_{RES} to comply with the Process Rules, not control of the Rules themselves. Control of the Process Rules is different. Generally, the actors who author and publish Process Rules are those who control the Process Rules as Resources. In an open society, laws and regulations are certainly Process Rules; they prescribe permissive and prohibited behaviors within complex systems (such as the varied Federal systems mentioned in the outset of this discussion). Internal corporate policies and procedures are Process Rules, controlled by the corporation itself. A manufacturer may publish Process Rules in the form of a user guide, the content of which is controlled by the manufacturer. We will explore in the later analyses of Rules used to design digital trust the varied sources of Process Rules and the tensions among control and trust in more detail.

In these early frames, recognizing Process Rules as a Resource to be used to hold the components of a system together is the key. We are still focusing only on the DM's direct knowledge. For the CIO, the Process Rules are the ones she helped author that describe the various components of the existing IT operating systems now proposed to be taken over by the vendor candidates.

Process Rules can build connections among any type of TDC_{CIR}, TDC_{RES}, or other TDC_{RUL}. Logically, mandatory pairings among Process Rules and other TDC_{RES} are required to make things work together. Indeed, many Process Rules are embedded into a TDC_{RES} structure by design. Something as simple, for instance, as a flat, three-pronged, U.K. electrical plug implements a Process Rule defining the type of outlet (and power source) to which the plug may be connected to accomplish the Work of delivering suitable power to the CIO's laptop; there is a logical, mandatory pairing of a process Rule with a Physical Asset. At the other extreme, complex Process Rules embedded into silicon chips installed in a fighter aircraft can express the controls for the circumstances in which a missile may be launched by the pilot. As with any other Resource, Process Rules will be added, deleted, or modified by the DM in the interactions among other TDC_{CIR} and TDC_{RES} as additional frames and layers proceed.

Process Rules are what make a system a system; they activate how Physical Assets and Human Resources connect. As we saw in the warehouse, a simple Process Rule for a tilt-tray conveyor kept things running.

What distinguishes Process Rules from other TDC_{RUL}? Process Rules are merely a subset of TDC_{RUL}. As the understandings of Work and Resources advance, Process Rules are selected from the larger inventory of TDC_{RUL} and paired with other TDC_{RES} to further define the TDT and better enable Work. They bind the full inventory of TDC_{RES} to work as a system. But a Process Rule also remains part of the larger TDC_{RUL} and can be important to later decisions in the trust calculations. For example:

> The posted speed limit on an interstate highway is a TDC_{RUL}.

> In designing a new car, computer sensors are included to read the speed data and, based on a GPS input, automatically slow the car if the speed limit is exceeded. The speed limit became a Process Rule

Process Rules are what make a system a system; they activate how Physical Assets and Human Resources connect.

embedded into the integrated operations of the car's system.

> ≥ If the car exceeds the speed limit due to a faulty sensor switch, the police will still enforce the posted speed limit and give you a ticket.

Process Rules are hugely important to digital trust! They are the Resources that enable the Net to function and give velocity and movement to digital information across the Net. Continually, improvements to the Net place a heavy focus on authoring and improving Process Rules and their integration into the Physical Assets. For example, new Process Rules recently announced have transformed the humble USB port on any device into a super-highway allowing labeling, ranking, and prioritization in the movement of hugely complex graphic files (such as movies or interactive gaming) to become possible with no functional change in the Physical Assets of the ports. Such innovations are what often drive any of us to purchase new toys—the keyboard still is the same, but the Process Rules empower new functions and services.

CODE

The second classification is *Code.* This includes any type of software, whether source code or object code, whatever the domain in which it is executed (servers, desktops, web browsers, embedded in devices, etc.). Code instructs computers what to calculate, how to compute, when to perform functions, and when not to do so. It is more precise than Process Rules; Code is the final, most granular expression of those Rules to the connecting elements of a system. Code is at the opposite end of the architectural spectrum, requiring specific, precise execution of 1s and 0s. Code enables a system to perform Work. Code is, without question, a distinct TDC$_{RES}$ classification inherent to information systems and devices. Yet the importance of Code to the trustworthiness of systems is a relatively recent evolution.

Some, perhaps many, readers of this book were not born at the time the warehouse system project landed on my desk in 1982. While software licenses existed as a form of commercial agreement, little concern had been expressed legally or functionally about Code embedded in the functionality of sealed devices included in delivered systems. But in the retail warehouse transaction, when the team discovered Code was embedded inside machines, we treated it like any other software, with fully negotiated license terms constructed as part of the agreement.

Today's environment is very different. Complex programs can be constructed with open source code modules, object-oriented programming enables rapid development, and automated patching of installed applications allows nearly continual remediation of the Code installed in or controlling any system. Applications, of course, can be licensed as independent programs, then downloaded and installed onto laptops, mobile phones, and mainframe servers. Entire companies conduct their business on software programs installed on remote servers accessible through Cloud-based providers.

The Internet of Things and similar innovations are increasing the ease with which Code is embedded into any physical TDC$_{RES}$. Your GPS display in your car is a simple example, factory-installed and ready to go with the first touch of your fingerprint to turn on the ignition. Yet, whether embedded or installed, the differences in Code can make all the difference in how we evaluate a system as

> Code enables a system to perform Work.

a TDT. Just think of the continued PC versus Mac battleground—the fight has always been all about the Code.

When Code is available as a TDC_{RES} that enables other Resources to operate as a system, the *initial* development of the definitions of the TDC and Work, along with a first sense of the TDT, can accelerate quickly. "[*your favorite operating system*] pre-installed" has sold enormous volumes of computers because, during a buyer's purchase decision process, the announced presence of Code made the computer easier to trust. But for more complex systems constructed of multiple components, such as the warehouse system, the trust decision process can consume enormous time. Why?

Because Code is the hardest possible Resource for which to acquire the Descriptive Specifications and Functional Specifications that communicate answers to the questions we want to ask about the provenance and design of the Code in calculating whether to award our trust. Much like being asked to buy real property in a far-off resort community without ever seeing the plot, it is very hard to learn enough about Code to make good decisions. Instead, there is every possible pressure to presume trust in Code.

Here, complexity and opacity are enormous obstacles. Yet if any TDT is a system or product of a system in the 21st Century, every TDT surely incorporates Code, if not in the TDT as a Resource, then surely in the process with which the TDT has been manufactured. Vendors insist functionality is the relevant measure of their products, whether the product is a Physical Asset with embedded Code, Code itself, or digital information that is accessed through Code. But in almost every scenario, vendors resist inquiries into the content of Code itself. In doing so, they also persist in demanding contractual terms of service that limit their liability if the Code components are defective.

The cruelty of this situation is exposed by the frequency with which Code patches are released to fix or correct vulnerabilities identified in Code that has already been placed into commercial use. Here the dilemma of Dead Man's Curve is most evident. Further complicating the challenges are the increased use of open source code and similar "blocks" that are accessible, enabling more rapid builds of software applications but putting into doubt the integrity of the internal design and the provenance of the Code employed. Indeed, an entire service industry has emerged that searches for "rogue" Code inside applications. Rare is the customer that can succeed in obtaining any disclosure that represents a Descriptive Specification or Functional Specification for Code that can be functionally integrated to their trust decisions.

What vendors will so often express in defense is that the capability of their Code to meet any such Specifications varies based on the TDC_{CIR} in which the Code will be used. Customers have different operating platforms, security standards, management oversight, and remedial capabilities (the list is much, much longer!) and the vendor argues that any of those could adversely affect the performance of their Code as a TDT. As a result, they cannot take the risk regarding the TDC_{CIR}.

That is exactly the point; there is a failure of communication between customers and vendors! In the absence of open, full disclosure of the TDC_{CIR} by the prospective customer, the vendor resists disclosure of the Descriptive Specification and Functional Specification for any Code included in the prospective TDT. The CIO had not fully described the operating assets within her systems (the TDC_{CIR} for any vendor's TDT), excluding any descriptions of all of the in-house Code assets that had been developed; the vendor responses had been similarly opaque.

But once we recognize Code is an inherent Resource to be evaluated in a trust decision, the dialogue has to evolve. Customers are not unaware of the continued weaknesses in commercial software; the steady stream of patches and announced vulnerabilities confirms they are operating on Dead Man's Curve every day. However, by classifying Code as a Resource, and recognizing Code is often the implementation at the most granular level of complex Process Rules, the possibility for a different communication emerges.

DATA

Finally, while Information is presented as a separate layer within the Trust Decision Model, digital information is also a distinct Resource classification. That may be a bit confusing, so here is the distinction—systems, as TDTs, require inbound and stored information to perform Work. Systems also produce as output all kinds of information, whether calculated reports, internal operating logs, security control data, etc. In our trust vocabulary, this class of information, whether inbound, stored, or outbound, is called *Data*. As a TDC_{RES}, Data is what a TDT uses to perform the Work. As output, whether as the primary product of computations or secondary performance reports, Data is also what a TDT creates. As we know very well, one system's output becomes the input for another. Indeed, even for each of us as computer users, the Data created by an application becomes the Data input we require to do our share in completing the Work.

Data is what a TDT uses to perform the Work. . . . Data is also what a TDT creates.

Digital information is everywhere in the Context; what we are looking for as Data to be a potential Resource is a subset of the universe of information that surrounds us. No different than any other $TDC_{RES,}$ Data is digital information that can be described by a Descriptive Specification and Functional Specification. Those Specifications, when they align to specific digital information, qualify that information as Data and then enable the Data to be paired to other TDC_{RES} and subject to TDC_{RUL}. Stated simply, Data as a Resource is digital information that aligns to the requirements for the kinds of information which can be inputted and used by TDTs in their operations.

In contrast, the Information layer in the Trust Decision Model is referring to the Decisional Information upon which we rely to calculate trust outcomes in out trust decisions. Decisional Information is what the *DM* needs to calculate trust; Data is what *a system* needs to perform the Work for which it has been trusted as a TDT. Decisional Information can include Data, particularly output information that records performance of a TDT against certain Descriptive Specifications and Functional Specifications. What distinguishes the two is the different use to which the information is being applied.

Thus, when the DM is surveying the Resources remaining in the Context (after the initial culling occurs), whether Data is present as a possible TDC_{RES} becomes another key variable in shaping the early TDC. Indeed, reliance on functional, conforming Data in using any TDT is more and more part of the deal. Is the Data known to exist? Can the Data be used to perform the Work successfully? Is the Data capable of being controlled? Complexity and opacity make those questions harder and harder to answer.

Does the Data satisfy all of the evolving elements for defining the TDC and the Work? Where is the Data? How was it developed and maintained? What controls have been used to assure its integrity? Can the Data move among other TDC_{RES} as part of a larger system to complete the Work? Will the Data measure up to the performance metrics by which we calculate the success of the Work? Once again, complexity and opacity endanger our decision process and put pressure on us to presume the trustworthiness of Data.

Decisional Information is what the DM needs to calculate trust; Data is what a system needs to perform the Work for which it has been trusted as a TDT.

ASSEMBLING THE RESOURCES

With the preceding breakdown (as shown in Figure 6-3), let us return to our CIO's story and the operating frames of her trust decisions. Moving beyond the ERM, below (Figure 6-4) is a more detailed inventory of the TDC_{RES} for her systems. This is still *very high level*, but the added Resource classifications (Process Rules, Code, Data) immediately generate a different perspective, illustrating how much more thorough we must be in expressing, as a customer, the qualities of the TDC (which include all of the TDC_{RES} in the status quo) and, as a vendor, the alignment of proposed products and solutions (as TDTs) with the TDC. The challenge is to identify and properly describe the Resources to enable the ability to line up the descriptions with the Work that needs to be done and, on another layer, the evolving TDT descriptions.

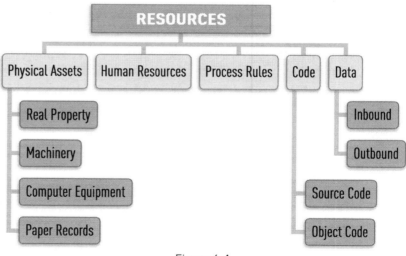

Figure 6-4

The differences between the RFP and what should have been included are now visibly obvious. But the CIO's experience is not uncommon. As technology invites more and more interdependencies, companies and organizations often discover they have not authored their Process Rules or Code, nor structured their Data, to enable the migration or movement of the related services to another actor. These Resources were never contemplated as something to be moved around or shared. As a result, when outsourcing, shared services, or the Cloud comes calling, companies are woefully unprepared to effectively evaluate their options and make strong decisions that can be trusted.

Now, go back to that last major decision you needed to make. Using the Resource classifications presented in this chapter, ask yourself: "Are all of the potential Resources I needed to evaluate in one of the five classifications?" They should be, with one exception: money. That's right, I am proposing that money is *not* a Resource for the purpose of shaping the definitions of TDC, TDT, and Work. Yes, certain potential Resources (such as a Porsche) will be excluded because they clearly are beyond a DM's financial means. But as any business executive knows, when money is involved, never say never. There are always ways of creating or finding capital.

Money still matters to the final trust decision, and the Trust Decision Model provides another, later opportunity to calculate the financial values. When you are undertaking to define the TDC and to find and assemble the TDC_{RES} to perform the Work, money does not yet matter. What matters is properly calculating where to draw the TDC boundary in order to fully identify the potential TDC_{RES} to use as a TDT to do the Work.

You might also ask, "What about intellectual property—patents, copyrights, trademarks, trade secrets, and know-how? Aren't those to be included as Resources?" Actually, they are all present in our Resource classes, just not dressed with those labels. The rules protecting intellectual property are part of TDC_{RUL}. Patents draw a circle around a defined bundle of Resources and the related statutes impose restrictions on the use of that bundle by others. Design patents are combinations of Physical Assets, Process Rules, Code, and Data; process patents emphasize bundles of Process Rules. Copyright and trademark law do the same, limiting uses of certain Data output by others. For example, copyright law applied to this book, authored as the output of several different computer systems, limits how much you can reproduce and distribute without my permission.

But asking the intellectual property question emphasizes an important point. When you calculate whether to trust a specific TDT, the Trust Decision Model anticipates that your decision will always consider whether the TDC includes certain Rules (TDC_{RUL}) paired to how you are defining the Work and the TDT. Indeed, the presence of some Rules may even be a mandatory pairing with certain Resources. For example, whether patent, copyright, or trade secrets laws exist will affect how you calculate your level of trust in any Resource. Since, through bad experiences, you have learned poorly paid workers in unsafe conditions tend to produce manufactured goods that cannot be trusted, you may require vendors that pay Human Resources no less than legally established minimum wages (Process Rules) or only operate manufacturing plants (Physical Assets) that conform to certain public safety and worker health protection regulations (Process Rules).

These TDC_{RUL} are only useful to you if they are meaningfully enforced. Just being a Rule on the books does not affect the calculation of trust. Instead, the real question is whether the Resources will create Data output that allows you to determine whether the legal rules, as TDC_{RUL}, are being enforced. To do so, the Descriptive Specifications and Functional Specifications for the

Resources must address whether the right Data is being generated to measure compliance. Yes, this remains complex, but the Trust Decision Model introduces a foundation on which to structure the complexity.

Here again, the CIO had contributed to the failure to communicate. Up to now, the company had steered away from distributed computing and virtual private networks across third-party infrastructure. A major reason had been the potential complexities of making sure sensitive corporate information could be adequately protected under the different laws of various "low-cost" data center locations. Yet the RFP did not address those concerns, nor the General Counsel's insistence that any outsourcing vendor would have to provide continuing security monitoring on their systems (in order to meet certain new Federal agency rules for their industry). The responsive proposals were predictable: the vendors leveraged their data centers in the "low-cost" locations and, since they were not asked, never indicated the Data output they could generate to enable the CIO to calculate legal compliance.

These weaknesses can be corrected, of course, but that requires consuming more time to properly author the Rules and yet another R & R by all concerned. This was the decision made by the CIO; the team went back to the conference room, ordered Chinese, and began to create a supplemental RFP that would be more inclusive.

THE FILM SO FAR

At this point, within merely two or three frames of our film, perhaps merely milliseconds in time for an everyday decision, a lot has occurred:

≥ An understanding of Context has been built, grounded on the realization that trust decisions begin by taking account of the surrounding Circumstances and Resources, including the Rules that may govern how Work will be performed.

≥ Circumstances and Resources, and their causal relationships with Work, have been unfolded, and the structures on which effective descriptions are built, the Descriptive Specification and the Functional Specification, have been introduced.

≥ Resource classifications have been presented with which to identify and classify Physical Assets, Human Resources, Process Rules, Code, and Data that may be considered further as components of a TDT (and as parts of a controlled system) with which the Work will be performed.

≥ Line drawing has been explained as a part of how trust decisions are engineered, and the initial rules for how to do so correctly (and incorrectly!) have been illustrated with the principle of indifference and the Rhett Butler Rule.

In the next frame, we complete the ranking of TDC_{CIR}, TDC_{RES}, and TDC_{RUL} and draw the lines required to create the initial description of the TDC. Then you will have the background on which to stack more detail into the layers defining the Work. After all, isn't it about time to get some Work done?

CHAPTER 7

DRAWING THE LINES

CHALLENGED BY THE CEO to use "this Cloud thing" to the company's best advantage, the CIO's initial survey of her own systems and the competing vendors created quite a bit of confusion. There were almost too many options of how Internet-based services could be employed, and all of them were offering operational and economic benefits nearly too good to be believed. As the supplemental RFP exercise began, she knew she needed to draw some lines that put some boundaries around the services that would be moved first.

In trust vocabulary terms, the CIO's initial survey was reviewing the Context. The global footprint of her operations, combined with the diversity of locations and systems configurations offered by the various Cloud vendors, identified an immense portfolio of Circumstances to be considered; her own system assets and those of the vendors (and the respective contractors, application licensors, and management teams of each) were a lot of Resources.

Her company's business activities covered three Federal regulated market segments, none of which included compliance frameworks that contemplated off-shore IT operations. To move ahead, the CIO had to select the Circumstances, Resources, and Rules that would define the boundaries within which the decision process would unfold ($TDC = TDC_{CIR} + TDC_{RES} + TDC_{RUL}$); every other place where the Cloud could have an impact needed to be taken out of play.

You likely have been there and done the same thing. Making decisions that can be trusted always involves drawing lines. Examining the decisions of others always audits how the lines were drawn. Knowing others will audit your decisions affects how you draw the lines. The CIO knew there will be questions testing her line-drawing. So do you, particularly on those decisions where you are a leader and there are others above and around you who may question your process.

In the prior chapters, we traveled through the early few frames, building a foundation for drawing the lines. The starting point is to observe the Context, defined by your direct knowledge and sense of what can be observed. You immediately exclude the Context elements that are not visible to your senses or of which you have no knowledge. The other Context elements are classified as Circumstances, Resources, or Rules and, if possible, further divided into subsidiary classes.

You also immediately exclude Circumstances with no causality on the proposed Work to be performed and Resources that are economically out of reach (subject, of course, to the "never say never" caveat). Resources that have possible causality on the proposed Work but cannot be controlled (such as electric power of a defined

Making decisions that can be trusted always involves drawing lines. Examining the decisions of others always audits how the lines were drawn.

voltage accessible through a converter plug) remain relevant as part of the TDC and perhaps even needed for the Work to be completed. Some Resources and Rules (but not Circumstances with known causality) may have already been excluded by applying the Rhett Butler Rule.

Certain Circumstances, Resources, and Rules have mandatory pairings established among them; succeeding with the Work requires alignment with those elements so they automatically are included as part of the TDC. You cannot fly a kite without wind. You cannot reach the top of the wall without a stepladder. You cannot obtain a building occupancy permit without installing the correct number of smoke sensor alarms.

For the remaining Context elements, their inclusion in the TDC requires ranking and line-drawing. Now the fun begins. Within the same moment of time, you or any DM are identifying the elements that will be included in the calculation of what is required to define and perform the Work. An error—leaving out elements that can measurably influence the outcome (causality) or including elements that will have no impact at all—alters both the quality of your trust decision and how others decide whether to trust your decisions.

Volumes of historic trust research attribute this sorting process to instinct but the capabilities of digital technology are now allowing us to see inside; the emerging awareness is that the rankings and line drawings at this point (and subsequent points in the decision chain) are actually being calculated using the layers of the Trust Decision Model—Resources, Rules, Information, and Time. Once you realize that essential truth, you can begin to make better decisions.

Rankings and line drawings . . . are actually being calculated using the layers of the Trust Decision Model— Resources, Rules, Information, and Time.

RANKINGS ARE MATHEMATICAL EXPRESSIONS

In the Trust Decision Model, rankings are mathematical expressions of the causality of each Circumstance, Resource, and Rule on performing the Work. They express the probabilities of each influencing success in the Work. To be ranked above the line is a calculation of this likelihood—whether expressed as a positive (this automated trading platform will enable faster day trading) or a negative (this single-factor authentication password exposes the network to hackers). Those Context elements that are assigned higher calculations of probability are those with which the boundary and description of the TDC is constructed.

In this frame of our trust decision film, if you are the DM making an everyday decision about your dinner options, everything is occurring internally. In the metaphor of the animation studio, the informal collaborations among the artists of the different layers become more serious. Descriptions of the Work must be more precise so that the positive and negative impacts of the Circumstances, Resources, and Rules on the Work, and among those elements, can be inputted. At the same time, precision in describing the TDC elements becomes more important to accurately describing the Work. So, rather than a single frame, a series of frames are needed to illustrate the decision chain, with energy concurrently devoted to developing multiple layers within each frame.

Like any mathematical work, the calculations are structured by Rules and Decisional Information. The Rules generate the type of Decisional Information to be gathered. The DM answers questions that provide the input needed in simple, binary structure (1s or 0s). Each Rule is authored with such granular detail that the Decisional Information can be expressed in that manner.

> *Rule*: Our Company only does business with domestic IT service providers.
>
> *Question:* Is Geneva Data (a Resource) an American corporation (yes=1, no=0)?
>
> *Decisional Information*: Geneva Data is a Swiss corporation (0).
>
> *Result*: Geneva Data is excluded from the TDC.

In the initial frames, the DM will freeze the existing description of Work (call it Work 0.1). Then, based on Work 0.1, the preceding process unfolds. Based on Rules, Decisional Information is collected by direct observation, and points are awarded, creating accumulative scores for each element.

Concurrently with each calculation, the DM evaluates whether the Circumstance, Resource, or Rule, if retained in the TDC, revises Work 0.1 and generates a new Work description (Work 0.2).

> *Resource*: An electric nail gun is in the room.
>
> *Question*: Should the prior description of Work ("Nail the wall frame together") be revised ("Nail the wall frame together using an electric nail gun")?

This step actually requires the DM to be asking questions about the historic impact of the variable element, in effect querying the stored performance records. In a few pages, we will learn what the questions are that are being asked to solicit and acquire that Decisional Information.

Once individual rankings are complete, the DM then calculates alternative outcomes using combinations of options. This begins to get interesting when we slow down the process and watch within each frame and within each layer. With each combination, the questions are gathering Decisional Information that fuels the next possible combinations. Using the trust vocabulary, the Decisional Information becomes Data for defining the Work.

Example One

Resource: The electric nail gun requires a grounded three-pronged outlet.

Resource: The wall contains a grounded three-pronged outlet.

Question: Should the prior description of Work ("Nail the wall frame together") be revised ("Nail the wall frame together using an electric nail gun supported by a functional power supply")?

Example Two

Resource: The electric nail gun requires a grounded three-pronged outlet for 220v power.

Resource: The wall contains a grounded three-pronged outlet for 110v power.

Resource: The carpenter's tool belt includes a standard 16 oz. hammer.

Question: Should the prior description of Work ("Nail the wall frame together using an electric nail gun supported by a functional power supply") be revised to ("Nail the wall frame together manually using any available hammer")?

The calculations may result in single elements (such as an electric nail gun as a Resource) being included until a second input (there is no power available) disqualifies its probability; the process is also looking for conflicts among pairings of TDC_{CIR}, TDC_{RES}, and TDC_{RUL} that can disqualify probability (what good is an electric nail gun if the contractor's company has a rule, based on safety concerns, prohibiting their use?).

In all of the calculations, sums are being concurrently calculated against "the line." Where is that line being drawn initially? In these initial frames, which only require a sketch, the line is drawn "low" for Circumstances and "high" for Resources and Rules. In other words, for Circumstances that can affect outcomes, the DM wants to be as inclusive as possible, including Circumstances with low probabilities of impacting the outcome (remember Circumstances are already present because of known causality). For Resources and Rules, the DM wants to narrow the field, including only those Resources most likely to succeed in performing the Work and only those Rules most likely to produce the same outcome. Resources and Rules are above the line only when there is a high probability.

Even within these few frames and layers, the process is dynamic, a continuing Rewind and Recalculation. The answers to initial questions become the Decisional Information for the next questions until the DM has acquired enough Decisional Information to calculate where to better draw the line.

This is the moment in the trust decision chaining where innovation finds its greatest momentum. If the available Resources can perform the Work pursuant to the Rules under the current Circumstances, the film skips quite a few scenes. But, if the Circumstances, Resources, and Rules above the line do not add up, the

This is the moment in the trust decision chaining where innovation finds its greatest momentum.

DM creates and tests the calculations of the probabilities by formulating and scoring unexpected combinations. Lacking a hammer, you observe a shoe on the floor and evaluate the probabilities. Lacking a domestically incorporated corporate entity, Geneva Data proposes to acquire a California-based holding company. Asked to evaluate retail sales trends from sales receipts, confronted by a rule requiring that personal information be encrypted, and lacking an encryption tool, you sketch out a revised version of the existing database (a Resource) to exclude the regulated personal information. In each instance, existing Resources are being calculated as alternatives. The decision to *trust* an innovative combination comes later in the process. But, to *create* the combination, one has to calculate some confidence in the probabilities ("I wonder if this might work"), to justify advancing the innovation beyond the current frame.

I hope it is becoming clear that the trust vocabulary enables us to express differently what innovation means. Much of humankind's history of innovation has involved the adaptation of Physical Assets and Human Resources (as Resources) to new combinations that perform Work. In other words, we create new pairings that become new systems, combinations of Resources used to perform Work not otherwise capable of being performed (i.e., new TDTs). In turn, each new innovation enables a revision in how Work is defined (creating Work 2.0). Our success with new TDTs and improved definitions of Work drive reforms in how Rules within a Context are authored ("Electric nail guns are allowed if operated by carpenters with 20 hours of training in their use") and how new Process Rules develop and mature.

This is where the freeze-frame, slow motion process has great utility. At each layer, the TDC boundaries (and the line) are being

> The trust vocabulary enables us to express differently what innovation means.

altered by how the probabilities of new combinations allow the definition of Work to be revised, which provokes the creation of new Rules (including Process Rules) that make things work. The process can be rapid, but it can also be time-consuming. If new combinations are not immediately imagined, the clock keeps ticking, increasing the lost opportunity cost of being unable to make a decision within the known Context.

This frame is also the point when a DM may evaluate the Context and conclude that, within the known Circumstances and in accord with known Rules, *none* of the existing Resources can be used to perform the Work. In other words, no Resources in the Context, either alone or in combination, are above the line. These chained decisions and pairings are calculations very similar to later, more complex trust decisions, but the current result is a negative outcome. There are no Resources within the Context for which the DM has direct knowledge of Anticipated Causality in performing the Work.

Again, this is where innovation launches. Commissioned by your spouse to hang the new, class picture of your twin fourth-graders, you have neither a hammer nor electric nail gun. No Resource is above the line. But you have direct knowledge of the weight of your shoe, the composition of the sole, the density of the drywall, and a sense memory of an old TV comedy in which an actor used a shoe. Suddenly a Resource in the Context moves above the line.

What occurs in a couple of milliseconds is near astounding. Work 1.0 anticipates a tool designed for pounding. There is a rough sense of the Resources that will work, with a Descriptive Specification and Functional Specification inferred by the Work description. A

> Because of
> its precise,
> granular nature,
> Code performs
> only the Work
> for which its
> has been
> programmed.
> Nothing more.
> If Code as
> a Resource
> cannot be
> used toward
> performing
> the Work, the
> Code falls
> below the line.

quick visual survey confirms no Resource meets the Rules of those specifications. Knowledge of the shoe is a Descriptive Specification. Knowledge of the drywall is a Descriptive Specification. The old TV comedy is a visual memory of a Functional Specification for a shoe as a nail-driving tool. The description of the Work is revised; Work 2.0 allows any tool with a functional weight and material density within a measured range similar to at least those of a manual hammer. The weight and composition of the shoe become 1s and 0s that are calculated against new Rules inferred by Work 2.0 and there is an anticipated causality that the shoe may work. Hence, the shoe falls above the line as a TDC_{RES}, even at the cost of the effort to remove it from your foot!

When executing trust decisions involving Code, there is a fascinating limit to the innovation that can occur at this moment. Because of its precise, granular nature, Code performs only the Work for which it has been programmed. Nothing more. If Code as a Resource cannot be used toward performing the Work, the Code falls below the line. There are no alternative uses of that Code. To create innovation with Code, even the coolest programs in the world need additional Code, new programmed instructions that adapt and revise what exists to create a new Resource aligned to the description of the new, desired Work.

This is not uncommon when trying to transport Data between two existing, autonomous programs; one needs new Code that connects the existing programs, allowing the Data to transition between the applications. The connecting Code may exist in the larger Context (such as an open source object package that creates an interface between two widely used commercial programs), but if the DM has no direct knowledge of the connecting Code as a Resource, both of the known component programs fall below the line. It is not possible to otherwise combine them to get the Work performed.

Similarly, for many other calculations that do not involve Code, when the initial Resources cannot be added up to perform the Work, that is again the moment of innovation or adaptation. Yet, just before that frame, and after the first calculation, the DM asks one other question: "Beyond my direct memory, can I acquire other Decisional Information that will demonstrate how the existing Resources can be employed to perform the Work?"

THE RIGHT DECISIONAL INFORMATION

So what Decisional Information does the DM need to gather about any Circumstance, Resource, or Rule in order to know how to calculate the probabilities and determine where to draw the line? Remarkably, at this early stage of the trust decision film, the Decisional Information required is comparable to the Decisional Information the DM will use to calculate later trust decisions, whether internally acquired or obtained from other sources.

The mathematical nature of the calculations means the questions we are asking, driven by the Rules, require quantitative, numeric answers. Even now, in first drawing the TDC boundary, the chained decisions are determining probability. To do so, there are five essential questions, each of which seeks metrics that matter:

> ≥ How often has the Work been achieved in the presence of the Circumstance, Resource, or Rule?

> ≥ How often has the Work been achieved in the absence of the Circumstance, Resource, or Rule?

The mathematical nature of the calculations means the questions we are asking, driven by the Rules, require quantitative, numeric answers.

> How often has the Work failed in the presence of the Circumstance, Resource, or Rule?

> What is the frequency with which the DM has directly observed a causality between the Circumstance, Resource, or Rule, on one hand, and the Work, on the other hand?

> How often was the Work accomplished with the Circumstance, Resource, or Rule having no observed effect on the outcome?

Each question is surveying historical performance information (output Data within any digital environment), to count outcomes. Was the Work achieved? Was the element present? Was the Work achieved without the element present? If the Work was not achieved and the elements were present, that outcome also counts.

The fourth and fifth questions involve counting observed relationships. The measurements always will be more useful when the denominator of total comparable Contexts is larger. A single successful direct causality (the hammer hit the nail the first time) bears little weight on the future probable effectiveness of the hammer. Over 20 million instances with only three failures enables a much more reliable calculation. If the DM lacks direct experience, this moment is when the DM may seek other sources of the Decisional Information required for drawing the line.

When a DM has no direct experience with a Circumstance, Resource, or Rule, these questions are not possible to answer. There is a buried "gotcha"; if you have had no experience, then you do not know to ask the question. The result is a more limited inquiry and, potentially, an improperly drawn line.

There is a similar, perhaps even disturbing, outcome when the Resource being considered is a black box—an asset (or system) for which the DM cannot identify the Resources, Rules or Circumstances. So many vendors do just that, offering systems as closed Resources that cannot be effectively queried by their customers. Functionally, it is the same as if the DM has no experience. The questions cannot be formulated against which to collect the Decisional Information.

This is where the war for control rises above the horizon. If a vendor can prevent a customer from asking the appropriate questions regarding how well the Resources offered by the vendor actually perform the Work, the vendor is disabling the customer's capacity to execute the trust decision about the vendor (and its systems) as Resources to perform the Work. The DM simply cannot access the historical records to know the answers—all that is visible is a black box.

Vendors have so many ways of constraining customers at this moment in the trust decision:

> "I actually don't know all of what's inside, but let me tell you, it sure goes fast."

> "Those are great questions; I will be sure to get someone in Product Design to get back to you."

> "I am not authorized to answer your questions. They would require us to disclose confidential

This is where the war for control rises above the horizon.

information we are not prepared to share; you will just have to trust us."

Yet, if a customer, as a DM, cannot acquire the right Decisional Information, then the ranking and stacking calculations become suspect, if they can even proceed at all.

RANKING AND STACKING

In these early frames, however, most trust decisions do proceed forward. Answering the preceding questions produces arithmetic counts—this is all that is needed at this point. For each Circumstance, Resource, and Rule, the DM now has objective mathematical content and can begin to populate more details in the respective Descriptive Specifications and Functional Specifications. Using the answers, each Circumstance, Resource, and Rule can be assigned values and, within their respective stacks, sorted and ranked top to bottom, based on the calculated probability of their impact on getting the Work done, separately and in combinations. Working only with direct knowledge and observed Context elements, the DM is narrowing the inventory of Circumstances, Resources, and Rules and then drawing the line. Those that remain become the TDC in which the process continues.

Living our daily lives, drawing the line is internal to how we evaluate the surrounding Context for selecting our breakfast foods, the best route to work, the proper template to use for the quarterly report, and the right app to download to create a visual slideshow. The process is buried inside the first frames of each routine decision.

In organizations and in business, however, the situation is different. If you are a leader making decisions, you want your decisions to be trusted and you want the decisions to be defensible when scrutinized by others. The questions presented in this chapter are vital weapons for formulating and building better decisions. They help you to collect and organize the Decisional Information required to rack, stack, and combine the Context elements. In turn, you then are able then to better draw the line, precisely identifying the Circumstances, Resources, and Rules you will include and the Resources and Rules to which you are indifferent (or even knowingly exclude under the Rhett Butler Rule). Some Circumstances may also be excluded as those to which you have determined to be indifferent. But those are not Rhett Butler Rule exclusions; instead, they are based on Decisional Information and line-drawing.

WHAT ABOUT THE LINE?

Each of the preceding essential questions has variations that you may ask in every TDC development process. The more complex the Work, Resources, and Rules (and, in turn, the more complex the Circumstances to be taken into account), the more questions you will need to ask. Yet, as complexity and opacity accumulate, a DM also needs to determine the critical mass of Decisional Information that is sufficient for proceeding with the trust decision process. That decision—which now allows you to draw the line defining the TDC—ends the decision chain represented by the opening frames of our film.

Working with these questions and the Trust Decision Model, you can improve the quality of the Decisional Information that you collect before making the determination of where to first draw the line describing the TDC. You are able to ask more pertinent questions. You are able to consider more varied combinations. In doing so, you are expanding your opportunities for innovation and success.

Where to draw the line, as a calculation of probabilities, varies. The answers to the essential questions are the input you need, but no magic algorithm is going to be found here or in the remaining pages. The science of probability mathematics offers nearly infinite strategies and analytical options. Instead, this chapter emphasizes the dynamics occurring at different layers—how the chained decisions to include and exclude Circumstances, Resources, and Rules change how you view and define Work and, in turn, how the evolving definition of Work alters the view of the TDC and its boundary. The questions also emphasize how early in the trust decision process the objective records of past experience displace any sense that trust is based on emotion. Everything becomes a calculation based on Decisional Information.

Let us close this chapter by returning to the challenges of boundary definition for the CIO and her team. Their initial planning overlooked one critical insight—the success or failure of their systems depended heavily on the internal rules with which the systems, devices, and applications worked as a singular, functioning, complex system that the company currently trusted. That information system was Wise's heartbeat. Millions had been spent, mostly under the CIO's seven-year tenure, developing internal applications and building process structures that leveraged the automation under her control. Those rules were critical as Resources, expressed both as Process Rules and Code. Any selection of a Cloud-based service provider as an alternate TDT had to account for those Resources, and she would have to assure the Board that those Resources would continue to drive the business toward additional wealth creation.

Imagine the CIO herself was able to order an R & R. Aware of the importance of those Resources, the CIO's team could have changed how Work was defined in the original RFP. They could have attached a listing of the in-house apps that would require support; the corporate policies, procedures, and controls that had been implemented in the design and operation of the overall system; and the metrics used to assure their continued execution. In the vocabulary of trust, these were TDC_{RES} and TDC_{RUL} that would have become mandatory elements in how the Work was defined. The line would have been drawn to include them above the line and, with that, the TDC would have been more fully constructed. This time, however, the supplemental RFP becomes the R & R. Now the CIO has a chance to improve the TDC.

But, with so much focus on the TDC, we have to ask—what has been happening at the Work layer? How will Work be described in the revised RFP in order to calculate trust better?

THE TRUST VOCABULARY

In this chapter, you will learn the following words:

Decisional Information Risk

Decisional Information Sources

Results

Risks (also shown as TDC_{RISK} or TDT_{RISK})

Tasks

CHAPTER 8

DEFINING WORK

ASSEMBLED BY THE CIO, the IT team managers at Wise were totally unsettled. This included the managers for Enterprise Architecture, Systems Engineering, Desktop Services, Server Farms, Outsourcing, Records Management, Information Security, Mobile Devices, and IT Legal. Moving to Cloud-based services had been announced as a mandate, not an option. No one really wanted to go there. But the original RFP had not been useful; the vendors had not delivered back the road map that had been anticipated. The CIO's briefing was concise, re-explaining the terms of the mandate and the boundaries she was proposing to target around the highest priorities to include in the supplemental RFP.

The team met the CIO's opening question with a dark, brooding silence, their heads bowed in thought, or avoidance. She imagined no one wanted to make eye contact and risk being asked to answer her question: "How will we measure success?" Finally, a voice replied, "But what are we being asked to do?"

So often in business and all of the other paths we travel, the destination is known. But *how* one gets from here to there is what making decisions is all about. Choices. Options. Do nothing. Go it alone. Select the right tools. Get the best results. Avoid the risks. Make the deadline. Complete the job. Succeed.

Every trust decision finds its origin at the moment there is awareness that an activity to perform or a task to complete lies ahead. In the trust vocabulary, of course, that activity is Work. To expand on earlier discussion, Work can be as simple as having a sip of soup or as complex as launching a rocket into space. Dismantling and relocating active IT systems and operations to a Cloud-based service provider with distributed data centers operating in three continents sometimes can make launching a rocket seem like child's play, but both are just Work, no matter how complex the tasks or the number of components to be assembled.

A CLOSER LOOK

As a concept, Work has nearly infinite complexity and dimension. It may be a single task, or a series of the same task repeated in sequence. Work may be a collection of tasks that must be performed in sequence, with structural routing, or branching across those tasks, with the order and execution driven by a series of if-then connectors. It may be a collection of tasks that we assemble into one bucket, but which may not be required to be performed in sequence nor in any structured pattern. Work can be physical activity or intellectual activity. Work may involve communication of content, recordation of activities, execution of transactions, or transfer of intellectual knowledge. Work may be the restraint or execution of negative controls—activities that prevent certain behavior, certain conditions, actions, or transactions. Work can be entertainment—virtually anything we do to amuse ourselves beyond staring at the landscape requires us to select and interact with other objects or people—a comfortable chair, a book, a film, a friend, or a favorite tavern. Work may be all of these variations and combinations and more.

Completing Work is the inherent, fundamental outcome about which you are making trust decisions. As introduced earlier, in nearly all our daily activities, you have three options when you have Work to do:

> The first option—do nothing. This, however, usually has severe consequences—you don't eat; you don't drink; you have no shelter in which to live; you don't get paid at your job. Doing nothing is always an option, but it leaves the Work, well, unperformed.

> The second option—perform the Work using only your own capabilities (e.g., your hands, your strength, and your mind). There are some chores for which you require no other assistance or devices to complete the Work. But, in truth, those tasks are few in number. Walking or running from here to there. Pulling yourself up into a tree. Thinking about and formulating ideas. Speaking. Listening. Sleeping.

> The third option—select and use tools that enable you to perform your Work. This option began early in our evolution, perhaps with the first time a human picked up a branch to dislodge an apple just beyond reach. Since then, our calculations have

Completing Work is the inherent, fundamental outcome about which you are making trust decisions.

continued to evolve. In every instance, we select tools because we trust them to improve the probability that the Work will be performed correctly; we trust them to perform the Work in a manner that meets or exceeds how we will measure success in doing so.

Faced with Work to perform, all of us—as individuals, teams, departments, corporations, and nations—extend beyond ourselves and into the surrounding environment to identify and acquire the tools, objects, resources, and information that we can marshal to perform the Work. We now know each of these assets are Resources. Each Resource that you select to evaluate becomes a TDT. A single TDT may perform all of the Work. You also may select a TDT to perform only one of the tasks that make up a complex unit of Work. Or you may be selecting complex TDTs composed of many Resources to perform only a single task. This book is a TDT you have selected for the Work of catching up to those who already understand that digital trust will become the key competitive differential during the next two decades!

In slow motion, formulating a description of the Work may seem to be a job that we already completed in the first frame. Yes, the Work layer was being sketched in the first moments but it is far from complete. By placing priority on defining the TDC (and awareness of the Circumstances, Resources, and Rules) as the focus of our first efforts, our sense of what the Work is may be further refined by our awareness of the TDC. Both TDC and Work are rough sketches at this point in the film, but the sequence is clear. We needed a cognitive sense of the TDC to make progress defining the Work.

For most decisions in our normal lives, the surveillance and configuration of the TDC and defining Work are nearly instinctive. But in business, the pressure to make decisions quickly can provoke shortcuts and omissions. By understanding what must occur in this frame for a good decision, and taking the time to invest the labor to compose a strong definition of Work, the later decisions in the process can actually occur more quickly.

"WHAT ARE WE BEING ASKED TO DO?"

In this chapter, we explore how Work needs to be defined to calculate trust effectively. Every day, we make hundreds or thousands of decisions to select and use tools. Prior to each selection and use, we must describe the Work. That description narrows further the inventory of TDC_{RES} from which to choose. The more precise the Work description, the more likely we will select and use the right tool for the job.

Each tool selection always includes some level of uncertainty. Sometimes the tools work just fine, but more often than we might wish to admit, our choices are less than ideal. The Work may require more effort than expected (a saw may be unknowingly dull, extending the time to cut up the firewood), the tool may be inadequate to do the work well (have you ever tried to eat peas with a flat knife?), or the information is too old or incomplete (like a soiled, ancient map), leaving you still lost.

I believe our level of dissatisfaction or disappointment with the quality of the work performed by any tool we select has a root cause—our inability to achieve precision and completeness in expressing the requirements for the Work. That is not a flaw, but it is our reality. The adverse effects we then experience expose, said euphemistically, the "opportunities for improvement." For example:

> When you are in a hurry, you may not use care to detail all of the criteria that the Work must satisfy in order for your undertaking to be successful. Deadlines have the same effect, limiting the time (and frames) devoted to building a more complete description.

> When you have limited experience, you may not have enough knowledge of the variables, circumstances, and complexities within the TDC that will challenge you in completing the tasks ahead. As a result, the criteria for what the Work must accomplish (and, in turn, the tools you will select as a TDT to do the Work) are incomplete.

> When you believe your own skills, strengths, knowledge, or capabilities can overcome the limitations of available tools (a sales performance dataset is missing three columns of data you feel you can calculate on a scratch pad; the light weight of a shoe to be used as a hammer can be offset by your physical strength), you still may select and use the tool only to discover your self-assessment was inaccurate (in trust vocabulary terms, you improperly described the Functional Specification for yourself as a Resource).

In any of these circumstances, our failures and shortcomings in executing the Work are logs we store inside our memory. They become the information that fuels how we learn—our experience builds our knowledge of the rules, criteria, pairings, and variables that may influence our effectiveness. Falling short in performing the Work enables us to rethink how we previously defined the Work (and, in turn, the requirements for Resources that could assist us).

On the next occasion when a similar task is presented, we call upon that experience to survey the TDC. We recall the prior experiences and use that knowledge to generate different requirements for defining success in performing the Work and, in turn, produce a new, improved, and different definition of the Work. Using that description, the TDT selection is more likely to be a better one than before; we have greater trust that it *will* be the right tool for the job. That is how learning connects with trust. Our experiences shape and refine the inventories of Rules we use to inform how we structure our next choices. The thousands of decisions we make to select tools generate histories of their effectiveness that inform future decisions by turning those histories into larger, more robust inventories of how we describe Work. It is a constant, dynamic, and complex exercise.

DOING SOMETHING NEW

The silence of the CIO's team revealed an awkward reality—everyone had experience building internal corporate systems with greater and greater complexity but not a single member of the team had any experience unbundling systems to engage with Cloud-based service providers. No one could offer the CIO a way of measuring success because no one had traveled that path before. Whether as a leader or as a follower, surely you have been in the same position—assigned the responsibility to get from here to there but with a sense you utterly lack the prior experience required to do so.

Our failures and shortcomings in executing the Work are logs we store inside our memory. They become the information that fuels how we learn.

The CIO pushed ahead. "Our CEO has pulled a number out of thin air. He believes we can use Cloud-based services 'to reduce annual corporate operating costs by at least $47.5 million.' This is no different than any other time we have been asked to reduce costs with IT; we just need to figure out how to use some new tools—Cloud-based services—we have never used before." Everyone knew her next words even before she said them: "Pizza or Chinese? It's going to be a long night."

THE TASK IS THE BUILDING BLOCK

Work is constructed from building blocks called *Tasks* in the trust vocabulary. A Task is a single action, event, or decision that contributes to the final outcome of the collected effort. It has two elements. First, there is a descriptive explanation of what action, event, or outcome is to occur. Second, there is an expression of how to measure whether the action, event, or outcome has been performed correctly. Those two elements—a description of the Task and a measurement of its performance—should be familiar. As required for Circumstances, Resources, and Rules, each Task needs a Descriptive Specification and a Functional Specification.

The words may be different than you have used in daily life but the concepts are essential to how to perform any Work. Imagine you are told to complete 100 repetitions of a "burpee" on the gym floor, but have no idea what movements are required. Now, imagine attempting a task you know how to perform, say a push-up, but you have no idea how many your coach wants you to complete. It is pretty difficult to do either Task successfully.

Both elements—the description and the measurement—are required to have a functional basis on which to undertake the Task. These simple truths are crystallized by the much touted management principle that "you cannot manage what you cannot measure." Edward Deming and Peter Drucker are perhaps the most notable sources for the concept. Jack Welch, as the CEO of General Electric, championed the principle within the broader management construct of Six Sigma, a process improvement methodology originally developed by Motorola in the 1980s.

Six Sigma measures the quality of manufacturing and business processes by instituting process controls to eliminate defects—the measurement of the absence of defects assigns a value, for which Six Sigma means 99.9999998% of the products are expected to be free of defects (3.4 defects per million). Today, Six Sigma is a global standard against which we define and improve process and measure the performance of Tasks. Six Sigma requires precision in the description of the Tasks and objective, measurable criteria by which to evaluate performance.

Six Sigma, however, also exposes another dimension of how to describe and think about the Tasks from which you compose a full description of Work—the need to control and avoid things going badly. When an adverse event occurs, the Work performance is compromised—there is failure. Tasks are not completed, incomplete, or improperly completed. Measurable positive outcomes are not achieved. Unfavorable losses, damages, or injuries are sustained. Six Sigma demands that any description of Work must include both an affirmative description of the Tasks to be achieved and specifications for how to control the potential risk of adverse events.

RESULTS AND RISKS

The trust vocabulary needs to expand again. *Results* are the affirmative description of a Task to be performed, with both elements—the

> "You cannot manage what you cannot measure."

description and the measurement—included. *Risks* are the negative description of the adverse outcomes and consequences that may occur in pursuing Results. Each Risk also has both elements—a description of the adverse outcome and measurements of the impacts. Each Task is defined by the Results to be achieved and the Risks to be avoided. Work becomes an aggregation of all of the Tasks.

For simple Work, such as hammering a nail, eating soup, or driving a car from here to there, both the description and a measurement of the Task are fairly simple to identify and compose into Results. The nail head must be flush with the surface; the soup must be transported entirely to your mouth; the car (and its occupants) must arrive "there" in one piece. Similarly, the opposing Risks are easy to identify and measure. The nail must not be bent or incompletely nailed into the surface; the soup should not dribble onto the table or your sleeve; the car (and its occupants) should not bear any marks of physical injury or damage, nor fail to arrive "there" in one piece.

In these examples, the TDT is the hammer, the soup spoon, and the car. Each is a TDC_{RES} that was selected to perform the Work. Once selected, the Resource's Descriptive Specification (TDT_{SP}) does not change—the hammer in your toolbox is still just a hammer. Until there is a draft definition of the Work, a relevant Functional Specification (TDT_{fSP}) is hard to construct. But as the Work layer is further sketched out, you revise the TDC_{RES} description. You survey the room, select the wall, knock on it to measure its composition, and learn the wall is composed of quarter-inch drywall. You check your pocket and you have a six-penny nail. Now, the hammer gains a Functional Specification—it becomes a hammer capable of driving a six-penny nail into quarter-inch drywall. Why? The definition of Work gained a Descriptive Specification for a Result ("drive six-penny nail") and a Functional Specification for that Result ("into a quarter-inch drywall"). Next, you compared the description of Work to your inventory of Rules for the kind of Work the hammer in your toolbox could perform (based on prior experience) (the $TDC_{RES\text{-}fSP}$), and you calculated an alignment between the two in order to generate a description of how the hammer could perform the Work.

Remember, at each frame, action is occurring on multiple layers. So the same process could work in a different order. When you first went to your toolbox and opened the cover, the hammer became a TDC_{RES} for which your prior experience generates its Functional Specification ($TDC_{RES\text{-}fSP}$). Then the description of Work may be the layer you quickly revise to add a suitable Functional Specification, and the hammer became a TDT, easily selected and trusted to do the job. Of course, if you only had an electric nail gun designed for masonry walls in your toolbox, the nail gun's Functional Specification would result in its disqualification as a TDC_{RES}.

Both the hammer and electric nail gun also have Risks associated with them. A hammer may smash your thumb; an electric nail gun's power may drive the nail into the drywall of the adjoining room. So merely describing how these Resources can perform the Work is not enough; you also must connect the Risks to the possible use of any Resource as a TDT.

To do so, you must unfold Descriptive Specifications ($_{SP}$) and Functional Specifications ($_{fSP}$) to show a bit more detail as part of describing each Task and each other TDC_{CIR}, TDC_{RES}, and

TDC_{RUL}. The same process generates greater detail for the TDT. For example, for a Resource being considered as a TDT, Results and Risks are present in both Specifications, as follows:

$$TDT_{SP} = (TDT_{SP\text{-}RSLT} + TDT_{SP\text{-}RISK})$$
$$TDT_{fSP} = (TDT_{fSP\text{-}RSLT} + TDT_{fSP\text{-}RISK})$$

In turn, each variable is merely a summation of its constituents; for example:

$$TDT_{fSP\text{-}RSLT} = (RSLT_1 + RSLT_2 \ldots RSLT_n)$$

Collectively, these improved descriptions of a TDT are weaving together in parallel a description of the Work the TDT can perform. This enables future, more precise, calculations of the alignment between a TDT and the Work to be completed.

Another way of visualizing the Work a TDT might perform is shown in Figure 8-1.

CONGRUITY IN DESIGN

The same expansion in these Specifications applies for Work, and for each Circumstance, Resource, and Rule within the TDC. We must identify both Results and Risks and incorporate the means of expressing their measurement into our understanding of what each is, and how each interacts with the others in the pairings that are constructed.

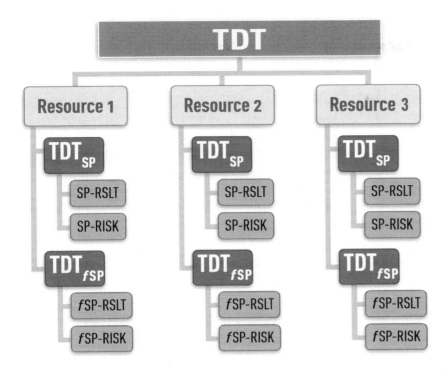

Figure 8-1

Especially for a single task, the preceding may seem complex. But the power of the trust vocabulary is that we are able to describe the TDC, Work, and any TDT with congruent structures. When Work involves multiple Tasks that are more complex and more inter-dependent, the "build" of the design accelerates and gains discipline. Separate stacks of Circumstances, Resources, Rules, Results, and Risks now can be more capably assembled, like children's construction blocks. Computer systems, software applications, the Hubble telescope, and any of the Mars rovers jump to mind as TDTs that perform complex Work requiring incredibly detailed integrations of these variables.

Building a complex description of Work is the same as building a TDC description; pairings are required. For a specific Task, we must

The power of the trust vocabulary is that we are able to describe the TDC, Work, and any TDT with congruent structures.

pair Results and Risks. The pairings occur between the Descriptive Specification and Functional Specification. But pairings also extend beyond the boundaries of a specific Task. A single Result may have multiple pairings to other Tasks, including mandatory pairings that document dependencies ("X must occur for Y to occur"). A single Risk may pair across multiple Tasks and have adverse impacts on multiple Resources and other assets. A mandatory pairing of a Risk and other Resources or Results means that, if the adverse event occurs, the next Resources cannot be used. When trying to build those pairings, it is as if our cel artists are drawing connecting arrows among and across different cels and different layers so that Work (and each of the constituent Tasks) may be properly described.

Later in this book, you will be introduced to the Trust Prism, a tool to gain control over the complexity that expands when these exercises focus on governing trust in digital information assets. But, in the current frames of our film, what should be intriguing you is that Work and the Circumstances, Resources, and Rules within the TDC all have consistent structures (Descriptive Specifications and Functional Specifications). While a lot is happening concurrently on different layers, they are connecting through the congruity of the Specifications.

DIFFERENT MEASURES

There is an added challenge when multiple stakeholders use different expressions of what Work (or even individual Tasks) should accomplish and use different measurements of success. But this is exactly what happens with nearly any digital asset—there are multiple stakeholders, each of whom has a vested interest in how Work is performed.

Imagine that a regional bank introduces a consumer-facing website to improve the abilities of their customers to build electronically the payment schedules, budgets, and other financial tools that give those customers greater control over their spending. The bank hires a developer to build the website. A very simple portfolio of the stakeholders and their varied definitions of one Task might look like this:

> ≥ Developer—The website loads within 5.00 seconds (the technical specifications attached to the development agreement never mentioned page loading speeds) and correctly and completely displays the portal page content, allowing customers to input their userIDs and passwords.

> ≥ Bank—The website loads within 0.80 seconds (consistent with other Bank-operated websites, which the Bank assumed the Developer had reviewed) and correctly and completely displays the portal page into which customers input their userIDs and passwords.

> Customer #1—The website loads within 0.50 seconds and allows auto-complete by Google Chrome of the userID and password so the customer can get directly to the secure landing page for his financial tools.

> Customer #2—The website loads within 3-5 seconds, but it does not matter since the customer needs another 15 seconds to find her paper sheet of passwords somewhere under her mouse pad.

None of these four stakeholders has the same expression of the Specifications for this rudimentary first Task. All of them have the same description of the Resource (the website), yet with nearly any single page-loading event, more than one stakeholder likely will be disappointed. What has gone wrong?

In this example, the specific Task the website must perform was to load correctly and completely display all of the Data (Work). Unfortunately the technical specifications for the Developer (TDT_{fSP}) omitted load-time as an expression of the Results. Obviously, both the Bank and the two Customers have three different measures stated in their criteria. The Work description (TDT_{SP}) was uniform—the webpage will load correctly and completely—but the variances in time metrics doom the webpage service to failure or, at the very least, to lots of grumbling, teeth-grinding, and lawyer fees.

For the CIO's team, the same issue was embedded in the profound silence that followed her question about how to measure success. Different stakeholders in the company historically had done battle over whether the IT shop had built the right solutions.

Her team was well aware of the numbers among their ranks who were newcomers, replacing others who lost their jobs after the most recent internal war on the quality of information security controls. Everyone knew the real reason for the war was the CIO's failure to get buy-in from the Board on the projected storage volumes after the additional encryption controls had been installed.

Indeed, the inability of multiple stakeholders to express, communicate, and achieve consensus on the Specifications for Work (and the TDTs used to perform the Work) is where the "root cause" of imprecision in defining Work often is revealed. The differences get exposed only after the Work begins and some are left feeling that their requirements were not considered or achieved. Under Six Sigma, imprecisions in describing Risks to be controlled by the TDT will doom a project from achieving the required functional efficiencies. How do they get to that point?

EXPRESSING WORK WITH RULES

Achieving precision, particularly across multiple stakeholders, requires that Work and each Task within Work (and the component Descriptive Specifications and Functional Specifications for each Task) be authored pursuant to established Rules. That's right. In the same stack of cels already illustrating TDC and Work, now the added layers of Rules become more conspicuous to the process. Within each frame, as evidenced by the Trust Decision Model, what is occurring is shaped and defined by Rules. The Work description is no different. Indeed, as we explore Work, there is synergy and interdependence among Work and Rules that deserves emphasis long before we explore Rules in depth. As you begin to build your description of Work, you also are interacting dynamically with Rules. Let's return to our freeze-frame analysis of the process.

Achieving precision . . . requires that Work and each Task within Work . . . be authored pursuant to established Rules.

Begin with the simple hammering of a nail into the wall to display your latest framed photograph of your twins. The first description of the Task is minimal: "Hammer nail." Next, you begin to compose a description of the Results: The nail should bear the weight of this frame and glass (weighing approximately 22 ounces) and be inserted into a standard drywall composition wall, behind which there is no stud or brick wall that will interfere with the length of the nail. Where do you find the Information that enables you to build the metrics and express the Results?

You access your inventory of prior experience and, in turn, from your prior history you put together your Rules for how to measure a successful nailing! You may have built that experience from how your parent taught you to use a hammer, from working on a job site as a handyman's assistant in your youth, or from the hundreds of wall-decorating moments that have preceded this moment in time. Likely it was a combination of all of these!

In the next moment, with the Results described and enhanced by metrics, you now observe and collect more Decisional Information. You evaluate the frame weight, the length of the hanging wire, and the standard width of the drywall. In doing so, you concurrently define the Results required to succeed and the related Rules. Next you have to select the proper nail.

Using the trust vocabulary, the nail is either a separate TDT or a separate Resource to be found in the TDC that enables the Work ("hammer nail") to be performed. In either case, you have to select one out of that big pail of spare nails you keep in the garage. For the nail, you calculate the size, weight, and length required, and determine whether the nail should have a head to help assure the hanging wire remains stable on the nail. You calculate, based on the weight and prior experience, the angle at which the nail should be hammered, and the length of the nail that should remain exposed in order to comfortably enable that hanging wire to be placed on the nail. All of these are metrics; all of these calculations produce requirements for expressing the intended Results. The calculations rely entirely on your observations, calculations you are executing pursuant to Rules you call up and rely upon to do so.

The next task is straightforward—how do you express a measurement of your completion? The nail should be of the defined size, weight, and length, and the nail should be inserted into the wall, to the correct length, at the defined angle. (Note, you are relying once again on the accuracy of your visual estimates of these measurements.) If you hang your frame and the nail sags, or the nail is not long enough to place the hanging wire, you may have properly performed the Work, but your measurement of a successful completion was not satisfied.

Concurrently, familiar with the contents of your toolbox in the basement, you also are developing the criteria for the hammer you must select as the TDT for doing the Work. In some respects the nail and hammer-to-be-selected are an on-the-spot, of-the-moment system for hanging pictures. Given the size, weight, and length of the nail, you have a sense of the types of hammers that will be suitable—the weight shall be one pound or less, the handle must be secure in the hammerhead, and the handle must be of a length and width comfortable to your hand and capable of being controlled.

All of this seems pretty simple—as you compose your description of the Results, you are formulating metrics that give your Results substance, detail, and accuracy. But those metrics, as part of the way Results are expressed, also are informing which Rules you select (or compose) and which Resources (the hammer and nail) you must employ to complete the Task consistent with your description. So, hammer in hand, nail properly placed against the wall, you are ready to perform the Task pursuant to the Rules, using the selected Resources that conform to those Rules, to achieve the described Results.

Allow the film to freeze right there to appreciate what has occurred. In the preceding moments, Work changed radically, transforming from a simple action into a complex portfolio of Results and Tasks that takes into account your prior experience and knowledge of the suitable Rules for installing a nail. Those Rules, in turn, take into account a full suite of Rules involving physics, engineering, muscular functionality, structural integrity, and manufacturing quality, all built from your direct, prior experience and stored and accessible as part of the larger inventory of Rules you carry around in your head.

Imagine a different scenario. As a professional interior decorator's assistant, you have been tasked with installing a full collection of a lawyer's diplomas and certificates on a custom, newly finished wall built with river rock and mortar at a cost of $50,000 for the wall itself. Your supervisor gives you an electric nail gun to use. Can you trust the nail gun to complete the Work successfully?

A quick check of your internal Rules confirms you have no prior experience on which to rely to define the Work properly. You have never nailed anything into a wall of rock and mortar and never used an electric nail gun. The nails you see pre-loaded in the gun look like small rockets, not the type of nail you previously have used for hanging pictures. The Task remains simple, "hammer nail," but you have no idea how to proceed because you do not have the Rules with which to properly compose a definition of Work that includes the required metrics for measuring successful performance.

Very slowly, move the film forward one more frame. Even without an ability to compose a description of the Results, your observation of the TDC includes features of the gun and the wall. Based on those observations, you are building an inventory of the possible negative consequences associated with the Task. If the gun cannot be controlled, nails may shoot fully into the rock, leaving nothing on which to hang the frames. The nails may split the rock, destroying the wall. A nail or a rock shard may fly into your face or other body parts. You could lose your job (and not even get your first paycheck)! Those, of course, are the Risks.

How do you describe those Risks? How do you express measurements of the Risks that relate to the description of the Results? How do your expressions of those known Risks influence the Rules that shape the full definition of Work? First, there is the optional consequence of doing nothing, allowing the framed collection to remain leaning against the wall, unhung, while you go for a bike ride. Second, any of the preceding misfortunes could occur, causing injury to the wall, your body, and your pride, and delaying completion of the task. For each, you have already formulated some measure of failure—embedded nails (requiring more attempts, more nails, and more of your labor), split rock, physical injury, or loss of income.

In composing any definition of Results, you also are composing and shaping a description of the Risks and, in turn, responsively selecting and shaping the Rules. These efforts are required to create a description of Work with which you can return to the rankings of TDC_{RES} and make further refinements by comparing the Specifications for Work and the available TDC_{RES}. The outcome is to draw the TDC boundary a bit more precisely, reducing the TDC_{RES} that are eligible candidates to be trusted to perform the Work as well as identify possible gaps where innovation can be fueled. Now, ranking the TDC_{RES} with this added set of calculations, the trust decision advances.

BACK TO BUSINESS

The hammer/nail gun/nail illustration is simplistic compared to what faced the CIO and her team. The brainstorming began as the pizza arrived. Tasks started being added onto the whiteboard; checklists were brought into the conference room; and some off-the-record conversations unfolded about why some of the earlier projects had blown apart over metrics and poor communications.

Three hours later, everyone was looking at spaghetti on the white-board—lines drawn between Tasks, dependencies erased and reinserted, metrics proposed and revised, and a "parking lot" of other topics still to be considered. While all of the content had relevance, no one had yet constructed a framework for answering the opening questions—what was to be done and how would success be measured?

This surely is a familiar scene for anyone in business or government. Time is passing and the costs of time are building. Deadlines will be announced. Interactions, even in these early frames, will become constrained into a more linear design. There will be no further opportunities for rewinds and recalculations.

What the CIO's team still lacked was a methodology for building a definition of Work that would support how to compose the RFP and eventually evaluate competing vendor proposals. While we can imagine they had a more complete inventory of the internal Process Rules, Code, and Data, assembling the criteria to measure the effectiveness of a vendor taking over was still eluding the team.

You have surely been in many similar meetings, whether assigned to the back bench or at the head of the table. Each stakeholder has their own set of requirements. Performance constructs do not count the same outcomes. Differences in professional experience produce irregularities in the questions asked and the ability to deliver secure good answers. Semantics are confused by acronyms and shorthand expressions. Few are able to translate their requirements into the one metric that matters—will the solution create greater wealth?

Eventually the chaos settles as the stakeholders, confronted by deadlines and mandates, develop shared vocabularies, create structures of requirements, and articulate measures of success that are glued together into a proposal. The team is building the Descriptive Specifications and Functional Specifications for the Work in order to identify the TDC_{RES} available in the TDC as possible TDTs—the tools with which the Work will be performed within the TDC_{CIR}. It is some of the hardest possible work to construct a full picture of the status quo (all of the TDC_{CIR}, TDC_{RES} [including Physical Assets, Human Resources, Process Rules, Data, and Code], and TDC_{RUL}, and all of the pairings among them) accurate and detailed enough to enable potential TDTs to be meaningfully evaluated to achieve a decision that can be trusted.

Whatever emerges is tested, parsed, calculated, and revised, again and again, as the trust decision proceeds. Vendor proposals, suggestions from team members, and critical reviews by senior management all pull and twist the first iteration, shaping and reshaping the elements, Rewinding and Recalculating how the requirements are expressed within each layer and how Decisional Information is gathered and processed against those requirements.

Think of the last big decision you needed to make as a leader. The proposals sat in front of you, carefully vetted by the vendors and your team members. The papers described the architecture of a proposed new IT system, a distribution warehouse, or a plan for combining the sales and marketing teams after the recent acquisition. Yet, even without opening the proposals, your experience had taught you questions to be asked, questions that may shake the confidence of those sitting before you.

As you peppered those in front of you with your questions, it is important to recognize what you were doing. With each query, you were auditing the quality of their decisions. Your questions examined whether they had properly evaluated the Context, the Circumstances, the Resources, and the Rules to reach their decision. As a leader, you were fulfilling an important role—making sure all of the Decisional Information had been identified, gathered, and inputted. A recommendation had been placed before you—were you confident your team had properly placed their trust in the recommended path forward? Your questions emerged from your prior experiences and the rules you have learned for what this type of project requires to succeed. You know the hard questions that need to be asked—they reflect requirements and rules you have learned from your own failures to look beneath the bridge.

If the team survived your first assault, the process Rewinds and Recalculates as you dive into the proposals themselves. Whether structured as financial data, project plans, draft agreements, or even video recordings of tilt trays, the information before you is the Decisional Information to answer your own critical question, "Can I trust the team's proposal as the basis on which to make a decision?"

As you review the projections and listen to your team's presentations, and in each chained decision you make, you are extracting, slicing, dicing and breaking information down into smaller and smaller portions. Those become the Decisional Information assets to be aligned to the Rules you have organized, Rules looking for simple, arithmetic calculations of "yes" or "no," "1" or "0."

THE WORK OF CALCULATING TRUST

But something else is happening, something that is very important. Calculating the quality of the trust decision is a separate task of Work itself! Each calculation is constructed of multiple Tasks, each Task requires Resources (notably Rules and Decisional Information), and those Resources must be trusted in order to properly perform the Work! So everything presented so far by this book has been serving *dual* decision chains. The first decision chain is the primary decision to trust selected TDC_{RES} assembled as a TDT to perform the primary Work (outsourcing selected IT services to the Cloud); the second decision chain involves the decisions whether to trust the Resources used as tools with which to make the primary decision. Decisional Information, therefore, is also used to perform the Work of calculating trust—if you cannot trust the Decisional Information, you cannot affirmatively calculate trust in the primary TDT.

Try making a decision, one on which your job depends, in which you have an uncomfortable gut feeling that you cannot trust the

Calculating the quality of the trust decision is a separate task of Work itself!

information you have been given. At that moment, the discomfort you experience is the manifestation of the *negative* calculation that you cannot trust the information as Decisional Information to make the primary decision.

Now, assume the information you have received seems functional, but you have concerns about the source. For the CIO, one vendor offered to generate the required performance metrics by using GovNowIT, an IT management service about whom the CIO knew nothing at all. Now there is a different target for her analysis—the CIO is making a trust calculation about the source of the Decisional Information, called a *Decisional Information Source* in the trust vocabulary.

In order to use Decisional Information as a tool to calculate trust in a primary TDT, a DM must affirmatively decide to trust both the Decisional Information Source and the Decisional Information itself. Each is a Resource to the trust decision process! For each, the DM has Rules to organize and Decisional Information to gather and input into the calculations against those Rules. It now becomes very interesting in our Trust Decision Model!

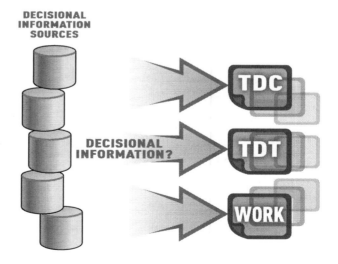

The interactions are fast-paced but visible. This chapter began by focusing on the film frame in which Work is being defined. But as the Rules for doing so are organized, the DM is concurrently asking, at different layers within the same frames, with lots of consultations among our virtual teams of artists:

> ⩾ "What is the Decisional Information that will be required to evaluate whether an available TDC_{RES} can be a TDT?

> ⩾ "What will be the Decisional Information Sources from which to obtain the Decisional Information?

> ⩾ "How can I determine whether to trust the Decisional Information and Decisional Information Sources?"

Why is this occurring? A DM cannot adopt a definition of Work (or a Task) if trusted Decisional Information about both a TDT and the future performance of the Work cannot be acquired. These three elements are chained together—a definition of Work suitable to support a TDT calculation requires Decisional Information to be available from a Decisional Information Source, each of which must be affirmatively calculated to be trustworthy. In effect, the Decisional Information Source is a TDT performing the Work of delivering a DM Decisional Information required to make the primary TDT decision.

Imagine the CIO and her team now drawing the boundary around the services to be included in the RFP as the Work to be performed. The existing information security policy and applicable legal regulations for one major division require real-time monitoring of intrusion attempts (a Descriptive Specification), including reporting on improper password challenges, use of blacklisted domain addresses, and cross-indexing to known IP addresses of competitive research facilities, to be updated every 15 seconds (a Functional Specification). In other words, for the Work to be outsourced successfully to a Cloud provider, the vendor must be able to deliver performance reporting that supports the current security functions of the company's operational Rules. Yet none of the proposed vendor candidates favorably responded to informal requests to confirm that type of security data is available from their platforms.

A CLEAR-CUT DECISION

No one should doubt the outcome—the CIO quickly concludes security services need to stay in-house and the entire project will be placed on-hold. There simply will be no Decisional Information with which to regularly measure that the outsourced Work (including bundled information security services) is being performed correctly. The same result occurs if a vendor offers that the security data will be provided by GovNowIT; no matter how attractive the sample performance reports appear to be, the CIO has no basis on which to trust the source.

The process is also true in our personal trust decisions—the definition of Work, Decisional Information, and Decisional Information Source decisions are chained together. For example, while shopping for a hammer (that nail is still waiting as the Work), you can ask a sales clerk or use a bar code scanner app installed on your mobile phone to scan the hang tag on a specific hammer (TDT), view the webpage content of the manufacturer, click and link through to consumer reviews and check consumer product reports. Each is a Decisional Information Source. To rely on what you learn, you have to calculate whether or not to trust each source and, if so, whether to trust the Decisional Information that is available from them.

Buying a hammer may again seem to bear little resemblance to determining the suitability of a merger, outsourcing to the Cloud, or building a $100 million distribution warehouse. Yet in the structure of how we make decisions, there is a precise overlay and consistency—how we develop and describe the Work and evaluate potential TDTs has remarkable symmetry and coherence among all of our decisions, small or large. What varies among all of the decisions in which we participate are:

> the volumes of TDC elements (Circumstances, Resources, and Rules) to identify,

> where to draw the line to establish the TDC boundary within the larger Context,

> the breadth and complexity of the TDC,

> the number and complexities of pairings to construct within the TDC in order to describe the Work,

> the range of possible TDTs available (or requiring development) to perform the Work,

> the volume and complexities of the Rules required to evaluate those pairings and options,

> the volume and availability of Decisional Information required by the Rules,

> the trust decisions to be made about the Decisional Information, and

> the trust decisions to be made about each Decisional Information Source (each of which requires the preceding elements to be constructed for each Source as a TDT).

Sure, this is complex; it is incredibly complex. Yet these frames in the film portray the most pivotal point in the trust calculations. These moments are when decisions blow up, and often quite badly, long before the trust decision itself is calculated. Here is where the fuse is lit for the explosive harm of a bad decision. As the Digital Age gains momentum, this point in the Trust Decision Model becomes even more important. There are three compelling reasons why this is so.

ALL DECISIONS ARE GROUNDED IN DIGITAL INFORMATION

First, as a leader and as a decision-maker, you cannot make any decision of consequence in the 21st Century without relying upon digital information. No way, no how, not going to happen. Your dependency on digital information is now inherent to how you conduct business and live your life, and the addiction is increasing. Whether buying a hammer or spending billions, more and more of the Decisional Information you require to make decisions will be digital, often generated as Data from Resources that are themselves performing the Work of doing so. Market price reports, labor efficiency data, the emission rates of different models of vehicles, the projected ROI from acquiring (rather than outsourcing) improved security services—all are Decisional Information required and used to calculate your decisions. To be effective in

First, as a leader and as a decision-maker, you cannot make any decision of consequence in the 21st Century without relying upon digital information.

making decisions, you must know how to calculate whether to trust Decisional Information that is digital.

TRUSTING DIGITAL INFORMATION REQUIRES TRUSTING THE SOURCE

Second, facing the distributed, globally massive complex the Net represents, you must evaluate the trustworthiness of each related Decisional Information Source. How can you trust information if you cannot trust the source? Now, more than ever before, Rules are required to define the attributes of the Decisional Information Sources you will rely upon to make your decisions.

A Decisional Information Source is like any Resource; both a Descriptive Specification and Functional Specification are required, expressing both the Results and the Risks of using the Decisional Information Source to deliver Decisional Information. To apply those Specifications, you will need Decisional Information again, but this time it is the input required to measure and evaluate your trust in the Decisional Information Source itself.

TO TRUST A DECISIONAL INFORMATION SOURCE, YOU MUST TRUST *ITS* SOURCES

Third, to trust a Decisional Information Source, you must evaluate *its* sources for the Information offered and make a trust decision on each. Now we slow the film even more. Consider how many sources of Data are called upon to generate real-time feeds of stock market activity and you get a sense of the complexity. By challenging the entire provenance of Decisional Information, evaluating the primary Decisional Information Sources as well as their sources, you are doing your job to assure the primary decision is calculated based on trusted information.

You assemble Decisional Information from diverse Sources and, for each, you rigorously ask if you can trust the Information.

This is the essence of the decisions you make; in business, doing so is the foundation of your success or failure. You assemble Decisional Information from diverse Sources and, for each, you rigorously ask if you can trust the Information. You have learned that not every source is reliable; even secondary audits can be required. As the assets at risk increase, so too does your scrutiny of the provenance of the information. Big Data, competitive intelligence, market analysts—all are pursuing the same activity. Each is aggregating Decisional Information which is only relied upon when the Sources (and their Sources) are calculated to be trusted. Only then can the Decisional Information be mapped against the Rules you have organized to define the TDC, the Work, and how you will measure success.

Is there a point at which this inquiry ends and moves ahead? Yes, and it is achieved by again applying the Principle of Indifference. A DM stops caring about the sources of the sources of the Decisional Information Source of the Decisional Information at that point when the inaccuracy of the Decisional Information will have such little potential impact on the primary decision that the DM becomes indifferent. In other words, there is a calculation that the Decisional Information, even if false, will not impact the success of the Work. When those calculations are *not* made, or executed improperly, *Decisional Information Risk* results.

UNDERSTANDING DECISIONAL INFORMATION RISK

Decisional Information Risk can occur at any point within the trust decision. It is the risk of presuming, rather than calculating, trust in Decisional Information. This risk most frequently occurs in the layers of the trust decision in which Work is being defined. Why? Because it is so much easier to make the presumption than to calculate trust in information, even more so when the information is digital. As mentioned earlier, deciding to trust information is real work!

What happens if trust is presumed? Mathematically, you are inputting an assumption into your calculations, rather than a statement of fact. The subsequent trust calculations go haywire if any assumed information does not actually align to reality. You know that from the hard lessons of earlier experiences—all of us have made decisions based on assumptions about certain information later proven to be wrong. But with the trust vocabulary and the Trust Decision Model, we can now isolate and see where those assumptions occur.

Within each frame, and at each layer, the decision chains are fueled by Decisional Information. The output from one frame becomes the input for the next decisions, chaining together. By slowing down the film and looking at each layer, questions can be asked at each moment about the trustworthiness of the Decisional Information (and its related Sources) in play.

Making assumptions is not inherently wrong; what is often fatal is being unable to identify when those assumptions are being made or to defend the decisions not to calculate trust. Think back to the questions you asked in making your last major decision. What Decisional Information did you rely upon? What questions did you ask about the Sources? What Decisional Information did you assume? What Decisional Information was improperly assumed? How did you challenge your team's reports? How were your decisions challenged by others? What questions focused on the trustworthiness of the Decisional Information and related Sources?

The due diligence, the audits, the cross-examinations—all of these steps in every major business decision are the same process. When

> Making assumptions is not inherently wrong; what is often fatal is being unable to identify when those assumptions are being made or to defend the decisions not to calculate trust.

they do not occur, the outcome has only one characterization—it is called "taking the risk."

"TAKING THE RISK" IS DECIDING TO NOT CALCULATE TRUST

"Taking the risk" occurs in two ways. As just discussed, Decisional Information (or its Sources) can be assumed to be trusted. The second path is to exclude the Decisional Information. Just like any other Resource, a DM can rely on the Rhett Butler Rule and make a conscious decision to put a certain information asset outside the TDC. Perhaps consumer reviews are not needed to choose a hammer. Perhaps the second validation audit will require too much time, so the financial study is simply tossed to the side. Perhaps it is too expensive to obtain a background identity report on every employee working in the vendor's data center.

Regardless of the justification, there is a very different outcome when we "take the risk" to not consider Decisional Information. Mathematically, rather than being assumed as a "1," the Decisional Information is a null set. It is treated as if it does not exist. As a result, the Rules embedded in a trust decision requiring the Decisional Information cannot be executed. There is simply no fuel with which to fire the Rule; there is only a "0." The calculations produce lower outcomes; trust is harder to achieve.

Trust can only be calculated with Decisional Information that is accurate, authentic, and factual. To assume those attributes creates Decisional Information Risk; to exclude Decisional Information creates Decisional Information Risk. In the Digital Age, either outcome is exactly what those waging the war to gain control of the information assets want you to do.

Complexity and opacity are the weapons of those who seek to win the war for control. If they can control digital information and the related systems (which are your Decisional Information Sources), they create barriers that impair your autonomy in affirmatively calculating trust. Expressed in our vocabulary, the bad actors are denying you the Decisional Information required in both of the decision chains. First, you are handcuffed from acquiring what is needed to evaluate the Decisional Information Sources and Decisional Information. Second, you are being forced to accept definitions of Work that cannot be effectively measured in calculating your trust in the primary TDT. At the bottom line, you do not have the Decisional Information about the TDT to measure how well the Work will be performed. You decide, instead, to take the risks. You are not acting "on your gut"; you are deciding not to calculate trust.

Let me emphasize that the primary trust decision process can continue. Decisional Information is a Resource and the consequences of that classification track the Trust Decision Model. But the calculations suffer, and the decisions become vulnerable:

> » Each time "1" is inputted on a presumption rather than a calculation ("Is this Decisional Information Source trustworthy? Is the Decisional Information trusted?"), the probabilities of successfully achieving the Work degrade. Why? There is an increased likelihood that the Decisional Information will later prove untrustworthy.

> » Each time Decisional Information is excluded by applying the Rhett Butler Rule, a "0" is inputted and the related Rule will not be properly executed.

As a result, the decision itself is less likely to be affirmatively calculated.

A DIFFERENT OUTCOME

The CIO was not prepared to take any of those risks. She reported to the Committee the vendor proposals simply did not include the details required to make a $47.5 million decision. Her report emphasized the reporting shortcomings and their compliance implications. She asked for more time to pressure the vendors and seek other bids, knowing she was actually covering her tracks at the team's failure to properly describe in the original RFP an accurate defined scope and measure of the Work.

The team dug back in. Their ERM was fully updated to include the added Resources that made their systems work—the Process Rules, the Data, and the Code. The RFP was re-issued, rigorous in the details required, but also comprehensive in describing the options of how the existing IT services might be divided and transferred toward Cloud services. Through her grapevine, four additional vendors were located, each of which had recently expanded from the Middle East toward supporting U.S.-based companies.

A vendor briefing was held, and the increased specifications enabled the vendor proposals, when submitted, to align to the company's performance and security data needs. The CIO's team developed detailed supporting documentation (records of the Decisional Information and decision process) and two vendor proposals were reported favorably to the Committee. Between them, the CIO recommended a "bake-off", to be based on certain test simulations her team had developed that would test and validate the vendor representations.

The Committee's response, however, was disconcerting. "That looks great, but you only have 90 days to get to a final decision. We are not going to fund any further evaluations; we need to begin seeing Cloud-based savings on our bottom line this fiscal year."

Ahh, time and money—the other two variables that can mess up a good trust decision. The CIO had thought she had won the battle, but she was at risk of losing the war . . . and her job. How would she make a good decision? In which vendor proposal would she place her trust?

THE TRUST VOCABULARY
In this chapter, you will learn the following words:

Functional Calculation

CHAPTER 9

TIME, MONEY, AND THE TDT

THE TRUST DECISION MODEL and trust vocabulary give us a new way of thinking about how we make decisions. Whether acting as a leader or team member, you now are gaining control of a different set of tools for discussing how decisions are made. You realize every decision is an affirmative, rules-based calculation, fueled by information and governed by mathematical input, not by emotion. You have learned that making any decision involves a chained sequencing of deliberations that are, in fact, micro-decisions in the process. Those deliberations are built of layers. Each layer captures and illustrates the combinations of variables the decisions must evaluate. The decisions move through a series of frames that, viewed individually, show the incredible interactions and dynamics occurring. By slowing things down, pairings, metrics, and calculations become more visible, empowering Rewinds and Recalculations that respond to the output of prior decisions.

But every decision requires an end-point, a moment in time at which you must decide whether to award trust. A target is required; to proceed, the DM must identify and finalize the TDT itself on which the final decision will hinge. Just like drawing lines to define the TDC boundary, now you must draw the line that becomes the boundary for the TDT. Once drawn, the TDT becomes a known asset and the decision is poised for calculation: "Can the TDT be trusted to perform the Work successfully?"

The CIO and her team now had to make that decision. In fact, they had multiple decisions to make:

> Can Vendor X be trusted?

> Can Vendor Y be trusted?

> If both Vendor X and Vendor Y can be trusted, which can be trusted more?

> If either vendor is trusted, how must we alter and manage our systems in order for the selected vendor to succeed?

> If neither Vendor X nor Vendor Y can be trusted, what happens next?

Beneath each decision were several uncomfortable truths. First, time was ticking away. The team had missed its first deadline; now a second deadline loomed. Despite building an improved RFP and receiving stronger proposals, there was no further time to Rewind & Recalculate. The new deadline even made the planned "bake-off" impossible to execute. Ninety days was barely enough time to work with the lawyers to negotiate the contracts. The team members would have to rely on the information that sat on the table before them. But they also knew, from hard experience, the "bake-off" would have greatly improved the possibility of achieving an on-time transition and turnover. Now, even post-contract, there would be no established, proven confidence that any of the proposed transition plans would be achievable.

Second, both vendors had submitted alternative configurations of their services, with the all-in pricing options of the alternatives proportional to the level of service reporting the vendor would offer. Each presented similar schedules—the more frequent and detailed a vendor's reporting of active performance data, the higher the price for the services. Only one configuration from each vendor would achieve the $47.5 million bottom line savings desired by the Committee, but there was a hitch. Performance reporting cost money and the configurations that hit the target offered only minimal reporting—each was still essentially a black box. If the CIO wanted detailed reporting on the vendor's services to support her information security and compliance functions, her company could never achieve the desired savings.

Third, a team member overhead at a conference reception that the company's largest competitor out of Asia, RHK Enterprises, was shifting entirely to Cloud-based services, with projected bottom-line savings exceeding $100 million, over twice the Committee's targets. Yet the CIO and her team had concluded that some of their existing services could not be shifted outside; the data was too sensitive and the need for control was too critical to put both compliance and operational functionality into the hands of a third party. They were troubled by the gossip; they could not figure out, if true, how RHK could migrate to the Cloud without facing indefensible substantial risks.

Now the importance of how to define the TDT properly comes into focus. The team's initial failings to do so had consumed time, provoked a new, firm deadline that constrained their final evaluations, and put at tremendous risk the post-contract ability to realize the projected savings within the current fiscal year. For the TDT to have a chance of hitting the Committee's demanded projected savings, the CIO would have to accept black box operations from the vendor, putting her at tremendous risk should an adverse event occur about which she lacked the necessary Data to initiate remediation and avoid potential sanctions and litigation. Yet it appeared that, even with no limits on time or access to performance data, the decision to exclude certain in-house services from the TDT (as described by the RFP) was being made differently by their competitor. What was RHK doing in Asia that allowed them to take the risks on security and compliance she felt she could not take?

Surely you have felt the same—the pressures of time and money inexorably can alter what you decide to trust and how to structure that decision:

> ≥ "If you don't pre-test the services before launch, can we get to the market faster?"

> ≥ "Why is it taking so long to make a decision?"

> ≥ "How much will it cost to conduct the vendor evaluations?

The pressures of time and money inexorably can alter what you decide to trust and how to structure that decision.

> "Can we get to the decision faster? What is holding you up?"

> "Once the vendor is selected, how long before we start seeing the savings?"

Time and money also become the ultimate metrics by which others will measure your effectiveness at making decisions:

> "Is new wealth being created?"

> "Is our existing wealth being best preserved? Have you done the most to maximize savings?"

> "Is efficiency being realized, creating more time for your team to do other work that will create other wealth?"

> "Will the Cloud-based outsourcing mean less over-time so I can finally spend this summer coaching my child's team?"

> "Will this leader's decision on the battlefield extend or end my life?"

The key to how you navigate the pressures of time and money is found in how you select and define the TDT—assemble the TDC_{RES}; acquire or create new Resources; identify TDC_{RUL} to be satisfied; organize, edit, and create new Rules; and structure the pairings and decision chains. Describe the target properly and you are far more likely to make decisions that will earn the trust of others.

After all, who was asking all of the preceding questions? The same people judging whether you can be trusted to make good decisions and be an effective leader. Are not those the same questions you ask when judging whether you can trust the decisions of others?

This chapter explores how to define the TDT and its boundary so that you can calculate a strong, defensible final trust decision. But you may be wondering: if money is such a controlling influence in business, and trust is so essential to decisions to create or preserve wealth, why is money excluded from the visual structure of the Trust Decision Model? In truth, it has been there all along, disguised as time. Yes, the trite phrase is true: time *is* money, but in ways you may have never contemplated.

THE SEQUENCE OF MONEY IN DECIDING TRUST

In the Catholic Church, the Devil's Advocate is assigned the responsibility to speak against a petition to nominate someone as a saint. That person is an investigator, commissioned to be a truth-teller who must stand against the positive attributes and be sure everyone understands the full history. While writing this book, a good friend served as my Devil's Advocate, the one each of us needs . . . and fears.

My friend challenged the Trust Decision Model with a cold, brutal skepticism, but his focus was not on history but on wealth. "You have not truly solved trust until you can account for the business case—you must be able to connect trust to the goals of creating and preserving wealth. How much money can trust create? How much will it cost to deliver trust? How will calculating trust create greater wealth than taking the risk without the calculations?"

His questions were provocative, and, more disturbing to my ego, he was correct. You likely have asked those questions in reading this far. I discovered the answers, and persuaded my friend to abstain from further objections, not by focusing on money but by travelling back to a time before money. As a species, humans were wired to make trust decisions long before they developed currencies. When their lives truly depended on making the right decisions to survive, what did they value in making decisions to trust other humans? How did they value the potential for tools to perform their work? What motivated our ancient relatives to select and use tools to perform work before there was money? What still remains as the fundamental asset by which we calculate the value of trust?

Time. It is the only finite asset each of us controls. In each life, in each workday, whether as individuals or as teams, we only have a defined amount of time in which to live our lives or perform our Work. In every business, each day delivers a defined amount of time in which to create new wealth. Tools have one value, whether as simple as a stone tossed at an apple or as complex as a distributed financial services network operating in over 150 nations—a tool delivers increased control over time.

When we affirmatively determine to trust a tool as a TDT to perform Work, we do so because using the tool will complete the Work in less time. The time saved is time we can use to do other things. An electric nail gun increases the velocity with which a carpenter works; either more walls can be built or the time saved can be spent playing ball or seeking out new work. A new warehouse system reduces the time required to locate, sort, transfer, ship, and track daily inventory shipments to retail stores. A global financial network enables us to execute transactions with a velocity measured in nanoseconds, rather than hours, days, or months.

In each life, in each workday, we only have a defined amount of time in which to live our lives or perform our Work.

Each decision to trust any TDT to perform Work includes a calculation of time as an asset.

The value of time is another mathematical exercise, adding, subtracting, and netting the measurements of time toward the trust decision. Each decision to trust any TDT to perform Work includes a calculation of time as an asset. To make those calculations, Decisional Information is required. To collect it, each Functional Specification (whether for a Circumstance, Resource, Rule, or Risk) must include and express measurements of time:

> ⧫ "How much longer will the strong wind slow our travel across the plains?"

> ⧫ "How much time will be consumed by transmitting Data to the Cloud-based servers of Vendor X (compared to keeping our servers on-premises)?"

> ⧫ "How much time is required to complete the paperwork required by the Internal Revenue Service? Can we save time by using on-line tax preparation software?"

> ⧫ "If the firewall is compromised, how much time will be required to restore services, re-generate new passwords, and document the incident in order to submit a claim?"

For each, Decisional Information is almost immediately translated into equivalent economic metrics by measuring and transposing the related expenses and revenues. But the fundamental asset is time—to decide to trust requires a calculation of efficiency and velocity valued against the alternatives. This is an essential principle in how we calculate trust; just imagine trying to make a decision to acquire a new assembly line in a manufacturing plant without asking about time savings and time expenditures.

It is important to emphasize that time is an inherent feature in how we express both Results and Risks. So often we think of the adversity of risk events in terms of physical or operational losses, damaged equipment, broken applications, or disrupted services. But the buried costs of risk events, so often overlooked in actuarial calculations of the probable costs of adverse events, are the time units consumed to restore operations, rebuild what is damaged, and retrain new employees, and the lost opportunities to create wealth during the time devoted to those rebuilding activities. To acquire those time units, money must be paid—salaries, replacement Resources, contractor support—and additional time invested in formulating and executing the strategies for recovering the lost opportunities.

In evaluating any Resource as a TDT for performing Work, "Will I gain control over time?" becomes an inherent, fundamental requirement we need to satisfy. To conclude that trust exists, a DM must affirmatively calculate that a TDT will deliver increased control over time. To do so, the DM must weigh, net, and input time value for Results and Risks, relying on Rules (to define how those calculations are to be made) and Decisional Information (and Decisional Information Sources that align to those Rules) to execute the calculations.

But money only becomes relevant *after* we have made a decision that a TDT will functionally satisfy the Rules described by Work, including the Functional Specifications for measuring time. In other words, we first must affirmatively calculate the probability that a TDT can perform the Work (and produce improved control over time) before money matters to us. If we do not achieve an affirmative result in those calculations, there is no trust and therefore no need to be concerned about money. The priority is to evaluate the TDT and determine that it is functionally capable of being

To conclude that trust exists, a DM must affirmatively calculate that a TDT will deliver increased control over time.

trusted. In the trust vocabulary, this is the *Functional Calculation*. That calculation is mathematical and relies entirely on everything that has preceded.

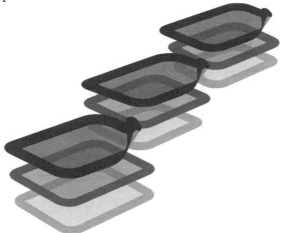

THE DECISION PROCESS SO FAR

Beginning with the first frame, the trust decision process has moved forward with multiple layers receiving attention in the time span of each frame. Observations about the Context inform how the next frames develop and, with each new frame, we add new layers to illustrate the moving parts of the process. Using the TDC, we define a boundary that frames the decision, identifying the TDC_{CIR}, TDC_{RES}, and TDC_{RUL} we need to be considered in the calculations. Within each layer, we assemble stacks of cels to create a full inventory of what exists within that layer. For each, we build Descriptive Specifications and Functional Specifications, express Results and Risks, and make required pairings. As a result, the TDC boundary is tightened and defined by preliminary calculations that exclude certain TDC_{CIR}, TDC_{RES}, or TDC_{RUL} from further consideration.

We also are conducting R & R at each layer: two steps forward and, sometimes, three steps back. We identify pairings to create calculations that combine results, netting and summing outcomes. Some work together; others do not, exposing the need to go back and revise what is there. In our imagined animation studio, those developing each layer exchange information, consult and collaborate, adding, subtracting, and revising specific cels to better illustrate the full TDC. When you are the DM, some of this is occurring in your mind, some of it requires you to record notes, accumulate information, build decision grids, and rank different pairings. For the hammer, all of this may occur in less than a second; for a $47.5 million Cloud-based service selection, hundreds of hours accumulated over weeks and months may be required from the entire team to progress across the timeline.

Work gains shape and substance through refinement of its definition. In other words, as we build a better understanding of all of the Tasks we require to be completed, we are also building depth, pairings, and relationships among them. We define and sequence Tasks so that the Decisional Information produced from one Task serves as the fuel for the next Task to begin. We develop Functional Specifications to express the Decisional Information required to evaluate how Resources will perform. We also construct criteria to evaluate the trust values of Decisional Information and their Decisional Information Sources.

We continue more R & R, which constantly and dynamically produce new, more complete iterations. Using the Rhett Butler Rule, we may determine intentionally to put some Resources outside the TDC. For others, we use Decisional Information calculations of very low probabilities to become indifferent and shift some Resources below the line. Circumstances keep changing; a light breeze becomes a strong gust and, suddenly the umbrella you packed will fail to keep you dry if it begins to rain. Some

Resources get excluded because they are incapable of producing Decisional Information required by the Rules. Others are tossed out because either the Decisional Information or related Decisional Information Sources are not accessible. In each case, there is no affirmative calculation; instead we look for other Resources that are equivalent in their probable contributions toward the Work and for which Decisional Information is accessible. We also may look for alternative Rules paired to accessible Decisional Information.

The actions reviewed above generate several important outcomes for our trust decision process. The TDC boundary becomes tighter as the interactions and movements of Decisional Information from frame to frame qualify and disqualify various TDC elements through chained calculations. The definition of Work is shaped more precisely. The Rules that will measure success become more expressive and aligned to the available Decisional Information. Some Resources remain beyond reach and are excluded; some Rules prohibit certain combinations of Resources; and some Circumstances change, frustrating the ability to perform any of the Work at all.

All along, from the first frame in which Work is recognized and the constituent Tasks first crafted, the TDT definition is gaining structure, substance, and detail. Resources and Rules are being paired and Circumstances evaluated. Some pairings may simply not make sense (a laptop with no battery cannot do Work without a power source); other pairings may provoke innovation toward how the Work can be achieved (a shoe for a hammer).

The TDT becomes a composition, an integration of Resources linked together by Rules to perform defined Tasks in combination

The TDT becomes a composition, an integration of Resources linked together by Rules to perform defined Tasks in combination and in sequence.

and in sequence. Whether or not it is digital, each TDT is always a system. The TDT becomes a solution, designed to achieve successful performance of the Work, built now of TDT_{RES} and TDT_{RUL}. The Results and Risks each Resource can achieve are measured against the Rules and summed and totaled using the available Decisional Information, and the calculations move the TDT toward being measured against the Work.

With the cels piled into sequenced stacks and the stacks assembled as layers and assembled into an entire folio, a DM now can view each frame as a separate assembly and calculation. The questions then pour out, each generated by a Rule that the DM uses as an evaluation tool: Is Work properly expressed? Has the TDC been fully surveyed? Are there Resources we once excluded that we now ought to bring back inside the TDC boundary? Has the line been drawn properly to include the Decisional Information with which all of the TDC elements and TDT components will be measured?

No different than the animation artist team, the DM is calculating alignment, symmetry, and execution. With each frame, scrutiny of the whole may expose misfits, gaps, omissions, or obstacles. Preliminary calculations generate more R & R. At all layers, and for each cel in each stack, dynamic adaptations are occurring. As the stacks are revised, another frame emerges. With each, the DM's evaluation is itself Decisional Information to the Work of the trust decision. Each evaluation is an output, a judgment of the quality of the full collection of moving parts measured against the Rules upon which the DM relies to complete the Work of deciding to trust.

Each DM evaluation then fuels further refinements in the requirements for achieving the Work. More precise expressions of the Work emerge, reflecting the impact, pairings, and changes among the TDC elements within the boundary. The DM also acquires more complete knowledge of the capability of the TDT to achieve the Work successfully, which serves as Decisional Information to generate more precise Rules. Each evaluation is always a calculation of probabilities and, once calculated, the output informs the beginning of composing the next frame. Alignment, symmetry, and execution Rewind and Recalculate until that moment when the Functional Calculation must be made: Will the TDT be trusted to perform the Work successfully?

THE FUNCTIONAL CALCULATION

On the second round, both Vendor X and Vendor Y stood out from the rest. X was a first-round participant; it was almost hard to believe its second proposal had come from the same vendor. Vendor Y was one of the new Middle East bidders that based its reputation on its success supporting some of the large global energy companies in the hostile and uncertain operating conditions in that part of the world. Each operated entirely different hardware platforms and geographic configurations, but their descriptions of their functional services both tracked closely to the new RFP. Too closely, in the CIO's mind; the "bake-off" had been designed to test whether the vendors actually could deliver against their promises. Surely you have faced a similar moment in making big decisions—the options seem promising, but you actually need to know more.

In truth, the CIO had not yet performed the Functional Calculation for either vendor. Her only real progress had been to disqualify the other bidders: software support services required by the RFP were not included; help desk services were only available from the Middle East vendors during their normal business hours; there were no details on how the security controls mandated by public regulations would be performed; warranty disclaimers and limitations of damages clauses in their boilerplate contracts left management of the risk of security breaches entirely on the CIO's team's plate; and none offered the performance data reporting packages that Vendors X and Y included (at least they offered the options). Resources, Process Rules, Descriptive Specifications, Functional Specifications, Rules, Risks, Decisional Information—all of these trust vocabulary terms align to the inadequacies within the rejected proposals.

What the CIO and her team were missing was the Decisional Information with which to assure in their trust calculations that the solutions offered by X and Y would perform to the RFP's description of how the Work needed to be executed (the Functional Specification). In responding to the Committee, a key feature of their strategy was to keep many of the active IT services in-house (largely to protect the value of the sensitive digital assets and better assure compliance); data storage, archiving, and software development were scheduled to be moved into the Cloud. To succeed, however, the data assets needed to move seamlessly from active systems to the Cloud and back, through secure virtual networks not previously deployed by Wise. Having never done so, many of the Rules (and the performance metrics they require) would be new for the CIO's team. The "bake-off" was more than a test—it also was a subtle effort to get the vendors to author the Rules.

FINALIZING THE TDT BOUNDARY

Remember the earlier point in the decision process—that moment when innovation occurs as the DM calculates TDC_{RES} that do not align to the Rules but adapts by acquiring or creating new Resources or Rules? The CIO's team was not there yet—in truth, despite the elegance of their slide presentation to the Committee, they did not even have the Rules assembled to assure the functional effectiveness of the Cloud-based services.

So often, as the Functional Calculation approaches, the holes and open spaces in the architecture of the Work and TDT are exposed. The component Resources are identified, but their integrated operation has not been fully thought through. The situation is no different than a building architect finalizing a home design and realizing the cold air return vent blocks the space where the toilet pipe needs to be installed. Rules are missing; Resources have not been fully described; mechanisms for generating or evaluating Decisional Information have been overlooked. It is where the need to R & R is most critical; it is also the point in time when R & R is most difficult to accomplish.

Yet that is what we do in our decisions. We rewind, revise, and hope to recalculate in time to still execute the Functional Calculation and not just jump and take the risks:

> New Resources are licensed to create the required Decisional Information.

> Consultants are employed to write necessary Process Rules.

> Second independent audit reports are sent at midnight by secure e-mail to validate the accuracy of Decisional Information.

> Lawyers are hired to craft agreements that enforce Rules defining where the boundaries are drawn between the systems of vendors and customers.

Each of these actions can be mapped into very specific frames of each decision and, with the Trust Decision Model and trust vocabulary, more precisely tied to specific layers and components. This is when the boundary and description of the TDT is finalized—decisions are made to determine, in total, "What will be the target of the trust decision?"

The decision chain that fills the next frames functionally splits into three parallel chains, with the output of decisions along each chain influencing the others. Imagine a movie screen split into three parts, with each camera following a different actor moving through the same activity. All of the pairings and layers are being considered, but the most influential decisions occur along these three chains.

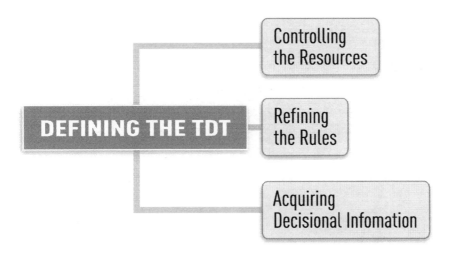

CONTROLLING THE RESOURCES

The first chain of analysis requires the DM to draw another boundary, separating the Resources that are part of the TDT (TDT_{RES}) from other Resources within the TDC (TDC_{RES}) that may be required for the TDT to perform properly.

> Your laptop needs electric power to perform the Work of writing the quarterly sales report. The laptop is the TDT; it requires the power as an added Resource but neither the laptop nor you can control the power availability itself. Deciding to trust your laptop is a distinct decision from trusting the electric company to not suffer a transformer blowout 10 minutes before your report is due. There are now two TDTs—the laptop and the power supply.

> Concerned about the electric company, you purchase and bring along to the coffee shop a portable, fully charged extra battery. Are there still two decisions—one for the laptop and one for the battery—or is there a single unified TDT consisting of the laptop plus the extra battery?

> The CIO knew that both Vendor X and Vendor Y would require her systems to continue operations. No Committee member cared about drawing boundaries—what they wanted was a unified IT system that would keep the company operating without disruption at lower costs. What the CIO and her team saw was a connected network of systems, each requiring trust decisions to be made individually and a larger decision (similar to the Committee's view) being made on the full post-contract operations.

How those lines are drawn requires refining how we define a system. I submit that the boundaries of a system (and, in turn, any TDT) are defined by the capability of the Resources of that system to execute

The boundaries of a system . . . are defined by the capability of the Resources of that system to execute the Rules paired to those Resources.

the Rules paired to those Resources. When other Resources are required which are not controlled by the TDT, the boundary falls between the TDT and those Resources and separate trust decisions are required for each.

> Trusting the power company is a separate decision; by recognizing the power supply as a separate TDT, you can make suitable pairings between them (the laptop requires a trusted power source) and separately decide to trust the laptop itself.

> Using the portable battery may or may not require two decisions. If the laptop operates Rules that, when the internal battery wears down, automatically seek power from a connected battery with a certain configuration, the laptop and the battery become a unified TDT. But if you must separately plug in the spare battery, then there are two TDTs.

> The CIO's concerns focused on how well her systems could govern and control the vendor systems in order that the Committee's perceptions of a unified system were met. To do so, she knew Rules were needed that her systems could execute against the vendor systems. If not, she would not have the control and would have to report that outcome to the Committee.

In a Cloud-based world of integrated systems, devices, applications, and data sources, the complexity of the line-drawing is obvious. But when a proposed TDT cannot control a Resource through the execution of Rules, separate TDTs must be identified (and the connected

But when a proposed TDT cannot control a Resource through the execution of Rules, separate TDTs must be identified.

descriptions, pairings, and line-drawings performed). The pattern is not unlike the parallel decision process for trusting Decisional Information—rather than evaluating an enormous blob of technology, people, processes, and data, the Trust Decision Model enables us to separate, isolate, and construct autonomous but connected decisions for the respective Resources as separate TDTs.

REFINING THE RULES

The Committee recognized what was happening. The "bake-off" idea exposed the CIO team's weakness—they did not know how to structure the Rules for transitioning to the Cloud. The fact the surviving vendors now were demanding premiums for performance data reporting had nothing to do with the reporting costs; their pedigrees clearly documented each vendor had existing customers that likely imposed even more rigorous obligations than the CIO had articulated so far. The premiums had everything to do with the vendors wanting to be paid for the time and assets that would be invested in teaching the CIO's team, through the "bake-off," how to manage their Cloud services (with particular attention to refining the Rules with which to do so).

There was a further complexity. Even if the Rules were authored by the CIO, neither Vendor X nor Vendor Y had offered to produce the Decisional Information to support a Functional Calculation of whether to trust their systems to do the job. Both had proposed contract language assuring only that "reasonable security controls consistent with industry best practices, including continuous firewall monitoring and incident reporting" were employed, standard lawyer words that offered no means to measure performance or execution!

The CIO had hoped to achieve something more with the "bake-off"—to qualify each vendor as a Decisional Information Source that she and her company could trust. Her security monitoring systems included continuous monitoring and incident reporting. To shift to any vendor, she needed to make sure that their reporting Data would work as a Resource to her own security monitoring services. She had Rules for the Data—sequencing, partitioning, encryption, XBRL tagging—and needed the vendor systems to prove their Data conformed.

So, on several layers, Rules had become challenging. The Rules by which the CIO governed her systems were not portable (to the extent they were even fully authored and published to the team); Rules did not exist for governing systems owned by the vendors so the entire assembly operated as a unified system; and Rules did not exist for conforming the vendor's performance data into the CIO's monitoring systems, if she could get the vendors to even move away from the ambiguity of the lawyer's contract language.

What this situation exposes is that, in the frames in which a TDT definition is being finalized toward performing the Functional Calculation, the Rules are frequently the TDT components requiring adjustment. By authoring Rules that enabled connectivity to be controlled, performance data to be reported and integrated, and objective measurements to be installed for evaluating security incidents, the CIO would be able to better define the boundary of the TDT each vendor system represented. But she could also achieve another goal—use the Rules to combine the TDT which a vendor system represented with her own legacy systems and present to the Committee a unified operating platform. In other words, she could deliver what the Committee wanted—a fully integrated system in which, under her leadership, the Committee could place its trust.

ALTERNATIVE SOURCES OF DECISIONAL INFORMATION

In the earliest frames of each decision, DMs rely solely upon their own senses to develop the TDC and then the Work description. Soon after, once personal knowledge is tapped out, a DM looks to other sources for the Descriptive Specifications and Functional Specifications required for all of the moving parts—Context, Circumstances, Resources, Rules, Tasks, and Work. The more complex the proposed TDT, the more complex the structure becomes. This becomes part of the third decision chain—adjusting the TDT description and boundary to enable the trust calculations to be fired in reliance on alternative sources of Decisional Information.

> Students selecting a professor for a required course will not just rely on the professor's bio and publications list; they visit RateMyProfessor.com, an open, crowd-sourcing teacher evaluation source, to acquire information from previous students. To do so, they are actually adjusting how they define the professor as a TDT to be someone who earns at least a three star rating from prior students.

> Prospective customers stonewalled by vendors will seek other information that can help them calculate whether their Rules can be satisfied— consultant opinions can count a lot.

Of course, before a DM can rely on the knowledge or information acquired from an alternative source, that source is a Decisional Information Source for which trust must be calculated as well. So often we presume trust in those sources, no differently than we presume the functionality of a Resource or a TDT, rather than calculating its trust. This is another variety of Decisional Information Risk, occurring in the parallel decision chain of constructing the decision itself. To offset that risk, two processes occur: the description of the TDT is revised so that its Rules include Rules that take into account outside Decisional Information and the Decisional Information (and its Sources) must be separately evaluated. Neither becomes part of the TDT but both are integral Resources to completing the trust decision.

To be helpful, one of the Committee members made a phone call to a long-time friend, a C-level executive at Vendor Y's largest client, Bluff Products. A quiet meeting was arranged with the CIOs and supporting team members from both companies. They held candid, oral, "off-the-record" discussions about Vendor Y.

The CIO and her team learned about Vendor Y's reporting services and the costs Bluff paid, and gained strategies for how to break the logjam over the contract language and author specific contract terms for the reporting services (not unlike the specifications for a tilt-tray message structure to a retail management system). Did the CIO or Committee member ever think to question the trust of the Bluff team as a Decisional Information Source? Not for a single second. Yet the entire reason for the meeting had been disingenuous; Bluff hoped, if the CIO's company signed up, they could press Vendor Y for lower fees for themselves!

Equipped with the new insights about Vendor Y, the negotiation team went back to both vendors offering the same counter-proposal (i.e., new Rules for the reporting services expressed in the agreement). There would be no "bake-off," but performance reporting services had to be included, with the full specifications required by the CIO's systems. Both vendors agreed, revising their services (the TDT) to conform to the counter-proposal and related Rules. The CIO felt they were reaching the end of the tunnel.

DONE DEAL? NOT REALLY

No trust decision can occur without a Functional Calculation. For trust to exist, the DM must reach that affirmative decision that the TDT can perform the Work successfully. But the DM also must conclude that the decision process that has been employed can be trusted! As stated earlier, in trust vocabulary terms, the decision process itself is a TDT for the Work of deciding to trust. Any failure to reach the calculated, affirmative end-point of either decision chain is simply choosing to take the risk, rather than determining to trust.

The problem, of course, is that nearly every trust decision will confront a point at which Decisional Information Risk arises. It is almost impossible to have no Decisional Information Risk. The CIO thought she had a done deal and was favoring Vendor Y with the strength of Bluff's references. But not really; she never made an affirmative decision to trust Bluff as a Decisional Information Source; that trust was *presumed*. Nevertheless, she moved ahead, setting up a final negotiation merely to fill in the pricing on the full-service offering.

When we freeze-frame any decision to move ahead in the presence of Decisional Information Risk, what occurs in the next moment is fascinating. There are only three options, each of which now carries more importance as the Functional Calculation approaches.

> ≥ Option One—Unable to obtain or validate Decisional
> Information, the DM inputs "0." That is, of course,

the correct result. There is a Rule; the Decisional Information is a null set, so the Rule cannot be calculated. Each Rule that cannot be calculated also means the Functional Calculation is more likely to yield a negative outcome.

⋙ Option Two—The DM resolves the Risk by inputting a "1" that has not been calculated to be true. Now the Risk is magnified; if trust is affirmatively calculated and "1" later proves to be inaccurate, the decision itself becomes vulnerable. The outcome is no better than failing to look under the bridge despite having been warned to do so.

⋙ Option Three—The DM eliminates the Risk by eliminating the Rule or Rules under which the Risk arises. It is simple to do; the DM merely writes the Rule or Rules out of the portfolio of Rules against which the trust decision is to be calculated. No more Rule; no more Risk. It has the same impact as any exclusion of any Resource pursuant to the Rhett Butler Rule; the field of options is narrowed by which to calculate an affirmative outcome.

When the "bake-off" was cancelled, the appropriate outcome was Option One: to keep the original Rule and input a "0." Vendor Y did not offer performance reporting to be tested before going live; so the Rule could not be satisfied. The Rule was valued by the CIO's team; proving functional integrity was important to safeguarding their compliance duties. But the CIO also knew that disclosing to the Committee there would be compliance risks while trying to achieve $47.5 million in savings would be unacceptable.

Relying upon Vendor Y's client as a Decisional Information Source was Option Two. The CIO could not verify the performance testing capability independently. She could rely on the other client as a secondary Decisional Information Source and input a "1" value for the rule requiring performance testing. But doing so shifts, not eliminates, the Decisional Information Risk. The Functional Calculation can occur, but reliance on second-hand information weakens the value of the reliance. How is that possible?

Put yourself in an auditor's role, looking at the soundness of the CIO's reliance on Bluff. What questions would you immediately ask? You would want to know about Bluff's trustworthiness and reliability in past collaborative exchanges; after all, Bluff is also a competitor. In this case, their true motive in offering favorable Decisional Information ("Vendor Y has strong performance reporting") was to gain savings in their own costs. The CIO presumed and did not test the reliability of the Decisional Information Source. How would you evaluate her decision to rely merely on a Committee member's friendship as the basis for making a bet to save $47.5 million? It is a sure thing—you would lose trust in her decision and in her team.

So while the CIO would input a "1" value, enabling the Rule to be satisfied, the input itself is vulnerable. That is why separate chained trust decisions involving Decisional Information Sources are so important. A DM must not only be able to defend the integrity of the trust decision in a TDT; the trust placed in the Decisional Information also must be defensible.

The CIO and her team never got comfortable with the other client's disclosures. So, in preparing their final recommendation, they chose Option Three; they eliminated the Decisional Information

> A DM must not only be able to defend the integrity of the trust decision in a TDT; the trust placed in the Decisional Information also must be defensible.

Risk by changing the Rules. Rather than a Rule requiring proof of integrity with pre-launch testing and validation, the Agreement merely required a Vendor's promise, articulated by the lawyers, to build reporting services after contract signing. The Functional Calculation was imminent; the contract revisions lined everything up. The Agreement terms were the Decisional Information that satisfied the new Rule.

But what really happened was the *deferral* of the Decisional Information Risk, not its elimination. Remember (from the warehouse lessons) that the Rules expressed in an agreement are part of the system and, therefore, part of the TDT. Thus, contract language incapable of objective functional measurement creates, rather than eliminate, risk. The new Agreement terms did not enable any Functional Calculation of Vendor Y's ability to perform the Work. The risk merely was shifted from the pre-decision process into the post-decision execution phase.

Imagine the Agreement now is signed, but Vendor Y stalls on its promises and blows smoke when pressed to build out performance reporting and testing. You know what will happen—finger-pointing, accusations, and counteraccusations will follow. All of these are entirely predictable when metrics-based, rules-based expressions of how to perform obligations are not explicit. The outsourcing may never be launched at all if the management and reporting capabilities are not first put into place.

Option Three—changing the Rules—can be a viable response to Decisional Information Risk. Indeed, it is how trust decisions most often evolve. But the right path can require even more effort; the more time passes, the harder it becomes to change the Rules before making a Functional Calculation that matters.

In the Trust Decision Model, when there is Decisional Information Risk that precludes a Functional Calculation, it is no different than any other frame in the film—a DM has the opportunity to Rewind and Recalculate. In acting properly with Option Three, a DM goes backwards to that frame when the Rules were added which cannot be calculated now. Then, the DM removes and replaces them with other Rules that do have trusted Decisional Information available from trusted Decisional Information Sources.

For example, imagine Vendor Y does have strong performance reporting capabilities that previously had been certified by the global leader in security testing (call them SecureTest, Inc.) as conforming to international best-practice standards. However, Vendor Y has resisted showing the actual format and structure of its reporting before contract signing; a prior customer prospect had misappropriated the reporting samples despite a confidentiality agreement and Vendor Y does not want to repeat its prior misjudgment.

Vendor Y reasonably could propose to the CIO that, instead of the actual performance testing, it will provide a signed certificate from SecureTest attesting to the standard of care and details addressed in Vendor Y's reporting. The CIO could rewind, replace the old Rule with a new Rule based on the offer, and accept the written attestation as Decisional Information from a trusted source (SecureTest). Now the rest of the Functional Calculation can proceed.

This is exactly what negotiations should produce—collaborative development of alternative Rules properly composed to support the Functional Calculation by requiring objective, measurable Decisional Information from Decisional Information Sources, each of which are calculated to be trustworthy. This adaptive editing,

R & R, and Functional Calculation *needs to happen* as teams develop each layer and move to each successive frame. It is how Decisional Information Risk can be filtered out of the trust decision.

Recall that, in the earliest frames, a DM is acting solely on directly known Decisional Information. But as the frames proceed, most decisions require Decisional Information from other sources; the higher the stakes and the more complex the decision, the greater the appetite for more information. This becomes the second critical moment in the trust decision—choosing among the three options when Decisional Information Risk stalls the Functional Calculation.

The same R & R process can be successful if the DM chooses Option One. If the Decisional Information does not support a Rule correctly (producing a "0"), the R & R can focus on finding alternative Rules that enable forward progress. The mistake often made in that scenario is to bypass the effort of doing the R & R. Instead, far too often in business, Rhett Butler appears again on the scene. Confronted with a null set, a DM intentionally shifts to Option Two or relies on Option Three to discard the Rule entirely (or replace it with one that cannot be functionally measured and relying on vague language [e.g., "reasonable security reporting shall be employed"] to assure future compliance). The result is consequential: affirmative trust becomes a less likely outcome.

ACHIEVING EQUIVALENCE WITH ALTERNATIVE RULES

When authoring replacement Rules to alleviate Decisional Information Risk, the critical strategy is to create *equivalence* in the values between the old Rule and the alternative Rule. That means a DM wants to select an alternative Rule or Rules that will produce

This becomes the second critical moment in the trust decision.

results in the Functional Calculation that are as close as possible to the results that would have been calculated affirmatively under the old Rule, had Decisional Information Risk not existed. What are the values that matter?

Remember how a Functional Specification requires measurements and expressions of probability? That is precisely the goal for achieving equivalence. The DM requires a mathematical means of calculating that the probability of succeeding in the Work when complying with the alternative Rule will be equivalent to the probability of achieving success under the original Rule. Therefore, the alternative Rules must measure up to all of the criteria that matter—the mathematical results must be functionally equivalent.

What is fascinating at this frame of the film is to look at all of the layers concurrently. As the Functional Calculation approaches and (under Option One) even following a calculation of "0" for any Rule, the R & R is not just a matter of changing the Rules layer, or just one cel in that layer representing one Rule. Instead, the pairings among all of the layers demand a recalculation to confirm that everything still, quite literally, adds up. Circumstances, Resources, Rules, Work, Tasks, Results, Risks, TDT—when one Rule is altered, the pairings and chainings fire new assessments across all of the layers. As a DM then moves again toward and through the Functional Calculation, the process can repeat itself.

That, at least, is the Trust Decision Model's theoretical construct. In reality, deadlines and other constraints limit or eliminate R & R, forcing linear decisions and conclusions. In some cases, Option One (inputting "0") for a single Rule can end the analysis; a DM can conclude that the TDT does not functionally align with the requirements of the Work, the TDC, or the metrics for measuring success. In other cases, Rhett Butler makes the call, relying on Option Two (presume "1") or Option Three to simply exclude the Rule affected by Decisional Information Risk.

Those are the only choices to make, and they apply both when deciding to trust the TDT and when evaluating the integrity of the decision process itself. By relying on Bluff's false information without validation of its trustworthiness (Option Two), the CIO and her team made the wrong choice. Just imagine the consequences if her defense to the Committee six months later is, "Well, we met Bluff's CIO at a bar and he said Vendor Y had strong performance reporting, so we took the risk of using the lawyer's phrasing."

"TAKING THE RISK" IS NOT EMOTIONAL

Now we can see that navigating the three options for how to respond to Decisional Information Risk is never emotional. Instead, when "taking the risk," a DM is engaging in fuzzy math, displaying neither courage nor audacity. Under Option Two, a value is presumed without being proven; under Option Three, a bad choice to eliminate a Rule or to substitute Rules without equivalent values has a similar outcome, changing the embedded mathematics required in the Functional Calculation. In either case, the Decisional Information Risk is merely deferred, not resolved. Should adversity occur, the time value of remediation will almost always exceed the savings realized using fuzzy math.

Good executives excel at making hard decisions by how they calculate Decisional Information Risks. Experience teaches what types of alternative Rules may provide equivalence in the Functional Calculation; the judgments that withstand scrutiny are those

When "taking the risk," a DM is engaging in fuzzy math, displaying neither courage nor audacity.

for which defensible, sound explanations are offered for how the mathematics were performed. As noted earlier, there are no magic formulae or algorithms in this book. What emerges at this point in the film is a better set of insights into how we unfold the decision process, how we account for the moving parts at different layers and cels, and what occurs in the R & Rs that occur.

If the Functional Calculation adds up, a DM then moves ahead and confronts the final substantive decision chain: What value will be paid or delivered to acquire the TDT to perform the Work with a probability of success that meets the Rules? Yes, time matters, but now a DM must decide whether to trade assets of value for the TDT. What will be paid for the opportunity to achieve success?

ABOUT THE MONEY

Imagine two different closing scenarios for the CIO, each involving a different, new vendor. Rather than continue the story with Vendor X and Vendor Y, it is useful to start "clean" so our focus is on the value proposition of the vendors and we are not trying to balance out defects in prior proposals.

In each of the following new scenarios, Wise proves to be a strong, competent potential customer for the vendors. The RFP described the Work fully, responsive vendor proposals arrived, and the team performed Functional Calculations through which they affirmatively calculated that they could trust the vendors to perform the Work. But money can make an enormous difference once the decision process nears the end of the film.

> ≥ Scenario One—Vendor T was the only one to produce
> a proposal that, as a TDT, survived the Functional

Calculation. Vendor T promised to be a strong service provider with a calculated probability of success in performing the Work to what the CIO's team felt met or exceeded Six Sigma standards. But quality had its price; Vendor T's service fees were nearly $20 million more than the amount required by the Committee.

> Scenario Two—The proposals of Vendor U and Vendor W (each a TDT) scored identically and positively; each would be a suitable service provider with a strong probability of functional success in performing the Work. Vendor U's pricing was in line with the Committee's demands; Vendor W offered pricing $5 million lower per year, potentially making the CIO a hero to the Committee.

Every transaction that creates wealth first requires an affirmative decision to trust. The Vendor to be selected will realize new wealth; its employees and contractors will have new sources of income as a result of the new contract. With either scenario, the Committee will be heroes, reporting savings of existing wealth, to be distributed to shareholders or invested in new sales and marketing assets to create new wealth. With the right choice, the CIO will continue her employment and perhaps allow her team a few more hours at home on the weekends.

Now money matters. Finally. Would you trust Vendor T despite the higher costs? Would you be suspicious of Vendor W's lower price? If you were the CIO, how will the Committee evaluate you and your team's recommendations? How will your team's loyalty and trust in your leadership be affected if you make a recommendation contrary to their own analyses of the best value?

THE TRUST VOCABULARY

In this chapter, you will learn the following words:

Expenses

Revenues

Risk Reserve

Trust Discount

Value Calculation

CHAPTER 10

DANCING THE TANGO OF WEALTH AND TRUST

MORE THAN ONCE you have now read that every decision to trust is a calculation of probabilities among three options—the option to do nothing, the option to perform Work alone, and the option to select a TDT with which to complete the Work. In each decision, the fundamental metric that is calculated is time. Work is being defined by how time is calculated. Is time gained by trusting the TDT to perform the Work? What is the value of the time invested in performing Work alone without paying to use the TDT? What time will be lost if the TDT fails to properly perform? If nothing is done at all toward completing the Work, what is the cost in time of allowing the status quo to continue?

In Chapter 2, the Trust Decision Model introduced the persistent presence of time as part of the process. You learned of two measures of time that mattered: the time expended to calculate trust, and the corresponding time value of opportunities lost waiting for trust to be calculated. The more time consumed in making a decision, the greater the time lost after acting on that decision in which to complete the Work with the selected TDT and create new wealth.

In Chapter 9, we discovered a third connection between time and trust, the essential truth that each trust decision calculates the value of a TDT by measuring time, not money. The choices among performing Work alone, selecting a single TDT, or picking among optional TDTs are first determined by the Functional Calculation. Arithmetically, the probable efficiency and productivity of a TDT in performing the Work must be affirmatively determined before the trust decision proceeds.

In both Scenario One and Scenario Two at the end of Chapter 9, the available vendors had passed the Functional Calculation. Vendor T, Vendor U, and Vendor W had each presented Decisional Information in their proposals, supported by extensive due diligence and validation exchanges. The CIO and her team had calculated that each vendor solution, as TDTs, would perform the Work of the IT services described by the RFP. But now the CIO had to calculate the economic value of trust—How much was she prepared to pay? How would she secure the Committee's trust in her decision to spend the amounts she proposed to recommend? What would be the economic value of making the right decision? What would be the economic impact if the wrong decision was made? Perhaps it is no surprise that the answers to those questions are found in calculating the value of time.

TRUST IS PROVEN BY A TRANSFER OF VALUE

Once an affirmative Functional Calculation occurs, a DM must calculate value, comparing the time value of the Resources under its control (which will be offered in payment) to the time value of the TDT. Money is only one possible Resource—Physical Assets (such as gold or equipment) or Human Resources (or their labor) can be offered in exchange. Today's economies are recognizing Data as an emerging Resource class offered as payment for a TDT (in substitution of money)—customer databases, sales performance records, big data analytics, and new digital currencies such as Bitcoin™. The DM may even offer units of personal time (such as attention to reading this book, or listening to a lecture) as payment for a TDT. For each possible Resource that may be offered, the DM asks the question, "Can I trade this Resource for the TDT and gain control of more time?"

In business and in life, every affirmative decision to trust is followed by a transfer of value. The transfer is the essential evidence that an affirmative decision to trust has been calculated:

> ⋙ A teenager may pay cash at the store for a new pair of jeans.

> ⋙ Two amateur photographers may trade equipment—a high-end camera case owned by one in exchange for a specific lens owned by the other.

> ⋙ Hundreds of millions of times each day, electronic payments are made paying for songs, books, films, and data with the transfer of control over digital information that represents money on deposit.

> ⋙ A CIO may approve $5 million per month paid to a Cloud services vendor in new support fees.

The transfer is the essential evidence that an affirmative decision to trust has been calculated.

> An automotive tire manufacturer may commit to a just-in-time continual inventory fulfillment contract in which only 50% of the wholesale price of the tires is being paid by a car company; the tire manufacturer is also receiving a database of the annual sales activity for the car model on which their tires are installed, listing customer names, addresses, and emails (which database has been shown by market sampling to generate an added revenue stream from after-market consumer purchases 37.5% higher than in previous years).

Examining this frame of each buyer-seller transaction, we discover there are *two* mutually exclusive, concurrent trust decisions. The DM, as a buyer (such as the CIO), is calculating the value of the TDT to them; the party in control of the TDT, as a seller or service provider, is calculating the value of the Resources offered in trade. Every transaction is nothing more than barter in which reciprocal trust decisions are required, with each side concurrently calculating the value of what is being offered and what will be received.

When currency printed and distributed by a nation-state is offered, the value calculation by both buyer and seller is straightforward. The marketplace's acceptance of cash is well-known; once received in payment (and tested for its authenticity, either by biting the gold coin, scanning a paper bill under ultraviolet light to detect counterfeit indicators, or electronically verifying the existing balance in an account paired to a debit card), cash becomes a fungible asset with fairly predictable value. The seller will have a calculated level of confidence the Resource being received can be used in a subsequent transaction as payment.

> Every transaction is nothing more than barter in which reciprocal trust decisions are required, with each side concurrently calculating the value of what is being offered and what will be received.

When the assets are any type of Resource other than money, including Data, the calculation of value becomes more complicated. For each, the associated time values must be measured and compared by both buyer and seller. If Resources are bundled together (e.g., Data + Server Use + Application), both sides must author ways of measuring the cumulative values to be integrated into the Functional Specifications and related pairings. The same Resources, once paid and transferred, also may have different values to buyer and seller. Sure, it can become complicated, even more so when the transactions involve multiple stakeholders offering different bundles of Resources. But these calculations are what produce an affirmative, mutual decision to consummate every deal. Each is a *Value Calculation* in the trust vocabulary.

For the DM acting as a buyer, the Value Calculation is a continuation of the trust decisions, chained to the outcome of the Functional Calculation. For the seller, the need for a Value Calculation drives new trust decisions on their side, each of which proceeds consistently with the Trust Decision Model: "What are my Rules for qualifying potential buyers? Can the buyer be trusted as a source of payment? Are the Resources authentic? What Rules exist to validate their quality? How do I trust the buyer's representations of its control of the Resources being offered? How do I know the Resources are available for transfer, free and clear of constraints on my use of them?"

Affirmative trust requires affirmative win-win calculations of gain—the transaction must enable both sides to gain. That may seem straightforward but the Trust Decision Model exposes that our instincts for a good deal are, in fact, mathematically driven.

THE RULES FOR CALCULATING THE VALUE OF TIME

For the DM acting as a buyer, any Value Calculation requires two layers of new attributes to be added to the Descriptive Specifications and Functional Specifications for the Work and the Results to be achieved. First are the new Rules which expand how Work and Resources are described. These Rules express the income and contributions to value that the TDT (and the component Resources included within the TDT boundary) must produce as Results and how those will be measured (including any minimum thresholds) (*Revenues* in the trust vocabulary). Second are new Rules for identifying and measuring the expenses and costs required to secure the Revenues, particularly focused on the Resources offered in payment (including any maximum limits not to be exceeded (*Expenses* in the trust vocabulary). Both these layers relate to how Results are expressed.

In parallel, there are new layers adding new Rules for measuring Expenses relating to the Risks associated with the TDT (and the component Resources) should a related adverse event occur. All of these Rules are being added into the appropriate layers for all of the moving parts, further expanding the inventories of Rules to be relied upon in performing the Value Calculation. A simplified illustration of this process is shown in Figure 10-1:

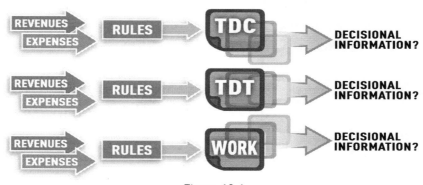

Figure 10-1

For each new Rule, related Rules express the Decisional Information requirements to fire that Rule and, of course, the criteria for its trustworthiness (and those for the related Decisional Information Sources). Imagine the CIO's team recognized the potential added Expenses which Wise will incur for internal staff allocated to managing the transition, as well as the impact those added duties would have on their availability to respond to their other assigned tasks, such as help desk support, patch administration, on-boarding new employees, etc. In order to better track all of those Expenses, a new time management system was acquired, and new task billing codes were developed. Operating costs per employee were calculated (as Expenses), based on units of labor time, as well as allocated and pro-rated costs for physical office space, computing equipment, and similar administrative costs not previously tracked.

Since many employees worked in the field, the CIO insisted that the employees be able to log-on and input the task billing system through remote devices. Concerned about possible overstatements and understatements by her team members of the actual time devoted to certain projects (in other words, she lacked trust in their reporting and the potential ease with which time reporting from personal cell phones, etc., could be manipulated by the employees), she also quietly worked with the Internal Audit group to set up a control that tracked access times to specific applications and log files her team members would require and use for certain tasks, and built simple comparative matrices. If the actual access times were less than 90% of the time reported by a team member, the CIO directly received a notification. Expense Rules, Rules for Decisional Information, Rules for Decisional Information Sources—all are interacting to create trust in the tracking of time and its related Expenses, in order to assure a continuing Value Calculation will be more precise.

An affirmative trust decision does not result if the Value Calculation fails to calculate a positive measure of the probability that wealth (measured in the value of controlling time) can be created.

As with the Functional Calculation and all the preceding chained decisions, the Value Calculation follows the same process. R & R can recur as often as needed, within the limits of deadlines and other constraints. Decisional Information Risk is also part of the process; missing or assumed values will require choices. This is the essence of how value is negotiated, with all of the stakeholders calculating, measuring, and expressing their sense of the values of the Resources to be transferred in the deal.

The mathematics are simple: an affirmative trust decision does not result if the Value Calculation fails to calculate a positive measure of the probability that wealth (measured in the value of controlling time) can be created. An unfavorable outcome in which projected Expenses exceed Revenues has the same impact as Decisional Information Risk or a calculated failure in the Functional Calculation; R & R is required to reach an affirmative trust decision. If the Value Calculation fails on either side of the transaction, the R & R can go back (whether by the buyer, the seller, or both) to any point in the lifecycle of the decision! The TDC, the TDC_{CIR}, the TDC_{RES}, the $TDC_{RUL,}$ the description of Work, the TDT—all can be modified, added, or subtracted, creating new pairings triggering re-execution of the decision chains that lead to the Functional Calculation and enable re-execution of the Value Calculation.

CALCULATING THE VALUE OF TIME MORE PRECISELY

To be effective in the Value Calculation, it is useful to emphasize two additional measures of time for which new Rules are appropriate. These are particularly important when considering the probability of Risk-based adverse events and calculating their all-in impact on whether trust will be placed in a TDT. Combined with the measures of time previously introduced, these measures enable frequencies and causalities to be better expressed as part of the Functional Specifications and in evaluating pairings among Circumstances, Resources, Rules, Results, Risks, Revenues, and Expenses:

Existing Measures

> The time spent to make the decision.

> The time of opportunities lost (failing to engage in productive exercise of the Work while you make your decision).

New Measures

> The time consumed to perform the Work.

> The time over which control is gained by performing the Work successfully (such as the cash payment received for doing the work, like an hourly wage).

> The time consumed by an adverse event occurring for which Risk was calculated (including the time consumed in performing repairs, replacement, remediation, and corrective actions).

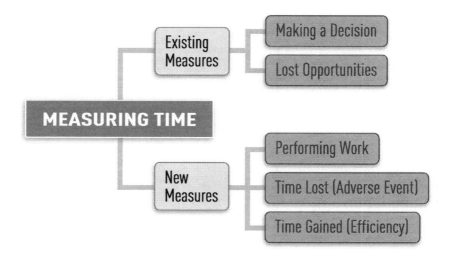

Each of these measures, of course, can be stated in an economic equivalent of the monetary currency of your choice. But the key to the Value Calculation is having the accounting mechanisms in place that enable these equivalents and probabilities to be mathematically expressed as Revenues and Expenses. When buried inside our heads as we make decisions, these moving parts are very hard to segregate—the rules for the measurements feel instinctive. But if we pause and look at the frame in which a DM calculates the outcome, the mathematics are visible: "Does the known value of X exceed the probable value of Y?" The answer is a sum of the Revenues less Expenses, virtually a balance sheet that can be calculated at any point in time.

Projects fail frequently, and recoveries from adverse events are more difficult to achieve, because one or more of the time metrics listed above are underestimated or overlooked. When that occurs, the results can be unpleasant. That was one of the CIO's key concerns: the time her team would devote to building and integrating the performance reporting services of any winning vendor.

Omissions and miscalculations also occur in measuring the value of the time saved by performing the Work successfully.

ACTIVITY	EXPENSE (IF ANY)	REVENUE (IF ANY)
Making a Decision	$ ( )	0
Lost Opportunities	$ ( )	$
Performing Work	$ ( )	$
Time Gained (Control)	0	$
Time Lost (Adverse Event)	$ ( )	0
Totals	$ ( )	$

For example, during the last 15 years, I witnessed and contributed to several dozen projects building electronic discovery ("e-discovery") capabilities inside companies (e-discovery is the process of identifying, preserving, and processing electronically stored information that has value in litigation or similar legal proceedings). Effective e-discovery enables corporate data assets to be located more quickly, filtered with greater effectiveness, and processed into files of responsive and relevant data faster and with greater accuracy.

Yet only once did I see a proposal for these projects calculate the all-in time savings such a system would create for other business projects unrelated to litigation! Projects always gave attention to the time measurements around litigation and legal fees (which are pure economic measures of time!). But the solutions could also help other departments improve their performance by reducing the time devoted to finding last year's sales reports, calculating the costs of medical care at high-risk field construction sites, and hundreds of other information-seeking Tasks grounded in finding and using Information for routine business decisions.

By overlooking the added Revenues and reduced Expenses the solutions could achieve, the total calculations were incomplete. Now, however, technology has unleashed capabilities to express and measure time that will enable improved calculations and, in turn, better trust decisions. The solutions are embraced within the tools portfolio presented in Part II of this book.

THE HIDDEN DISCOUNT FOR DISTRUST

Before turning to the outcomes in Scenario One and Scenario Two, there is one more dimension to how value is calculated. As a business discipline, risk management only has one source of funding—the net profits at the bottom line. From every dollar, euro, dinar, yen or other form of income received, a company must set aside some portion of their income as a risk reserve. In the trust vocabulary, to pay for the Expenses of Risk-based adverse events that occur, some wealth is kept available and accessible as the *Risk Reserve*. This Risk Reserve may be used to pay insurance premiums, legal fees, incident recovery costs, marketing expenses following a data breach, or other similar Expenses. The goal is to create a cushion of assets against which those Expenses can be incurred. In international financial services, doing so is a mandatory requirement, with the amounts of the Risk Reserves proportional to the assets under management and the presence and use of trusted systems and controls. In other industries, the amounts and controls are more discretionary. Of course, if the Expenses of an adverse event exceed the amount of available Risk Reserves, a catastrophe can ensue.

But, on the other side of any transaction, in the frame in which the Value Calculation occurs, there is an added, hidden value a DM introduces which operates in parallel to the Risk Reserve. The Value Calculation, in subtracting Expenses, assigns values to the probabilities of Risks occurring as well. These values are built into *a hidden discount for distrust*. In effect, a DM is protecting itself against the possibility a Risk-based adverse event occurs as a result of its trust in, and use of, a TDT, creating greater Expenses offsetting the projected net Revenues the TDT is expected to produce. This is the final element in the Value Calculation, called the *Trust Discount* in the trust vocabulary.

For example, imagine your company is close to acquiring a smaller competitor. The competitor is the TDT. Final, late-night negotiations are focused on the potential lawsuits against the TDT stemming from a since-abandoned engineering design claimed to be the basis of several injuries from consumers. While you have worked hard to establish the right acquisition price, you have a nagging concern some of the engineering records may not be what they seem. As a result, you ask for a further reduction in the price—in doing so, you are creating a discount for the possibility you have misplaced your trust in the TDT (and the integrity of their engineering records). This is the Trust Discount. It is equal to the price reduction you calculate as a projected net present value of the potential Expenses should your trust decision is flawed.

The Value Calculation, in subtracting Expenses, assigns values to the probabilities of Risks occurring as well.

> The Trust Discount ... is present as part of every Value Calculation.

This Trust Discount is often hidden, but it is present as part of every Value Calculation. I illustrate this principle in my classes with a simple exercise. I present two cereal products, each containing raisins. One is a popular brand; the cereal is inside a sealed cardboard package. The other product is sold in a transparent bag through which the contents are visible. The second product is 75 cents more expensive. Declaring the news just reported rat feces had been found in a child's breakfast, I ask, "Would you prefer to pay less for being unable to see the product (a discount for distrust) or pay more for the chance to confirm visibly you are truly buying raisins?"

There is always some delta between the best possible value of a TDT to a DM and the amount actually determined to be paid. That amount can be paired to a single variable in the trust decision or can be an accumulation of multiple discounts. Using the trust vocabulary, however, we can investigate more thoroughly, moving beyond instincts. Perhaps a Descriptive Specification lacks suitable Rules; perhaps the Decisional Information Source for specific Decisional Information has been presumed trustworthy (a "1"); or perhaps there is limited knowledge about frequency or causality to effectively calculate the probabilities of certain Results. Regardless of the basis, the manner in which our sense of uncertainty is expressed is in the value assigned to the Trust Discount. If that uncertainty is large enough, the Value Calculation fails. If there is time, R & R begins again.

EXECUTING THE VALUE CALCULATION

For the CIO, time had expired. In either scenario, a decision was required, a decision she hoped the Committee would trust. But the decision was also one for which she feared her team might abandon her and put at risk her ability to achieve the intended outcomes.

Scenario One

Vendor T passed the Functional Calculation with ease. On each metric the CIO's team had developed, Vendor T delivered performance logs, specifications, documentation of ongoing maintenance, and sample data reporting formats and test files, beyond even the minimums the RFP had requested. Vendor T had figured out easily that the CIO needed help with this transition; having previously migrated other newbie customers to the Cloud (and profitably), Vendor T had a terrific sense of what the CIO would need (as Decisional Information) to support a recommendation of its proposal.

But the target of $47.5 million in savings set by the Wise Industries Board was completely unrealistic. Vendor T had developed strong analytics on what was required in the first few years to make this type of transition work and the time required of T's staff to hold a client's hand was a cost no RFP ever anticipated. Training, mapping data structures, testing security protocols for incident responses, producing compliance documents, integrating performance data reporting—all of these (as Tasks) were part of the larger Work, had never been mentioned in the RFP, and the related Expenses needed to be charged to the clients.

Vendor T also knew the increased scrutiny that the regulators covering Wise would apply to Vendor T's systems and controls; experience had built up a good understanding of the related expenses of producing architectural and performance data for the regulators that the CIO had never before been required to generate. As a result, in the role of the seller, Vendor T had calculated its annual service fees to be nearly $20 million more than the CIO had requested. The $47.5 million in savings had been the CIO's Value Calculation; the $27.5 million in savings proposed by Vendor T (reduced by the added $20 million in Expenses) was their Value Calculation of its services to Wise.

But Vendor T recognized, standing alone, its price would be difficult for the CIO to accept. So Vendor T opted to be more fully transparent in their proposal to the CIO. It acknowledged these types of migrations are difficult and often involve unexpected investments of time and potential adversities. Rather than submit a low bid that would win and then charging new fees for each add-on, Vendor T identified all of the preceding factors (training, documentation, etc.) and expressed them as new Tasks. For each, Vendor T precisely described the Tasks, listed the Resources required, submitted added Descriptive Specifications and Functional Specifications, and expressed the Results to be achieved and the Risks that could be avoided. Vendor T emphasized these new Tasks, while more expensive, added greater value by illustrating, with comparable metrics, the staff and cost savings of other clients (including internal and external legal, consulting, and audit fees) who had previously elected to obtain similar services from Vendor T. An independent audit of those savings by a well-known, global consulting group was also included.

Vendor T had artfully amended how the CIO had defined the Work in the RFP, executing an R & R with its proposal. New Tasks were added, new Resources expanded the TDT description, new Results to be achieved (and new Risks to be navigated) were identified and valued, Decisional Information was delivered to support the amendments, and a trusted Decisional Information Source was provided. The CIO and her team quickly recognized Vendor T had helped them immensely. The Work definition was more aligned to what a Cloud migration of this nature required, and the added Resources, Results, and Risks made sense. But there were two dimensions of near "magic" to Vendor T's proposal.

First, Vendor T had identified and provided metrics regarding the internal time demands on the CIO's team the migration would require, both with and without the added Tasks. The team had overlooked the added complexities involved; the internal "burn rate" was much higher, regardless of the vendor selected (representing a contraction in the projected savings). Vendor T equipped the CIO with a better expression of the all-in costs (as Expenses) the Committee needed to anticipate.

Second, while the service fees were higher, the CIO had actually reduced a hidden trust discount included in her Value Calculation tied to the uncertainties in her own mind. Vendor T's candor had been impressive; by describing the Tasks and related Expenses, as well as the indirect Revenues realized by lowering direct spending on lawyers, consultants, compliance, and auditors (costs completely overlooked in the CIO team projections), Vendor T improved her confidence in the recommendation that was going to be made.

If these interactions are slowed down, even more of the R & R occurring in each frame and at each layer can be visualized. The CIO had to expand her description of the TDC to include new Resources—specifically the added personnel within Vendor T, and her own staff, that would be required to absorb the added migration-based Tasks. The definition of Work was revised to include those Tasks. For all of the preceding, added Rules were articulated and integrated into the Descriptive Specifications and Functional Specifications regarding the skills, capabilities, and performance metrics, as well as Expenses associated with each Human Resource. The TDT description of Vendor T's full services was revised, with both new Results and new Risks included, and relevant controls applied against those Risks (such as the compliance audits by regulators). New decision chains were assembled and executed, both for the TDT and for the trust decision process itself. A Functional Calculation was affirmed and a new Value Calculation completed.

The uncertainties plaguing the CIO also are more easily exposed. She knew a major migration involved many Tasks new to her team, but they did not have direct knowledge within the Context of the Resources required (both from a vendor and the team itself) to perform those Tasks. Those Resources were placed outside the TDC boundary; had Vendor T not addressed them, the attendant Expenses likely would have been disastrous. She lacked the Rules with which to calculate the contributions of those Resources to the Work; she had neither the Decisional Information nor Sources with which to gather the Rules. Her sense of emotional uncertainty merely disguised what can now be seen as Decisional Information Risks which accumulated to create a functional trust discount—"Even if a vendor fully aligned to the RFP, what was missing that could undermine the trust to be placed in that vendor?"

Vendor T addressed those concerns. While the proposed direct Expenses were higher than originally projected, the CIO planned to illustrate to the Committee unexpected Risks (including Decisional Information Risks) that neither they nor she had originally contemplated the migration would confront. She could explain the Expenses associated with those Risks and provide trusted Decisional Information from a trusted Decisional Information Source that Vendor T's new definition of Work actually created other unexpected savings in Expenses (for the lawyers, consultants, and auditors) that improved the company's bottom line. The CIO was confident the Committee would approve the recommendation of Vendor T. She was still proposing a plan that would drop nearly $30 million annually to the bottom line and the new Tasks better assured her team they would be remain employed!

Scenario Two

With complex RFPs, two vendors will never score identically against the grading criteria. Remarkably, that was exactly the outcome after two weeks of RFP reviews by the CIO's team. Her immediate concern was that the criteria themselves were not composed accurately. Perhaps the metrics were not expressed with sufficient precision. Perhaps Vendor U and Vendor W had conspired behind the scenes to submit identical proposals; after all, there was very little competition in the market for Cloud-based services that supported the regulated industry of the CIO's company. The parallel grades themselves created authentic concern (i.e., Decisional Information Risk on steroids!). Regardless, time did not permit the CIO to focus any further on those concerns; the team had produced documentation showing both vendor proposals aligned to the RFP. She had to focus on cost.

Vendor U had offered to perform the same Work for $5.0 million less per year—how could she figure out whether or not to believe them? If she chose Vendor U and the future was flawless, she would be a hero to the Committee. If she selected the lower price and Vendor U failed to deliver, she would be accused of cost-cutting for the sake of cost-cutting and suffer the consequences. Hindsight can be very cruel that way.

Accepting either Vendor proposal made a 20% reduction in her staff inevitable; if she made the wrong choice, she would not have the Human Resources with which to recover. The $5.0 million would be diverted elsewhere by the Committee quickly; she would have to beg for any funds needed to rebuild if the Vendor failed, if she even was lucky enough to keep her own job. While higher in cost, she sensed there was a lower risk in selecting Vendor W, if not for the company then at least for herself and the sanity and loyalty of her remaining staff.

When this moment is frozen, the dynamic interactions between the Value Calculation and the Functional Calculation are vivid. Each of the critical decision points in the Trust Decision Model influences how the Value Calculation proceeds. Unaware of the complexity of sub-Nets within various Cloud vendors, the team had not drawn a boundary around the geographic locations that were suitable and unsuitable for their corporate assets (a TDC_{CIR}). Vendor U based their proposal on the use of a new data center subcontractor in Khazacki (a fictitious country) that offered them very low pricing on excess capacity; Vendor W anticipated the CIO would insist on North American locations when negotiations turned to the issue and had priced its proposal accordingly.

Expecting their team could control security at their firewall, the RFP had no Rules requiring vendors to use "clean" machines, certified as secure and free of malware, nor any Rules mandating security management consistent with the same protocols the CIO had endorsed. Vendor W did both and had higher costs embedded in its pricing; Vendor U did not and its pricing was lower.

The CIO had insisted the RFP require vendors to describe training needed for clients to use their services; Vendor U had done so, but merely estimated the class time at 20-50 hours per employee; Vendor W affirmatively stated 40 hours were required. Was Vendor U close enough to have been scored equally on the training? Could the adequacy of their training be presumed (a "1")? What was the possibility the CIO's team will require added learning (and from what sources) to work with either Cloud vendor? Within the time remaining, the CIO had no sources to which to turn to acquire answers (Decisional Information) to these questions (each inferring new Rules the CIO wanted to apply).

NO HAPPY ENDING

In Scenario Two, there is no happy ending. The lower pricing offered by Vendor U had provoked the CIO to sense a basis for distrust—if both proposals also had the same pricing, the decision would be easier. Now she was struggling to connect the dots between the lower fees Vendor U proposed and the gut feeling something was being missed which made the lower cost too risky to accept.

Were the CIO to reject Vendor U's lower cost option, she lacked the Decisional Information with which to defend her team against the inevitable questions from the Committee, "If the vendors scored comparably, why reject the lower cost proposal?" If she chose Vendor W and the higher costs, more than one Committee member would critique her continued insistence that further IT service cost reductions would expose the company to risk-based adverse events of substantial magnitude.

She had made that argument time and again, but never been able to show any supporting evidence of the linkages between spending and security disasters. In every other company in their industry, IT funding was going up and hacks and security incidents were still occurring. None of the Committee truly believed going to the Cloud could create greater risks, especially if $47.5 million could be liberated for the marketing and sales of their new products.

With either option, the CIO would appear before the Committee without the Decisional Information with which to defend her Value Calculation. But the true origin of her problems began with poor decisions taken long before in how to compose the definitions of Context, Work, and the TDT in order to more accurately calculate the value of time and costs, as well as an inability to find Decisional Information Sources in which to place her trust.

THE FINAL DECISION POINT

The Trust Decision Model is nearly complete; there is one final decision point. It occupies the frame immediately prior to the decision itself whether or not to trust a TDT. For the CIO, the duration of this current frame had seemed endless. Throughout, at every earlier point, there is an opportunity for new Decisional Information to fuel R & R involving one or more cels in one or more layers. Yet deadlines and other constraints will always require any decision to reach a conclusion. Regardless of the velocity of the entire decision process, in the moment before the decision itself, there is one question remaining, "What have I missed?"

THE TRUST VOCABULARY

In this chapter, you will learn the following words:

Process Calculation

Risk of the Unknown Risk

CHAPTER 11

T MINUS AND HOLDING

AS DAWN CAME, the CIO had not followed the advice of her mentor to make every major decision before going to sleep. To the contrary, despite all of the planning, evaluations, and negotiations preceding this next Committee meeting, both the complexity and the enormity of the consequences were haunting her. This had become not just another outsourcing or technology partnership deal; the decision required a confidence in the recommended path that she had not been able to achieve. She was troubled by the rumor that RHK, their top competitor, not only was following the same strategy, but was poised to achieve twice the savings her team believed to be realistic. Those headlines would turn investors away from her company's business quickly. Over coffee, she idly turned on the news and clicked onto live coverage of the latest launch of new crew members to the International Space Station.

We are all familiar with final space launch preparations. As the minutes tick toward launch, the astronauts sit upon an enormous maelstrom, perhaps the most powerful concentration of force and energy humans can engineer and build that is not a nuclear weapon. With years of preparation, teams distributed around the globe look anxiously at the clock, checking displays, meters, sensors, circuits, visual signals, audio signals, and heartbeat monitors. They constantly are assessing, measuring, validating, and calculating data, synchronizing verbal reports and commands toward ignition and lift-off. Then the quiet, controlled voice of Mission Control announces, "T minus 10 minutes and holding."

What happens next is remarkable—the entire launch and support team of hundreds of scientists and technicians executes a review of the complete history of all that has preceded that moment. The substantive records and incoming data are examined, audited, questioned, compared, and measured to determine if the elements are in place to support the final calculations. With human lives and enormous investments on the line, the demand for absolute accuracy and precision is immense; the redundancy of repeating prior calculations is never questioned. Every possible metric that can be measured is subject to review, mathematics are recomputed, and the probabilities for success are again scrutinized.

No matter how small in measurement, any deviations, variances, anomalies, or missing data drives urgent analyses, more questions, and further calculations. Results are ingested back into the algorithms and checklists, totals are added up, and the question is asked again, "Are we prepared to decide whether to launch?" No emotion is tolerated in these exercises. The data gathering and measurements are entirely mathematical. The launch teams are not making the decision to trust the spaceship! They are using the countdown hold-time to question whether they have collected and validated the trustworthiness of all of the Decisional Information required to make that decision.

Each engineer, scientist, specialist, physician, radar operator, and astronaut join together in searching for any evidence that they should *not* trust their systems to successfully launch the spaceship. Are there Circumstances that have changed that require moving them above the line to be part of the TDC? Are all of the Resources accounted for? Are the measurements of their suitability to perform the required operations being received? Are those measurements accurate? Have all of the sensors been checked for errors or indications of instability? Are all of the blanks in our calculations filled in by Decisional Information? Are all of the Decisional Information Sources online and authenticated? Are there any changes which require us to pair differently the combinations of Resources, Rules, and Decisional Information on which we intend to rely to make the decision?

No matter the stakes, in every decision to trust, the same final frame is inherently part of the decision. When the decision process is placed on hold, a time window opens in which we examine the integrity of the decision process itself. Whether for a nanosecond, minutes, or even months, a DM pauses to examine the Context once more, seeking any sensory information that suggests one further R & R is needed before making the final trust decision or, perhaps, deciding not to proceed with the trust decision itself.

THE RISK OF THE UNKNOWN RISK

Whether for a space launch, the CIO's recommendation on which vendor to select, or your own decision on a transaction or hiring selection, this frame is always present. Even after a DM has performed an affirmative Functional Calculation and Value Calculation, there lurks the possibility that something has been missed—observational data about the Context, the Circumstances, the Resources, the Rules, the TDT, the Work, or the Tasks that provoke the DM to conclude the final trust decision itself is not ready to be calculated. In that moment, a DM is looking to identify and classify what is termed in the trust vocabulary as the *Risk of the Unknown Risk*. If X is the Unknown Risk, and trust is always a calculation of probability, then the Risk of X is always present—it is another means of expressing the inherent gap between the trust that may be capable of calculation and perfect trust. The launch hold gives the entire organization and collective of systems and sensors an opportunity to gather Data that slices off some portion of the Risk of X and converts it into a known Circumstance, Resource or Rule requiring an R & R.

When found, that Data serves as Decisional Information looking to connect to a Rule. If the Data is recognized as such (for instance, evidence of an engine ignition not firing, an oxygen leak, or excess moisture inside the flight suit of an astronaut experiencing his first launch), the flight team can go to the Rules layer that relates to that type of Data and endeavor to connect the Data to the Rules. It is no different than any other frame or decision chain; the new Data received at one layer is informing the structures across the other layers and stacks. In suspending the countdown, Mission Control, as the DM, opens up the moment and freezes time to allow discovery of a Risk of X and calculation of its impact on the trust decision itself.

If no anomalies are recognized, the countdown proceeds. Finding something, however, triggers another round of R & R. Flight and launch sequences are actually built to anticipate that a Risk of X will be identified. For every launch, a "launch window" is calculated in advance, a period of time during which, even after a Risk of X is identified and remedied, the flight can still safely launch and meet the mission objectives. When the hold begins, it allows the launch crews time to identify, dissect, and evaluate any Risk of X (or multiples), make decisions about how to adapt, and then proceed to liftoff within the launch window.

Once a DM connects the Data to new Rules to be considered, the recurring parallel evaluation is needed to calculate whether the Data can be trusted as Decisional Information to be used with those Rules. The sources of the Data must be evaluated as well to determine if they are trustworthy Decisional Information Sources. For any space launch, success depends on the effectiveness of the processes employed during the hold to scour the Context for any Data that can reduce the Risk of X as a variable in how trust will be calculated. But in so many business decisions, deadlines and other constraints deny or jeopardize this moment.

In making a trust decision, the worst possible outcome is for a DM to be conscious of a Risk of X (i.e., there is new Data identified in the Context) and then be unwilling or unable to alter the decision process. To move ahead flaws, if not destroys, the trust calculation. This is *why* launch sequences include a mandatory hold—the entire team has one last chance to make sure there is no Risk of X they can identify. Even if the Data is isolated, the team must evaluate whether to delay the launch or apply the Principle of Indifference and proceed ("Just a little extra perspiration from the newbie; cleared to light the candle."). Watching the launch coverage, the

This is *why* launch sequences include a mandatory hold—the entire team has one last chance to make sure there is no Risk of X they can identify.

CIO realized her restless night had been consumed by the same reasoning sequence, a self-imposed hold on her decision, in order to ask again and again: "What have I missed?"

THE PROCESS CALCULATION

Here is where we find the penultimate link in the decision chain. At "T minus and holding," the DM is making a *Process Calculation*. But the DM is not evaluating the TDT itself; rather, the DM is evaluating whether the Rules governing the trust decision process have been followed. As with the Functional Calculation and the Value Calculation, the Process Calculation must produce an affirmative output in order to move to the next frame. It is a "go/ no go" decision as to whether the DM is prepared to execute the trust calculation. A DM must be able to trust the decision process in order to calculate properly the trust to be placed in a TDT. So the DM asks one final time, "Can the decision process itself be trusted as the basis on which to proceed?"

All of the rules discussed in exploring the Trust Decision Model apply equally to the decision process as Work; as noted earlier, that process is itself a TDT—a tool that a DM uses to make good decisions. There are line drawings, valuations, determinations of indifference, and pairings among Circumstances, Resources, and Rules. There are trust decision chains about Decisional Information and Decisional Information Sources, all shaped by a definition of the Work to compose the Rules properly, acquire the accurate Decisional Information, and be prepared to calculate a trust decision about the TDT. In every trust decision, T Minus and Holding opens the window during which the Process Calculation can occur.

THE FINAL TRUST DECISION

The Trust Decision Model now reaches its end-point. An affirmative Process Calculation positions a DM to calculate the final decision to trust, or not to trust, the TDT. Three different outcomes are measured: the Functional Calculation, the Value Calculation, and the Process Calculation. The DM must determine the TDT can perform the Work; the DM must determine using the TDT will create value; and the DM must determine the decision process itself can be trusted. Only if each chained decision is affirmative can the DM proceed to make a final trust decision with confidence.

Of course, no trust decision is absolute or perfect. All are calculations of probabilities. The Risk of the Unknown Risk is always present; with every decision, boundaries are drawn to exclude variables, sometimes with calculated precision and sometimes with the knowing disregard of Rhett Butler. Circumstances shift; Resources are altered; Rules are changed; Decisional Information Sources become unreliable; Decisional Information becomes unreliable; the Expenses of Resources accumulate or shrink; the availability of Revenues improves or fades away; time is gained in which to conduct further R & R; or time runs out, allowing no further audits of the decision chains that have preceded. With each, there are causations upon the TDC, the TDT, the Work, and the decision process itself that will not be calculated into a specific trust decision. Only after our decisions are made can we assess the outcomes of the accuracy of our computations.

The actual Results educate us about Data and Risks that should have been measured differently and, in turn, how we should author new Rules for the next occasions. The trust decision process and the knowledge and wisdom of experience connect at this critical junction; the end of one decision, and the Results of placing trust in a TDT (or not), informs the manner in which the next decisions evolve. Yet we tenaciously seek to reduce the Risk of the Unknown Risk in every trust decision we make. We are wired by evolution to do so.

But now our acceleration into a digital world is creating unexpected, substantial, additional stresses on how we make trust decisions and how we decide whether to trust the decisions of others:

> As designers, engineers, owners, operators, and users of systems that are amazingly complex, we pursue achieving trust in their capabilities as TDTs no differently. With greater complexity and structure in the dimensions of a TDT and the Work to be performed, each trust decision becomes more complex.

> As leaders, executives, IT architects, policy authors, team managers, regulators, and individual users, we are shifting how we make important decisions and how we use technology as we do so. Our instincts are adapting to expect the availability and reliability of digital knowledge in real-time, delivered on our command from information systems that must themselves be trusted, operated by often unknown entities and controllers.

≫ Without really thinking about it, we are measuring time differently. The time available to make good decisions is compressing; the competitive advantage in making decisions more quickly is more often measured in milliseconds or nanoseconds rather than minutes or days. The ubiquity of technology and digital information is morphing our expectations to expect trust decisions to be made in less time, with greater confidence in the calculations, while still accounting for and calculating the probabilities and causations of more and more complexity.

≫ To compete, companies are building global information systems and digital operating platforms and accessing enormous volumes of digital information assets. All of this is designed to align to specific Rules, no different than a building architect must harmonize the different regulations for the components of a home. Yet divergent, inconsistent and increasing volumes of public laws and regulations authored by nation-states, together with the private rules of dominant components of the infrastructure of global commerce (financial, shipping, communication, transport, service), are imposing costs, increasing complexity, and creating new compliance risks that threaten the efficiency with which these global platforms realistically can be operated.

Concurrently, complexity and opacity are creating greater Risks of the Unknown Risk, not fewer. These forces are working as unseen barriers, restricting us from the Decisional Information and Data our Rules require to calculate trust decisions with confidence. They have the same effect as a radar sensor going dark 20 minutes before launch, a proposed service vendor submitting a proposal lacking measurable reporting data, or an automated securities trading system failing to immediately display order volumes—they foreclose us from acquiring all of the Decisional Information required to make good decisions.

For some, these tensions are degrading performance, making decisions more difficult, consuming more time, and increasing the probabilities for miscalculations. Each Decisional Information Risk that results has another, more sobering, impact—each creates a window of opportunity for the decisions to be questioned by senior management, peers, team members, or customers. For others, mastering the dynamics of these digital shifts and conquering the inherent, burgeoning complexities has become the strategy with which to survive and prosper.

It was a miracle the CIO and her team had progressed this far. The days preceding the Committee meeting were typical for the closing strokes of any big deal translating the terms onto the final papers—long nights, countless pages of revised specifications, phone calls, messages, and dozens of compromises and accords with the preferred vendor. But, as she turned off the news and headed out the door, she now understood she had two decisions to make. She realized she could only announce the second decision naming the vendor if she could be confident her team had not missed anything of consequence. She had only one option to announce to the Committee.

On the other side of the world, another, very different launch was occurring at RHK Enterprises. Their corporate press release described $110 million in annual savings, exceeding by more than 20% the initial internal forecasts of the savings to be gained moving IT services to the Cloud. RHK's Executive Vice President knew the market would be pleased as she pushed "Send" and delivered the press release to the world.

Two companies. Ferocious competitors. Comparable objectives. Identical, intensely complex trust decisions. Careers, corporate wealth, and market leadership on the line. Different outcomes. The balance of this book presents the tools and strategies that make the difference.

PART TWO

DESIGNING DIGITAL TRUST

CHAPTER 12

INTRODUCTION

IN RHK ENTERPRISES' corporate suite, the celebration was enthusiastic. Investors had responded dramatically, triggering nearly a 3% growth in RHK's market capitalization and a nearly equal compression in Wise Industries' valuation. Financial reporters were queuing up for more on the story, and several portfolio managers had called to schedule in-depth briefings. Behind the curtain, the RHK reengineering team already had constructed economic models to respond to the inevitable customer pressure for better pricing. Every announcement of greater profits had the same result. This time, the projections were in place to deliver pricing adjustments to existing customers that also would attract new customers from RHK's competitors, with Wise Industries the biggest target. Without changing a single product, the net income growth for the next three years promised to be outstanding!

Having started several years earlier, RHK's current and future competitive success now ran on a new architecture. Quietly, with executive leadership and substantial dedicated funding, RHK had constructed a business model that awarded the greatest value to the information assets controlled by the company. In contradiction to the advice of its accountants, lawyers, and many former division managers, RHK rapidly had achieved a sustainable competitive advantage over Wise and others by committing to design and build something entirely new—an infrastructure that delivered digital trust across the company. Their strategy implemented engineering principles and tools that were already being adopted more widely within their ecosystems by both suppliers and customers. Digital trust was transforming how the company acquired raw materials, manufactured products, delivered services, and created wealth.

In Part I, you learned how we make decisions, and how, both as leaders and followers, we evaluate whether to award our trust to the decisions of others. Now, the lessons and understandings gained in Part I establish a foundation for discovering how, in the Digital Age, we can engineer and deliver *digital trust*. Part II's tools will empower you and your teams to achieve something exceptionally valuable—the means to build a new, enduring bridge between the complexity of human trust decisions and the precision and certainty of computational trust! Those who do so first, whether as nation-states, corporations, or communities, will not only shift the momentum in the prevailing wars, but also gain substantial, measurable competitive advantage.

In Part II, shifting our attention away from Wise Industries to the opposite side of the globe, you will be introduced to the design principles, strategies, and critical tools that you, like RHK, can use to achieve those outcomes. While the story of Wise and RHK is fictional, the innovations presented in the following pages are real. They are the backbone for the integrated capabilities and solutions we will need to shift the momentum in the war for control of information and the war against trust.

The three tools you will discover are visually compact and elegant. Each is so simple you will be able to sketch them out on a dinner napkin or a classroom whiteboard. But do not let the simplicity of their visual presentation be deceptive; in the background, the solutions are powered by connections to diverse, rigorous disciplines, including modal decision theory, Bayesian network modeling, Procrustean geometric visualization, probability mathematics, jurisprudential theory, behavioral science, economics, political science, and current best practices in the engineering and design of IT architecture, project management, DevOps, information governance, information security, and mobile computing.

Looking further ahead, you will learn in Part III about the signature innovation for managing and governing digital trust to sustain competitive advantage—the Trust Prism. The dynamic, volatile changing landscape of the rules within a single, global market will test the agility and velocity with which systems, devices, applications, and information adapt. The Trust Prism enables effective management of digital trust through continual governance with velocity, control, and reliability.

Imagine Tony Stark, Iron Man in the Hollywood films, instructing his computer to display a 3-D, rotating holographic image of the Trust Prism displaying the trustworthiness of the national power grid. The room is filled with a functioning representation of the trust levels each system, device, application, and node is achieving. With a wave of his hand, the Trust Prism expands, isolating individual layers, and Stark selects and dissects the continuing streams of transactional data, communication and operational logs, and metrics for detailed analysis. He opens and closes application windows, inspects digital gauges and measures of economic and computing performance in real-time, and searches for weaknesses or vulnerabilities to be strengthened in real-time. That is the power of the Trust Prism; it creates transparency into how complex systems operate and how we can design them to be trusted.

Now you have a glimpse of the power of the Trust Prism that is waiting for you, a single asset that integrates all that can be built using the Trust Decision Model and the strategies, principles, and tools to be presented in this Part II. We began in Part I by unfolding the map of the Trust Decision Model. To begin here, visualize a tool belt already loaded up and ready to go to work designing and building digital trust.

CHAPTER 13

FACING THE CHALLENGE
OF DIGITAL TRUST

NEARLY FIVE YEARS AGO, the RHK Innovate team was assembled for the first time. The CEO and Executive Vice President attended the Project Innovate launch meeting personally. They presented, in detailed and very expressive language, the ambitions of the Board and their confidence in the team to attack and conquer the challenges. The mission was stated simply: to create a new platform from which RHK could launch and sustain competitive dominance across the entirety of a single global market.

The Board had concluded that, within the next decade, RHK's ability to create and control digital information would be the most critical measure of the company's success or failure. Big data analytics, alternative digital currencies, Internet of Things, continual government surveillance, well-capitalized attacks and defenses battling over access to corporate intellectual property—all of these were markers of the emerging operational and economic value of any organization's digital assets. To survive and to prosper, control had to be transformed from a "best guess" to a certainty. RHK's digital assets had to become functional as property, assets to be created, managed, preserved, and traded with the same ferocity and value as any other asset within the company's control. The Innovate team was commissioned to identify and overcome whatever barriers or obstacles, internal or external, inhibited achieving those objectives.

The team was composed of representatives from every operating division and each administrative functional group. Motivated to justify the trust placed in them by the CEO and the Board, the team quickly embraced a near ruthless ambition to succeed. A separate development center for Project Innovate was built out with all the traditional tools for project planning installed, tested, and ready to turn on. Work groups were created, staffed and balanced with representatives from different divisions. Communication funneling mechanisms were set up, through which group reports could be consolidated and published for review and comment. The budget officer approved any submitted requisitions without question; the ease was almost unsettling to the team, clear evidence of the intent of the Board to succeed. "Limited resources" would not be an available excuse on this project.

In the earliest days, "rules of the house" were adopted, mapping best practices in authoring laws, standards, and best practices to their internal deliberations and production. Rotating chairs assured no one operating group dominated the dialogues; consensus-oriented decision processes assured all views could be expressed; and detailed documentation recorded all outcomes, creating a structured foundation of rules and requirements from which Project Innovate would rise.

The team's first report to the supervising Executive Vice President was stunning, a two-sentence expression of the consensus achieved to express Project Innovate's objective differently. "Our mission will be to create *trust* in our digital assets, not control. We can only justify investing in control for those assets that can be trusted." The Innovate team had concluded, running on 20th century carryover technologies and business processes, that no corporate employee, executive, supplier, contractor, customer, or regulator was able to affirmatively express trust in any of RHK's electronic information assets. Building that trust, in all levels and across all dimensions of the corporate ecosystem, was recognized as the critical objective. The Innovate team was stunned to discover the proportion of the company's resources devoted to assuring that information assets with which decisions were made were factually accurate. They were even more dismayed to realize the levels at which those resources at every level of the business were routinely diverted from their primary jobs in order to search for, find, filter and validate information and its accuracy as one of those dreaded "and other duties as assigned." From the lowest paid worker to the CEO, and across all of the connected networks of vendors, financial institutions, inventory suppliers, distributors, retailers, communication services and customers, enormous volumes of time were devoted to determining whether information could be trusted as a resource with which to make business decisions.

A CONSENSUS TO DESIGN TRUST INTO GOVERNANCE

To succeed, the Innovate team concluded that trust had to become something measurable, designed into every aspect of corporate governance and not merely a feature of the IT infrastructure. Trust had to be capable of being proven, not presumed. There was no other option; the IT team emphasized that every network, system, device, and application was rigorously tested already to assure its

Trust had to be capable of being proven, not presumed.

probability of success from an engineering perspective. The CFO, internal audit, and compliance team members emphasized that validating information consumes enormous time and resources, and they were often tasked to fill the gaps when information is inaccessible or not capable of being trusted.

Jung Singh, an attorney assigned to Project Innovate from the Legal team, expressed a contrasting view. She explained to the team that much of Legal's work was devoted to finding alternative versions of truth among the existing information assets in order to minimize adverse settlements and fines. Committing to any type of "single truth" metric for evaluating how information would be trusted would compromise their flexibility as advocates in response to compliance examinations, enforcement actions, litigation, and even in internal investigations.

The COO became personally engaged, pointing out that nearly all of the risks handled by Legal could be mitigated (and perhaps eliminated), if accurate, more granular performance data indicating non-complying deviations could be created and accessible. He emphasized that properly designed surveillance and monitoring embedded within the operating systems could identify data that were markers of risk in advance of adverse events actually occurring. "If social networks can calculate the probability of someone announcing a new relationship before she asks him to 'go steady,' surely we can do the same . . . *if* we can trust the information we rely upon to conduct operations and run the business."

DIGITAL INFORMATION WAS A PRODUCT WITH VALUE

Digital information, to be valued, had to be viewed no differently than any other RHK product worthy of the value paid by their customers. Just as Six Sigma was used across all operations, and just as IT Engineering rigorously tested the systems, devices, and applications, new requirements and testing criteria needed to be composed and used to sustainably assure the quality, reliability, authenticity, and accuracy of digital information. But the "elephant in the room" became quickly obvious—creating the right functional operating metrics to show how new levels of trust created favorable economic outcomes for RHK and its shareholders. If the returns on the investments that would be required could not be reliably projected *and* achieved, none of them would remain employed.

The Project Innovate team was absolutely correct—achieving digital trust has no value unless doing so creates new wealth. There must be a compelling business case. But the RHK Innovate team also recognized what we learned in Part I; time is the unappreciated metric for measuring the value of digital trust. Out of their initial scoping and brainstorming, a Statement of Need was constructed that accompanied their initial two-sentence report. The conclusions persuaded the Executive Vice President to authorize the Innovate team to proceed.

> Achieving digital trust has no value unless doing so creates new wealth.

MAKING THE BUSINESS CASE FOR DIGITAL TRUST

The 11 critical conclusions presented in the Statement of Need appear below. These express the business case for digital trust at RHK, but I believe they also apply to the current global landscape and markets in which we all participate. As you review these, consider whether they are equally true for your company or organization. Much like the policy platform of a major political party, these are the 'planks' on which to build solutions.

We can no longer presume to have trust in digital information required to operate the business and make decisions.

Every decision taken in this company, whether by human or machine, is fueled by information. To use any information, two actions are required:

> First, the information must be acquired and accessible to the decision process.

> Second, the information must be validated as useful for the decision—this requires affirmative, calculated determinations of its factual accuracy, integrity, and provenance.

Every decision taken in this company will rely, in some measure, on digital information assets over which the company maintains or acquires control. To rely on those assets, affirmative trust must be calculated, not presumed.

Time is a finite resource with which to create wealth. At every exchange point of information within the company and between the company and our stakeholders, time consumed to acquire, access, and validate information (including digital information)—the process of deciding to trust—is a controllable expense.

Digital information creates risk when trust is presumed, rather than affirmatively calculated, at any exchange point within the company's functional ecosystems, whether or not controlled by the company. Ports, gateways, application interfaces, OSI layers, shared databases, transactions data, payment activities—each are friction points at which digital information trust can be scrutinized. The value of digital information risk is proportional to the level of trust that is proven at each friction point.

Risk originates from three root causes:

Risk exists when an existing rule is not performed.

Risk exists when there is an absence of a rule with which to control known threats or vulnerabilities.

Risk exists when information required to execute existing rules cannot be properly accessed and used for those purposes.

Engineering which creates transparency to non-performance, exposes omissions of rules, and documents when required information is missing will reduce risk and improve the functional reliability of the related assets, including digital information.

The Net is built upon private assets (networks, routers, services, devices, applications), and is not part of the public domain. The values of these assets to RHK and our trading partners and customers are inherently calculated by the net economic value of efficiency—measures of time and productivity offset by the direct and indirect costs of their use. In order to use any one or more of these assets in our business, any digital asset (including those we create) must demonstrate positive net economic value.

When positive net economic value can be demonstrated, automating any rules-based action, including creating trusted records of performance, is superior to relying upon human performance of those rules.

Every digital asset (including information) is currently engineered, constructed, and used pursuant to explicit, known rules. Any failure to comply with the rules bundled with those assets creates compliance risks. These compliance risks are no different than any failures to comply with public laws and regulations, corporate policies and procedures, commercial contracts, or other rules by which the performance of the company and its components are measured—the probabilities and costs of related adverse events can be calculated and controlled.

Compliance with explicit, known rules is economically efficient if trusted digital records are created to document compliance. Digital assets (including information) should be engineered to comply with known rules, including public laws and technology standards, and create compliance performance records that can be trusted.

The Statement of Need serves as a manifesto for how to connect economic measures of wealth to the returns on investment that can be achieved by engineering and building digital trust. While new innovations have improved, and will continue to improve, the physical velocity of transit for data moving from here to there, as a global community, we have not seriously addressed how to improve the velocity and accuracy of our decisions whether or not to trust information.

Indeed, at many levels within technology's current infrastructure, the velocity of data can only be improved by reducing the time invested in scrutinizing the data's integrity. Message headers, encryption, metadata—all of these increase data velocity at the price of disabling the receiving device or app from affirmatively calculating the utility of the information asset. This is a Decisional Information Risk—the receiving party is both presuming and deferring its calculation of the data's utility (the data is a TDT) until after the transfer has been executed. Technologically, the outcome is no different than opening up electronic mail with embedded malware; it is too late to remember to look under the bridge.

By connecting information, time, resources, rules, results, risk, and wealth, the Statement of Need accomplishes something important—it creates a foundation from which to connect building digital trust to the purpose for any business to exist—to create new wealth. The Innovate team now had to build on that foundation. Just like an architect, whether for office buildings or information systems, the team needed to formulate a portfolio of design principles.

TRUST HAS ALWAYS BEEN EVALUATED IN HINDSIGHT, IN REACTION TO CONFLICT

The problem, of course, was that no one had ever focused on the trust value of information in design; virtually all substantive digital information had been presumed to be factual. Sure, systems included identity verification and packet validation mechanisms, and encryption was used at several layers to secure integrity. But questions about the trust value of the actual business records within information systems, stored documents, performance logs, and communications only arose reactively, when key data objects were in conflict with applicable rules, prior knowledge, or other data objects being relied upon in analysis and making decisions. IT teams focused diligently on the reliability of processes, but never extended probability mathematics and similar mechanisms for measuring reliability toward calculating the trustworthiness of the information within those processes.

After several long periods of creativity and brainstorming, consensus was achieved. A portfolio was assembled, titled *Digital Trust Design Principles*. The principles reflected the team's central conclusion, extracted from the Statement of Need: the time consumed making decisions that are fueled by digital information is the highest cost in every business process. To achieve digital trust replaces that high cost with strength, compressing the time, improving accuracy and probability in the decision, and raising the levels of compliance with the rules shaping the boundary within which the decision must occur.

The Digital Trust Design Principles gave the team confidence they could build trust and gain control. There was one thing more they were eager to report—the company could accelerate their business to operate at the speed of light. At the top of the new principles was the most important—the Velocity Principle.

The time consumed making decisions that are fueled by digital information is the highest cost in every business process.

THE TRUST VOCABULARY

In this chapter, you will learn the following words:

Mobile Rules

The Velocity Principle

CHAPTER 14

THE VELOCITY PRINCIPLE

RECALL THE DILEMMA of Dead Man's Curve presented in Chapter 1 and the question it represents: when should we decide to stop patching existing infrastructure and invest in building something new? The RHK Innovate team recognized the Board's ambitions to control information and the team's own agenda to engineer digital trust were something new. As explicit business objectives, they were almost in direct conflict with the realities of the 20th Century IT infrastructure on which the company and the larger global market all relied.

RHK certainly did not control all of that infrastructure. The networks, major backbone and storage systems, domain name systems, encryption keys—all of these were assets manufactured and operated by others. To succeed, the company needed to design solutions that worked on that infrastructure, routing around the patches. The totality of the Net is no different than any other system; it is constructed of Resources and Rules. RHK would have to innovate its trust solutions within the boundaries of the related Rules of the Net.

RHK, as a business, was comparable to any commercial 18-wheel-trucker trying to navigate Dead Man's Curve. The company wanted to achieve greater velocity, increasing the volume of content carried while preserving the integrity of the content at all points along the path of transit. But speed only has value when one is able to travel safely. That became the Innovate team's dilemma—accelerate trust, improve control, and minimize risk to RHK's assets and operations. If the infrastructure was not theirs to control, the solution had to be found in how the digital information itself was packaged, transmitted, received, processed, exchanged, and stored across all the systems to which RHK connected. The team faced the fundamental opportunity to build the entire business toward operating at the speed of light. The Velocity Principle conquers that challenge!

> ## THE VELOCITY PRINCIPLE
> The velocity of information is proportional to the transparency of its governance.

The Velocity Principle reflects several of the team's early realizations, expressed here in Trust Vocabulary terms:

> Information is always a TDT, a tool acquired and used to make decisions that are Tasks, the building blocks of Work.

> Information begins as a Resource with Anticipated Causality for completing the Work and within the control of the DM (or capable of being controlled,

by licensing or purchase, for example). With those qualities, Information qualifies as a TDC$_{RES}$.

To progress further, a DM develops definitions for the Work (i.e., one or more Tasks using Information to make one or more decisions), and for the TDT that will enable the Work to be performed. Each of these definitions includes Descriptive Specifications and Functional Specifications, all identifying Results and Risks, that will support both a Functional Calculation and a Value Calculation. Together, these become expressions of the Rules that Information, as a TDC$_{RES}$, must satisfy to be selected as the TDT to be used to perform the Work.

A DM then prepares to perform a Functional Calculation. Recall that a Functional Calculation evaluates whether Decisional Information aligns with the Rules. As discovered in Part I, when seeking digital Decisional Information, we must perform separate, chained trust decisions and evaluate the Decisional Information, the Decisional Information Sources, and, as appropriate, the systems (and their exchange points) through which the Decisional Information itself has passed. Whenever any Decisional Information fails to align to the Rules, Decisional Information Risk arises, requiring a DM to exercise one of three available options to navigate to the starting point of the Functional Calculation. R & R may be required in exercising those options.

A DM then performs a Functional Calculation, computing whether the known Information meets the Rules, inputting Decisional Information and adding outcomes up to calculate an answer to the question, "Can the Information be trusted as a TDT in performing the Work (i.e., making one or more decisions)?"

Next, a DM collects the Decisional Information required for a Value Calculation, identifying both Revenues and Expenses related to the Information as a TDT. Here, the Innovate team broke things down with new granularity, realizing:

> Every activity described in the preceding sequence is actually consuming time, creating Expenses paired to the specific Tasks of calculating the utility and value of Information to perform the Work of making decisions.

> Information has velocity. When Information is to be used as a TDT, it is moving from some location of storage or being created by new input. With either option, no different than cargo inside a truck, Information enabling Work moves constantly from here to there. Every connection point between networks, systems, devices, applications, organizations, and people becomes a border crossing at which trust in the Information must be either presumed or calculated. While trust is being calculated, Information loses velocity, waiting to move further while the Work of deciding whether to trust the Information is performed. In turn, the primary Work of making a decision that relies on that Information as a TDT is further delayed.

While trust
is being
calculated,
Information
loses velocity,
waiting to
move further
while the Work
of deciding
whether to trust
the Information
is performed.

As a result, using the varied measures of time (see Chapter 10 and the related discussion), the all-in Expenses of calculating trust were far higher than ever previously understood. Internally within RHK, the team identified numerous points in the work flow of many processes where applications, devices, employees, and managers were duplicating the performance of Functional Calculations for the same Information (and for relevant Decisional Information). Externally, business transactions with its trading partners experienced the same duplication of friction points as RHK's information was questioned as to whether it could be trusted as the basis for making deals. Cumulatively, these measures of the Expenses were substantial. As a TDT, any Information became much more expensive. The Value Calculation for Information as a TDT also acquired more complexity, requiring added Decisional Information and Decisional Information Sources.

Finally, the added Expenses meant that the Work itself had to create greater Revenues to offset the more visible, and previously unaccounted for, Expenses. The definitions of the primary Work (and the metrics for success, including Revenues) had to be paired directly to, and offset by, the Expenses of calculating trust.

As with the Functional Calculation, the Value Calculation rests upon Decisional Information chained to other decisions about Decisional

Information Sources and Decisional Information Risks. The fact that the Value Calculation focuses on time metrics and economics does not alter the pairing of those decision chains or the manner in which Decisional Information Risks must be navigated. The Trust Decision Model continues to define the process.

A DM then performs the Value Calculation, computing whether the known Information, if used to perform the Work, creates Revenues exceeding Expenses. A favorable outcome advances toward T Minus and Holding, one final look at the integrity of the process. Then, and only then, can a DM calculate whether to trust the Information as a TDT to perform the Work needed to make a decision.

Of course, at any point in the preceding, absent deadlines or other constraints, R & R is always possible following unacceptable calculations, adding even further time and labor to the process.

There was redundancy in the trust decisions about Information as a TDT and the Decisional Information each trust decision required.

As the Innovate team mapped and dissected the decision processes within RHK and its networked ecosystem, the redundancies they discovered gave them one further insight into the implications of the Velocity Principle. At every exchange point, each DM was organizing and applying many of the same Rules to evaluate the Information as a TDT (and the related Decisional Information). Each DM's related decision chains were nearly identical in every analysis, irrespective of the identity or role of the actor evaluating the Information or the nature of the decision. Yet, despite the redundancy and similarities, Information repeatedly lost velocity while each separate trust decision was executed.

"What would happen if we could eliminate the redundancy of those trust decisions?" asked the Records and Information Manager on the team. "Could we increase the velocity of Information? Would that not improve the velocity of making the business decisions that require the Information, and reduce Decisional Information Risk?"

FORMULATING THE RULES FOR VELOCITY

Those questions sparked a flurry of activity in all of the Project Innovate pods and workrooms. While at the outset they knew that the entire Net was structured to automate trust decisions in physical devices, organizational identities, IP addresses and router ports, and that complex means of distributed computing were ever more robust, the notion of creating similar systems for validating the provenance and substance of Information as factually objective, authentic assets that were reliable as TDTs had not occurred to the team. Yet, when the Innovate team's open source research group evaluated the entire body of research on trust, security, and privacy, that exact trend came into focus.

COMMUNICATING THE PROVENANCE OF INFORMATION

The team realized the lethargy of Information and the accumulated volume of Expenses rooted in redundancy were grounded in the inability of current protocols and systems to pass along to successive custodians and users of Information the Decisional Information required for making trust decisions about Information as a TDT. In other words, across networks and systems, the same types of rules-based questions were being asked to qualify the trustworthiness of Information, and similar, if not identical, Decisional Information was being sought, often from the same Decisional Information Sources. The answers, once calculated, were not visible downstream. The critical missing quality was transparency.

For example, within the mortgage finance division, the problems were enormous. An individual borrower application might trigger over a dozen different inquiries (such as those of the lender, title insurance, home insurance, flood insurance, and homeowners' association) for credit score data from different actors within the process, each executing its own decision chains about whether to place trust in the borrower. Within the international transport division, electronic data interchange had made great progress in standardizing information assets and their meanings; however, redundancy still persisted among the decision chains of all of the actors tracking the Information recording the status and control of merchandise in transit (and its related Revenues and Expenses).

The impact of the Velocity Principle emerged from the realization that the downstream trust decisions in any business process were redundant when looking back upstream at the overall process. At each exchange point, a downstream DM was seeking Decisional Information about the Rules by which the Information had been created, managed, stored, and made accessible. In other words, that DM was trying to evaluate how the Information had been governed previously (and how well it had been governed), prior to that moment at which that DM gained access to the Information. If that collected historical record could somehow be packaged with the Information (much like a passport accompanies you in your international travels), the Information would gain velocity.

The critical missing quality was transparency.

This insight generated the team's second realization. If a record could itself be designed as a trusted Decisional Information Source to meet the trust requirements of downstream DMs, then the velocity of the Information could be accelerated even further—the trusted record of the provenance of the TDT, as Decisional Information, would achieve its own velocity.

Have you ever stood nervously at a Customs and Immigration desk as the officer scrutinizes your passport? She is looking for the attributes of trust, and the indicators of distrust, in your passport as a portable, physical Decisional Information Source. The same is true with improvements in drivers' licenses in many parts of the world—holographic imagery, signatures imprinted across driver photos, bar codes—all serve as attributes to better assure the authenticity of the license (and deter the ease, and increase the cost, of forgeries!). But the Customs and Immigration officer and a police officer now do more; they also digitally access additional Decisional Information Sources in order to evaluate your authenticity and the integrity of the provenance reported by your passport as a Decisional Information Source.

The Project Innovate team concluded its ambitions required building the same type of asset, a Decisional Information Source that would give velocity to digital Information used as a TDT to make any decisions. The Source would contain data (as Decisional Information) that recorded the same kinds of records—creating transparency about the provenance of Information as a TDT, capable of moving with the Information. This Source could serve as a trusted TDT to each successive trust calculation and decision, amended and updated by those very decisions. The result would be a complete record delivering Decisional Information about Information required to do Work, two assets—the Information and a trusted record of its governance—working to jointly support the trust decision chains of multiple downstream DMs.

There was one big "if": how would RHK motivate customers, suppliers, and even regulators to collaborate in enabling the Velocity Principle? Inside the company, the team was confident senior management would provide the necessary momentum for putting the new systems and controls in place. Given the imprimatur for the Project, the typical budget battles and turf jealousies would be snuffed out at the top.

But the team had performed several mappings of where the digital assets under their control had originated. To the surprise of many, much of the Information in their control used to make internal decisions came from external third parties. The Information was either a primary Resource, acquired for the value of the Information, such as licensed market data used by Marketing or legal research services used by Legal, or a data byproduct that originated from a primary transaction (e.g., sales of goods, purchases of inventory, contractor employment, etc.). At the same time, there was continuing, increased demand for RHK to generate outbound Information assets that other supply chain partners and vendors could use in their own decisions. RHK's outbound data was equally relied on by others downstream. In other words, the company was interconnected at every operational level—governance, finance, operations, inventory, distribution, transportation, retail, legal, human resources, IT—receiving and transmitting Information assets in these digital ecosystems. Enabling the Velocity Principle would require collaboration with even competing companies and entities. Unless others outside the company joined in the implementation, there would be no progress toward improved velocity.

COLLABORATING TO ACHIEVE VELOCITY

Think back to when the first trans-continental railroads were built, and even before, as national railroads were being constructed across the United States and other regions of the world. Do you recall the fabulous iconic image of the two teams laying the Pacific Railroad coming together, a perfect alignment of infrastructure . . . to enable velocity? In contrast, time and time again in the earlier history of railroads, the gauges of the railroads were built to different widths. This meant that the train cars could not smoothly move from one system to another, and shipments and passengers had to be off-loaded and reloaded at junction points to enable their continued travel.

What made the Pacific Railroad so different? There was a commitment to standardization—a commitment that enabled competing rail-laying teams to move in concert with one another and, while engaging in competition, work toward a realization of greater wealth by enabling interdependency, linkage . . . and velocity. No longer were railroads built with competing gauges—soon standardization transformed rail transport, and those who did not standardize were eliminated from the marketplace.

For that transformation to occur, the competing teams (and their respective engineers) did something different than before—they exchanged their technical requirements, published those requirements to the forges and manufacturers of the rail equipment itself, and committed to rely on those requirements as the basis for conducting trade. They were creating standards, uniform Rules for the infrastructure.

Earlier in my career, I studied the history of rail development to remedy some substantial gaps in my knowledge of international

> What made the Pacific Railroad so different? There was a commitment to standardization.

trade and transport (Steven Usselman's book, *Regulating Railroad Innovation*, is exceptional). Governments confronted enormous challenges as new railroads and new equipment, previously not regulated by any published rules, were failures—explosions, derailments, fatalities, loss of goods and materials. In the absence of rules and driven by the opportunity to create wealth, those building the infrastructure and the transport vehicles compromised on security and safety. But in the cauldron of an open market, without regulation, there was absolutely no incentive for collaboration, the formulation of standards, or the authorship and publication of safety criteria.

However, a "tipping point" lay ahead when the formulation and publication of rules became advantageous to the community, including among competitors. Things changed significantly when that point was reached, and standards were authored and published. Businesses expanded, fueled by the interconnections made possible by the shared adoption and enforcement of those standards as Rules. The new wealth was created with such momentum that, nearly a century after the 1920 end point of Usselman's analysis, much of America's landscape today reflects that accumulated wealth. Many of the railroad towns remain dominant commercial hubs.

There are obvious parallels between the evolution of railroads and the Net. Both transport goods—on the Net, we are transporting information. Both began in social cauldrons of innovation. Similarly, the Net continues to expand, faster than exponentially, because of the standardization of the essential architectures and transport structures, packets being the digital railroad cars of the Net.

Yet, at the mid-point of the second decade of the 21st Century, enormous volumes of conduct persist that imitate the earliest railroad operators—proprietary, non-standardized, exclusionary systems of non-conforming assets and carriers. We see nation-states attempting to regulate the infrastructure, digital manufacturers, and carriers with inconsistent, often self-protecting, rules and regulations that create, rather than break down, barriers. Despite the uniformity of Rules for the infrastructure of the Net, the continuing need for safety and security for the Net, the Information, and the stakeholders is now driving global momentum toward new formal laws and regulations. As this book reaches publication, we are seeing this in new EU regulations, new Federal US legislation, and new Chinese technology standards for securing servers and routers used in financial services, to name but a few.

TRANSPARENCY ANSWERS THE TOUGH QUESTIONS

The Project Innovate team asked tough questions:

> ≫ What becomes the catalyst for driving competitors to create rules for new infrastructures to be designed and constructed collaboratively?

> ≫ When standards are developed, how are they published, communicated, and adopted?

> ≫ How does any system view different sources of rules: formal law, regulation, case decisions, technology standards, agency publications, proprietary interfaces? Does the source matter to a system's mechanical execution of processes that conform to specific rules?

> ≫ When does it become advantageous to author standards and eliminate non-conforming assets,

systems, protocols, data formats, and transport infrastructure? Who decides it is the time to do so?

> When are nation-state laws and regulations barriers to the velocity of commerce?

The Velocity Principle emerged from this cacophony of questions. The Innovate team realized that achieving the transparency of governance for Information provided answers to each question:

> Competitors will collaborate when the Revenues gained from standardization exceed the Expenses of authoring, enforcing, and conforming to multiple, non-conforming, autonomous Rules.

> Standards establish transparency and consistently improve velocity (for any asset, including Information) when compliance with the standard is capable of objective measurement and validation. Adoption of standards occurs when the Revenues gained exceed the Expenses incurred by the status quo.

> Systems are insensitive to the sources of Rules. What matters is the precision with which the functional processes that the systems perform can be aligned to the Rules and the potential for certainty that compliance can be achieved in design (no different than an architect working within a building code).

> In the long term, uniformity and certainty in the Rules is always preferred to dynamic volatility,

no matter the "field of play." When any business competes, standardizing and ensuring uniformity in mandatory Rules external to the company (i.e., the TDC_{RUL}) is more efficient, resulting in lower Expenses than those incurred conforming to non-standardized Rules.

> Governments will stop authoring new Rules (inherently limited to the boundaries of their enforcement capabilities) when the private sector authors and enforces standards effectively and without reliance upon governments to do so.

The Project Innovate team concluded that achieving digital trust in the Information assets controlled by RHK would require collaboration among the full community of those with whom RHK exchanged Information, including competitors and regulators. Indeed, digital trust had to be mutual and reciprocal, and was going to require a compelling business case that resonated across the board.

In his outstanding book, *The Speed of Trust*, Stephen Covey came close to anticipating the contribution of *digital trust* to the speed of business. Covey realized the existence of trust accelerates transactions, partnerships, and business decisions. But his analysis, brilliant in all respects, emphasized the role of trust in interpersonal relationships—the human interactions that enable business to occur.

THE VELOCITY PRINCIPLE EMPHASIZES THE EXCHANGE POINTS AMONG SYSTEMS

The Velocity Principle takes a different focus, emphasizing the value of digital trust to the speed of business within the stark

Digital trust had to be mutual and reciprocal, and was going to require a compelling business case that resonated across the board.

reality of a world that creates and transfers wealth across global digital networks and systems. Every exchange point across which Information transits is a point at which the velocity of Information can be accelerated. For a single e-mail, those points are numerous. Across RHK's ecosystems, there were tens of thousands of systems boundaries and exchange points at which velocity could be measured and expressed.

Remember that every system boundary is defined by its Rules; as Information reaches each boundary, the inspections and negotiations that occur are aligning the Information (and the record of its provenance) with the Rules of the next downstream system. Compliance allows entry; non-compliance is a "fail." A single packet's non-conformity can provoke a rejection and request for retransmission.

Transparency of governance became the single answer to all of the following questions that the Innovate team asked in their brainstorming:

> How can we program our systems, our devices, our applications—and even the information assets in transport between and among complex systems—to enable and facilitate trusted relationships?

> How can we engineer those systems to reach beyond defensive security management and enable the data assets to be trusted themselves—objects in commerce that can be evaluated for their reliability within the milliseconds within which transaction engines make decisions?

Compliance allows entry; non-compliance is a "fail."

≥ How can we enhance data in transit and at rest so that it gains authenticity, rather than expose the data to potential degradation in its reliability as more systems and applications touch the data over time?

≥ How will we navigate the momentum for larger and larger transactions in data (what we now call "big data deals") against an increasing inventory of quality control criteria around security, management, records management, and similar topics?

≥ How can digital information be valued as property?

≥ How can digital information be governed as property in a world in which nation-state regulation is losing its effectiveness in governing corporate entities and protecting corporate assets?

THE VELOCITY PRINCIPLE
The velocity of information is proportional to the transparency of its governance.

Many will view the transformative power of transparency as a direct contradiction to business principles of confidentiality and the tradition of connecting nondisclosure to competitive advantages. Yet, when Decisional Information about any TDT can be made more reliable, and the Decisional Information Source can be trusted, the velocity of the decision whether to trust the TDT accelerates and the subsequent Work performed using the TDT accelerates. The coincidence of Information existing in a digital form as a TDT (especially as a tool used to perform the Work of making important decisions) does nothing to alter the essential truths embraced by the Trust Decision Model presented in Part I of this book.

While the emphasis in Part I was on the CIO as a leader making a big decision, the routines of any organization involve thousands of decisions each day. Indeed, each machine automated to perform a specific process (such as tilting a tray bearing merchandise at a specific packing station) uses Information. The Information must align to the Rules to perform successfully as a TDT in each and every use. Engineered into the systems are calculations of those alignments.

Of course, each exchange point across which Information travels attenuates the complexity of the alignment calculations. Each point (whether between servers, devices, or applications) is inherently an opportunity for the governance of Information in motion to be compromised. Such is the simple and compelling reason for encryption and virtual private networks operated with encryption—the encryption tools eliminate exposure of the Information to potential compromise. It is also why operators of the Net's infrastructure carefully negotiate the Rules for lines of demarcation in their responsibility and control for digital assets. If Information is corrupted or lost, the line drawing enables greater precision in assigning liability.

THE VELOCITY PRINCIPLE ENABLES VALUE TO BE CALCULATED BASED ON TIME

The Velocity Principle embraces the importance of time as a metric in evaluating the value of digital Information. While across and between systems, packets can move rapidly, the definition of appropriate velocity will vary with the business decision being made. For instance, one of Google's many distinctive features is that it publishes the total time required to secure the results for each search—clear evidence that time matters to the acquisition of Information. In a corporate acquisition, however, the buyer may spend months evaluating Information offered by a seller to determine its reliability as the basis for calculating the value of the business.

In both instances, auditors rigorously are evaluating the records of governance and provenance—is the Information authentic? Were the systems through which the Information traveled secure and controlled? How functional were the measures of governance? These questions are the building blocks of trust; answering those questions favorably is a prerequisite to placing trust in the Information as a TDT. In judicial courts, the judge and jury do the same—the law invites them to weigh the credibility of a witness or specific evidence in making a determination of whether to rely on that witness or evidence in measuring the truth. Until that evaluation has occurred, Information stops dead—it does not move.

NEW WEALTH CANNOT BE CREATED WHEN INFORMATION LACKS VELOCITY

The Innovate team concluded, both for RHK and the other companies and organizations through which its Information flowed, the deceleration of Information had become a major source of lost income. Remember, every transaction is intended to create wealth. When that transaction's momentum pauses, the ability to generate new income is delayed. Look again at the precision with which Google calculates time; nanoseconds and milliseconds add up. But there is something else the Innovate team observed—Google was being transparent in showing the effectiveness of its governance systems at finding, recovering, filtering, classifying, sorting, and presenting Information assets.

When a source of Information includes the Decisional Information enabling the governance of that Information to be evaluated more readily, the time required for that evaluation is shorter. When the Decisional Information is presented in a consistent format or structure, the time required can be reduced further. When the Decisional Information is presented in a format that enables evaluation to occur automatically, through code-based evaluation processes, the time required further compresses. Each of these compressions improves the velocity of the Information and reduces the time the DM consumes determining whether to trust the Information to support the Work.

21ST CENTURY REGULATIONS AND MARKET FORCES ARE DEMANDING VISIBILITY

Through the 20th Century, corporate governance globally was dominated by a veil of discretion and secrecy regarding how a company created its wealth. That lack of transparency was a major target for 20th Century governmental regulatory reform and continues to drive mandatory disclosures. The complex array of regulations that now govern a business, whether in the United States or other nations, has transformed the knowledge base we possess about a company's processes, strengths, and vulnerabilities. The regulatory schemes largely do not alter the essential business of a regulated entity; instead, the new rules demand more visibility into the trustworthiness and integrity with which digital information assets documenting a company's conduct are created and maintained.

Similarly, market forces from investors have been pressuring corporations to be more transparent regarding their governance and operations. Standards are evolving, and metrics are being developed, by which a company's governance can be better evaluated as a pre-condition to making new investments or sustaining existing investments in that company. Stated using our trust vocabulary, the investment of any investor is a trust decision regarding the company as a TDT. Investors make their investments by assembling rulebases of Rules and gathering Decisional Information required by those Rules. The trends toward evaluating governance are actually chained trust decisions about the governance systems a company employs; each system is a TDC_{RES} that may be separately considered and scored. Doing so requires the same qualities of visibility and transparency being required by governments.

From the 40,000-foot level, larger trends and shifts are visible in how transparency is evolving. Many of these are uncomfortable, creating a reality of Orwellian surveillance that permeates our workplaces and our personal lives. Yet, we are becoming a culture that monitors, measures, and acts upon collected digital information with continually increasing focus and granularity. In the simple act of acquiring Information to perform Work, we are asking our devices, machines, and code to extend their functions and act as our surrogates and agents in the initial decision chains to qualify Information to be trusted. Doing so requires access to the records that surveillance and monitoring create—Decisional Information that fuels trust decisions whether to rely on, or change, the status quo.

The Project Innovate team concluded they could explain how the Velocity Principle achieved competitive advantages for those

Rather than
persist in
20th Century
resistance to
transparency,
the opportunity
needed to
be embraced
to expose
Decisional
Information.

that would embrace it. Rather than persist in 20th Century resistance to transparency, the opportunity needed to be embraced to expose Decisional Information. Doing so increased the velocity of the decisions of others whether to trust RHK's Information. Internally, packaging the Decisional Information would accelerate trust decisions within the company. Externally, looking upstream, even the simple purchase order sent to a supplier becomes easier to trust and faster to execute. Looking downstream toward those who generated RHK's revenues, greater transparency meant faster decisions to purchase from RHK. Everyone wins.

Let us look at the Innovate team's realization a bit closer. Doing more—formatting both Information and Decisional Information in standardized formats, enabling the Information to be automatically evaluated, and delivering access to performance records that confirm adherence to the Rules—delivers further velocity. This is because you are positioning your Information to be more rapidly qualified for consumption and used as a TDT by your trading partners (downstream DMs using the Information as a tool to make decisions). You are enabling your Information to be more rapidly evaluated and pushed through the downstream trust evaluation decision process. In doing so, there will be an inherent competitive advantage over the competitor that does not do so. Why? Because you are reducing the time your trading partners require to evaluate your Information, accelerating the momentum with which they calculate their decision process and make the ultimate affirmative decisions required for the transaction that relies on that Information.

EBAY™ ILLUSTRATES THE VELOCITY PRINCIPLE IN ACTION

Consider eBay™. As consumers using its platform, we see the Velocity Principle in action. For buyers and sellers, the added transparency into reputation, performance, past transaction history, and other data that eBay™ delivers accelerates our pre-qualification of a counterparty. What eBay™ is doing enables velocity of the commercial transaction by informing the pre-qualification process. Experience taught the company the Rules upon which consumers relied to make trust decisions. Enabling online purchases of goods that a consumer cannot physically examine from sellers unknown to them was hard to achieve. But eBay™ persisted, learned the Rules which buyers required, and created the Decisional Information required to meet those Rules.

Product descriptions, item condition, item specifics, shipping terms and conditions, seller identity, seller volume of activity—each of these add information content to align product views with a buyer's trust criteria. Further experience surely helped eBay™ also understand that consumers welcomed the chance to access feedback information—crowdsourcing opinions on a seller's performance. Sellers wanted to know the same about their customers. The terms of sale became relevant next, and eBay™ developed rules requiring exchanges, product returns, and the means of addressing defects in packaging, product delivery, and product quality (as compared to the information description on which the consumer relied). Today, eBay™ dominates for many reasons, but one of the most powerful is its success at inserting greater velocity directly in the consumer's evaluation of products and vendors.

MERGERS AND ACQUISITIONS ARE MEASURING TRUST IN INFORMATION

Now consider another realm. Within business-to-business acquisitions, such as corporate mergers, the transactions lawyer is, more and more, working as an information broker. The conventional transaction agreement (e.g., to purchase a company or its assets) is actually a brokering of information and its impact on the wealth creation value of the transaction to both buyer and seller. The seller is offering historic information regarding its business operations to inform the buyer's determination of the suitability of the proposed price. But the buyer wants more—the buyer seeks assurances regarding the governance systems through which that information has been created and maintained.

The buyer wants to know about the records management process, the information security management, and the seller's reliance on standards and other identified criteria that have shaped the seller's information governance practices. The definitive contracts authored through the negotiations of the transactions lawyers contain terms that preserve for the buyer an opportunity to hold back a portion of the purchase price pending the opportunity, post-closing, to validate the accuracy of the representations and the integrity of the data in representing the condition of the business and the basis on which the purchase price was calculated. In opposition, of course, sellers resist disclosure, seek to minimize due diligence, and negate or exclude the reserves buyers may seek to offset information inaccuracies that degrade the accuracy of the purchase price. The time consumed addressing the inherent distrust between the parties actually imposes substantial Expenses that neither sidetracks nor incorporates into their acquisition cost models.

The pre-qualification of Information for its reliability is a vital period *in time.*

Again and again, as we look at how Information moves between individuals, entities, organizations, systems, devices, and applications, whether across the living room or across the Net, the pre-qualification of Information for its reliability is a vital period *in time.* The economic cost of that time can be measured and, if that cost can be reduced, the profitability of a business (and any transaction) can be increased. Improvement is achieved when the transparency of the governance of the Information accelerates to an earlier moment in time the affirmative decision to trust the Information. This is actually true for any TDT, but critically true for digital Information as a TDT. Every transaction is executed more quickly the sooner Information required to complete the deal can be trusted.

VELOCITY AND TRANSPARENCY IN SUPPLY CHAIN MANAGEMENT

We are seeing similar transparency in supply chain management on a global basis. More and more, customers are seeking Information about the complete governance of the production chain to verify and validate—with less and less tolerance for delay—the continued availability, quality, and timeliness of raw materials or components that will be integrated into the finished product. Production data is being used to route around failure in the supply chain. A supplier disrupted by a labor dispute, a shortage of mined ore, or a violent storm—all are identified more easily, and alternative suppliers can be called into action more readily. The result is a lowered actual cost of risk, and an accelerated resilience around adversity.

That same level of transparency, when embedded across the functional infrastructure of Cloud services, becomes invaluable to assuring commercial success without replacing the global digital architecture. As the Project Innovate team began to test the Velocity Principle against trending business models, its value to Cloud services emerged as perhaps one of the most important qualities. In contrast to the CIO at Wise, RHK's Project Innovate team took the opportunity to proceed differently.

Every Rule relating to the governance and utility of Information must be portable.

Building on the Velocity Principle and the commitment to achieving digital trust, the team realized that every Rule relating to the utility of Information must be portable, capable of being performed equally well by contractors, service providers, and RHK's own full-time employees. The team recognized that, while the Cloud introduced tremendous flexibility in how Work could and would be allocated and balanced among contractors and suppliers (and even customers), the company required consistency in how its processes and assets were to be governed. The Rules required a new quality—mobility.

THE IMPORTANCE OF MOBILE RULES

Mobile Rules have nothing to do with using wireless telephones; instead, in our trust vocabulary, a Rule is "mobile" if its requirements can be performed by any actor responsible for its execution on a company's behalf. If control of Information (or any other corporate asset) was transferred (say, to a Cloud service provider), Mobile Rules travel with the Information, enabling consistent governance irrespective of the system in which the Information may be processed or at rest. Similarly, if RHK was a receiving party downstream from a supplier, Mobile Rules are also valuable. Imagine a supplier uses Mobile Rules with Information in its control that is sent to RHK in connection with a shipment in progress. The Mobile Rules (and the records of their execution) create Decisional Information about the shipment that RHK can process with greater velocity. Quite literally, RHK would be able to know and evaluate the Rules concurrently with the Information.

This is where RHK began to gain real advantage over Wise; RHK relied on the Velocity Principle to justify authoring and revising the business rules of the company and its systems as Mobile Rules. Mobile Rules were visualized as standards, capable of execution by any actor, generating records of their application that would be consistent, functional Decisional Information about the Information to which the Mobile Rules had been applied. Their success requires transparency; the Velocity Principle emphasizes the Decisional Information's visibility—the greater that visibility, and the easier with which trust could be calculated affirmatively at each exchange point, the higher the velocity with which the Information as a TDT could be put to work.

The Board delivered a mandate to build control; what the Innovate team launched with the Velocity Principle was a means to connect the consequences of building trust with improving velocity and creating wealth. Recall its initial report: "We can only justify investing in control for those assets that can be trusted." Any property—physical, tangible, real, digital, intangible—when governed carefully, has greater intrinsic value than property poorly or sloppily maintained. Whatever the asset, when valued by auditors or as the object of a commercial transaction, our human instincts focus on asking questions to acquire Decisional Information about the quality of that governance.

For example, "New in box," a common descriptor on eBay™, conveys the same type of Decisional Information for each item; a color photograph representing the item for auction is additional, confirming Decisional Information regarding how the seller has managed that item. Ratings of the seller by previous buyers are the same, with Decisional Information that is used to calculate the likely authenticity of the image and descriptions. For each record, potential buyers have developed their own Rules, both for the item they may wish to buy and for qualifying the seller as a Decisional Information Source for the Decisional Information about the "governance" of the item.

Every single transaction in commerce, if calculated as a trust decision, requires the same evaluations. Investigating the governance of an asset is asking questions about the TDC in which the asset, as a TDT, has existed. When that TDT is Information, the questions focus even more closely on provenance—what has been the TDC in which the Information has progressed up to this exchange point? The Velocity Principle demands that Decisional Information about each TDC be accessible to a DM.

In its mandate for control, the RHK Board actually was demanding something else—it sought to eliminate decisions that proceeded in the presence of Decisional Information Risk. When opacity and complexity prevail, the provenance of Information is inaccessible; decisions (as Work) must proceed despite questions persisting regarding the reliability and trustworthiness of Information. What troubled the Board was the frequency with which decisions were proceeding past T Minus and Holding, despite uncertainty regarding the Information.

By expanding its vision of how RHK acquired, used, and conveyed Data as a Resource used to make decisions, the Project Innovate team recognized there was an alternative to attacking Decisional Information Risks with a counterpunch of adding increased layers of control. Instead, the team proposed to calculate and demonstrate the economic gains trading partners and customers would realize by sharing in implementing Mobile Rules that powered the velocity of Information. The team proposed that everyone would benefit from reducing Decisional Information Risk; the critical next step was to build a demonstration of Mobile Rules.

Under the team's house rules, every decision aimed for consensus. While the preceding strategies took weeks to formulate, one question was still pending: "Will the development and use of Mobile Rules to create transparency in the governance of Information align with our legal and compliance obligations, whether statutory, regulatory, or contractual?"

When the then-current Project chair cornered Jung Singh, the Legal team member, her answer was a predictable one: "It depends." The chair was succinct in his response: "Make your answer 'Yes!' Legal, Compliance, and Audit will not stop our momentum. You have one month to build a bridge across the Chasm of SIAM."

THE TRUST VOCABULARY
In this chapter, you will learn the following words:

Chasm of SIAM

Compliance Rulebase

Rulebase

SIAM Words

CHAPTER 15

BRIDGING THE CHASM
OF SIAM

SIAM DOES NOT refer to the historic name for Thailand or to the Society for Industrial and Applied Mathematics. Project Innovate's IT engineers coined the term to refer to an annoying propensity of legal rules to be so ambiguous in their requirements to make compliance difficult, if not impossible, to achieve with any confidence. "SIAM" referred to any word or phrase used in a rule that employed "**S**emantically **I**ntentional **A**mbiguous **M**eaning." "Reasonable; appropriate; suitable; material; as necessary; properly responsive to; commercially acceptable"—these are but a few of my favorite SIAM terms. These are called *SIAM Words* in the trust vocabulary. They are endemic in rules authored by lawyers, particularly those rules relating to all things digital.

THE CHASM OF SIAM

As often happens on teams like Project Innovate, the Information Security team members arrived one morning to find a whiteboard decorated with an editorial cartoon of the Chasm of SIAM, and the phrase stuck.

The *Chasm of SIAM* was that gap between the ambiguity of SIAM Words and the precision required by IT systems, devices, and applications—when IT engineers tried to cross that chasm, they knew their death (at least, the death of their tenure) was almost certain. Why? Because engineering compliance with SIAM Words was always, at best, an educated guess. The lawyers were always hiding behind the ambiguity of the rules. They resisted expressing any confidence in any particular proposed solution. If a solution later failed and was found to be legally inadequate, the engineers would be placed in the cross-hairs. "It depends" was nearly always the preferred advice and counsel the IT team received.

The risks seemed even more substantial when new technologies or new data structures emerged. The recent cascade of new innovations like social media, Cloud services, the Internet of Things, and block chaining, as well as security technologies responding to the increased volume and success of adverse attacks, had been particularly frustrating. The lawyers simply did not demonstrate any willingness to craft corporate policies and procedures for those technologies that met the demands for precision IT engineers required—the developers wanted specifications that provided direction about how to navigate the legal rules, not ambiguities. So, committed and expected to build the solutions, in trust vocabulary terms, the engineers made up Rules that paired Resources, Results, and Risks (including their interpretation of the Risks of failing to comply with the SIAM legal rules).

A software developer begins any project the same as a building architect, asking, "What do you want the solution to accomplish? What are the requirements?" Yet, within RHK, the IT team had concluded, long before Project Innovate, that the volume of SIAM Words that Legal authored in response to those questions was inversely proportional to the maturity of a technology—the newer the technology, the greater the ambiguity expressed in the company's related legal work product (such as corporate policies, procedures, contracts, and other legal instruments they were asked to develop). Of course, the higher the volume of SIAM Words, the more the IT engineers made up new Rules to work with the Resources, including existing systems, devices, and Data.

The Legal team members accepted the Chasm of SIAM cartoon with a good-hearted chuckle. Responsible for protecting the corporation's legal exposure, they actually valued the presence of SIAM Words, whether in formal statutes and regulations or in their own work products. The ambiguity created flexibility for them once "the cow manure hit the circulating air blades at a high rate of speed." As advocates for the company, responding reactively after an adverse event occurred (whether allegations of an "unsuitable" work place, failures to disclose "material" facts, or claims that "commercially reasonable information security controls" were not employed), every SIAM Word in a binding legal rule was an opening, not a constraint.

SIAM WORDS PRESERVE LEGAL FLEXIBILITY

SIAM Words created opportunities for the Legal team members (and the outside lawyers they hired), to present their case that the company's procedures *were* "suitable" or "commercially reasonable" or that facts not disclosed were *not* "material" to investor decisions. Legal saw each ambiguity as an opportunity to filter the facts to show that corporate behavior fell "above the line" and did not violate the applicable legal rules. In other words, semantic imprecision allowed the lawyers to argue the company's actions did *not* justify any fines, sanctions, or adverse awards—its behavior was "close enough" to avoid the penalties.

To Legal, SIAM Words were always a defensive weapon to minimize the potential economic harm to the company in the face of adversity. They saw no incentive for authoring rules with precision; doing so only would increase the likelihood of success in any adverse audit, examination, or legal investigation. Increased precision in any rule would create a "bright line" against which the company's behavior could be evaluated more rigorously.

SIAM Words are ubiquitous in legal work products. Statutes, regulations, and agency guidelines are the starting point. The legal work products created by lawyers that govern the guts of a business add onto the pile. Websites and consumer-facing legal instruments, such as privacy policies or website terms of use, add further volume and complexity. All of these connect together, linking and chaining the rules for transactions, processes, and relationships. The accumulation of SIAM Words creates for any of us more and more confusion as to what conduct complies or violates which rules.

Even technology standards, particularly those structuring best practices in business processes (such as information security management and IT service management, to name just two), use SIAM Words to describe the duties and responsibilities of the actors subject to the rules. So, in both law and technology, SIAM Words make it difficult to objectively assess whether there is compliance with what the rules require. Ironically, that is precisely what many technology standards are designed for—to provide a framework or boundary within which an independent auditor can validate the conformity of a company's systems or processes (i.e., a TDT) with the rules expressed by a specific standard.

Legislators and public agencies defend the use of SIAM Words as an appropriate means of providing regulated companies with flexibility in structuring their compliance. Officials will emphasize that their rules apply to companies varying in size, with different inventories of resources with which to design their compliance. The vagueness of SIAM Words purportedly allows each regulated business a range of motion in which to structure its solutions, suitable to its capabilities as well as the level of risks created by its operations.

Regulators (those in agencies responsible for enforcing statutes and regulations) also will leverage SIAM ambiguity to gently pressure the companies they regulate, over time, toward adopting new technologies. Solutions for online identity validation in 2002 may have been "reasonable" and "appropriate" at that time.

Today, however, with the full range of new attack vectors and warfare for control, those solutions nearly universally are judged to fall below the line of what is "reasonable" and "appropriate." In trust vocabulary terms, the older technologies, as Resources, now lack the Functional Specifications to control the Risks associated with their use in the current Context. Regulators now encourage new, more responsive solutions (i.e., new TDTs), through informal guidance and recommendations that do not require companies to formally amend the existing SIAM wording of their rules. As a result, antiquity drives the Resources to fall below the line drawn by the regulators that describes the TDT suitable for performing the Work of complying with the Rules.

Unfortunately, the companies being regulated are never sure when the regulators may draw that line differently. This is one of the real frustrations of aligning technology, as Resources, with legal Rules. For the technologists, it feels the same as a sports official having the discretion to alter the boundaries of the field in the middle of play. While there are those in business who may dream of a world without regulations, others are more willing to accept the presence of Rules, as long as the requirements expressed by the Rules are stable. Indeed, just as Rules set the boundaries for systems, so too can Rules define, and provide a foundation for, a market to exist in specific goods and services. Securities markets, brokerages, commodity exchanges, and, more recently, information exchanges, exist because of the Rules that provide their structure. They work well because all of the Rules are built with sufficient precision to allow the competitive activities to proceed—"game on" is a successful product of explicit Rules.

Ironically, the Legal team always seeks precision when authoring Rules by which vendors and suppliers will be held accountable.

Those Rules are expressed in the relevant commercial agreements. No different than the warehouse distribution center agreements discussed in Part I, contracts have become increasingly complex, built from attachments, specifications, blueprints, and working models to express fully the requirements a vendor or supplier must satisfy. Due diligence to assure that a vendor or supplier is able to comply with those agreements also has become more rigorous. For example, information security questionnaires and on-site due diligence inspections routinely require inspecting, documenting, and validating of over 120 specific topics. Stated in the trust vocabulary, the TDTs offered by the vendors are described by Descriptive Specifications and Functional Specifications, and the Work to be performed is similarly detailed, expressing the Tasks and corresponding Results, Risks, Revenues, and Expenses, including Rules for the metrics and reporting services to be provided.

ENGINEERING AWAY FROM SIAM WORDS

In an unexpected consequence of Moore's law (which states that computer processing power will double every 18 months), as new technology and innovations proliferate, the tensions between ambiguity and precision drive the sides of the Chasm further apart. Rather than enabling new computing power (and the ability to achieve velocity), with Rules that offer increased precision, more and more Rules for new technologies are expressed in SIAM Words within every level of legal work product. Given this situation, when implementing solutions, connecting the digital Resources of trading partners, and structuring the flow of Information required by the commercial agreements, IT teams proceed to write the rules needed to make things work.

The result is a shift in how digital trust is achieved—the IT engineers are becoming the more influential authors of the Rules that

The IT engineers are becoming the more influential authors of the Rules that govern digital assets; the lawyers are becoming secondary players.

govern digital assets; the lawyers are becoming secondary players. In any business or communication relationship, the interdependency of Information flows requires parties to establish mutuality in the related Rules. Computing essentially requires each side to create and transfer identical duplicates of any Information in motion. To do so, the parties have to play by the same Rules. The sender for message 1 is the receiver for message 2. Reciprocity and equivalence in execution are essential for each party to acquire the Data their Resources require to perform the Work. There is no strategic advantage to imposing SIAM Words when building and executing relationships; the parties (and their related technologies), require precision.

Gradually, the reciprocity required to transfer Information has driven IT engineering teams to abandon SIAM Words and to adopt more equal, measurable expressions of their obligations. Technical specifications exchanged among the parties describe Rules that apply equally to all concerned. These are the Rules that state the meaning of each data field. Directories assign precise meanings to each data set within each data field. The Rules became the basis for structuring digital assets of immense volume and complexity. The engineers and computer scientists build these Rules to enable connectivity and velocity. They are doing so without consulting Legal, and have been doing so for quite some time, executing with predictability, certainty, and precision.

Public authorities are caught in the middle. They attempt to craft Rules broad enough to provide flexibility across a pool of regulated entities. But they also need the Rules to have sufficient specificity to enforce those Rules in a meaningful way against bad actors. States also recognize their physical boundaries are borders on their legal systems that constrain their enforcement authority.[*]

* As I write this book, fascinating and troubling debates are unfolding as to the power of nation-states to enforce Rules against actors that have no physical presence within their boundaries. Cyberterrorism and privacy/data protection are just two of the battlefields in which the powers of the nation-state to assert control and enforce its Rules are being tested.

The Chasm of SIAM degrades the velocity for Information. Remember, at each exchange point through which Information transits, inquiries are made to evaluate whether the Information complies with a defined set of Rules. Each is a trust decision. Each inquiry requires Time; if there is uncertainty as to the alignment between Information and the Rules, Decisional Information Risk arises. More Time is consumed. Every SIAM Word in that set of Rules further provokes an "It depends" that must be resolved for the Information to move through the exchange point. It is no different than an immigration officer calling over a supervisor to make a call on approving entry when a passport is not consistent with an online database that has been consulted.

The Chasm of SIAM degrades the velocity for Information.

The trust vocabulary continues to be very useful to explain how the Chasm degrades velocity. For example, when courts hear cases and reach decisions, a judge or jury are calculating how a particular collection of established facts aligns to the Rules, many of which include SIAM Words. They are considering those facts as Data (a Resource), Decisional Information required to be gathered and validated in order to evaluate compliance against specific Rules. In a US jury trial, before deliberations, the court will read to the jury a written statement expressing those Rules. Much of the Data presented as evidence describes TDC_{CIR} and TDC_{RES}. The court is evaluating whether a defendant (as a DM), properly performed the Work; the analysis often evaluates whether the DM properly selected a TDT. A DM's awareness of Risks, and the causality between identified TDC_{CIR} and a TDT, is considered. Lawyers battle to influence whether and how a jury should apply the Principle of Indifference to disregard certain evidence as the jury calculates its decision. Generally, if the defendant has no knowledge of the Risk of the Unknown Risk, the court will not impose liability. In other cases, ignorance will be no excuse; the defendant is presumed to have knowledge of the Rules.

The same process occurs at every exchange point across the nearly infinite complexity of the Net, calculated for every byte of Data in motion. Data does not move without a trust decision at each exchange point. While the DM may be human, that person is interacting with Code that is executing instructions line by line to apply Rules. The bulk of the trust decision process then unfolds behind the scene: A TDC is defined and validated. Pairings and dependencies among Resources, Rules, and Circumstances are identified and validated (or not). Decisional Information Sources are identified and validated as trusted. Decisional Information from those Sources is organized and processed through defined, chained trust decisions. When Decisional Information Risk is exposed, the probabilities of defined Results and known Risks are further calculated. R & Rs occur; if the Rules produce a "0," new Rules and new Data may be assembled and processed. A T Minus and Holding sequence is performed.

Data then is evaluated for its completeness, accuracy, and integrity—in other words, additional Rules calculate whether to place trust in the Data as a TDT for Work waiting to be performed. Data elements are compared to historic, comparable records to assure there is alignment. Descriptions are compared to actual content. All must be predictable, certain, and precise or the gate remains closed. Complex mathematics calculate the probabilities—a single false reading from a sensor within the network across which Data has passed may be sufficient to close the gate; multiple false readings from other sensors may earn only indifference and be ignored. Data that is not affirmatively trusted is rejected or embargoed; downstream transactions and Work waiting for that Data are delayed or entirely aborted.

There is no room in cyberspace for SIAM Words. Code, in executing trust decisions, simply cannot process "It depends." Instead, engineers take their best guess at constructing a set of instructions and Rules that Code *can* calculate and execute. Any SIAM Words that remain in the Rules are shoe-horned by engineers into a set of instructions capable of calculation and automation. Sometimes it goes the other way—the Code is shoe-horned into the Rules. In either direction, Six Sigma and other metrics-based control practices require the precision and measurements that SIAM Words do not articulate. The Chasm of SIAM is overcome; a bridge is built. Data sustains its velocity. Work is accomplished. This is what engineers do. They learn not to ask Legal for approval.

BUILDING A BRIDGE ACROSS THE CHASM

Project Innovate required a new collaboration. Stung by the Project chair's mandate, Legal asked IT Engineering to create a dissection team (a project name for brutally breaking down existing processes). Its mission: to teach Legal how IT Engineering built those bridges. As it turned out, the dissection was easy. Once they exposed the status quo, the answer was immediately apparent—the lawyers had to learn how to think like engineers.

When confronted with a SIAM Word, the engineers consistently build a translation. They realized that, for every SIAM Word, there was a Resource that was the target to be evaluated as "reasonable," "appropriate," "suitable," etc. That Resource could be a human actor, a machine, a process, or a type of record. Each SIAM Word

> Code, in executing trust decisions, simply cannot process "It depends."

was a disguised expression of how outcomes were to be measured or, in trust vocabulary terms, the Results that the Resource needed to achieve. The engineers were building both Descriptive Specifications and Functional Specifications for the Resources to have confidence that the Results were achieving the measurement expressed by the SIAM Word.

It actually was amazingly simple: "X [a Resource] was Y [a SIAM Word] if...." It took only a few examples for everyone doing the dissection to be working on the same page:

> The system [X] was appropriately secure [Y] if....
>
> The driver [X] was negligent [Y] if....
>
> The loan approval [X] was suitable [Y] if....
>
> The personal information [X] was adequately secured [Y] if....

The team also quickly recognized that many SIAM Rules included multiple Resources as targets and multiple, conjoined SIAM Words. For example, in 2000 when RHK began transferring EU consumer information to its Arkansas data center, Legal had given IT Engineering this sentence, known as the "Security Principle," extracted from the United States Safe Harbor Principles:

> "Organizations creating, maintaining, using, or disseminating personal information must take reasonable precautions to protect it from loss, misuse, and unauthorized access, disclosure, alteration, and destruction."

The Safe Harbor Principles can be studied in depth at www.export.gov/safeharbor.

IT had dismantled the Rule into a chained sequence of Rules on which they had relied for nearly 15 years to assure the RHK CIO that RHK complied with the Security Principle. Each of the following illustrates (in vastly simplified form), the results of their deconstruction. They used the same process for translating any SIAM Words into functional requirements against which to build solutions.

The first step was to give meaning to each noun, explicit or implied. Figure 15-1 reflects the IT team members' conclusion that:

> ⪼ "Personal Information" was defined to include not only the original EU Databases but also any new Databases constructed including the same Data.

> ⪼ "Organization" included not only the US business (RHK-D) but also the holding company and other subsidiaries that may use the Personal Information (each designated as a separate actor, A-1, etc.).

> ⪼ "Precautions" had no further definition in the Security Rule. So, the IT team treated it as a SIAM Word (Y-1) and defined it to mean a designated set of processes (Process A, Process B, etc.) to be reasonable (Y-2).

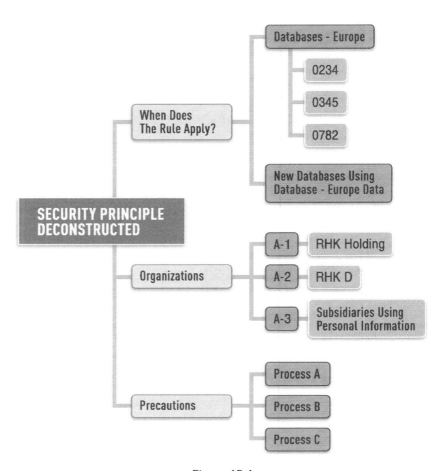

Figure 15-1

Next, for each process (create, maintain, use, disseminate) identified in the Security Principle, the IT engineers required further description to know when an action taken with Personal Information (PI) was within the boundary of those descriptions (Process A is creating PI).

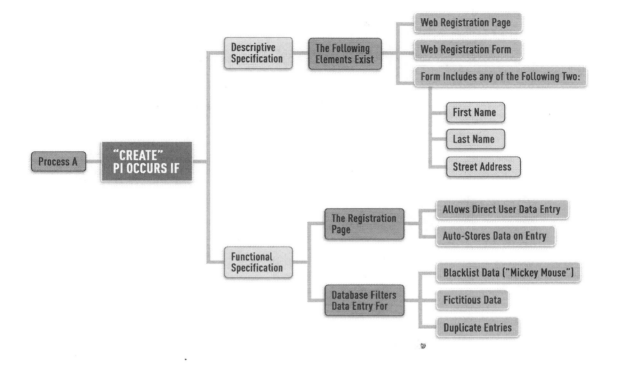

Figure 15-2

Figure 15-2 is just one illustration of one process, including both a Descriptive Specification and Functional Specification (vastly simplified for this purpose).

Now, since PI has been created, the protections against loss must be used, of which Process B is one example (see Figure 15-3).

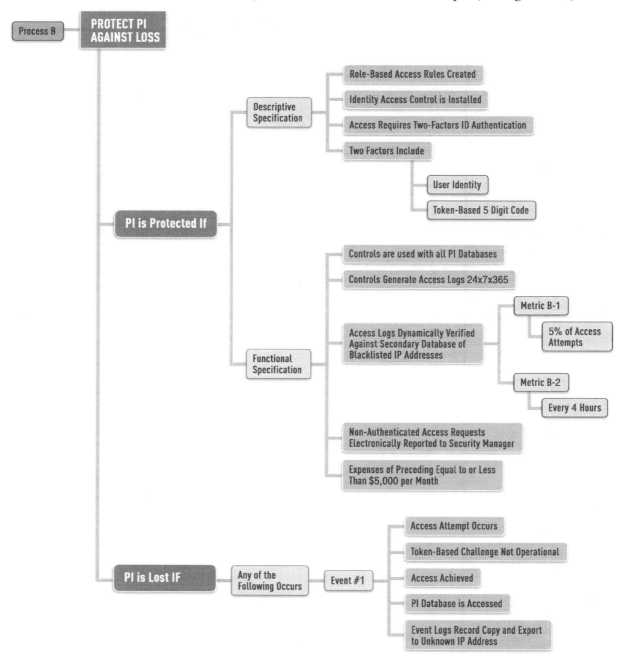

Figure 15-3

Notice that the Functional Specification uses several elements to translate "reasonable" (Y-2) into operational Rules. First there is a specific Result, exemplified by the Task of operating Process B (a Descriptive Specification). Second, within Process B there must be secondary Tasks that are capable of being measured (dynamic validation against blacklisted IP addresses, which serves to protect PI against "loss"; yes, "loss" is yet another SIAM Word, discussed below in connection with Figure 15-3. Third, how well Process B protects PI against loss must be calculated (relying, in this example, on the number of instances of dynamic validation, expressed as a percentage [Metric B-1], occurring in a defined period of time [Metric B-2]).

Notice also that the Functional Specification in Figure 15-3 includes Expenses. When measuring Revenues or Expenses for individual Results or Risks, the economics can be challenging. Nonetheless, when evaluating compliance with SIAM Words, financial factors are very important. Boards of Directors care, as do regulatory authorities during an examination. IT Engineering at RHK had started measuring Expenses for their IT solutions long before Project Innovate, but now they had even more specific accounting to generate with much greater detail.

As noted earlier, the Security Principle includes certain terms not otherwise defined in the Safe Harbor (shown as X-1 to X-4 in Figure 15-4 below). Many legal rules do this; they rely on the "common sense" meanings for words and do not provide further definitions. IT Engineering required each of these words to undergo the same transformation into more precise expressions, just like any SIAM Word.

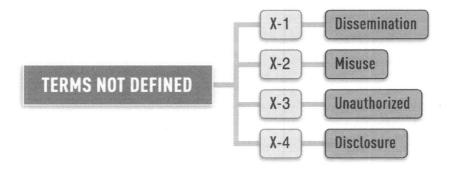

Figure 15-4

But X-3 is still missing something. To know what actions are "unauthorized," logic requires knowing first what actions are "authorized." So, even though the Security Principle does not include those words, IT Engineering required more definitions to be developed in order to implement compliance.

Now, putting the pieces together, all of these translations from the exact language of the Security Principle became functional. To comply with the Security Principle, the engineers authored a defined set of Rules, the execution of which could be mapped to specific Resources (systems, devices, applications, and PI within the control of actors A-1, A-2, etc.). In trust vocabulary, this is a *Rulebase*, literally a database of rules. The phrase is not new to computing; a Rulebase is recognized as part of a rule-based system, which takes specific actions based on the interactions between input (Data) and the Rules. This is the foundation for artificial intelligence, as exemplified by IBM's Watson or Google's automated automobiles. Sensory data is inputted, Rules are organized and processed, and trust decisions are made directing which chess piece to play, or whether to accelerate or brake.

A Rulebase designed to comply with any TDC_{RUL}, whether a statute, regulation, corporate policy, or commercial agreement, is a

Compliance Rulebase. It aligns a TDT's design and operation to the requirements of the TDC_{RUL}. In our continued migration toward automated business processes, including the automation of trust decisions, Compliance Rulebases are vital. They enable the Chasm to be bridged. SIAM Words are translated by a Compliance Rulebase into requirements and metrics (Descriptive Specifications and Functional Specifications) that power the alignment of a TDT to perform Work as designed.

By using the notation examples in the preceding figures, IT Engineering developed a Compliance Rulebase to enable alignment with the Security Principle. A-1, A-2, PI, Process B, Metric B-1, Process B Expenses, and X-1, X-2, X-3, and X-4 could be paired. Additional TDC_{CIR}, TDC_{RES}, and TDC_{RUL} could be mapped; additional pairings and dependencies were recognized and controlled by either existing Resources or new Resources developed as innovations. Existing systems and processes and innovations were mapped to Rules in the Compliance Rulebase. The end result was IT Engineering's ability to demonstrate structured processes that executed the SIAM Words of the Security Principle.

SIAM Words are translated by a Compliance Rulebase into requirements and metrics … that power the alignment of a TDT to perform Work as designed.

BUILDING EVIDENCE OF COMPLIANCE

Internally, Legal merely had passed along the Security Principle (along with other related Rules), and asked IT Engineering to take care of whatever was required. The documentation IT Engineering created gave them a basis to report back to Legal and the CIO that they had done their job—RHK was in compliance. But IT Engineering had built something else without fully appreciating its value. The same internal documentation of design was useful as substantive evidence of RHK's compliance with the Security Rule.

By mapping and structuring the Compliance Rulebase, they created records of the care with which they had interpreted each SIAM Word. IT Engineering's ongoing performance logs and metrics were additional evidence, factual Data that, having been properly designed, regulators and trading partners could trust as Decisional Information demonstrating alignment to the Security Principle. IT Engineering had engineered transparency; by creating and documenting design architectures and performance metrics to align to a Compliance Rulebase, they had applied the Velocity Principle to the Personal Information assets of RHK. Those records were objective testimony for the provenance of the PI.

Jung Singh got very excited. What she understood was that, both in common law and civil law nations, court opinions served as authoritative interpretations of the meaning of SIAM Words. The collected published opinions explained, in the circumstances of each case, whether the conduct of a party conformed to the meaning of a SIAM Word, taking account of the same variables discussed to this point. Indeed, entire legal practices were built on navigating the precedents represented by those cases and battling on whether a court's alignment of a SIAM Word to the specific TDCs, Rules, Resources, Results, Risks, Revenues, and Expenses was justified. ("This case is just like *Dewey v. Cheatam*, your honor." "But in the Erie Railroad case, your honor, there were no warning lines painted on the platform; the case is distinguishable." You have seen enough courtroom dramas to get the point—this is what lawyers are paid to do.)

As the dissection team worked further, Jung Singh realized that if she looked at case law differently, she could be invaluable to the IT Engineering team and Project Innovate. She decided that each case decision could be viewed as a mash-up of "pairings" of the moving parts of a trust decision; the results could be deconstructed into elements that the IT team could better map into Compliance Rulebases. As an attorney, she knew where to find the substance of what came after the "ifs" on the diagrams she reviewed with the IT team members. Case law, agency guidances, published legal best practices—these became design resources that generated increased density and precision to the Compliance Rulebases, not merely knowledge assets to employ as weapons for advocating against sanctions and fines.

Legal, Compliance, and Audit were not about to stand in the way of the momentum of Project Innovate; they were going to join IT on the front lines, shifting from serving as reactive, defensive cost centers toward adding value to the bold vision of building digital trust. Two important insights emerged from the dissection of the status quo. First, it was clear that achieving and sustaining digital trust required *predictive* confidence in the certainty of how specific conduct aligned with legal rules. Stated in trust vocabulary, the Results had to affirmatively produce Data as Decisional Information to allow the calculation of a TDT's performance of what a legal rule, as a TDC_{RUL}, required.

Rules that employed SIAM Words did not contribute to developing forward-looking trust in the related TDTs or the Data or Information they produced. Instead, just like IT Engineering had done for years, existing *external* SIAM-expressed rules (statutes, regulations, association rules, etc.) had to be deconstructed and aligned to the "X is Y if..." model. In addition, the Legal team members realized they had to move forward and engage with the design process for implementing Rules within the *internal* control of RHK, such as corporate policies or specific procedures, and do the same by constructing new Rules for new innovations and data types. Legal

> Achieving and sustaining digital trust required *predictive* confidence in the certainty of how specific conduct aligned with legal rules.

could author all of these Rules differently, as part of the company's systems, to eliminate SIAM Words and directly provide "hooks" to the Compliance Rulebases that IT Engineering had constructed.

Second, the evidential value of the documentation created in design, and the ongoing operating logs recording the metrics of performance, could not be understated. They were critical to RHK's future ability to demonstrate its compliance with both internal and external Rules. From their inception, the documentation and logs had to be considered and treated as what they were—records that were objective evidence of the good faith with which the company designed and governed its compliance with any applicable Rules. In trust vocabulary terms, those records are the Decisional Information for any third party evaluation (whether governmental or commercial) of RHK's compliance with the Rules. Instead of offering "it depends" to preserve defenses, Legal could help IT Engineering create documentation and logs that would be persuasive, affirmative evidence of RHK's good faith to comply. Compliance and Internal Audit are always being pushed to reduce the contingent set-asides for litigation and enforcement (the risk reserves discussed in Chapter 10); now the probabilities used by IT Engineering could be mapped against those economics, producing authentic savings in operating costs and reduced set-asides.

RHK's outside counsel, and perhaps even its General Counsel, would be furious that Project Innovate would be making recommendations that would slice the Legal budget dramatically while improving profits. Jung Singh realized, however, that this was the right way to proceed. First though, under the house rules, she needed Project Innovate's buy-in to her solution—the Rules for Composing Rules.

THE TRUST VOCABULARY
In this chapter, you will learn the following words:

Assets

Attributes

Costs

Rules for Composing Rules

CHAPTER 16

THE RULES FOR COMPOSING RULES

PREPARING HER PRESENTATION for the dissection group, Jung Singh knew it was a dress rehearsal for a later presentation to the full Innovate team. The attorney wanted to demonstrate that she had been learning about trust alongside everyone else—she needed to convince Project Innovate to trust her creation, the *Rules for Composing Rules* (the *RCRs*), as a useful tool for building digital trust.

She had brainstormed the RCRs in order to author Rules more effectively and cross the Chasm of SIAM consistently. While doing so, she realized the RCRs had another critical role—they could change how new digital assets (systems, devices, applications, Data) might be evaluated as TDTs within other trust decisions. For new third-party services (in potential mergers, joint ventures, or Cloud-based services), new licensed, external data assets (the due diligence on new Big Data analytic services was piling up), and new interfaces among existing RHK services, the RCRs created an entirely new vector from which to analyze the Rules bundled within those TDTs. They enabled rules-intensive analyses that would assess how well any TDT aligned to the Compliance Rulebases against which RHK conducted its business and, in doing so, expose those Rules with which the TDT did not align. Using the RCRs, RHK could address those shortcomings *before* signing agreements, either by adding new contract terms or adjusting the value of what would be paid.

The attorney had one further insight. At each exchange point within its systems, RHK was performing the same type of validation Tasks— Data in transit (and the Decisional Information about that Data) was being measured against the Rulebases to calculate whether to trust the acquisition and use of that Data for downstream Work and Tasks. If the RCRs were deployed across RHK, compliance controls could move closer to, and perhaps into, those exchange points. That would better automate the Tasks of validating the Data and increase the velocity and trust with which those Tasks were performed across RHK's networks tens of thousands of times each hour. In other words, rather than repeatedly transmitting Mobile Rules, IT Engineering could embed their execution into the related automated Resources (such as sensors, applications, and devices).

Bridge the Chasm of SIAM. Improve the validation and assessment of new TDTs against Compliance Rulebases. Achieve more accurate valuation and improved reliability in transactions for digital assets or services. Automate the validation and compliance of Data in motion. Improve velocity. Build digital trust. Increase control over digital assets. "Not a bad inventory of Results to achieve," she observed.

If we reflect back to the Wise Industries CIO, several of those are the outcomes with which she struggled in evaluating Cloud vendors. Her own policies and procedures (Rules) were not expressive enough to be easily transferred to the vendors. The vendors (in all of the scenarios except the very expensive Vendor T) failed to meet her requirements for performance data and reporting. She and her staff had been extremely concerned about the time that would be consumed post-contract signing developing services that would meet those requirements.

TESTING THEIR TRUST IN THE RCRs

The dissection team and the full Project Innovate team endorsed the Rules for Composing Rules but noted that they needed proof that the RCRs would be workable. They formulated a test, to be performed like any lab experiment. They assembled two teams with comparable skills. Each team had to design the path forward for adapting RHK's security privacy controls to comply with a forthcoming, inevitable change in the EU privacy rules. One team worked with the proposed RCRs; one did not.

In addition, as a global business, RHK knew that information security had multiple legal, geographic boundary-based Rules with which RHK needed to align its systems, processes, and larger ecosystems. Both teams also had to build solutions that generated automated red flags for potential legal vulnerabilities, as well as operating records demonstrating Six Sigma compliance with the legal rules. One team succeeded; one did not. The RCRs made the difference.

EXPRESSING THE RCRs

Jung Singh presented the RCRs as eight questions for evaluating any Rule or any Rulebase. She reminded the team that every TDT is a system, and every system can be illustrated as shown below (Figure 16-1).

Figure 16-1

She proposed bundling a TDT's components into three classifications: *Assets*, being the Resources and Rules of the TDT, *Attributes*, being the Results to be achieved and known Risks to be avoided, and *Costs*, being the Revenues and Expenses for the TDT. With those added labels, she presented the RCRs:

WHEN DOES THE RULE APPLY?

It is critical first to describe the context in which Work is to be accomplished. Many external Rules work the same—expressing when the Rules apply. Pursuant to the Trust Decision Model and trust vocabulary, this RCR is consistent, calling for descriptions of both Context and TDC. You will recall that these descriptions are interacting with other layers, including the description of Work (which is expressed by the Attributes) and a description of the TDT (which is expressed by the Assets).

This rule anticipates expressing any conditions precedent required as part of the TDC ("X must exist to do Y"; "X must occur before Y"). Each is either a TDC_{CIR} or TDC_{RES}. For computer programmers, these are some of the most difficult chains to construct; the next Task in any process may require dozens or hundreds of prior events to be sequentially executed successfully before firing.

Each predicate Task is governed by other Rulebases; each generates Data reporting successful execution of the Task to trigger the next Task in the sequence. In our normal, day-to-day activities, we do not think much about this chaining of Tasks and Rules to one another; however, in the digital space, the omission of a single dependency can be the "bug" that collapses an application or system's functionality.

WHO IS THE ACTOR TO PERFORM WHAT THE RULE REQUIRES?

Work must be performed by some Resource. In composing Rules, the Resource that performs Work is the *actor*. When you are the actor, in an activity such as hammering a nail, the actor is simple to identify. But actors need not be humans; networks, systems, devices, applications, and Data also may be actors. Indeed, when using the RCRs to compose Rules, a TDT (or a Resource within a TDT) is usually the actor. For a specific Task, more than one actor may be required to perform the Task to achieve the Results. What is important is that an identified target exists against which we can apply the Rules being composed.

WHAT IS THE ACTION THE ACTOR IS TO PERFORM?

Work can be a single Task, but we have learned that most Work is far more complex, involving connected chains of Tasks, dependencies, and other variables. But each Task involves at least one action to be performed by the actor. This rule is satisfied by a verb—some action taken, or some action restrained. Clarity and precision are important; as the bank website example illustrated in Chapter 8, the absence of precision rapidly can denigrate any meaningful evaluation and agreement by the stakeholders with an interest in the Work. A test of the measure of precision that is required is to be able to identify the moment in time when the action begins and the moment when the action ends. The times displayed by Google in publishing search results are illustrative of the precision that can be achieved.

Consider the various actions described in the single sentence of the Security Principle (X-1 in the preceding chapter): create, maintain, use, disseminate, take precautions, protect, [prevent] unauthorized access. Each is a separate action in the string listed in the Principle, but in practice each describes many different Tasks within the RHK systems. This RCR requires the engineers and lawyers to map between the TDC_{RUL} and the TDT_{RUL}, aligning the different Tasks to each action in the Principle.

WHAT IS THE OBJECT OF THE ACTION?

When an actor is directed to take, or refrain from, a defined action, there is always an *object* of that action—an item of tangible property (e.g., a building, an airplane), a person (or class of persons), a network, a system, a device, an information asset, or the actor itself. The action is taken in relationship to the object. To comply with the Security Principle, for example, RHK (actor) takes (action) precautions (objects). As with describing the action, any imprecision or omission in a Rule describing the object will place an actor's ability to perform in alignment with the Rule at risk. The actor (or person or entity controlling the actor), must speculate: "Is Z the object against which I am to take action?"

But what is a "precaution?" The term jumps out as a SIAM Word because the official language of the Security Principle provides no further definition. Indeed, the actual object is a collective subset of all possible precautions, namely "reasonable precautions." This exemplifies a particularly troublesome doubling-up common to legal Rules and increasingly replicated in the authoring of technology standards. First, one must determine "precaution [X] occurs if", for which, in any information system, there can be dozens of controls, interconnected and concurrently being measured to protect personal information. Then, one must work through "precautions [X] are reasonable [Y] if." Calculating Y, of course, requires interacting with, and building pairings among *when, actor, action,* and *object.* As we have seen, each can have multiple elements in the answer to the related RCR, making the expression of both X and Y in the preceding more complex.

When lawyers are evaluating how evidence lines up against legal rules, they are following the same analysis but have the luxury of working with hindsight. One or more identified TDC elements ("the rain was pouring"), may trigger supplemental questions ("Did you have an umbrella?" "Was the umbrella designed for the intensity of the wind?" etc.), which can draw new answers, creating relationships among the moving parts not previously considered. The IT engineer, however, must anticipate all of those relationships, conditions, and pairings when mapping Rules to the Resources within a TDT and, more precisely, to the Code that instructs its operation.

This becomes a critical distinction; it is where Jung Singh saw Legal's best potential to improve the engineering and advance the

Case law
could be
deconstructed
into more
precise
architectures,
identifying the
relationships
and pairings
that courts
recognized in
rendering their
opinions.

levels of trust. Case law could be deconstructed into more precise architectures, identifying the relationships and pairings that courts recognized in rendering their opinions. These moving parts then could be used in identifying X and Y, proactively and by design. Statutes, regulations, agency releases, court decisions, commercial contracts, corporate policies, procedures, and handbooks—all of these were TDC_{RUL} that needed to be mapped and aligned to TDT_{RUL} and the TDT_{RES} to build complete specifications. In doing so, each of the preceding RCRs (when, who, action, object) could be defined with much greater precision while producing an unexpected benefit—doing so would enable RHK to demonstrate it took account of (and designed its systems and controls to comply with), the rule of law. The Compliance Rulebases that related to those TDC_{RUL} were actually evidence themselves, proof of their compliance programs.

HOW WILL PERFORMANCE BE MEASURED?

The attorney realized that the clarity with which an action is expressed had to be complemented with precision in expressing how that action will be measured. This RCR requires observable, quantitative expressions of measurement to be part of any Rulebase. As illustrated by the Security Principle, so often measurements of actions are expressed in the imprecision and subjectivity of SIAM Words. To cite just three examples, "reasonable," "satisfactory" and "appropriate", when used as performance standards, disguise the failure of a Rule author to embrace precision. For the purposes of calculating trust, the measurement of any action (as a Task) needs to be quantitative. Something has to be counted, weighed, scored, or valued—an arithmetic expression of completion is required.

The attorney reviewed her list: when, actor, action, object, measurement. These were powerful building blocks for bridging the Chasm. If "X is Y if" is the starting point, she was excited that these five RCRs could be used to map amazing amounts of legal reasoning into more structured Rulebases and Compliance Rulebases that IT Engineering was building to calculate digital trust.

But she felt her solution still was incomplete. No different than any other lawyer, Jung Singh read the headlines. Legal disputes and enforcement actions increasingly were being won or lost based on the discovery of digital records inside a company's own systems. She was well aware of the vulnerability within RHK itself.

OVERLOOKING THE DIGITAL EVIDENCE OF NEGLIGENCE

Long discussions within Project Innovate had exposed an uncomfortable reality—many compliance investigations, security incidents, and systems failures were traced to improper reliance on Resources (notably Human Resources) to "do the right thing." Over four decades of IT innovation and change had drilled testing and acceptance criteria into the specifications for any project. Yet two persistent trends were circled on one of the project whiteboards— the failures of people to perform all of their Tasks in the ordinary course of business (such as filing emails out of their Inbox), and failures to effectively monitor and analyze performance reporting data generated by the systems (such as ignoring external attacks from an unrecognized IP address until a certain minimum number of attacks had been launched). Both were sources of Risks that investigations determined to have been the root cause of several adverse losses.

So often, constrained by budgets, headcounts, and counterpunching the crises of the day, investigations showed that, while systems were

> For the purposes of calculating trust, the measurement of any action (as a Task) needs to be quantitative.

generating performance Data, no one was able to see the clues or recognize their significance. The staff policies described how to file the emails, but no metrics were in place to monitor and measure compliance by each employee. Sniffers and similar controls on corporate networks were observing unauthorized activities (such as database access logs recording IP addresses from which queries originated), but the IT teams, pressed to complete the next innovations, lacked the bandwidth to pay close attention.

As an attorney, she realized the computers were producing enormous volumes of useful evidence, much of which was even being measured, but numerous losses still occurred. What had proven truly disruptive to RHK's bottom line in its U.S. operations had been its e-discovery expenses. Regulators, opposing counsel in civil litigation, and even the teams negotiating commercial transactions had read the same headlines. They voraciously pursued any digital records that would contradict RHK's standard denials and defenses. RHK had learned fast, and was making the same demands on anyone adverse to its interests. But the costs were staggering. Everyone was battling to find the evidence of someone else's negligence within the vast digital repositories. The real issue, however, was an inherent lack of trust by opposing litigants in RHK's disclosures of its operating records. "We are not using our own Data to govern ourselves effectively," she muttered.

Based on these observations, she crafted three more RCRs. "Now we will use our Data to govern, and we will be able to crow about it," she smiled. Buried in the Legal group, the attorney was unaware of how well she was aligning RHK to global trends in how investors are evaluating and scoring corporate governance systems (discussed earlier in Chapter 14). Companies create wealth with consistent

The real issue, however, was an inherent lack of trust by opposing litigants in RHK's disclosures of its operating records.

production, minimized risk reserves, and strong customer loyalties that reflect lower trust discounts in the calculations of what to pay for a company's goods and services. In other words, companies are measuring performance and remedying imperfections. The same values behind Six Sigma have been transforming the demands of investors for transparency into the qualities and measurements of corporate governance. The new RCRs were the cornerstones on which RHK could sustain and nurture the trust of those investors toward higher valuations.

HOW WILL PERFORMANCE BE REPORTED?

Each Rulebase must identify how performance of each Rule will be reported; it is insufficient for performance Data to merely be stored. If the Data has worth as a record of how well systems and processes are performing, then some actor (human or machine) must be capable of receiving and evaluating the Data. This RCR requires that the Data must be produced *and* organized, not merely stored passively within the network. The attorney's continued work on Project Innovate was sobering; she had not realized how much surveillance was going on across the information systems and the larger supply chains through which RHK did business—inventory networks, distribution networks, financial systems, customer service field agents, employee email filters, keystroke logs, cell phone tracking. But the Data was not being connected rigorously to performance metrics, and evidence of errors, malfunctions, intrusions, or performance negligence was not evaluated actively by Resources that were capable of intervening and minimizing the potential for Expenses tied to Risks.

TO WHOM WILL PERFORMANCE BE REPORTED?

Can the actor
be trusted
to evaluate
the Data
effectively and
make strong
governance
decisions?

This RCR requires an actor (human or machine) to be accountable for supervising performance reporting and assuring that the related TDT is working and firing accurately. That is management's task in any organization—to acquire performance Data, evaluate it, and make suitable adjustments as needed. Of course, when management makes those adjustments, it is acting consistently with the Trust Decision Model. It is evaluating Data as Decisional Information for calculating existing Rules for a TDT, adjusting its description of the TDC, evaluating and adjusting its descriptions of Work (and specific Tasks), and related TDT specifications, editing related Rulebases (and adjusting the Resources and Rules of a TDT), and Rewinding & Recalculating to affirm the validity of the edits in sustaining trust in the related TDTs.

More is needed than merely identifying an actor to receive the performance reports, however. This RCR requires a separate trust decision: can the actor be trusted to evaluate the Data effectively and make strong governance decisions? Does that actor have the Resources (time, manpower, analytical tools, etc.) to take effective actions based on the Data? For example, auditors evaluating corporate information security management systems are trained to focus on this separate trust analysis. It is not enough for companies to have best-of-class information security tools in place that are designed to manage security risks (such as identity access and management). The auditors also seek objective evidence that management takes action with performance data, rather than allowing that data to aggregate and collect dust in the virtual equivalent of digital file drawers. If there are adverse events, auditors want to confirm that management investigated the related data, and that it then took suitable remedial and corrective actions.

Jung Singh realized that a separate trust decision analysis required going back to the top of the RCRs and applying them consistently. To evaluate the trust that can be placed in those receiving performance reports, RHK needed to ask the same questions and formulate the answers. It needed to draw lines to define when investigations, workarounds, and remedial and corrective actions were appropriate. It also had to compose metrics and integrate them into the Rulebases. The management controls were emerging as separate TDTs composed of Resources (including Human Resources). She knew that, as with any TDT, a Value Calculation was required—were those controls, if implemented as TDTs consistently with the RCRs, generating Revenues exceeding Expenses?

WHAT ARE THE INCENTIVES AND SANCTIONS FOR PERFORMANCE?

Economists study how incentives motivate behavior. Their scholarship and science is well-founded in human behavioral theory. People, communities, and organizations perform better when presented with positive incentives. Yet, the attorney was perplexed. There seemed to be a contradiction between the affirmative, wealth-creating calculations of trust and how we, as individuals, groups, and organizations, administer and enforce our rules. Modern legal systems and most corporate governance models operate on a presumption that people can be expected to behave in conformity with the rules—the systems and models offer no direct incentives to comply.

> "Doing the right thing" was merely a moral standard, providing no direct, affirmative incentive for doing so.

Centuries of experience demonstrate a different truth—compliance is often a calculated decision, weighing the possible gains from non-compliance against the possible sanctions and other adverse consequences of being caught. Just as trust is a calculation of probabilities, so is the decision whether or not to comply. Indeed, nearly all formal legal systems rest on the principle that the state has the power to use force to impose sanctions—either the loss of property, the loss of freedom, or, in extreme circumstances, the loss of life—in response to non-compliance with the rules.

That perspective—to emphasize the negative sanctions—has crept into and across so many different bodies of rules that govern our conduct in commerce, government, community, and society. Somehow, "doing the right thing" was merely a moral standard, providing no direct, affirmative incentive for doing so. Yet rulebooks are filled with disciplinary and punitive sanctions, and enforcement resources, including those of Legal, Compliance, and Internal Audit, focus more toward the prosecution and enforcement of those sanctions rather than the detection and recognition of positive, conforming behavior.

The RCRs had to align with the essential economic principles favoring the value of positive incentives. The attorney concluded that, if affirmative calculations of trust created wealth (whether measured in time or money), they had to contemplate that the new wealth will be more effectively distributed to those who properly performed the Work. Sanctions still had a role; others, including investors, wanted to see evidence that improper conduct was not tolerated. But her instincts guided her to a different conclusion—if the incentives are properly designed, there will be dramatically fewer instances in which sanctions would be considered, lower investigation costs, fewer searches for electronic evidence contradicting claims of conforming behavior, and higher investor valuations rewarding governance. Such a design would feature incentive distribution based on objective Data demonstrating conforming performance of the Work at or exceeding the defined metrics.

There is a causal relationship that makes this final RCR fairly important. Any seller must provide sufficient incentives across its entire production process to motivate the performance of Rules-based controls, distribute those incentives to the actors in that production process, and monitor and manage the process to assure continued, proper execution. Success in doing so results in a product or service that earns your trust as the customer and, in turn, induces your decision to pay value for that product or service. If the process works, the value that you, as a consumer, transfer (in the purchase price, subscription fee, or any other barter of assets) will exceed the net actual production cost to the seller and enable it to retain a portion of the payment as profits, to be shared with the investors or shareholders in the seller's enterprise. In the attorney's design, payments made by consumers must fund the incentives delivered back through the entire process. Every contributing TDT must enable an affirmative Value Calculation; Revenues must be calculated to exceed Expenses.

A ROADMAP FOR COMPLIANCE

The RCRs were designed to bridge the Chasm of SIAM, creating defensible documentation of how TDTs enabled by IT systems aligned to the TDC_{RUL} that measured compliance against SIAM Words. But the attorney recognized the RCRs also transformed how the Legal team would create work product following Project Innovate's conclusion. There was no doubt that digital records were becoming substantive, preferable evidence in evaluating compliance issues. Now, Legal had an opportunity to anticipate and encourage that outcome in all of their work. Corporate governance policies, operating procedures, employee manuals, website terms of use—all could align more closely to the reality that Data created by using the RCRs would be functional as evidence of compliance, trusted as objective documentation of the company's business.

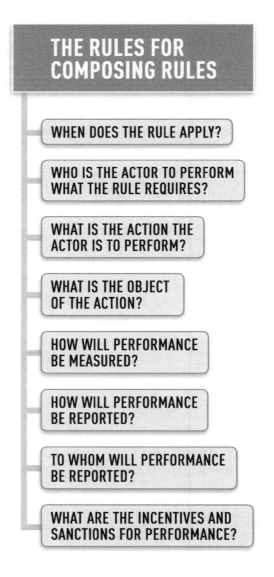

THE RULES FOR COMPOSING RULES

- WHEN DOES THE RULE APPLY?
- WHO IS THE ACTOR TO PERFORM WHAT THE RULE REQUIRES?
- WHAT IS THE ACTION THE ACTOR IS TO PERFORM?
- WHAT IS THE OBJECT OF THE ACTION?
- HOW WILL PERFORMANCE BE MEASURED?
- HOW WILL PERFORMANCE BE REPORTED?
- TO WHOM WILL PERFORMANCE BE REPORTED?
- WHAT ARE THE INCENTIVES AND SANCTIONS FOR PERFORMANCE?

Imagine using the RCRs to structure compliance with any typical legal rule or regulation (an external TDC$_{RUL}$). Each word in the TDC$_{RUL}$ that has a defined meaning, such as "PI" in the Security Principle, first is aligned to known Resources (see Figure 15-1). SIAM Words then are deconstructed, with the TDT Resources mapped to the RCRs. TDC$_{CIR}$ and TDC$_{RES}$ are identified and systems programmed to recognize their presence and navigate the appropriate Rules. The external TDC$_{RUL}$ is paired functionally to the Compliance Rulebases for the TDTs performing the Work. The documentation becomes a constructive, useful demonstration of the company's good faith in creating precision and control.

In the real world, away from Wise Industries and RHK Enterprises, this is very much the direction in which companies and regulators are proceeding. Struggling to secure effective resources for enforcement, public agencies are turning to big data analytics to discover non-conforming behavior. In order to rely on the corporate data assets as evidence, regulations are being published that require IT system architecture design documents, governance controls, and remediation records to be preserved and accessible for review. As just one example, in late 2014, the U.S. Securities and Exchange Commission published Regulation SCI, a 700+ page release setting new rules for "System Compliance and Integrity."

THE FOUR REASONS THE SPEED OF LIGHT CAN BE ACHIEVED

For four reasons, I believe that the RCRs are the core of the new Rules for business at the speed of light. First, the RCRs accelerate the velocity and efficiency of engineering to this new, growing interdependence between the public and private sectors. In any company, driven at first by the costs of e-discovery and now by the pressures of designing compliance across diverse geographic rule systems, IT and Legal are recognizing that the sources of the Rules are irrelevant to the governance and IT systems of any company. The Rules may be expressed in legal work products or technology specifications. What matters to the systems is that the requirements be expressed with a precision that ultimately allows calculations of execution to be arithmetically computed. The RCRs create a common set of criteria by which we can author and publish the requirements.

Second, the RCRs are powerful evaluative tools for auditing the quality of existing Rules and the TDTs implementing them, particularly those Rules *not* mapped into automated systems. For example, when we view existing policies, procedures, or commercial agreement terms through the filter of the RCRs, SIAM Words become immediately conspicuous. As noted earlier, while 20th Century drafting strategies favored imbalances in the precision of those legal work products whenever possible, the interdependent qualities of the 21st Century's reciprocal, bilateral, or multilateral commercial relationships no longer tolerate those imbalances. We must compose the rules of engagement differently, and the RCRs guide that process.

Existing legal work products, particularly commercial agreements, often are burdened by SIAM vocabulary. Recall the terms that one vendor offered to the Wise Industries CIO in Chapter 5; she did not have any predictive confidence the vendor would produce functionally meaningful reporting. By contrast, more and more research is advancing toward automated negotiations and contracting, without the burdens of imprecision that result when lawyers draft agreements. In another direction, software tools are enabling automated authoring of commercial agreements, composing the rules expressed in the contracts from terms and provisions used in prior contracts. All of these are implementing reforms toward precision and the ability to automate execution of Rules. The RCRs empower those authoring the contracts and implementing technical specifications to fully articulate what is required with clear, actionable language.

Indeed, one of the unexpected outcomes of just-in-time manufacturing and similar digitally-intensive supply and demand marketplaces is that the digital precision entwines commercial actors in a codependence that favors affirmative, immediate resolution of errors and non-conformities rather than litigation. These bumps in a relationship, when they occur, are metrics-intensive; the parties see evidence of error and act on that evidence. If the related Data is mutually trusted, the parties in any commercial relationship are able to create the workarounds that allow assembly lines and supply channels to continue with minimal interruption. Interpreting whether conduct violates the ambiguity of SIAM Words becomes inefficient to the economies of business. Quite simply, the expenses of switching to another supplier or customer (literally known as 'switching costs' in economic research) now also require building and executing affirmative trust decisions across the IT Resources and Data assets, as well as building trust (and pricing) for the primary goods or services. These Expenses make resolution of the bumps much lower in cost than changing to a new primary relationship. The RCRs help drive beneficial collaboration and efficiencies that enhance wealth creation.

Third, the RCRs pressure those designing systems (who are themselves TDTs) to understand that the design documentation and performance logs are evidentially valued. For nearly three decades, and likely before then, software developers have griped about creating documentation. But now, and into the future, there is even more pressure for them to do so with care. The records contribute to the transparency of governance and, in turn, to the velocity of information and the downstream business decisions that await. In one recent set of major lawsuits involving Toyota (and faulty accelerators), an analyst issued an expert report that provoked nearly $1.2 billion in settlements by Toyota within days. The report disclosed the contents of developer documentation which showed how known industry standards for software design had not been implemented.

Finally, the RCRs impose on senior management the responsibility to prove its value as the company's senior leadership cadre. The RCRs connect to how it will be judged in an increasingly digital, transparent market. Every day, the company's investors, regulators, customers, employees, and the business and trading partners are making those trust decisions—can management be trusted to govern effectively? The RCRs were tools that could strengthen those stakeholders' trust in RHK.

The Project Innovate team began to work together closer than ever before. Faced with the complexity of information systems, governing legal systems, and a new appreciation for the sources and authorship of the Rules, they realized that the scalability of the RCRs and truly achieving digital trust required more. Not every single Rule can satisfy each of the RCRs. To do so would create a portfolio of sentences with a complexity that would make James Joyce's writings appear simplistic. Instead, the team needed a larger framework on which to use the RCRs, allowing dependencies and structures among and across all of the Rules. That framework was provided by the remaining Digital Trust Design Principles.

THE TRUST VOCABULARY
In this chapter, you will learn the following words:

Trusted Information (T-Info)

CHAPTER 17

THE DIGITAL TRUST
DESIGN PRINCIPLES

THE VELOCITY PRINCIPLE was important to expressing the business case for investing in digital trust, emphasizing the interactions among Time, Information, and governance. The remaining Digital Trust Design Principles developed by Project Innovate went further. They provided a framework for choosing among the priorities and trade-offs required in focusing Resources and using the RCRs to construct improved outcomes. The Project Innovate team leaders realized, however, that the Design Principles could help RHK achieve even more.

When Project Innovate launched, it was clear that the economic concepts and business models focusing on emerging markets defined by geographies and national borders were becoming obsolete. New markets were emerging, their boundaries and dimensions defined by transactions in which digital Information was the primary asset of the deal itself rather than a by-product of transactions involving other manufactured goods or professional services. Originally, electronic data had no independent value other than serving the needs of business to track transactions and historic analysis. But the new information markets were different. In these marketplaces, digital Information was the product itself, offered in trade as payment for cash, goods, services, and even other Information assets.

Data licensing, big data analytics, market intelligence, Cloud services, predictive modeling—all of these activities have an insatiable appetite for Information that can be licensed, bartered, bought, or sold. In every deal, the Information is a TDT no different than any other TDT. The deals are like any other—every transaction first required an affirmative decision to trust. Functional Calculations, Value Calculations, Process Calculations, Risk Reserves, and Trust Discounts are equally in play. Rules for those computations are evolving rapidly and Information that does not measure up will be substantially discounted or overlooked, in the same way you would pass on a hammer with a loose head. It was clear to Project Innovate's team that the corporations empowering their Information to be trusted would be first in line and best in class in these new marketplaces.

Project Innovate's discussions also focused on the enormous global battles regarding the acquisition, control, and use of personally identifiable information, and the persistent non-payment or inadequate compensation paid to data subjects for the acquisition and use of their personal information. In the team's view, the inevitable movement to the Cloud potentially would expose RHK's corporate operational records and information to the same type of exploitation. In other words, RHK's vendors would treat them like vendors are currently treating data subjects! There was little question that, without imposing the controls called for by the Board, the market, rather than the company and its stakeholders and investors, would benefit. In this context, the Design Principles gained vital importance.

UNFOLDING THE DESIGN PRINCIPLES

The Design Principles build upon a critical assumption—every business decision requires digital Information as a Resource with which to make that decision. In the trust vocabulary, that Information will be classified as either Data (such as raw inventory material used in a calculation) or Decisional Information (used to evaluate another TDT, such as a hammer, a Cloud service provider, or a rocket into space). With either classification, trust in the Information itself must first be calculated for it to be useful to the business decision. In other words, an executive, a manager, an operating system, or a set of individual processes or controls within an application no longer could presume trust when making any decision. Exposing every decision to the Design Principles was going to have an impact across the company far beyond merely achieving the Board's original control objectives, reaching and influencing the full portfolio of thousands of daily decisions made within, and for the benefit of, RHK. Why? Because every decision, large or small, requires affirmative *digital trust* in order to make a good decision.

The same perspective is true for nearly any 21st Century business operating anywhere in the world—even a street artist or fruit vendor connects to the Net in some manner to purchase supplies, deposit earnings, or acquire a permit to operate. For Project

Every business decision requires digital Information as a Resource with which to make that decision.

Innovate, this insight was transformative. Individually, each Design Principle may seem reasonable, and even, perhaps, a bit ordinary when measured by traditional business management practices. Taken together, however, the Design Principles were going to become inherently strategic for RHK. Applied across the company and its ecosystems, the Design Principles delivered a new, unique structural decision framework that emphasized rules, information, and calculations—rather than emotions—across all business decisions, as well as enabling those making decisions to prioritize their choices for where achieving digital trust would create the greatest new wealth.

With daring, the team proposed that the Principles must apply equally across the business, not merely to Information under the company's control. Its ambition was to embed digital trust into how the company acquired, created, used, sold, and transferred all of its Resources, not merely Information. Looking upstream to RHK's supply chains, every Resource was a TDT for which digital Information was required to calculate and execute the acquisition of that Resource. Looking downstream to its markets, distribution networks, and customers, every good, product, and service delivered by RHK became more competitive when RHK's digital Information aligned to the trust requirements of its customers. At the same time, looking toward the emerging new markets for digital Information, RHK would be creating a new product line built from the trusted digital Information the company controlled. Within RHK, the Design Principles were poised to become the foundation for abandoning Dead Man's Curve and building something new.

Project Innovate

Digital Trust Design Principles

The company will build and sustain the capabilities to calculate trust for any TDT acquired, created, used, sold, or transferred in its operations.

The company will calculate affirmative trust in:

> any TDT acquired, created, used, sold, or transferred in its operations;

> any Information used to make decisions to acquire, create, use, sell, or transfer any TDT (including other Information); and

> any TDT used to make those decisions.

The company will use a TDT only when the value of Resources is calculated to exceed the value of Rules.

The company will use a TDT only when the value of Results is calculated to exceed the value of Risks.

The company will use a TDT only when Revenues to be achieved exceed the value of Expenses to be incurred.

The company will author and publish all Rules for TDTs using the Rules for Composing Rules, until the Expenses to do so are calculated to exceed the Revenues produced.

The company will govern all TDTs with transparency, until the Risks are calculated to exceed the Results of doing so.

The company will author all Rules for TDTs so that they map and align to published and recognized external standards, until the Expenses to do so are calculated to exceed the Revenues produced.

The company will author all Process Rules for TDTs to enable their automated execution, until the Expenses to do so are calculated to exceed the Revenues produced.

The company will calculate the functional and economic value of all Information pursuant to these Principles.

MEASURING THE VALUE TO CONTROL *TRUSTED* INFORMATION

The rotating Project chairs unanimously agreed to limit the Design Principles to 11 in number (including the Velocity Principle). The Principles reflected the shared view that RHK could not achieve digital trust immediately across all of its Resources and operations. Choices were required and calculations of Expenses and Risks would shape the priorities. But the team's painstaking internal negotiations and consensus building to whittle all of the substantive analysis and strategies down to 11 left exposed a pressing question: "How will we consistently measure value with the Design Principles?"

In the beginning, RHK senior management's focus emphasized achieving control. Digital trust was not on the radar. The Design

Principles obviously took the company much further, but doing so required structuring valuation questions into every transaction, operation, and activity. When did the value of digital trust affect the deals and how would RHK measure those impacts? The problem for the team was more challenging because the broader financial accounting profession had not developed consistent valuation models for digital assets.

The team concluded that a DM calculates the value of any TDT (including Information) by combining and netting two separate characteristics:

> The value of any TDT is proportional to the probability the TDT will perform the Work accurately. When the TDT is Information, the Work is the decision to be made using that Information.

> The value of any TDT is proportional to the accuracy of applicable prior trust decisions.

In other words, merely calculating the probability that a TDT will perform the next unit of Work (or individual Task) successfully is not enough! A DM also must evaluate how strongly to trust comparable prior trust decisions (and earlier decision chains), and separately calculate the quality and accuracy of those decisions. After all, if a TDT previously failed to accomplish the Work, any DM instinctively reviews and analyzes the prior trust decisions to evaluate where things went badly. That process (in effect, an R & R of the entire decision) is inherent: the greater the accuracy of our prior decisions, the greater our trust in the integrity of our current decisions. The less accurate our prior decisions, the more diminished our trust in their integrity as the basis for new

For further information on the economic valuation of digital information, and a dive into the rabbit hole of current debates, search "data valuation" or "economic value of data."

decisions. This exercise is comparable to a Process Calculation at T Minus and Holding except that it is performed retroactively.

This requires evaluating how well prior decisions' TDTs achieved the expected Results (i.e., performed in alignment with the Rules creating the TDT_{SP} and TDT_{fSP}), while not incurring any TDT_{RISK}. Now, all of the frequency measurements and causality calculations that are part of the Trust Decision Model discussed in Part I come into play. The team realized the mathematicians and quants working for RHK would have all they needed for those calculations *if* they created and preserved the transparency of the Data from prior trust decisions and tracked the Circumstances, Attributes, Assets, and Costs. Doing so would provide the Data as a Resource that would enable the measurement of probabilities and causalities across decisions and the recognition, alignment, and/or differentiation of the comparable and non-comparable TDCs. If the records of prior decisions could not be accessed and chained together, there would be a failure in transparency and Decisional Information Risks would arise.

For organizations, nothing is more critical than preserving the ability to evaluate prior decisions and then adapt current and future decisions to achieve greater reliability. Project Innovate realized that building a new architecture using the Design Principles as a foundation meant progressing toward digitally capturing and using institutional knowledge rather than relying on individual, personal knowledge and the oral history of best practices. The Design Principles went far beyond Six Sigma; they empowered RHK to be forward-looking in making better decisions, leveraging the same concepts of granular metrics to assure higher quality in overall functional performance while creating new digital Information assets that were both trusted and valuable.

For organizations, nothing is more critical than preserving the ability to evaluate prior decisions and then adapt current and future decisions to achieve greater reliability.

STRIKING THE RIGHT BALANCES

The critical ingredient the Innovate team incorporated across the Principles was a requirement for explicit measurements and calculations; presumptions of trust would exist only when their impact was below the line of indifference. As happens with all trends in automation and computing, the Innovate team projected enormous initial gains, followed by smaller, incremental improvements. This line of reasoning generated the following corollaries to the Design Principles:

> For Assets, the value of Resources (measured in terms of probability, not economic cost) is balanced against the value of Rules. Too many Rules requiring human execution or expressed in SIAM Words, and a TDT creates too many Risks.

> For Attributes, the value of Results is balanced against Risks. No TDT is affirmatively trustworthy if the Risks are calculated to be more likely to occur than the intended Results.

> For Costs, Revenues are balanced against Expenses. Of course, many TDTs may operate successfully (pursuant to the Rules for the Work), and not create short-term net Revenues. The Principles impose a responsibility to assure that every TDT eventually creates wealth. Transparency is essential to enable effective calculations.

Automating Rules into Resources would shift into digital form the records of both successful and failed outcomes for use as Decisional Information for future decisions. With every transaction, RHK would create new Data with new value. Structured against known Rules, the new Data would enable automated evaluation and improvement. RHK would exclude fewer variables because of indifference or computational complexity. Rules called upon in future trust decisions would have persistent access to historic records as Decisional Information and the accessibility of the records would mean less future Decisional Information Risk.

MAPPING THE EMOTION OF TRUST TO A CALCULATION

Through the formulation of the Principles, the team concluded that every emotional expression of trust ("I trust them with all my heart") is actually a verbalization of the assessed outcomes of prior calculations of trust. Historic affirmative Results improve trust; hit-and-miss reliability degrades trust. Rankings of any Context element and its subsequent influence on a trust decision connect directly to the quality of prior experience and prior decisions.

Now the team understood the critical reason why *digital trust* was so vulnerable—the pace of innovation was moving faster than the formulation of Rules that any stakeholder used to calculate trust. Each new innovation is a new TDT. When prior experience or trusted sources cannot produce the Rules required to align and calculate the Assets, Attributes, and Costs for the TDT (and its components), calculating trust becomes impossible. The challenges of Rhett Butler-based exclusions and Decisional Information Risk are magnified further when the Rules themselves are incomplete or absent.

When Rules are absent, the Process Calculation at T Minus and Holding fails. There are too many unknowns. Mathematically, as a negative value the Risk of the Unknown Risk freezes the calculations. Moreover, when a new TDT places at risk Resources that

Every emotional expression of trust ("I trust them with all my heart") is actually a verbalization of the assessed outcomes of prior calculations of trust.

are higher in value, a DM instinctively assigns greater value to the Risk of the Unknown Risk, making it even harder to calculate affirmative trust.

As TDTs, digital innovations (including new kinds of digital Information) gain velocity when a DM can calculate higher probabilities of achieving intended Results (as Tasks and Work). The key is to have the Rules in place, accessible to a DM, and available for performing those calculations. This is how a Process Calculation gains its value, demonstrating that Rules exist and have been used. Having more Rules does not hinder the adoption of something new; what matters is the frequency and effectiveness with which a TDT automates the execution of those Rules and creates accessible records. The more comprehensively a Process Calculation considers all possible Circumstances, Resources, Rules, and Costs, the smaller the Risk of the Unknown Risk's impact on the trust calculation.

For digital Information to be trusted as a TDT the transparency of its governance is essential. That requires an ongoing execution of known Rules throughout the lifecycle of the Information prior to reaching any exchange point. A DM does not accept Information as a TDT without validating both the presence of Rules and the evidence of their execution. These are all required for an affirmative Process Calculation. Therefore, in the trust vocabulary, *Trusted Information (T-Info)*, is Information documented to possess four qualities:

> ⪰ the Information is digital;

> ⪰ the Information has been affirmatively calculated
>   as trustworthy;

> the Rulebases used for that calculation are identifiable and accessible (i.e., transparent); and

> the records of that calculation are identifiable and accessible.

BEING FIRST IN LINE

Therefore, investments to control Information are best justified when Information, Rules, and Decisional Information can be bundled and made accessible to a DM concurrently. Rather than avoid Rules or wait for others to author Rules, the Innovate team was convinced that RHK needed to embrace the strategic posture of being first in line to author the Rules by which it would govern its digital Information. The team also realized that the winner in any market or ecosystem would be the first to automate the execution and governance of those Rules.

To enable those strategies, the team designed two additional tools, the Unified Rules Model and the Unified Information Model. Together with the RCRs and the Digital Trust Design Principles, these tools further accelerated the ease of aligning Rules and Information and introduced the precision required to bundle and create the accessibility RHK required.

Investments to control Information are best justified when Information, Rules, and Decisional Information can be bundled and made accessible to a DM concurrently.

THE TRUST VOCABULARY

In this chapter, you will learn the following words:

Execution Layer Rules

Formal Law Rules

Formal Principles

Implementation Layer Rules

Interpretations

Public Layer Rules

Unified Rules Model

CHAPTER 18

THE UNIFIED RULES MODEL

THE FIRST OF THE NEW TOOLS, the Unified Rules Model, emerged out of another brainstorming session. The RCRs had been well-received, but Rules composed using the RCRs had to fit together like the struts and trestles of a bridge over the Chasm of SIAM. Everyone agreed that RHK was like any large, global business and faced Tower of Babel complexities—executives, lawyers, service providers, regulators, and customers all authored their rules in different languages, structured their rules differently, and used diverse—and often conflicting—measures to calculate conformity and compliance. To succeed with the Digital Trust Design Principles and implement the RCRs, all of the stakeholders had to speak the same language, see the full picture, and work on the same page. How could those outcomes be achieved by RHK and by the full complement of external stakeholders within the ecosystems in which RHK did business?

The brainstorming session started with Jung Singh wiping away the Chasm of SIAM cartoon and starting fresh. The whiteboard soon filled with new questions:

> With so many Rules, Rulebases, and Compliance Rulebases to build and consider, how do we organize the Rules into a coherent structure everyone can access and navigate?
>
> How can any of us visualize and navigate the relationships among different Rules and their parent-child dependencies?
>
> How can the variables be tracked that trigger which Rules apply to different trust decisions about different TDTs in different TDCs?
>
> On the Net, how can we identify and map these Rules in order to leverage the potential of technology to automate compliance?
>
> Moving forward, how can we organize and structure the process of authoring Rules—in internal operations, commercial transactions, trading networks, and across governing nations and multi-national regions—in order to create and sustain a competitive advantage in building trust? How can we do so to enable *digital* trust?

Those questions may sound hauntingly familiar. Virtually any company is confronting a similar list today. You already may have asked some of them yourself or been assigned to come up with the answers. The reality is that multiple professional disciplines are pursuing the same agenda—building the Rules with which to

Multiple professional disciplines are pursuing the same agenda— building the Rules with which to create and calculate trust in digital Information.

create and calculate trust in digital Information. However, much like each continent once was inaccessible to the residents of other continents, so too are the rules developed by each profession often inaccessible to other disciplines and practitioners. The challenges are made more complex by the global diversity of our work forces and our ecosystems, with multiple native languages, trading systems, business cultures, and varying levels of government oversight and control inherent to the totality of any business.

ORGANIZING THE RULES

To answer those questions, the Innovate team realized that it needed new tools. Imagine the team already had the Trust Decision Model and Trust Vocabulary (introduced in Part I) available and had completed the Design Principles and the RCRs. All of these were Resources for performing the Work of designing digital trust across the business. Each new tool would be an added Resource. Collectively, all of these Resources needed to deliver cohesion and connect together.

The light bulb turned on: collectively, these Resources, both the existing ones and any new tools required as new Resources, were a TDT. The Work was to engineer digital trust and create T-Info. The team had multiple Tasks to perform as part of the Work for which these Resources were required. Behind the questions on the whiteboard lurked the Rules for this TDT.

The Unified Rules Model and the Unified Information Model were innovations responding to those Rules. They would help the team assemble and connect all of the Resources together, creating a unified system and process that could, itself, be trusted by all of the stakeholders to perform the Work. So, like the animation team described in Part I (but unlike the CIO at Wise Industries), Project Innovate fired up its Trust Decision Model, working across the frames of film and layers to create new descriptions of its Work, the component Tasks, and the Results to be achieved to better describe what the new tools, as innovations, needed to accomplish. The team assigned its highest values to the following Results:

> The tools will enable team members and ecosystem partners to better visualize all of the variables and complexities to be navigated in building digital trust (Circumstances, Resources, Rules, Costs, Decisional Information, and Time).

> The tools must support the global communication and collaboration requirements of our Resources and those of our ecosystem partners.

> The tools will formalize the Design Principles and enable team members and ecosystem partners to achieve greater consistency in the design and management of Information (and the Resources used to perform Work in which the Information is employed).

> The tools will improve the transparency of how Rules are applied to Information and, in doing so, improve the velocity with which Information is evaluated as a TDT in trust decisions.

> The tools will improve the granularity and accuracy with which Rules are applied to Information by other Resources, enabling accurate reporting and calculations of the effectiveness of those applications.

The tools will improve the capability of Resources to automatically evaluate optional sources for Information (systems, service providers, etc.) and calculate similarities and differences that affect the calculation of trust in those sources with greater transparency.

The tools will better enable identification and isolation of Rules not being properly executed, in order to improve remediation and corrective action and to reduce Risks.

The tools will better enable identification and isolation of Information for which Rules have not been authored in order to assure the continued utility of the Information.

The tools will better assure that output performance reports (as Data) are properly generated to enable the calculations of due execution of the related Rules.

The tools will improve the mapping and routing of output performance Data to Rules, better assuring that ongoing documentation of due execution is created, preserved, and accessible to ongoing calculations of trust and the governance of related Resources.

The described Results were littered with SIAM Words ("better assure") and the team realized it needed to complete a lot of work to translate these Results into metric-based Rules. But the new tools had a more fundamental purpose; they enabled the Rules to connect to Information assets with granularity and precision.

Once those connections were in place, the team could layer in the metrics.

To better understand and explore the Unified Rules Model and the Unified Information Model (presented in Chapter 19), for the remainder of this and the next chapter, we will step away from the fictional RHK story and focus directly on the tools themselves.

THE UNIFIED RULES MODEL

The *Unified Rules Model (URM)* is a visual, interactive tool that connects and integrates into a unified structure all of the Rules that historically have been distributed and siloed among law, technology, business, and personal behavior. The URM is structured to function at a global level; it is not limited to the use of any specific human or machine language, nor is it confined to the structure of any specific legal or information system. It can be adopted and used by all who author and manage compliance with Rules, whether in government, industry, education, social, or cultural organizations. In the same manner that software development has been transformed by the use of a Unified Modeling Language, the URM transforms how we will develop and execute Rules in the next generations of the Digital Age. In describing the URM, I have told colleagues, "This model can be presented as a single image and explained in less than five minutes, but it will take a lifetime to master." That single image appears at the end of this chapter; its components unfold between here and there.

THREE FUNDAMENTAL CAPABILITIES

The URM contributes to all of the Results defined by efforts like the Project Innovate team's mission. Before presenting its components, however, three fundamental capabilities deserve emphasis:

≽ First, the URM enables a portfolio of existing Rules applicable to a TDC or TDT to be organized into a coherent collection, regardless of the source or authorship of the Rules. Within any TDC, the URM enables the functionality of that specific collection (whether or not structured as a Rulebase) to be objectively assessed in order to expose the flaws in the design, implementation, or enforcement of those Rules with accurate, and perhaps brutal, transparency.

≽ Second, the URM enables new Rulebases and individual Rules to be designed with architectural structure and integrity. In 1987, John Zachman, in a landmark white paper (listed in References and Additional Sources), was inspired by building architects to first imagine and describe the field of information architecture. He recognized that those designing information systems also needed to embrace visualization as a tool for expressing and structuring the design and complexity of those systems, as computing evolved rapidly away from single machines toward systems and networks of machines, devices, applications, and data. Zachman appreciated building architects' ability to use visual tools—blueprints—to support communication and consensus among all of the stakeholders and participants in the construction of a new building. He advocated that using comparable visualization tools would enable information architects, owners, contractors, operators, and users of information systems to communicate, collaborate, and construct a shared understanding of the system or application to be built. In doing so, Zachman unleashed the imagination of his and succeeding generations to work differently.

Today, we globally invest billions in the design and construction of new physical buildings based entirely on digital visualizations of their structures. The stakeholders place their trust in the accuracy and integrity of those digital images. The images illustrate how the buildings conform to the complex and often disparate rules for construction, electrical services, plumbing services, landscaping, flood plain management, safety and health, and functional integrity. Advanced architectural software products electronically annotate a design to document conformity with the applicable rules, as well as identify when one or more components of the building conflict with the related rules. Rules drawn from autonomous sources are reconciled and unified in the background of those applications.

The URM enables the same level of confidence to be achieved in structuring and integrating the Rules for complex business systems (e.g., health care, financial services, transportation, pharmaceutical manufacturing, food production, and IT computing, among others), and guarantees the operation of those systems pursuant to those Rules.

≥ Third, the URM enables the performance of systems, processes, and resources to continuously inform our ability to assess the performance of the Rules and accelerate our agility in revising Rules to sustain and improve velocity. The wired infrastructure that the current Net represents cannot sustain itself relying upon the slow pace at which nation-state governments evaluate, update, and enact new Rules. The Net requires a more agile responsiveness to revise Rules when they fail to achieve their purposes and Risk-based adverse events occur. The URM (working in combination with the other tools) enables mapping of the enormous volumes of operating Data generated by our systems, devices, and applications with greater specificity to the similarly massive volumes of Rules by which those assets and the Information flowing through them are governed.

These three functions are ambitious; however, I fully believe we can achieve them. The URM expands our individual and collective abilities to create, design, and build complexity with visual tools.

> The URM expands our individual and collective abilities to create, design, and build complexity with visual tools.

THE IMPORTANCE OF SAFETY TO DECIDING TO TRUST

The science and art of building architecture also evidence another domain that the URM taps into and advances—the public interest in assuring that a building design (and resulting structure) conforms to the published rules for assuring the safety, soundness, and functionality of the building itself. We have a comparable issue in the business world. Beneath all of our concerns about the integrity and security of information lurks a persistent question: "Will I (and my company) be safe in accessing, opening, or relying upon this information?"

Building codes did not originate from the imagination of bureaucrats. Instead, each requirement for each component of any building evolved out of experience (including accidents, collapses, fires, explosions, earthquakes, floods, and similar misfortunes), engineering, and science, driving an articulate expression of what would enable that component, and the building as a whole, to achieve its objectives. Modern constructions—whether residences, skyscrapers, or industrial manufacturing plants—are integrated systems of amazing complexity. Structural loads for different materials and designs; spatial use load capacities; plumbing services; electrical services; environmental heating, cooling, and air quality control; lighting; window structure and safety requirements; accessibility for disabled residents and visitors; wiring and structural facilities for high-end computer data rooms, digital conferencing, and everyday desktop computers—all are within the body of knowledge any architect must master to be successful and all are addressed in, and the architect is held accountable against, published building codes, regulations, permitting and inspection processes.

While there is the opportunity for great creativity for the architect, each design—and, hopefully each construction—is, in its essence, an alignment of that creativity on top of, and integrated into, a foundation and infrastructure of rules. Each blueprint is the visual expression of that alignment. Each drawing is the basis on which the stakeholders in a building's success make their decisions to invest in the evolution from a design to a completed structure. The drawing must be sufficiently detailed to enable building inspectors charged with enforcing the rules to be able to see, inspect, and confirm that the design conforms to the relevant rules and that, during and through construction, the as-built building also conforms.

As briefly referenced earlier, current software-based architectural tools have deconstructed and reassembled into Rulebases various Rules collections that govern building design, from the most parochial local building codes to international standards and rules of physics and engineering associated with specific components (such as weight loads and wind velocities). The result is that, as the architect selects each component of a building, the software calls up and electronically aligns the Rules applicable to that component. If the architect digitally assembles a design in conflict with the Rules (for example, selecting the wrong size nut for a specific bolt, or installing an elevator that does not meet local building code rules), that conflict is exposed immediately and the architect must resolve the conflict before proceeding.

Similarly, public authorities are using software programs to electronically evaluate blueprints submitted for proposed new buildings and calculate their conformance to all applicable building codes. What enables these tools to work effectively is that each component of a proposed building has a digital identifier drawn from an International Organization for Standardization (ISO) directory. Those codes then are associated with the collected, applicable Rules. For example, the local building codes have been parsed into Rulebases so that, for any element within a code-based Rule (component, connection rules, load-bearing weight rules), the Rule is separately identified and maintained. The Rules directories are connected so that, for each ISO-based code, the relevant Rules (and dependencies) can be precisely associated with each component.

Taken as a whole, this process is known as Building Information Modeling (BIM). BIM is dynamic, global, mature, and continuing to grow in its capabilities. It does more than merely enable virtual designs and three-dimensional modeling; BIM empowers project teams to develop inventories of components, objects, and assemblies (such as an elevator mechanism, a restroom design, or an entire floor or building module), and then use those inventories to visually design their buildings with greater efficiency and confidence, with each instance being based on a shared definition of the relevant parameters and building constraints. In effect, BIM builds trust in the buildings that result, each of which is a TDT. BIM merely is applying object-oriented programming concepts to the physical objections and operational functions of the building; the Rules are bundled together with the components, creating modules suitable for rapid, consistent assembly.

In the background, however, the BIM software applications do so much more, creating digital capabilities for exchanging vital information among connected subcontractors and team members; generating simulations that test the performance and capabilities of alternative design configurations against predicted performance metrics; developing competing construction and build schedules to evaluate total costs, timetables, and execution parameters; and enabling the as-built drawings to be adjusted and conformed, thereby accelerating the completion and approval of the building for use. After the ribbon cutting, the BIM tools support ongoing performance management for a building, working from sensors, controls, and other data gathering tools built into the building for such purposes.

What is intriguing is that many of the objectives achieved with BIM are ones for which, until the URM, no methodology or tool has existed to enable comparable integration and management of the rules for information systems, process modeling, and compliance—all of which are essential to digital trust. The URM is the foundation for achieving similar (and perhaps greater) functionality across the full portfolio of activities for which we use information technologies. There is no reason Information cannot be awarded the same qualities of trust we place in the buildings in which we live and work. To do so, we must construct and maintain our Rules for Information differently.

The URM offers a visual, dynamic, flexible, and scalable architecture into which we can structure and manage both existing and future Rules. Doing so allows those Rules to connect more clearly to the digital capabilities of the Net and supporting information technologies and advance connection, compliance, and execution.

A UNIFIED STRUCTURE OF LAYERS

The URM organizes all of the Rules governing Information into three layers (shown in Figure 18-1). In the following pages, we explore these layers and their relationships. The power of the URM is that it enables a DM to organize Rules applicable to any TDT, not merely digital Information! For any trust decision in business, there are multiple sources of Rules to be identified, organized, reconciled, and applied. The URM is useful across the full diversity of those decisions and their Rules.

Figure 18-1

Public Layer

The first layer is the *Public Layer*, which consists of the official, published rules of governments. The constituent rules are what

> The URM offers a visual, dynamic, flexible, and scalable architecture into which we can structure and manage both existing and future Rules.

we consider as "the law." The Public Layer is organized first by geographic regions (such as Europe, North America, the seas), then by individual nation-states and their subsidiary jurisdictions (i.e., states, provinces, territories, counties, cities, towns, villages, homeowner associations, and neighborhoods). Public Layer Rules also are authored and administered by regional coalitions of nation-states (such as the European Union and the Asia-Pacific Economic Cooperation forum), or global coalitions (such as the United Nations or subsidiary organizations like the International Atomic Energy Agency). The unifying element of the Public Layer is the sponsorship and ownership of a rule by a government or entity composed of governments. The Public Layer is divided into two sectors—the *Formal Law* and the *Formal Principles*.

PUBLIC LAYER

FORMAL LAW

Formal Law

Formal Law Rules are the constitutions, statutes, and regulations published by legislative or executive functions within a governmental entity. The Formal Law Rules are maintained in a layered hierarchy in almost any nation. The first sub-layer is defined by a national constitution. The next sub-layer consists of the statutes crafted by legislatures. The statutes either authorize or direct the executive branch to author regulations consistent with the statutes, and those rules—the regulations—make up a further sub-layer. The constitution, statutes, and regulations are the structural elements for most nation-states with organized law. There is generally a hierarchy among the sub-layers; the authority to author regulations is granted by statutes; the authority to author statutes is granted by a national constitution.

PUBLIC LAYER	
FORMAL LAW	FORMAL PRINCIPLES

Formal Principles

The Public Layer also includes *Formal Principles*. While not formally approved or authorized by legislative or executive action, Formal Principles are considered as part of "the law of the land." For example, in nations that derive their history from Great Britain, many of these principles make up the "common law," including, by example, the body of tort law—the right to bring a court action for personal injury or property damages resulting from an action, or failure to act, that causes such injury or damages.

In other nations, principles of natural law are recognized as having legal status by those authoring Formal Law. Agencies, courts, and other governmental authorities confirm the existence of these principles through their publications. For example, the United Nations Universal Declaration of Human Rights expresses a catalog of essential rights (e.g., the right to work, the right to education, and the right of freedom of expression) that can be classified as Formal Principles. However, in many regions and nations, Formal Principles (including those described by that Declaration) are *not* expressed or ratified by Formal Law; their existence is validated, if at all, by Interpretations (discussed in the next section).

Privacy is a preeminent example of a Formal Principle (and integral dimension of digital trust) that has evolved, generally moving from a recognized Formal Principle into Formal Law, but that movement has been inconsistent. Globally, the privacy rights of data subjects expressed in Formal Law vary dramatically, with the EU consistently taking the lead, developing reforms in Formal Law to respond to each new generation of technology. In early 2015, the world was waiting for the EU to finalize an entirely new scheme of Formal Law, the General Data Protection Regulation. Elsewhere, political inertia, power struggles, or cultural conflicts are barricades to responsive reforms. The consequence is that the Rules falling under the privacy umbrella, to the extent that they exist, are distributed among both Formal Laws and Formal Principles.

PUBLIC LAYER	
FORMAL LAW	FORMAL PRINCIPLES
INTERPRETATIONS	INTERPRETATIONS

Interpretations

Interpretations are the publications from a governmental entity that explain how to administer and apply any specific rule or regulation, or evaluate whether one Formal Law (or its application), is in conflict with other Formal Laws or Formal Principles. Both Formal Law and Formal Principles are continuously interpreted in the ongoing operation of governments. In each case, Interpretations are subsidiary to other Rules; they are, in fact, interpreting the application of those Rules in varied circumstances, conditions, or configurations. Described using the trust vocabulary, Interpretations pair and align Circumstances, Resources, Rules, and Costs.

Formal Law and Formal Principles have a parent-child relationship to Interpretations. The choice of those words is intentional; parent-child is also a critical concept in object-oriented software programming and development. Regulations are the children of statutes; Interpretations are the children of the higher layers. For example, published judicial opinions are Interpretations. The opinions of courts have varying weight in shaping the manner in which Rules of the Public Layer are construed, based on the judicial traditions and rules within different legal systems. In many democracies, courts serve as auditors of the legislative and executive branches, with the authority to overrule or declare certain Rules (or their application) to be illegal. In other systems, the courts have lesser authority, but when acting as a venue for resolving disputes, conflicts, and enforcement actions, the courts are still acting as part of the government.

In addition, executive agencies and other publicly sponsored research bureaus or similar entities have the authority to publish guidances that interpret how Formal Law should be understood and applied. Guidances are not formal regulations, but they can be nearly as influential to both the regulators and those they supervise. They assist regulated entities in shaping their behavior to comply with Formal Law and help the agencies prioritize the use of their own enforcement Resources. Agencies publish all sorts of variations of guidances—white papers, frequently asked questions, "best practice" checklists, and model agreements, to name several; however, few are developed through any formal processes of drafts, reviews, public comment, and analysis. Instead, the agencies' professional staff authors and publishes the guidances directly.

When viewed more closely, many Formal Law regulations and Interpretations are the published outcomes of trust decisions. Presented with specific TDCs and TDTs, the authorities are calculating the alignment of SIAM Words found in 'parent' layers to those TDCs and TDTs—the authors are just making trust decisions differently. Circumstances, Assets, Attributes, and Costs can all be taken into account—does the TDT (as described) align to the Rules within a defined TDC?

Courts are always looking backwards, assembling historical facts and evidence required as Decisional Information. They pair and align Context elements to create descriptions of the Circumstances, TDT, and Work performed (or not performed) to evaluate whether an identified Rule was executed. Was the conduct reasonable, appropriate, or suitable to the circumstances? A court is merely calculating "X is Y if," without explicitly using mathematics.

The resulting decision, published as an opinion, expresses new Rules that interpret the alignment between a parent (such as a Formal Law or Formal Principle) (which is "Y") and the moving parts. In trust vocabulary language, it is stating, "When TDC is A, and TDT is B, and Work is C, the Result (X) does (or does not) comply with the existing Rule (Y)." In common law and in some civil law nations, prior Interpretations (such as previous decisions considering other fact patterns under Rule Y) also can be important influences on how a court expresses its reasoning. But behind the court's words in concluding whether the current case aligns to, or may be distinguished from, other prior Interpretations, is a trust decision process. The court is identifying the moving parts and calculating outcomes. Similarities are identified and measured. Distinctions are identified and weighed. Results are computed. Determinations are made whether X complies with Y.

As I complete this book, innovations are being announced here and there that aggregate and dissect the content of judicial opinions differently. The goal is to identify patterns, and develop predictive analytics, regarding how certain judges may evaluate specific combinations of the moving parts in reaching specific outcomes. Essentially, big data analytics are dismantling the content of the opinions, finding patterns, and extracting the Rules judges have employed. The results can be unsettling, exposing biases that specific justices may not explicitly recognize they have. But the innovations are simple to explain using the trust vocabulary—they are identifying the TDCs and the Results, creating pairings, calculating probabilities, and exposing the Work and TDTs that are acceptable (or unacceptable) based on Rules upon which the courts rely.

Agency Interpretations are looking forward into the future. Their publications present model scenarios (describing TDCs) and provide guidance as to which TDTs and Work will or will not comply with a Rule containing SIAM Words: "In the following conditions, the following behavior will (or will not) be the basis for enforcement action under Rule Y."

As noted earlier, these Interpretations help both sides prioritize and align their respective Resources to assure responsiveness to the parent Rules. The agencies use Interpretations to focus their enforcement assets; regulated companies rely on Interpretations as the most precise guidance available for bridging the Chasm of SIAM and gaining confidence that their conduct (as Work) and the Results align to a Rule. In other words, they can trust that compliance will be recognized and sanctions will not be imposed.

The Implementation Layer

Beneath the Public Layer is the *Implementation Layer*. This layer contains the written and unwritten Rules that enable relationships and transactions to exist, operate, and thrive within the boundaries of Public Layer Rules. These Rules are additional "children" of the parent Rules expressed in the Public Layer. The Implementation Layer is similarly constructed with different sectors.

> Agency Interpretations are looking forward into the future.

By design, Public Layer Rules often do not identify fully all of the requirements needed to govern certain conduct, transactions, or types of property. Instead, public policy favors expressing only certain minimum requirements. This is the genesis of contents of the Implementation Layer—the additional Rules, not in contradiction of the explicit Public Layer Rules, that subsequently are created to fully develop and execute the related relationships and transactions. At times, the Public Layer Rules anticipate these additional Rules in silence; at other times, the Public Layer Rules are explicit in describing those minimum requirements (e.g., "SCI companies shall execute agreements addressing the following topics" or "Companies shall adopt and conform to published, recognized standards for information security controls").

PUBLIC LAYER	
FORMAL LAW	FORMAL PRINCIPLES
INTERPRETATIONS	INTERPRETATIONS

IMPLEMENTATION LAYER	
BUSINESS RULES	TECHNOLOGY RULES
INTERPRETATIONS	INTERPRETATIONS

The Implementation Layer has two coequal sectors—the *Business Rules* and the *Technology Rules*. This division is historical, reflecting a separation in how the Rules within each sector have been authored and maintained to date. But the division is *not* structural; coequal means that the Rules within each sector have equal contributions and functionality in any Rulebase and an equal contribution to how trust decisions are made. Culturally and operationally, these sectors are blurring together in the 21st Century; the division between them now is more like a dotted line, the qualities of which we will examine shortly in more detail. Business Rules are increasingly composed for implementation with specific technology (whether as simple as access and identity management or as complex as automated trading decisions for stocks and other securities); Technology Rules more frequently are identifying the Resources and Work that align with Public Layer Rules in a manner historically the exclusive domain of lawyers (such as BSI 10008, a standard published in 2008 by the British Standards Institute stating the Rules for evaluating the admissibility of digital evidence in the courtroom).

The Business Rules

In Western cultures, lawyers are the dominant authors of the instruments within the Implementation Layer that publish Business Rules; in other regions, executives dominate. The instruments are the tools of commerce and organizational governance: contracts, agreements, licenses, codes of conduct, articles of incorporation, bylaws, corporate policies and procedures (on all possible topics— records management, employment, ethical rules, trade practices, occupational health and safety, purchasing practices, etc.), and marketplace rules (such as the rules governing the world's major stock exchanges). These instruments are the building blocks that express the terms of engagement and provide the controlling structures for relationships among government entities, corporations, businesses, cooperatives, guilds, unions, and alliances. Of course, the same structures are present for non-business entities such as neighborhood clubs, civic associations, family groups ("Rules of the House"), property users ("Dublin Recreation Park Rules"), and consumers.

As noted earlier, Business Rules in the Implementation Layer are not written only by lawyers. Corporate executives and managers also will compose and author Business Rules, describing and articulating detailed requirements for the procedures of business. In civil law countries, there remains, based on my own three decades of experience, a preference for having these instruments authored by non-lawyers.

Regardless of their authorship, Business Rules have an important hierarchical quality—they help *navigate* the Public Layer Rules. In most instances, companies and business organizations compose their Business Rules with a conscious awareness of the Public Layer Rules. The use of the term "navigate" is fully intended here. Business Rules are not always authored to *comply* with Public Layer Rules, but they are composed with an *understanding* of their requirements. That is an important distinction, particularly when the Public Layer Rules include SIAM Words for which Public Layer Interpretations do not provide further precision or certainty.

It is important to be blunt here: many lawyers craft Implementation Layer work products to take advantage of the imprecision in Public Layer Rules. To do so, they calculate the probabilities in their heads: "What language in the Implementation Layer product (such as a contract) creates the smallest obligation while still being defensible under the Public Layer Rules?" When attorneys conducts legal research, they seek Public Layer Interpretations that have connections (or pairings) to the related TDCs and Work for which they are authoring their work products. If explicit Interpretations exist, they may constrain the flexibility but create certainty. However, when SIAM Words lack precision, the attorneys go to work.

In many respects, an attorney is applying unconsciously some RCRs to evaluate and measure what a defined set of Public Layer

Many lawyers craft Implementation Layer work products to take advantage of the imprecision in Public Layer Rules.

Rules requires. If, for example, the laws do not require specific tools ("What is the object of the action?"), no defined metrics exist for calculating compliance ("How will performance be measured?"), or an agency lacks enforcement resources ("How will the rule be enforced?"), the attorney will craft related policies (as Implementation Layer Business Rules) to present a veneer of good faith, proposing Resources to be paired with those Rules in varying combinations.

Their business clients calculate the Costs (both Revenues and Expenses) of alternative expressions crafted by the lawyers, balancing and netting Results versus Risks (including the Expenses incurred later for legal fees defending their conduct and the probabilities of enforcement actions). The value of time becomes particularly visible in the internal discussions—the time required to build compliant processes (and create and preserve suitable documentation) will be measured against alternative uses of that time to create new Revenues and "just take the risks" regarding how well their Implementation Layer Business Rules align to the Public Layer.

It is useful, using the trust vocabulary, to understand how an agency or court views this activity. At the Implementation Layer, the corporate policies and procedures are Rules, children of the Public Layer. The corporate policies (as Rules) and corporate Resources are the Assets of a TDT; the TDT is the corporate system or process that must align with the Public Layer Rules. When evaluated, the regulatory agency or court is making a trust decision, asking "Does this TDT align to the Public Layer Rules?" The public entity is evaluating, within a defined TDC, whether the TDT properly performs the Work required by the Public Layer Rule; the attorneys defending a company argue that the TDT is within the boundary contemplated by the SIAM Words within that Public Layer Rule. The regulatory agency or court's decision becomes a new Public Layer Interpretation.

The 21st Century is witnessing an important transition in the priorities for creating wealth. Using technology to automate the execution of Rules, compliance is becoming less expensive than non-compliance. But that means that the Implementation Layer also must be engineered to include the Rules against which technology is designed and used. Policies, procedures, contracts, and manuals expressing the Rules governing Human Resources were sufficient in the 20th Century, but automating compliance now requires similar instruments expressing the Rules for technology.

The Technology Rules

The converging impacts of communication, transport, and publishing technologies that shaped the final decades of the 20th Century introduced levels of interdependence and interactions among our governments, businesses, neighborhoods, and families. 21st Century mobile, always-on technologies are further accelerating that trend. But, even before the Net, the need to connect and interconnect our systems, products, power sources, transportation vehicles, currencies, and tools fueled the formation of communities in which we developed a second type of implementing rules—the standards that enable technology to implement activities authorized under the Public Layer Rules and the Implementation Layer Business Rules. Standards began as the expressed policy architectures for building physical objects of amazing diversity and complexity (such as railroads in the 1800s), but they increasingly are published as expressions of the global measures of due care and diligence with which we construct business management processes and technologies.

Using technology to automate the execution of Rules, compliance is becoming less expensive than non-compliance.

Standards are the primary layer of the Implementation Layer Technology Rules. In many respects, for the global Net, standards are no different than statutes or regulations; they are the controlling Rules for an enormous volume of the technical operations of digital networks, systems, devices, and data structures. Those composing the standards are no different than attorneys or executives composing Implementation Layer Business Rules—they are navigating the requirements of the Public Layer in order to build and operate systems as TDTs. Standards enable companies to engage in business activities and transactions that are permitted by law; standards are never authored to enable companies to engage in activities that violate public law. They also are composed on occasion to enable activities not yet subject to statutes or regulations (for example, there were no laws governing Net-based communications when the first standards for message structures were formulated), but even then they are acting with an awareness of the Public Layer.

Beneath technology standards is an additional portfolio of child instruments similar in function to Business Rule instruments (e.g., policies, procedures, guidelines, service level agreements, interconnection agreements between networks and systems, data sharing agreements, etc.). All of these play the same role—expressing Rules with greater specificity in order to implement higher parent Rules. On the business side, the Rules emphasize the behavior of Human Resources; on the technology side, the Rules are aimed more specifically at the remaining Resources—Code, Data, and the additional Technology & Physical Resources.

There is a dynamic, shifting synergy between the Business Rules and Technology Rules in the Implementation Layer—think of it as a porous, dotted line that separates them. Generally, the Business Rules express the directions in which an organization or community will direct its behaviors, practices, and capabilities; the Technology Rules govern how those objectives can be functionally built and executed with, and across, known technologies. But technology standards also have been published to enable business practices not yet actually in play; sometimes it takes putting the standard in place, even across a small community, for the practice to begin. In doing so, the synergies reverse; the capabilities unlocked by the publication of a technology standard can provide the inspiration and imprimatur for crafting and adopting new Business Rules.

The preference for implementing innovation through Code and Data is shifting the balance between Business Rules and Technology Rules. While displayed as equally sized classes in the URM, that visualization does not reflect the trend toward authoring Implementation Layer work products to fully contemplate the use of information technologies, rather than view the technologies as supplemental add-ons. As a result, the work products of professionals on the technology side slowly are absorbing functions that historically were authored by those on the business side. For example, Six Sigma and similar measurement-based management methodologies logically require measured, technology-based Rules in preference to policies based on, or directly employing, SIAM Words.

Interpretations

Like the Public Layer's Formal Law Rules and Formal Principles, both Business Rules and Technology Rules are supported by *Interpretations*, particularly within corporate management systems. One or more offices or operations have the responsibility to interpret, in specific conditions, (a) whether and how the policies expressed in the higher levels (such as employment non-discrimination policies) are to be applied, or (b) whether certain conduct violated existing Rules. Within corporations, these Interpretations often are published as supplemental procedures to the corporate policy. The semantic and process analyses underpinning the development of these Interpretations is no different than in the Public Layer; within different TDCs, the suitability of different pairings among Resources, Rules, and Costs are evaluated and appropriate children Rules are authored and published.

Added sources of Interpretations are the multitude of informal advisory opinions and decisions made in navigating daily collisions between fact patterns and higher-level Rules. These Interpretations are authored when a specific TDC/TDT/Work pairing has not been fully addressed in those Rules. Companies and organizations constantly pause to ask the kind of questions for which the answers are Interpretations: "Can we do X under the ABC agreement?" "Does our hiring policy allow us to employ Fred's brother?" "Are we required to use two-factor authentication to satisfy our network access control policies?" Certainly a great deal of the advisory work performed by lawyers inside companies is responsive to these types of questions. The answers are new Rules, paired to the described TDC/TDT/Work pairing. These Interpretations further supplement and enrich the scope and application of both the Public Layer and any higher Implementation Layer Rules.

For Technology Rules, the portfolio often expresses Interpretations in high-level design architectures of a specific system, device, or application. These architectures are drafted with an awareness of the standards that apply (both for the overall target as well as specific components), but do not go into enough detail to enable execution without additional Rules.

Currently, a key point of differentiation between Business Rule Interpretations and Technology Rule Interpretations is the level of documentation with which new Rules are documented. Technology Rules require lengthy, technical documentation in order to move to the final URM layer; one simply cannot build Code of any complexity without formal documentation. However, many Business Rule Interpretations are informal—they are the daily decisions that management makes in meetings and in hallway conferences. With increasingly mobile work forces exercising shorter job tenure, companies are finding that the failure to document these decisions formally degrades their internal "institutional knowledge." The solution is to require digital capture of documentation, thereby formalizing and enabling its later recall. But that cannot be done well unless there are the Rules in place for doing so.

The Execution Layer

Execution Layer Rules prescribe the detailed, precise steps of getting Work done in order to fulfill and comply with all higher layer Rules. Execution Layer Rules are, by far, the highest volume of Rules that exist. They govern the specific Resources that will perform, or be used to complete, the Work—be they Human Resources, Technology & Physical Resources, Processes, or Information.

These Rules define the exact processes to be employed with those Resources and specify the Data required, and the Data that will be produced, in performing the Work. Execution Layer Rules tie everything together with precision; these are the ones for which the RCRs are most demanding. At the higher layers, some SIAM Words can persist, but at the Execution Layer the ambiguity of the parent Rules must be replaced with metric-based precision for trust decisions to be calculated well.

There are four sectors of Execution Layer Rules, based on the assets that a Rule targets (these track the Resource classifications presented in Part I).

EXECUTION LAYER RULES			
HUMAN RESOURCES	TECHNOLOGY & PHYSICAL RESOURCES	PROCESS	INFORMATION

Human Resources Rules

People perform Work, whether loading a truck, operating a lathe, typing a letter, developing computer software, or operating computer programs. For each, there are Rules that govern the performance of that Work. Those Rules are organized into this sector; they are the contract of performance between the employer and the employee for the Work the person is required to perform, and they articulate how we will measure and evaluate that performance.

Technology & Physical Resource Rules

This sector includes the Rules that define how we expect physical, tangible assets and information technology assets to operate together (versus how the humans will use these Resources). This sector is not limited to computing—it includes the Rules for any tangible, physical assets that perform Work or are used to enable Work to be performed by Human Resources. Buildings, vehicles, computer devices of all sizes, product packaging with sensor-sensitive labels, RFID tags attached to pallets and containers to track their location, software applications—all of these are governed by Rules within this sector.

Process Rules

This sector includes the Rules that structure the Work performed by all other Resources into consistent processes, workflows, or lifecycles. That is right; Process Rules are both within the URM and a Resource. Rapid standardization is occurring in organizing processes into repeatable sequences of Work. That standardization is a function of the Rules themselves, creating the priority, sequencing, logic, dependencies, and controls that enable processes to exist and function smoothly. Technology's presence in our lives continues to shape how we craft our processes and, in turn, author the related Rules. Even for activities requiring no computer, such as hammering a nail or sipping soup, when asked to describe the process, we are evolving toward more detailed ways of expressing the execution rules. Now we are inclined to be more specific and methodical, expressing Process Rules that incorporate the metrics and reporting that the RCRs contemplate. We are increasing our focus on process and, in doing so, also analyzing and structuring the logic, the patterns of connection, and the efficiencies of alternative configurations of various available Resources into optimal processes that allow us to perform Work more productively. We are constantly seeking new velocity and precision.

Information Rules

Information is the fuel that enables Work to be performed, whether characterized as Data, Decisional Information, or T-Info. Whatever the combination of other Resources assembled to do the Work, Information must be acquired and processed for the Work to proceed. As discussed in Part I, we first use our senses to acquire and record Information about the surrounding TDC. As we engage with, and connect to, TDC_{RES} and TDTs, we also favor those Resources that collect and transform the Information required by the Work.

Of course, IT Resources do even more—processing and outputting Information that enables Human Resources to perform less Work or execute the Work with greater efficiency. Machines use sensors, video cameras, lasers, radio frequencies, content analysis, and other tools to observe and record Data they require to execute the decisions and actions allowed by the Rules governing their behavior. But Information enables all of this to occur only when there are Rules that describe and qualify the Information required by the other Resources.

For example, Execution Layer Rules control and shape the inbound Data each specific Task requires within a larger description of Work, as well as the outbound Data to be reported about the performance of Resources and TDTs when completing the Task. For digital assets (e.g., networks, systems, devices, applications, and Information), these additional Rules for outbound Data are critical to enabling their management, optimizing their performance, and identifying flaws, failures, or persistent shortcomings (i.e., the realization of Risks) requiring remediation or corrective action. Even non-digital Resources, however, cannot be managed effectively without outbound Data reporting their performance. For those non-digital Resources, that Data is reported by other means (e.g., visual observation, oral reports, etc.).

Execution Layer Rules can be numerous for Human Resources! Just think about how many Rules you learn and master in order to drive a car from here to there, operate a lathe or press on a manufacturing floor, or do your Work making decisions as an intensive consumer of Information. When the Resources are machines, such as printing presses or steam railroad engines, the volumes of Execution Layer Rules further increase because they must be mapped into and executed by the machine with persistent precision. The Rules of mathematics, physics, and other sciences that we navigate in doing Work must all be identified and integrated into the design and functionality of our machines.

Of course, when information technology is introduced, Execution Layer Rules morph into even greater volume and complexity. That complexity is what enables IT to perform consistently, repeatedly, and successfully against the Rules we author. Each line of Code is a separate instruction to be executed; any single application can contain tens of thousands of lines of Code. Each component of any system may include dozens of applications that must operate simultaneously in order for the components to Work cohesively, constantly seeking inbound Data and generating outbound Data, all defined by the Rules expressed in Code. Just take a look at the list of programs on your desktop computer to get a sense of that magnitude—they are just the tip of the iceberg.

The quality and substance of Execution Layer Rules will determine where governance will succeed or fail.

Information architecture; information systems engineering; software development—all of these professional disciplines involve authoring Rules. Their Work is creating Execution Layer Rules, defining and shaping how the Rules in each of the four sectors of this Layer shape how people can interact with and use technology to complete defined Work and Tasks, and direct technology to perform Work aligning with known, prescriptive Rules. In the 21st Century, our dependence upon information technologies continues to increase; ultimately, and sooner rather than later, the quality and substance of Execution Layer Rules will determine where governance will succeed or fail.

When comparing the Execution Layer with the higher layers, you may have observed that Interpretations are conspicuously absent. Their omission here is entirely logical and intentional. Execution Layer Rules are the final word on how Work is to be performed. The Rules are granular in their level of specificity, focused on specific Tasks, and express how we expect Tasks to be performed and how we will measure their performance. Should Results indicate that performance of one or more Execution Layer Rules is not achieving the metrics expressed by the related definition of Work (or a specific Task), we make changes in the related Execution Layer Rules rather than author and publish Interpretations. While it is inevitable that some Interpretations are made without changing the Rules, the Unified Rules Model does not accommodate that method of governance. Instead, by emphasizing their absence, the need for revising Rules to improve Results is more explicit.

COMPLETE VIEW

Here, then, is a complete view of the layers and sectors of the Unified Rules Model.

PUBLIC LAYER			
FORMAL LAW		FORMAL PRINCIPLES	
INTERPRETATIONS		INTERPRETATIONS	
IMPLEMENTATION LAYER			
BUSINESS RULES		TECHNOLOGY RULES	
INTERPRETATIONS		INTERPRETATIONS	
EXECUTION LAYER RULES			
HUMAN RESOURCES	TECHNOLOGY & PHYSICAL RESOURCES	PROCESS	INFORMATION

The URM structure is intentionally designed with very large, generalized layers and sectors. This structure allows big picture perspectives in evaluating TDTs. In business and in our regular lives, we often confront situations in which, to evaluate where Rules may need improvement, we must lay out and analyze all of the existing Rules. The same is true in designing an innovation; like a building architect, we must identify and organize the Rules into structured Rulebases (even if we do so without the formality of a database structure and try to do so in our heads). The URM enables visualization of these processes. As Rules are identified, sorted, and aggregated into the appropriate layers and sectors, many of the Results described by the Project Innovate team are being achieved by the URM.

SOME KEY OBSERVATIONS ABOUT THE URM

Several further observations are appropriate to offer at this stage:

> As mentioned earlier for the Public Layer, none of the layers or sectors of the URM reflect *any proportional sizing* based on the volume of Rules within each layer or each sector. Until a specific Rulebase is developed, it is not responsible to suggest any particular visual sizing of layer versus layer, or sector versus sector. However, properly using the RCRs, experience suggests that the Execution Layer, once populated, will have the largest number of Rules, with the Rules for Technology and Information being the largest in overall volume. This outcome may surprise some, particularly with the general awareness and increasing volume of Public Layer Rules addressing security, privacy, and control. But compliance with those Rules, many of which are SIAM-intensive, requires density and precision to be built at the Execution Layer.

> The layers *do not create or require a rigid hierarchy*. But, within and across the layers, hierarchies certainly will exist. The URM enables us to identify and audit those structures, to pair and match the parent and child Rules, and to improve the structural integrity with which we achieve governance outcomes (Results) and avoid adverse events (Risks). So often, when a Rulebase or Compliance Rulebase is evaluated with the RCRs, gaps become visible—parent Rules at one layer lack any child Rules in the Implementation or Execution Layers.

The mechanisms for measuring performance and assuring execution are missing, creating compliance and governance Risks. The URM responds to this by encouraging the design of logical parent-child structures into Rulebases, which has enormous benefits toward improving governance:

> If there is a Public Layer Rule, what are the connecting Implementation Layer Rules?

> If there are Implementation Layer Business Rule Interpretations, have those been mapped into Execution Layer Rules to assure the consistency of our operations?

> If Execution Layer Rules are directing Resources to generate outbound performance Data, are those reports properly rolling up into the higher layers of governance to demonstrate proper execution and governance?

Therefore, as new Rules are authored and published (itself a Work effort), the URM and RCRs work collaboratively as Resources that enable quality control. A "good" Rule can be linked and chained across the layers. If that structure cannot be visualized, the Risks are no different than relying solely on SIAM Words to express requirements.

≫ The URM is designed to *function globally*, without regard to the governance requirements of a specific legal system or size of organization. The URM provides an architecture that, at first glance, is deceptively simple. But that simplicity enables us to assemble and analyze any Rulebase with far greater focus on the structural relationships among the Rules and their alignment with the RCRs. Evaluating the source (statute, corporate policy, contract, application code, etc.) and the Resources, the proper placement of a Rule within the layers and sectors can be easily determined. Doing so has an important implication: a Rule is being decoupled from its source and viewed autonomously. No single professional or author of a Rule has exclusive authority to interpret what a Rule requires. Instead, once placed within a specific layer or sector, the URM design and the RCRs drive additional questions that enable more thorough expressions of what is required for compliance with that Rule. For example:

> With a Public Layer Formal Rule (such as a regulation), are there Interpretations that must be identified and evaluated for their applicability and requirements?

> With an Implementation Layer Business Rule (such as the rules of a commercial agreement), does the Rule require us to acquire technology to perform the Work? Is the Rule explicit regarding any connecting Technology Rules (i.e., "A company handling personal information shall implement security controls that may be certified under ISO 27001")? Do Technology Rules exist that enable the Business Rule? If not, must those Rules be authored to

bridge between the Implementation Layer and the Execution Layer?

With an Execution Layer Rule, do related Rules describe, connect, and pair to Rules within all four sectors for the Resources engaged (Human Resources, Technology & Physical Resources, Process Rules, and Information)? Does the Rule have an explicit parent connection, allowing the outbound Data to document how performance of the Execution Layer Rules advances and accomplishes the governance objectives of the higher layers? If not, should the company author and publish a more tangible, explicit Implementation Layer Business Rule by which the Execution Layer Rules will be managed?

The URM eliminates SIAM Words as the final expression of how to measure compliance.

These types of questions are not easy to ask, nor are they easy to answer. That may explain why they so often are overlooked or given short attention. But the questions illustrate an important feature of using the URM—to encourage and require authoring and maintenance of Rules at the Public Layer and Implementation Layer with the same design structure and integrity that we are accustomed to using when authoring Execution Layer Rules. Yes, for the Digital Age, the URM eliminates SIAM Words as the final expression of how to measure compliance.

USING THE URM

In its simplicity, the URM enables visual distribution and viewing of a business process' existing folio of Rules. Much like the current culinary practice of "deconstructed" dishes, in which the components of a familiar dish (such as apple pie) are disassembled and reassembled, the URM allows the content of that folio to be broken apart. Rather than having a collection of all of the Rules known to management, the URM then enables us to sort the folio's contents, assigning each Rule into a layer and, as applicable, a sector. As we do so, the URM allows us to develop associations, groupings, and clusters among different Rules. When a Rule directly references or cites a parent ("These regulations are adopted pursuant to Revised Code Sec. 1234.56"), that association is obvious. But some Rules are more challenging to map, not unlike the experience in middle school of learning to diagram the structure of a sentence. But finding those chasms or logic gaps in a folio of Rules is exactly how we can and must improve governance to build digital trust.

Once we have sorted Rules among the layers and sectors, we can repeat the process, enabling identification of logical relationships for the Rules within each sector and among the layers. A unified view of the folio that allows us to organize, structure, and access the entire Rules inventory, the URM enables us to see the full picture of the Rules that govern our Work.

In doing so, the gaps and chasms (including any Chasms of SIAM) become more visible and show us where to focus to improve the governance of the related Resources. Similarly, given the chance to construct a new Rulebase rather than evaluate an existing folio, the URM helps developers more accurately account for and evaluate the Public Layer and Implementation Layer Rules. They then can design the Execution Layer Rules (literally authoring the Code of an application itself) with a sense of the relationships to the other layers. This improves the ability to provide a proof that the Code and Process Rules conform to and execute the requirements of the higher level rules.

THE PREREQUISITES FOR UNLEASHING THE URM

The full design power of the URM requires, as prerequisites, certain additional, supportive Resources. These added Resources enable the URM to be integrated with other emerging design technologies, whether used to design buildings, products, processes, or information systems.

Uniform Naming Convention

We must develop a uniform naming convention that identifies any Rule consistently within and across the URM. The naming convention will assign a unique identifier to each Rule, one that stays with the Rule and becomes the reference number upon which we rely throughout the Rule's existence.

One of the biggest challenges in migrating existing Public Layer Rules into a structural model such as the URM is the complete absence of consistency in how specific statutes, regulations, and interpretations are indexed, labeled, and organized. Different, comparable jurisdictions (nations, states, counties, cities, towns) have adopted individualized naming structures for their rules. Statutes are organized into articles, chapters, sections, and the like, with each uniquely named and structured for each jurisdiction. Text titles are non-uniform; numeric references are non-uniform; and sub-sections of statutes are identified with different schemes.

For example, Ohio and Indiana are adjoining states, each with a "Code" in which statutes are organized (Ohio calls it the "Ohio Revised Code"; Indiana calls it the "Indiana Code"). Ohio's statutes for motor vehicles are set forth in Title 45; laws governing the licensing of motor vehicles are in Chapter 4503; and the statute requiring the owner of a manufactured mobile home to pay a real property tax is in Chapter 4503.06(A). Indiana's statutes for motor vehicles are set forth in Title 9; the statute for requiring mobile home owners to pay real estate taxes appears in IC9-17-6-15.1(a).

Adoption and application of a uniform naming convention to existing laws is extremely challenging. In the United States, a National Conference of Commissioners on Uniform State Laws (or NCCUSL) works to develop uniform statutes that individual states may enact. If enacted by the states as developed, these statutes can accelerate uniformity enabling interstate commerce and regulated entities to operate with greater efficiency and predictability. However, each state has the discretion to act with regard to any uniform law NCCUSL recommends. A state may enact the uniform law as written, approve modifications to the uniform law, or simply elect not to enact the uniform law at all. The process is consensus-based and, on more than one occasion, the final work of NCCUSL faces sufficient opposition at the state level that uniformity never results.

The United Nations Commission on International Trade Law (UNCITRAL) functions in a similar manner. Focusing on topics as varied as international commercial arbitration, electronic commerce, credit transfers, and cross-border insolvency, UNCITRAL develops and approves model laws that nation-states may enact. But their adoption is entirely at the discretion of each country and, for various political and economic reasons, certain model laws never progress forward into enactment.

Indeed, both NCCUSL and UNCITRAL often struggle merely to sustain uniformity in the content of drafted legislation. On many occasions, competing forces at the drafting venue will recommence their hostilities at the enacting level, resulting in amendments and modifications that create non-uniformity in the approved, enacted versions. Even when uniformity outweighs the nonconforming

The costs
of manually
charting and
mapping how
to conform
a business
process to
differing Public
Layer Rules
across multiple
jurisdictions
are intensive.

attributes of any Rule in the Public Layer, the absence of a naming convention makes it more difficult to organize the various laws into an architecture that allows us to chart and map similarities and differences. While commerce and government are not crippled by the inability to do so, the costs of manually charting and mapping how to conform a business process to differing Public Layer Rules across multiple jurisdictions are intensive. The difficulties that currently exist in achieving global privacy compliance are an obvious example.

But creating a shared naming convention *is* possible and computationally feasible. To be successful, a naming convention for Rules should embrace the same principles for developing and enhancing its content that have enabled open source code to be successful. The Open Source Initiative describes open source as software that can be freely used, modified, and shared. While there is still ownership, the licensing of open source allows continuous modification and refinement. Open source is growing in its appeal, particularly in large, multinational businesses, because of the ease with which the Rules expressed and executed by the Code can be examined, assessed, and modified.

Tens of millions of Rules exist globally. A successful naming convention must allow flexibility and rapid evolution of improvements, in contrast to the rigorous, consensus-based means with which Public Layer Rules and Technology Rules (standards) are approved. The likely strategy for evolving a uniform naming convention will be organic, beginning in the smaller communities, associations, or political districts where consensus is easier to accomplish, adoption is easier to promote, and the complexity of the Rules to be named is lower and less daunting. That is actually how many standards begin, and it is a proven method with which to proceed here.

Properly designed, a naming convention can exhibit a taxonomy—a structure—that both functions for machine-based processing and analysis and also has human-readable, comprehensible elements. It allows each identifier to open a portal to useful information about the Rule:

> Convey the geographic region or systems within which, and for which, the Rule has been adopted.

> Communicate context and ownership, identifying the layer and sector in which the Rule resides, and, within each layer and sector, the more specific sources and authors of the Rule.

> Illustrate the structure of a Rule, and its relationships to other Rules.

Differences between two comparable identifiers (for example, the identifiers for the Ohio and Indiana mobile home taxation rules) may help isolate their differences and similarities. The identifiers, and the larger taxonomy, also provide a framework against which we can associate other layers and Rules. In effect, a naming convention reinforces the URM bias to enable each Rule to be a logical parent or child within the structure.

Controlled Vocabulary

With no fanfare or broad, global announcements, the Net has been driving remarkable transformations in the language and vocabulary for describing the capabilities of any Net-based Resource. A critical aspect of automating processes (and authoring Rules that enable automation to be performed consistently) is developing accuracy in the meanings assigned to specific symbols, combinations of symbols, words, and phrases. Rules, in their essence, are merely instructions. At the Execution Layer, enormous investments have been made to develop and maintain the Resources that deliver controlled vocabularies—data dictionaries, relational tables, and vocabulary models.

The results are often astounding to discover. Under the United Nations sponsorship, robust vocabularies exist for structuring and expressing the terms for international trade and commerce. The Object Management Group (OMG) has adopted the Semantics of Business Vocabulary and Business Rules (SBVBR), a standard that enables the interpretation and use within computer systems of both formal and natural language descriptions of Rules within a business. In Europe, a continent divided by multiple languages and bound together by the strength of a single currency, significant work is underway to develop uniform rule modeling languages. A Simple Rule Markup Language (SRML) and the Semantic Web Rules Language (SWRL) also exist, each allowing business rules and processes to be expressed and enabled across the Net.

In some respects, the URM concept itself is quite modest. It merely invites leveraging the enormous progress already achieved to develop the consistent vocabularies for IT-enabled governance upward across all layers of rulemaking, establishing and extending across all of society's governance systems a structured, consistent architecture. What is required is to assure that nouns, verbs, and metrics have precise meaning. The problem is not easy; for example, the word "document" has different meanings under the American legal rules governing evidence, the ISO standard for information security, and the ISO standard for records management practices. The challenge of a controlled language will not be solved until we can reconcile those meanings so that, when a specific word, phrase, or identifier is used in a Rule, we have clarity regarding its intended meaning.

In effect, there is an ongoing struggle between those who are defending the value and utility of SIAM Words and those who are engineering automated processes that, by their very nature, require the precision of controlled vocabularies in order for Rules to be authored and executed as intended. Think back to the first pages of this book and the discussions about control, trust, and those vested in protecting the profitability of patching Dead Man's Curve rather than building something new. The struggles to establish controlled meaning are the trenches in which the war for control is the most vicious.

Consistent Rule Structure

One further predicate is required: a consistent template architecture within which we can express Rules. To be useful and *not* political, rules must be complete expressions. Rules that omit critical elements do nothing to enable efficient alignments and compliance with the related activities, actions, processes, actors, or assets that the Rules are intended to govern. Either a Rule is authored with all of those elements in place or it is designed to be supplemented by related Rules (as parents or children) that enable the emerging Rulebase to be complete. Conversely, Rules that are orphans, without a proper place within a larger governance architecture, do little to advance governance.

What does such a template include? The Rules for Composing Rules (RCRs) suggest the elements. The RCRs can be effective across all of the URM layers, providing clear, objective, measurable guidance for composing strong Rules that allow us to calculate trust decisions based on those Rules more effectively. A Rulebase for a TDT,

> The struggles to establish controlled meaning are the trenches in which the war for control is the most vicious.

built on the structure of the URM, using the RCRs, and implementing uniform naming conventions and consistent vocabulary, is the final product.

RETURNING BACK TO THE FUTURE

At the outset of this chapter, the Project Innovate team expressed the Results they required to synchronize the tools into a coherent TDT for engineering digital trust. The URM is the first of two tools designed to respond to, and achieve, those Results. But the URM does not address all of them; the second tool finishes the job.

That tool is the Unified Information Model.

THE TRUST VOCABULARY
In this chapter, you will learn the following words:

Activity Description
Activity Description Information
Content Elements
Content Layer
Descriptive Elements
Descriptive Layer
External Evaluations
External Performance Metrics
Evaluation Layer
Internal Performance Metrics
Navigation Layer
Unified Information Model

CHAPTER 19

THE UNIFIED INFORMATION MODEL

ACROSS ALL OF ITS WORK, Project Innovate had accomplished a great deal. Originally tasked to control the information assets of RHK, it had gone much further. In doing so, the importance and role of digital Information in the future of its business evolved. The team realized that soon all Information useful to the company would be "born digital." In electronic form, Information was not only an essential fuel required for all decisions; Information was becoming a new kind of property, the value of which RHK would measure by the quality of its Information creation and maintenance governance practices. Calculating the quality of governance required further Information, all digital, to fuel the trust decisions evaluating that governance.

In the same manner it had recognized the layers of Rules, the team realized Information existed in layers. It hypothesized that each Information layer fueled different layers and segments of the decision chains within any trust decision, enabling the Rules within those layers and segments to be fired. If trust was a rules-based decision, and the team wanted to complete its work to enable affirmative calculations of trust in Information, it needed further structure in order to align Rules more precisely with Information.

Dissection teams independently created white-board visualizations of these layers. Then, as before, the "rules of the house" stimulated dialogue, collaborative exchanges, and movement toward consensus. While information science and knowledge management had made enormous progress using their professional disciplines' precepts, those representing the team's other disciplines viewed the structure of Information with less precision. Across any decision chain for a TDT, Information was observed to serve different purposes during different frames, often working concurrently to advance the decision process at different layers. The team struggled to categorize and classify those layers.

TRUST REQUIRES TRUTH

From one of the dissection teams, a realization emerged that changed the conversations—trust requires truth. Information is only useful to business decisions if it can be confirmed to be factually accurate. Calculating trust in Information requires reaching a conclusion on the probability that the Information is an authentic record of an event, a transaction, or any element of the TDC. To be trusted, Information must be truth. When there is less than the full, accurate truth, Decisional Information Risk is again present. As with other insights, the team realized that every trust decision for any TDT has the same requirements for the Information required by the Rules. When Information is the TDT (such as an inventory list or customer profile used to process shipments), the need for validation of truth is even greater. As Sonmi-451 stated in David Mitchell's *Cloud Atlas*, "Truth is singular. Its 'versions'

Information is only useful to business decisions if it can be confirmed to be factually accurate.

are mistruths." To affirmatively calculate trust, Information as a TDT requires an affirmative calculation of the probability of its authenticity.

THE UNIFIED INFORMATION MODEL

The *Unified Information Model (UIM)*, adopts a structure similar to the Trust Decision Model and the Uniform Rules Model, anticipating the sequential processes and layers. For it to be useful in any trust decision, the UIM requires Information to be viewed in layers. The top layer supports the early frames of any trust decision. If a trust decision progresses, the additional UIM layers present additional Information as fuel for the Rules that drive later sequential decision chains.

At the same time, each frame of a trust decision generates new Information as outputs that may be bound together and carried sequentially to the next frames and decision chains. The same process unfolds within each trust decision, with Information, properly validated at each exchange point, ultimately supporting the Functional Calculation, Value Calculation, and Process Calculation of any trust decision.

As in the prior chapter, the UIM is best understood by focusing directly on its structure and utility apart from the story of RHK Enterprises. However, as you read through this chapter, imagine how the Project Innovate team might be integrating the UIM with the other tools to achieve its objectives. You also may think back to the CIO at Wise Industries and the challenges she faced. Consider how she and her team might have navigated those challenges if the URM and UIM, along with the RCRs and Digital Trust Design Principles, had been part of their strategic arsenal.

The full image of the UIM appears later in this chapter; as before, its components are unfolded between here and there.

The Descriptive Layer

The Trust Decision Model emphasizes that the early frames focus on acquiring descriptive information about the Context, drawing lines that shape the TDC and identifying the TDC_{CIR} and TDC_{RES} that are known and visible. Recall that a TDT nearly always is constructed of multiple Resources. The *Descriptive Layer* is where the related Information for those Resources is placed and classified.

DESCRIPTIVE LAYER

The actual classification of a TDC_{RES} or TDT (whether as a Physical Asset, Human Resource, Data, etc.) does not affect how we gather and organize related Information in the Descriptive Layer. And, as with the URM and other tools presented in this book, the UIM works equally well for any TDT, whether or not the TDT is itself digital Information.

In order for a trust decision to proceed forward, a DM first develops a description of the various moving parts requiring evaluation (the TDC, TDC_{CIR}, TDC_{RES}, a specific TDT, etc.). The DM will use the Information organized in the Descriptive Layer to develop and refine the related Descriptive Specifications and Functional Specifications that the trust decision calculations will require. For the purposes of what follows, imagine that you have progressed to that point in the process, perhaps just before T Minus and Holding, where you are calculating whether to trust a specific digital sales report for the Southeast Region you found on a server somewhere within the global network of your business. That report is now the

The UIM works equally well for any TDT, whether or not the TDT is itself digital Information.

TDT. Ahead of you on your calendar is a meeting with the Board—you need to trust the report as truth to succeed in your meeting.

DESCRIPTIVE LAYER		
DESCRIPTIVE ELEMENTS	CONTENT ELEMENTS	ACTIVITY DESCRIPTION

Descriptive Elements—The first sector of the Descriptive Layer, labeled as *Descriptive Elements*, includes just that—the Information that presents factual, descriptive qualities and characteristics of the TDT. Descriptive Elements are objective; Rules exist that express the features and qualities we need to identify. The Rules and related Descriptive Elements are paired together, in that the Rules tell us what Information we must gather or access to assemble the Descriptive Elements that the TDT requires. The actual Rulebase assembled for any TDT is, of course, shaped by the interactions and progressions across the layers and frames of the Trust Decision Model; it is as dynamic and susceptible to R & R as any other part of the decision process.

For books, magazines, and other content assets now created and preserved digitally (each being a TDT for someone), the density and diversity of the Descriptive Elements is astounding. Think for a moment about this book. Whether you are reading a physical version or an e-book, the Descriptive Elements are similar, as are the related Rules. Information fields identify the book's key attributes—primary title (*Achieving Digital Trust*), secondary title (*The New Rules for Business at the Speed of Light*), author name (Jeffrey Ritter), date of publication (2015), physical page count (#), digital size (#GB), ISBN number (physical version), ISBN number (electronic version). These Information objects are the

Descriptive Elements that anyone uses for this or any book. They are immediately visible and are part of the Descriptive Specification for this book, indispensable for finding it at any point in its lifecycle—search, locate, retrieve, purchase, open, use, store, etc. The cover images are part of the Descriptive Elements as well—in retail publishing, publishers very much want you to judge (and buy) the book by its cover! What Rules do you have for how a book cover communicates Information?

Content Elements—The Descriptive Layer's second sector, *Content Elements*, includes Information providing more substantive detail for a TDT. For a Physical Resource, this may be the Information under the "Product Specifications" tab on a retail site, or the list of ingredients on a sealed box of morning cereal. When Information is the TDT (such as the sales report or this book), Content Elements introduce additional descriptive details of the content, such as an executive summary or the descriptive content on the back cover. Content Elements also can be authored and assigned to a TDT by third parties, such as librarians (or a third-party service provider on which they rely, such as OCLC, which maintains a global catalogue on library holdings, listing over two billion holdings, www.oclc.org). A book's Dewey Decimal Classification number is a Content Element. The number enables the unique placement of the book into library catalogues, and provides a structural and relational description of the content to other books. Indeed, OCLC lists over 40 fields for its fixed-field elements from which to construct a data record on a content asset.

For the sales report, and so many other Information assets required in business as TDTs, omissions, inconsistencies, or errors in the Descriptive Elements and the Content Elements are often major obstacles in finding the right asset. The emerging discipline of Information Governance is nothing more than a more systematic, technology-enabled business process for authoring and executing the Rules to develop better Descriptive Elements and Content Elements for Information and Data assets. In many respects, the functional need for both Descriptive Elements and Content Elements is emphasized by the difficulties of navigating the obstacles. When these two sectors are incomplete (based on the relevant Rules), Decisional Information Risk is the outcome and the Expenses increase as Time is consumed overcoming the obstacles. The sales report is missing the name of the supervising regional director; do you still submit a request to bring it up on your screen, only to find that the report never was reviewed by the director? Time is consumed, and decisions delayed, when Descriptive Elements and Content Elements are inadequate.

Activity Description—The Descriptive Layer's third Sector, *Activity Description Information (ADI)*, includes objective Information about the origin, transit, access, and management of a TDT. For TDTs that have nothing to do with digital, ADI is often important to our trust decisions. "Made in China" is ADI for a hammer; current courier services provide real-time transit tracking of merchandise; "stored in a smoke-free home" appears in some eBay seller product descriptions. These Information assets are responsive to the Rules of DMs that focus on the origin and handling of the TDT prior to its possible acquisition by a DM. What actions have occurred with respect to a TDT? ADI is the record of provenance for any TDT.

Of course, in the digital space, ADI is intense in volume and detail for nearly any Resource or TDT, whether a network, system, device, application, or other Information. Your keyboard has become a surveillance device capturing ADI at the keystroke level;

> Time is consumed, and decisions delayed, when Descriptive Elements and Content Elements are inadequate.

the Internet of Things is nothing more than an ADI capture grid. Characterizing the provenance that is evaluated at every exchange point, ADI about TDTs is pivotal to how we build our descriptions and evaluations. When it is absent, there are even further barriers, no different than when a visa permit is not included in your passport at a border crossing.

For the sales report, the omitted name of the supervisor actually was hiding a second Rule requiring ADI: "The report must be reviewed and approved by a supervisor." Even if the name was present, you still want Information to confirm that those supervisory activities were completed to assure that the ADI, if it exists, is responsive. If not, Decisional Information Risk results. Assume you have acquired accurately both the Descriptive Elements and Content Elements (the supervisor's name does appear in the right location), but the version control sheet does not contain the ADI indicating the supervisory activities were completed. You are likely to suspend further evaluation of the report as a TDT while you call the supervisor to ask him directly.

For information systems, the Content Elements are always present; the transparency of the related substantive Information is where the battles for control can be brutal. The same is true for ADI; service providers are more than pleased to deliver the sausage; they rarely want you to have the ADI describing how the sausage actually was produced. But these Information Sectors hold and convey Decisional Information initially so important to how trust decisions are made with respect to digital assets, particularly Information as a TDT. That is why the battles for control exist—the ADI is vital to determining the truth regarding the authenticity and quality of a TDT.

Service providers are more than pleased to deliver the sausage; they rarely want you to have the ADI describing how the sausage actually was produced.

Today, virtually any digital file (the primary Content itself) will have metadata generated and associated with it. That metadata sits within the Descriptive Layer. Users may or may not have the ability to edit or supplement the metadata; for many reasons, including preserving the objective authenticity of the primary Content, more and more metadata is created automatically by the applications and secured against editorial revisions. Metadata enables management of the file, both within the application and in larger efforts to organize and manage digital assets.

Achieving the stability and functionality that is required to do so in a manner that works across different formats, systems, networks, and institutions is essential. It is also darn hard to do. The Dublin Core® Metadata Initiative (DCMI) is perhaps the most ambitious undertaking to do so, emerging from the same OCLC community and its stakeholders that control the library catalog systems (www. dublincore.org). The DCMI designs metadata standards, best practices, descriptive vocabularies and ecologies that will develop descriptive, high-quality data records to sustain the availability of information with legal, cultural, and economic value. This is essential to librarians' and other custodians' ability to organize information assets and integrate them across platforms, systems, or networks; their success enables other users to access additional, related knowledge, and to construct relationships among information assets.

Advancing the DCMI's ambitions requires vocabularies and dictionaries. These semantic tools enable expression of the bibliographic information in a consistent manner, with defined meanings and values. Much of the work to develop these vocabularies currently is executed under the sponsorship of W3C—the World Wide Web

Consortium (www.w3c.org). W3C is enabling the emergence of a global web of linked information—the Semantic Web. Linking data requires descriptive vocabularies that enable the Descriptive Layer Information to be stated consistently, but live, functional capability across the Net requires something more—Rules for handling the Data to which the bibliographic data relates.

Under W3C's sponsorship, enormous, global efforts are underway to develop those Rules. The resulting products are known as Resource Descriptive Frameworks (RDF) and RDF schema, supported by Simple Knowledge Organization System (SKOS), Web Ontology Language (OWL), and the Rule Interchange Format (RIF). All of these enable the functionality of relationship building among Information assets—known as *inference* within the Semantic Web community. RIF and its implications for structuring Rules within the URM are enormous.

What is also impressive about the Semantic Web is that it realistically anticipates that Information is evolving away from the formal structures of books, articles, other physical objects, and their electronic equivalents. Instead, the Semantic Web envisions, and enables, the evolution of different architectures. Those architectures will require Information from the Descriptive Layer and each of its Sectors. Indeed, as Information assets become more numerous and functionally both smaller (text messages, photo images, and blogs rather than books and magazines) and larger (enormous databases that enable big data transactions), the Descriptive Layer content becomes even more vital to the further automation of searches that end users are conducting to find, evaluate, and calculate whether to trust Information needed to perform the Work.

Within the Descriptive Layer, there is no precise hierarchy among the three sectors. As any trust decision advances, a DM's labors to define the TDC, the Work, and the TDT inherently are making multiple, concurrent demands for Descriptive Layer Information to be used as Decisional Information for Rules within the decision chains. Collectively, the sectors within this Layer function collaboratively in their interactions. As each frame of the decision process progresses toward defining the TDC, TDT, and Work with greater precision, these sectors offer all of the responsive Information required by the related Rules. Almost.

The Evaluation Layer

EVALUATION LAYER		
INTERNAL PERFORMANCE METRICS	EXTERNAL PERFORMANCE METRICS	EXTERNAL EVALUATIONS

The distinction between a Descriptive Specification and a Functional Specification suggests the next Layer of the UIM, the *Evaluation Layer*. This layer presents the Information that describes how a TDT performs the Work (and/or specific Tasks within a larger description of Work). Much of the Evaluation Layer Information serves as Decisional Information for Functional Specifications; the Information here is what a DM relies upon to calculate whether the TDT will produce the Results (and avoid the Risks) defined by the Rules for the Work. There are three sectors; in contrast to the Descriptive Layer, however, the divisions between these sectors are more explicit. In this layer, the source of Information becomes important to identifying the appropriate sector for the Information.

Internal Performance Metrics—This sector includes Information generated by a TDT from its own Resources. A tilt-tray conveyor system may count the number of trays per hour via an integrated bar code reader; the digital tablet on which you may be reading this book is monitoring and automatically reporting the pace at which you complete each page; a search engine may generate a report on the time required to perform and generate results. Each of these are examples of *Internal Performance Metrics.*

Internal Performance Metrics are measuring the performance of the TDT itself or its component Resources, so it is important to align the metric and the TDT (or Resources) being measured correctly. For example, if you are reading a printed copy of this book, there are no Resources with which the book generates any type of metrics-based Information. If you are reading an e-book version, your device may display, as a percentage, the progress achieved in consuming the book's Content. But that is not a measure of the book's performance in meeting your Rules for the book as a TDT; instead, the metric is measuring your performance rate at consuming the content. Properly designed, Internal Performance Metrics align to the Functional Specifications for a TDT. They are measures that allow us to calculate progress toward the Results to be achieved in performing the Work (including Revenues and Expenses) and to fulfill the RCRs for measuring and reporting performance.

Within modern management, the Information in this sector is comparable to Key Performance Indicators (KPIs). But the characterization of this sector as *Internal* emphasizes that we must design a TDT's Resources and Rules to generate the performance metrics from within the boundaries of the TDT; reliance upon any external Resource is structurally differentiated within this Layer.

That distinction is important to how we achieve velocity in our calculations; if we do not require an external source, then we do not need a separate trust decision on that source as a Decisional Information Source. Fewer decision chains mean faster calculations.

External Performance Metrics and *External Evaluations*—The two remaining sectors accommodate the Information from the external sources. In many instances, a DM must rely upon external sources to deliver Evaluation Information that fuels a trust decision. A DM who relies on internal observations of a TDT's performance is still a source external to the TDT; hence, the sensory gathering a DM performs creates Information placed within these sectors.

Regardless of the source, objective, measured Information is an *External Performance Metric*; subjective evaluations that lack metric-based reporting ("Jack Bainbridge is a great CEO."; "Their software seems super-fast and reliable.") are *External Evaluations*. The distinction is important when thinking through how a trust decision relies on Evaluation Layer External Information.

When acquiring External Performance Metrics, a DM is accessing Information that is purportedly objective truth—some counting of events or transactions has occurred, just like Internal Performance Metrics. A DM still must evaluate the source (is the speed gun used by an officer a reliable tool for measuring the speed of a vehicle?), but a DM also can evaluate the Process Rules through which the metrics were calculated. (Indeed, many defense counsels have defended their clients on speeding tickets on that very basis, challenging whether an officer followed the proper protocols for using the speed gun.) However, External Evaluations ("He was driving faster around Dead Man's Curve than I have ever seen") do not expose the Process Rules used to reach conclusions nor contain any objective Information about how the Evaluation was calculated (e.g., how many times has the witness observed cars on Dead Man's Curve?). As a result, a DM (such as a judge) must ask different questions of the source, and may never get alternative, objective metrics with which to R & R the trust decision (e.g., was the ticketed driver was actually speeding?). The result is, of course, Decisional Information Risk emphasizing the absence of Evaluation Layer Information.

Crowd-sourcing evaluation platforms (such as a movie with a 3.5-star rating, which has averaged the ratings by 123,127 consumers) are an interesting cross-over, converting multiple External Evaluations into an External Performance Metric that aligns to certain Rules a DM may select for evaluating a TDT ("We only go to horror movies with at least three-star ratings"). In many respects, the capacity to count subjective evaluations and migrate toward objective metrics that technology enables is indicative of how we are, on a global basis, seeking similarly to evolve. Increasingly, our trust decisions tie intimately to metrics.

Indeed, across the Evaluation Layer, the mathematical influence on trust decisions is both direct and substantial. Here is where a DM acquires the Information that allows the calculation of Functional Specifications within the trust decisions. While Evaluation Information from external sources is not bound structurally to a TDT in the same manner as Internal Evaluation Metrics Information, the practical reality is that a DM functionally creates that binding in the trust decision process. In other words, the Evaluation Information is considered as part of the TDT itself, integrated with the other Information used to make a trust decision about the TDT. The UIM reflects that integration—a trust decision for a TDT always requires Evaluation Information.

Evaluation Information is considered as part of the TDT itself.

Remember that, until a final trust calculation occurs, a DM still has not actually used a TDT to perform the Work. But, as a DM progresses through the Trust Decision Model, the Functional Specifications for the TDT continue to require added Decisional Information as those Specifications grow richer in definition and precision. If not generated by a TDT, or from a DM's direct sensory collection, the Information must come from other external sources before the required calculations are made. The Rules for calculating trust in those sources logically will vary based on whether a DM is seeking Descriptive Information or Evaluation Information.

Even partially unfolded to this point, the utility of the UIM to any TDT trust decision is worth illustrating here. Consider your passport. It is a TDT for crossing national borders. An immigration officer relies on this TDT to perform the Work of validating your identity. Its size, color, national symbol, internal page coloring, and imprinted patterns communicate Descriptive Information. The stamps affixed to the pages and the Information within the stamps (such as locations, dates, order of appearance) communicate ADI about you. Security techniques used to assure the authenticity of the passport (such as sealed photo casings, signature images embedded in clear plastic, holographic images, etc.) communicate Internal Performance Metrics; these features of the TDT will preserve evidence of tampering or alterations. Yet most immigration officers are trained to presume most passports cannot be trusted; they rely on their own inspection (External Evaluations), as well as External Performance Metrics in the form of database reports automatically called up by a swipe of the bar code on your passport to verify the ADI.

All of these steps occur as one process, governed by disciplined Process Rules. After all, you and the officer are being viewed by a video camera, which is itself automatically analyzing the collected visual Information against defined Rules describing the Functional Specifications for how the officer and you should behave. As discussed earlier, of course, any Information asset crossing an exchange point undergoes a comparable analysis. But, whether the asset in transit is you or digital Information, the Process Rules for the trust decision integrate all of the Evaluation Layer Information into the same evaluation of the TDT.

The Navigation Layer

NAVIGATION LAYER

Some TDTs are pretty simple, like a hammer or an e-mail from the regional supervisor confirming he did approve the report. Other TDTs, particularly complex digital Information assets (e.g., relational databases, digital encyclopedias, transaction logs, keyboard stroke logs, etc.), are more complex; using them requires some type of navigation. The *Navigation Layer* presents the Information that allows the navigation of a TDT. In a book, this might be the table of contents, something we often review to evaluate the responsiveness of the book to the Work we need to complete. In digital space, the Navigation Layer is more complex and, with the capabilities of the Semantic Web and related Descriptive Layer Information, both dynamic and a bit volatile.

Since the Semantic Web and related technologies are enabling greater detail in the Descriptive Layer, the overview that a table of contents or similar guide (think of the site maps most websites still offer) provides may be unnecessary or not detailed enough. As anyone knows, using any search engine, we can conduct searches directly into the content of a collection of data assets (such as the files in your desktop folders), without relying on any Descriptive Layer or Navigation Layer Information. However, the functionality of doing so is becoming increasingly challenging as the sheer volume and density of digital assets continue to expand (without culling, disposition, or other efforts to reduce those attributes).

But the Navigation Layer still is important. First, this layer already is installed in and used with much of the tangible, fixed information assets we continue to use—books, magazines, user manuals, rice cooker instructions, etc. We expect to find Navigation Layer Information in those assets; the fact that the same information may exist in a digital asset that could be searched without reliance on the Navigation Layer does not dilute our use of that layer when evaluating and working with tangible materials.

Second, for many Information collections, and particularly for Rules inventories (such as statutes, civil codes, regulations, administrative publications, etc.), there has been a lack of progress in structuring the type of consistency in the Navigation Layer Information that the Semantic Web is achieving within the Descriptive Layer. Given the importance of this Information to our decisions to trust, this lack of consistency is astonishing. Remember the discussion in the prior chapter regarding the need for a naming convention as a prerequisite for the full potential of the URM to be realized? We now have a comparable call for a Navigation Layer for the Rules.

Several years ago, NASA was researching alternative uses for satellite capabilities beyond research and military functions. Global legal information (GLI) was identified as one of the most promising targets for using global communication capabilities to enable access, transfer, and use of that information. NASA used GLI to demonstrate large, massively scalable data services that could have global demand. The Net, in many respects, displaced the momentum of NASA's work. The United States' Law Library of Congress assumed responsibility and the Global Legal Information Network (GLIN), emerged, with national governments contributing their official legal documents into a Net-accessible database. GLIN is an outstanding example of a vision that is possible leveraging the Semantic Web, enabling disparate, non-uniform Information assets to be integrated into a much larger, and more functional, Resource. But its status is uncertain and the number of nations using it as an archival mechanism is quite limited in comparison to its potential.

Imagine that you, as a DM, have acquired the Descriptive Information and Evaluation Information required by your Rules but the Navigation Layer is non-existent, rendering you unable to confirm further that you can navigate to the critical Information needed within that sales report you need to consult prior to your upcoming appearance before the Board. You are not even making a trust decision about the report because the absence of a Navigation Layer prevents you from calculating the Functional Calculation. Similarly, because of the uncertainty of the time required to slog through the report, you cannot accurately calculate a Value Calculation. The report is worth far less if you cannot find the relevant Information before the Board meeting at which your recommendation is expected.

The Content Layer

CONTENT LAYER		
CODE/RULES	FACT	FICTION

The final layer is the *Content Layer*. If a TDT is a Human Resource,

Technology Resource, or Process Rule, the specific details about the TDT fill this layer. In reaching this layer, all of the Rules have been satisfied to this point; as the frames of the trust decision progress, a DM has traveled from the Descriptive Layer to the Evaluation Layer and then to the Navigation Layer. Then the moment comes when the TDT is directly there. If the TDT is Information, the Content falls within three possible sectors. For this layer, our analysis begins at the right side.

Fiction—The first sector is *Fiction*. While films, novels, and short stories certainly are Information that sit within this sector, it has a far more important role in business decisions and processes. Fiction is Information that we have not affirmed to be fact. Remember, trust requires truth. If Information as Content cannot be calculated affirmatively to be truthful and authentic (within the likelihoods of probability defined by the related Rulebase for those calculations), a DM cannot rely upon that Information as a TDT. In computing and in human decisions, the outcome is a null set; the Information is treated as if it does not exist. Big data analytical engines do the same thing with inbound Data at the exchange point; if the Information (as primary Content for the analytical computing Work) is determined not to meet the applicable Rules for ingesting it, the Information is embargoed or filtered out. In other words, it is treated as fictional.

Facts—Of course, *Facts* are what businesses use to make their decisions. As noted in the prior paragraph, when calculating trust in the factual authenticity of Content, probability remains relevant. There is always a Risk of the Unknown Risk that restrains a DM from treating Content as absolute Fact. For any trust decision, the line of demarcation between Fact and Fiction is often difficult to calculate. Now all of the Context and TDC elements become engaged: Circumstances, Resources, Rules, Results, Risks, Revenues, and Expenses. All of the URM layers and prior UIM layers are engaged: What do the Rules require in order to calculate whether Information as a TDT is Fact or Fiction? What UIM layers and sectors contain Information required by those Rules?

Code/Rules—The final sector of the Content Layer is a basket for the Content that is expressed as Rules. The addition of Code in the title emphasizes the importance of software to the Rules for Information. *Code/Rules* includes instruction manuals, procedure guides, and the source and object code of software applications; all are Information, but they are neither Fact nor Fiction. So, within the UIM, they each are classified as Code/Rules. As a DM, you expect any Code or published Rules to be accurate and functional as Information assets, but they are not evaluated based on authenticity. Code/Rules is a Resource, of course, but uniquely structured by the same semantic and language elements with which other Content is constructed. Code, in particular, will also be a part of the Execution Layer Rules, delivering instructions to machines and devices on how to perform Work with other Information and Resources. As noted earlier, to determine to trust Code as a Resource or TDT, a DM navigates the upper layers of the UIM the same as any Resource or TDT. But Code also is Information and also belongs in the UIM. Especially in the 21st Century, Code, as Information, has become one of the most valued TDTs of all, and the most vulnerable to poorly executed trust decisions.

USING THE UIM

The full Unified Information Model looks like this.

Code, as Information, has become one of the most valued TDTs of all, and the most vulnerable to poorly executed trust decisions.

DESCRIPTIVE LAYER		
DESCRIPTIVE ELEMENTS	CONTENT ELEMENTS	ACTIVITY DESCRIPTION
EVALUATION LAYER		
INTERNAL PERFORMANCE METRICS	EXTERNAL PERFORMANCE METRICS	EXTERNAL EVALUATIONS
NAVIGATION LAYER		
CONTENT LAYER		
CODE/RULES	FACT	FICTION

The UIM enables the pairing of Rules to Information and vice-versa. This capability works both for evaluating whether to trust Information as Data (a Resource), or as Decisional Information; in either case, the UIM creates awareness that those evaluations often focus on the higher layers (and the corresponding Rules) rather than the Content Layer itself.

In discussing the challenges of achieving digital trust during the last few years, so often the structure of Rules applicable to specific business processes and assets proved incomplete. The Rules have not connected to, nor taken full advantage of, the layers of Information that exist and can be used to support trust decisions. Instead, we have continued to use SIAM Words as the performance metrics, leaving to future risk managers and regulators the responsibility to establish greater precision in the metrics of defining acceptable and expected performance. Similarly, complex systems are generating Information as output Data; however, it is underutilized, sometimes viewed as performance reporting only for one Task or set of Tasks, rather than being leveraged to support larger trust decisions regarding an entire system as a TDT.

The UIM and the URM empower us to use the Digital Trust Design Principles and the RCRs as a collected set of Resources working as a single TDT to achieve digital trust. Yes, that's right—when we apply the Trust Decision Model to calculate whether these are viable tools for performing the Work of achieving digital trust, the outcome needs to be an affirmative trust decision! Behind the curtain, countless hours have been spent building a Compliance Rulebase against which this TDT was constructed as an innovation, with each Resource complementing the others, leveraging existing IT engineering Resources to create something that enables the Work of engineering trust to gain velocity, improve accuracy, and produce the transparency required with which the resulting products, systems, and solutions can be more effectively evaluated.

Information, of course, is the required fuel. The UIM enables the engineering and trust decision process to recognize more accurately how any specific Information asset will be used within any specific frame (and even within the different layers within a frame) of a trust decision. That asset may serve multiple functions, subject to different Rules for each function. The UIM creates transparency into the functions of that asset, whether we have classified it as Information, Data, or Decisional Information. By placing it in different UIM layers and sectors within different trust decisions, we can express the demands on that Information more rigorously as Rules, and can enrich the utility and power of the Information.

T-Info can exist in any UIM layers or sectors; after all, T-Info is functionally equivalent to factual truth for the purposes of calculating trust. But T-Info only exists when we have affirmatively calculated the Rules for being trusted and can support it with accessible Data that provides the required transparency. The UIM achieves those requisites by providing a better sense of the dynamics and pairings among different assets.

THE FINAL CHALLENGE

The Project Innovate team now faced its final challenge. It had confidence in what it created, but now had to pull the strategies, principles, and tools together to demonstrate it could accomplish the true objective for achieving digital trust—creating new wealth for RHK and its shareholders. It was time to respond to the blunt demand of their Executive Vice President: "Show me the money."

CHAPTER 20

CREATING WEALTH WITH DIGITAL TRUST

THE TRUST DECISION MODEL. The Trust Vocabulary. The Statement of Need. The Rules for Composing Rules. The Velocity Principle. The Digital Trust Design Principles. The Unified Rules Model. The Unified Information Model. Essential truths about business. Essential truths about human beings. Strategies to survive and strategies to dominate. The Project Innovate team had accomplished far more than ever imagined. No one was surprised by the investments that the effort had required. But in trust vocabulary terms the team now had to live up to the values expressed by the Design Principles and show that Revenues would exceed Expenses and RHK would achieve new wealth when digital trust was achieved.

ACHIEVING VELOCITY WITHIN ECOSYSTEMS

RHK was a center point within the company's networks of suppliers. RHK was also a point of origin within the global distribution and retail networks through which its goods and services were delivered into the market. Indeed, like any global business, RHK connected into many different business ecosystems. In the 20th Century, an "ecosystem" was a physical, land-based space defined by environmental conditions and interdependencies among living things, for which geography, topography, biology, and environmental conditions shaped the boundaries. A biological system was just like any system; once the components changed (e.g., desert sands replaced rain forests), governed by different rules (including the rules for survival), new system boundaries replaced the previous ones.

In the 21st Century "ecosystem" has gained an additional meaning; the term now also defines virtual digital spaces that are as multi-dimensional and multi-layered as their physical-space counterparts. Networks, systems, devices, applications, and Information establish similar inter-dependencies and pairings as in biological ecosystems. The boundaries for any digital ecosystem are the same as for any system; they are defined by the limits of the Rules that can be enforced by the system's Resources. Changing the Resources means changing the Rules; do so and a different ecosystem is present. For a simple example of the complexity, think about the last time you switched mobile phones with different operating systems.

The Project Innovate team realized that Data had been moving within digital ecosystems with the same fluidity that molecules of air move within biological ecosystems. But the fluidity of Data was a function of the presumption of trust nearly everyone had placed in Information. RHK was not alone in struggling with the rapidly accelerating Expenses for securing and validating Data at every exchange point. Those Expenses were degrading corporate net incomes everywhere, throughout every part of the digital ecosystems in which RHK did business, for all trading partners in all directions. Each supplier, each customer, each joint-venture partner, each licensee, and even each regulatory authority that operated, controlled, and used the components of these digital ecosystems were doing the same thing—patching Dead Man's Curve.

The Board mistakenly had presumed that the solution to gaining control of its corporate Information meant stronger walls, greater defenses, and fewer interactions with the outside world that would expose their systems to threats and malicious actors. The team realized that RHK had to engage with its ecosystems differently, opening the gates to pursue greater, rather than less, interdependence. The competitive opportunity was to share its work within those ecosystems, positioning RHK as a superior "pairing" partner through which T-Info could be acquired and shared. Doing so would lower the trading partners' Expenses by helping them achieve faster, more confident trust decisions in the reliability and functional value of Data that RHK touched. Those lower Expenses meant less friction at the exchange points and, in turn, greater transactional velocity for everyone.

The economics were fascinating. RHK and its partners classified their spending on information security, e-discovery, and GRC (governance, regulation, compliance) as Risk-based Expenses; all of these were being incurred to avoid greater adverse impacts on profits from adverse events—a breach of consumer personal information, a lawsuit ruling based on product design negligence or regulatory laxity, or a degradation of investor confidence because of poor corporate governance. In every company, these were funded by Risk Reserves.

As Data flows increased between RHK and its suppliers, customers, and regulators, each of them were incurring added Expenses to keep up. Each had to validate its trust in RHK's Data by conducting extensive security assessments, negotiating agreements with detailed terms allocating risks of loss, increasing the IT security monitoring staff to examine logs and performance data for anomalies and, as a backstop to those tools, setting aside additional cash allocated to Risk Reserves (for example, to pay for cybersecurity insurance). Each trading partner was factoring every currency unit of these Expenses into larger Trust Discounts they were demanding. Suppliers required higher prices to offset their spending on security and related costs; customers demanded lower prices to reflect their Trust Discounts (and free up the cash required to pay for their own IT security costs). Whether upstream or downstream, within each ecosystem, the optimal pricing for both sides was being offset by the combined economic costs of the patches.

LOOKING UPSTREAM

Looking upstream (toward Resource suppliers, such as those supplying raw materials; production inventory; financing sources; and other TDC_{RES} required to operate RHK's business), Project Innovate realized RHK could lower Expenses to acquire or use those Resources if it could accelerate the velocity of Data coming into the company and calculate that Data to be T-Info earlier. The Data was a concurrent supply asset moving in parallel to the actual Resources being acquired. Compressing each measure of Time in processing that Data created lower overall Expenses. Every inbound Data asset was crossing multiple exchange points within (and therefore controlled by) RHK. At each, there was friction (and Expense) to implement protections against such Risks as malware, spam, and non-conforming Data. The Expenses pressured RHK to negotiate for lower prices, essentially embedding a Trust Discount (based on Data-based Risks) into how RHK established pricing for the primary Resources flowing into the company.

The Innovate team theorized that helping those trading partners create and deliver Data already aligned to RHK's Compliance Rulebases for validating Data could create new velocity and lower Expenses. It was no different than just-in-time manufacturing; to make that work, quality control shifted from the manufacturer's inbound docks to the supplier's facilities. Now, the product requiring quality assurance was the inbound Data, which was itself Decisional Information for managing the flow of inbound goods and services. Both the suppliers and RHK would benefit if that Data conformed to shared, full Rulebases from inception.

LOOKING DOWNSTREAM

Data flowing from RHK headed in a number of commercial directions. First, supporting RHK's internal operations, there were the Cloud-based service providers receiving Data, processing Data, and creating accessibility to Data for RHK and its trading partners. Second, distribution, transportation, and retail partners received outbound Data, often serving as Decisional Information for their related transactions in goods and services. Third, RHK's customers were both corporations and individuals, purchasing wholesale and retail, direct and online.

Commercial retail operations had incurred substantial, unexpected headaches to comply with the new PCI requirements for credit card processing; now the team understood those as Data-based Expenses directly funded out of Risk Reserves against the possibility of fraudulent cards and identity theft. The same was true for major corporate customers of RHK's manufactured and processed products; their trading partners all shared interdependencies on the Data flowing between them, yet everyone was incurring comparable Expenses and embedding Risk Reserves and Trust Discounts into their pricing negotiations.

The Data-based Risk Reserves and Trust Discounts were diminishing the actual price of goods and services in all directions even though no one was able to say precisely how much those prices were affected. Realizing this, the team then could see potential economic opportunities and in every direction. Reduce those Expenses for suppliers and raw materials, and RHK could acquire other operational services at lower costs. In turn, RHK could reduce its internally redundant Expenses, aggregating savings that would allow it to set more aggressive retail pricing for its goods and services while concurrently increasing the loyalty of existing customers and attracting new customers. Focusing on digital trust meant igniting and motivating all of the ecosystems in which RHK existed to work toward collaboratively building digital trust. Win-win-win in all directions, upstream and downstream . . . at least theoretically.

ACHIEVING VELOCITY WITH GOVERNMENT

The Data interchanges with public sector agencies and regulators, including judicial disputes, presented a different challenge for the Innovate team. Unlike commercial relationships, at first glance RHK lacked the potential to create favorable economic outcomes. There were no pricing models with the public sector that the company could manipulate. But the Legal dissection team, with a little nudge, started looking at the total Expenses incurred to create and submit Data to meet mandatory legal regulations for reporting and disclosure on corporate operations. The results were alarming.

Previously, RHK had counted only the direct Expenses incurred within Legal (including payments for outside law firms and technology support firms such as e-discovery process vendors). Recently, Legal had submitted more funding requests to bring technology into these processes, but the projected returns on investment kept falling below the line; the CFO office forecasted Expense reductions that were not competitive with other spending proposals.

The dissection team began digging deeper into the full portfolio of Legal's activities—analyzing email chains; broadcast emails tied to specific reports; "seek and find" exercises within non-Legal departments responding to requests from Legal, Audit, and Compliance; report development time within those non-Legal departments, including supervisor mediations of drafts and revised drafts toward the final published report; supplemental due diligence (a T Minus and Holding activity); and the start and finish times for queuing and review prior to senior management sign-off. Everything changed when the team initiated similar dissections on the non-Legal departments, tracking and allocating a ratable share of the time spent on each of these activities, tracing the Resources expended, and adding up the cumulative Expenses.

The team discovered that the activity-based costs for finding, assembling, validating, and publishing Data to regulatory authorities were far greater than had been calculated previously by only focusing on Legal. At every level of the business, from job applications to leveraged financing transactions, creating regulatory disclosures constructed from corporate Data assets and validating their integrity to avoid potential added enforcement audits or sanctions was time-intensive! Increased regulations, including rules such as the SEC SCI Rule, were compounding the volumes of Data accessible to public authorities (including, but not limited to, U.S. operations), and every department was diverting Resources to build and maintain that accessibility. To sustain operations in some nations, the transparency required by the governments was intensely intimate.

As RHK was shifting more and more to outsourcing models with its upstream suppliers, and its downstream customers did the same toward RHK, the team uncovered added Data-based Expenses that had not been previously considered by the CFO in calculating savings. Upstream and downstream, the outsourcing contracts imposed new, added duties on a service provider to create and maintain operational Data for a customer that the law required the customer to maintain. RHK was demanding these services from its suppliers and was responding to customer demands to do the same.

These shifts created an enormous opportunity for expressing the value of achieving digital trust. In effect, the service provider was becoming the author and custodian of Data that the customer then acquired and integrated into its regulatory disclosures and reporting. (You may recall this is the same problem that the Wise Industries CIO faced. She had struggled to secure from the vendors the performance data reporting she was required to maintain for the supervisory authorities overseeing her company's affairs. Only Vendor T was prepared to do so, embedding the added internal costs into the calculated fees.) Yet both parties were incurring Expenses to do so, for which no direct Revenues were attributable.

The dissection team computed that the actual Expenses for regulatory reporting and responding to enforcement accessibility simply had not been counted accurately—it had discovered a "black hole" of enormous value. As the aggregated economic numbers grew larger, and as the duties to create and maintain Data suitable to regulators became more and more redundant around the same Data, so did the opportunity to envision velocity within the ecosystems by achieving reciprocal affirmative calculations of trust.

In so many agencies, the public auditors had been incredibly skeptical, testing and kicking corporate reports to see if they were as good on the inside as the attractive graphics on the outside cover. The agencies, in receiving downstream delivery of Data from a company, did not presume trust; instead, they presumed distrust. Companies had more and more of a burden to demonstrate their Data was accurate, controlled, and reliable.

Achieving digital trust acquired a compelling new objective. RHK could gain added competitive advantage by earning the trust of the public sector in the quality of Information that was produced under the Design Principles. Indeed, when RHK tracked the percentage of business records accessible to official authorities, government emerged as the largest external consumer of digital Information assets under RHK's control. Digital trust was not limited to improving internal business records and commercial interchanges; the public sector agencies existed within the same ecosystems and were consumers (and creators) of the same Information flows.

For official authorities, assuring integrity is an enormously important part of advancing the public interest. Their Work requires them to consume Information to measure whether Public Layer Rules are being met by markets, professional services, product quality, environmental emissions, vehicular operations, etc. No different than in a wealth-creation transaction or business decision, their functions cannot be executed unless there is first an affirmative calculation to trust the Information on which they rely. To that

Government is the largest external consumer of corporate Information assets.

extent, public sector agencies shares similar motivations to lower the Expenses they incur to overcome their presumption of distrust. If they can achieve trust in the Information with greater velocity, they can focus more on enforcement.

The team realized it could leverage deploying the Design Principles across RHK's supply chain Information flows to improve the regulatory Information flows; the ecosystems were nearly identical once RHK viewed government as an active participant within the TDC boundaries of each ecosystem. Indeed, outsourcing and further expanding RHK's engagement within the business ecosystems created new, unexpected opportunities to add value by aligning Information and Data into consistent, unified reporting formats (supported by Execution Layer Rules and performing reporting) that could gain the trust of the public sector.

Project Innovate audaciously resolved to change the game by developing Compliance Rulebases focused on exchange points within their ecosystems. Official authorities were merely another set of exchange points, interfaces through which Data had to be validated for transit. Increasingly, public officials wanted to see those Rulebases, inspect documentation, and validate the performance data. Instead of resisting disclosure, the team concluded that RHK should open the curtains with authorities, inviting scrutiny of the Design Principles and their implementation. By doing so, RHK could reduce the overall Expenses of regulatory reporting, create new Revenues upstream and downstream (by reducing the related Trust Discounts and Risk Reserves of its supply chains and customers), and direct internal Resources (notably Human Resources) away from regulatory reporting and toward creating new wealth. The team was confident that engineering digital trust would achieve these economic outcomes.

THE ACTIVITY-BASED COSTS OF DECIDING TO TRUST

The black hole the Project Innovate team uncovered was not an anomaly or, from an accounting perspective, a particularly new thing. Years previously, executives across the broader business world had realized that the finite time assets of labor were not being tracked as efficiently as possible. In response, in the 1980s a management accounting practice called *activity-based costing* (also known as ABC accounting) was developed. ABC accounting provides the means to identify specific costs and converted untraceable "overhead" time (and the related costs) within any black hole into more precisely identified expenditures.

ABC accounting requires two components, both of which can be unwieldy to develop and maintain. First, there must be an accurate inventory of the possible activities that an employee (or other Resource) may perform during a defined time period. Second, once that inventory exists, ABC accounting requires accurate, detailed reporting of time expenditures by activity in order to enable accountants to "do the math." Task-billing codes familiar to so many professionals emerged from these accounting methods.

Historically, both components proved problematic. It was possible (though not easy) to build an activities inventory, but it was difficult to record and track how black hole time units were allocated among those activities. Many workers/timekeepers actually found the recording activity was another, unwelcomed "other duty as assigned" that did not improve their productivity, adding more paperwork and taking time away from regular duties. Inconsistencies among workers in recording their activities; mischaracterizations of time to disguise less productive activities—these and other functional problems constrained ABC accounting's utility, so much so that it fell out of favor in many sectors in the last years of the 20th Century.

But the omnipresent use of technology in nearly every task within a business has enabled a resurgence in the value and utility of ABC accounting that has not yet been fully leveraged. The "if you cannot measure it, you cannot manage it" business culture has taken hold, of course. But there is something more—machine-based surveillance and classification can eliminate the added Expenses of recording how Time is consumed. As previously discussed in Part I, this is now an essential function of IT technology, measuring the Time for any Task.

Today, putting aside the moral or ethical debate about the acceptable levels of surveillance, the same monitoring, measuring, and economic calculations can track our activities as Human Resources within our organizations. Two shifts make this functionally efficient: the increased level of our interactions with devices and applications and the nearly exclusive "born digital" quality of Information in business using digital devices. Auto-classifications of data assets, keystroke logs, wireless building networks tracking employee ID locations, and RFID wristbands worn by warehouse workers now are routine.

These technologies are inspiring a resurgence of ABC as a business strategy—gathering Decisional Information to evaluate performance, tracking and classifying behavior, and calculating the level of trust that each Human Resource can earn (or lose). The Internet of Things is no different; stories are now commonplace of refrigerators auto-generating grocery deliveries based on the frequencies with which bar-coded items are removed, and of home climate controls sensing the body heat levels in a specific room each minute and adjusting the room temperature accordingly.

Project Innovate recognized the tsunami of surveillance technology as a natural extension of Six Sigma, leveraging those technologies' capabilities and generating greater efficiency and productivity. Connecting the dots among human effort and both commercial and regulatory reporting allowed the team to calculate different denominators of the "all-in" costs of the status quo. The team finally had a way to address the question: "What were the Expenses of deciding to trust Information?"

The activity-based costs that emerged were very different than those previously considered. Continued surveillance was not the team's goal; a few case studies, even for the CEO, would show how much activity-based time was consumed inefficiently. The economic modeling that was exciting occurred when new Revenue models showed that the synergies of shared quality standards for Data within ecosystems produced positive results. The investments for building and sustaining digital trust now showed entirely different returns on investment.

Within each division and department, authoring and automating the Rules upon which RHK relied to evaluate Data used in making decisions created greater availability of Time for Human Resources to make better decisions. Technology Resources could be used better to execute consistent decisions that could be trusted. Information assets emerged that better served the requirements of the ecosystems and their residents; new markets were opened in which the trusted, verified Information assets created new revenues.

Helping RHK's business partners, customers, and regulatory authorities achieve greater trust in its Data assets would accelerate decisional velocity for everyone. To succeed, RHK was about to change the rules of the game for each relationship. The team realized RHK needed to show, with transparency, how each commercial entity realized greater wealth by implementing the new Rules. For the regulatory actors, the key was to show how affirmative trust in RHK's Data could reduce the agencies' direct enforcement costs, allowing agencies to focus their funding on others for whom the low-trust presumption was more deserved. Built on the foundation offered by the Design Principles, the new Rules would empower agencies to calculate independently their affirmative trust in RHK's Data. To succeed, RHK needed to persuade the agencies to abandon Dead Man's Curve and build something new.

ACHIEVING COMPETITIVE ADVANTAGE

The final Digital Trust Design Principles had been crafted with a deceptive intent. The Principles were never intended to be consumed exclusively by internal audiences. Instead, the team's report recommended RHK share the Design Principles with customers and suppliers across its ecosystems. The team intended the Principles to become the basis for new dialogues regarding the value of digital trust in these relationships and the importance of mutually creating and sharing T-Info as a Resource in its businesses. The Design Principles needed to appear at the front of every future specification, and evaluation criteria had to be built from new Rulebases. Upstream and downstream, collaboration and consensus on creating and using T-Info in harmony with the Design Principles would place RHK in a position of influence and control. The lessons of the last two centuries of human history had been learned: those who write the rules best control the outcome of the game.

Those who write the rules best control the outcome of the game.

Moving forward, the Principles required that each new business process and solution be viewed as a TDT, responsive to the concerns expressed in the Statement of Need and advancing the corporate objectives to achieve and sustain digital trust. Project Innovate realized every Resource (raw inventory, component parts, computing services, Human Resources, consulting, Data, etc.) that RHK acquired or consumed required trust decisions. Whether hired, purchased, leased, or built from scratch, the company used the same decision processes! The Design Principles applied to far more than just Information. They delivered a more formal framework to guide every RHK business decision.

Measuring new TDT specifications against the Design Principles (for *all* existing and future goods and services) was going to be provocative—virtually any commercial agreement would require new negotiations placing Information, ecosystems, and trust directly on the table. Suppliers would prefer RHK as a customer because the suppliers would incur fewer Expenses by demonstrating the trustworthiness of their Information and Resources. They also would receive Information from RHK that they could use more quickly in their own decisions and systems. Customers would prefer RHK as a supplier both for the fewer direct Expenses required to trust RHK Information and Resources, and the lower retail prices on goods and services offered by RHK.

In addition, now the barter value of Information could be calculated, not merely presumed, and, as a result, Information would gain exchangeable, economic equivalence. T-Info controlled by RHK would be, quite literally, as good as gold. Building on the Design Principles was going to allow RHK to demonstrate the direct economic value of its Information and systems to the other side of any exchange point, reducing friction and increasing velocity in all directions.

The same approach would apply to regulatory exchanges. The Project Innovate team recognized that public officials would not abandon their presumption of distrust for some time; yet several agencies indicated interest in a different type of dialogue. They were prepared to reduce the intense scrutiny of RHK's IT systems and process records. Preliminary discussions confirmed the obvious—RHK's systems and process records were Decisional Information Sources to the government DMs evaluating whether to trust RHK's primary Information (Content/Fact) as objective evidence of compliance. Agencies were intrigued; if RHK committed to align its corporate systems to published standards that would allow independent third-party audits, the agencies might be able to reduce their Expenses challenging both the factual records and the relevant systems.

The concept was analogous to audit opinions on financial statements (such as the SEC relying on auditor opinions), only applied to technology services. Continued evolution by RHK consistent with the Design Principles could accelerate the velocity with which the public sector placed trust in both RHK's systems and Information. In turn, if RHK shared its learning curve within its ecosystems, the suppliers and customers also would be positioned to have similar dialogues with their respective regulators, making RHK a valued trading partner indeed.

THE FINAL RECOMMENDATION

When California's Dead Man's Curve was finally replaced, the new highway was not the act of an imperious central state government mandating the abandonment of obsolete infrastructure. Instead, intensive collaboration extended over years, engaging all of the stakeholders. Building something new required building a consensus favoring the new Rules on which the new highway would be constructed; accomplishing that consensus was an essential investment in order to achieve the interoperability and velocity objectives that were on the planners' drawing boards.

The team realized that it could not author the new Rules alone, despite RHK's market dominance. More and more, standards development within technology sectors was beginning to express detailed, structured Rules for business processes, information security, information governance, and, as important as any of the preceding, the operation and use of mobile devices. But, in every instance, there was always a compelling business case for creating wealth that preceded the launch of the deliberations to create new standards. (Recall that standards are part of the Implementation Layer of the Unified Rules Model—they enable business practices that are permitted by Public Layer Rules).

There was also something else—standards do not emerge spontaneously. They always begin with a first draft. Every standard starts out as an innovation—a set of Rules with one of three alternative origins. First, the Rules already were in use somewhere, enabling improved Results (including reducing Risks), with sufficient value to justify collaborative expansion across larger ecosystems. Second, those Rules created such a powerful competitive advantage for the early adopters that their competitors initiated the standardization process to try to normalize the rules of the game. With either of those origins, the standards were normalizing the Rules and, as a result, advancing the engagements, interdependencies, volumes, and wealth creation achieved within the related ecosystems. As with abandoning Dead Man's Curve, the velocity demands of commerce always reach a tipping point when the Rules become vulnerable to adaptation.

Third, and far less frequently, a collection of sponsors with a shared challenge (Risks outweighing Results), and no solution, come together to create a new innovation in the form of a set of Rules expressed in a standard capable of broad adoption. But even then, there is always a rough draft, some sketch expressing the Rules to be authored in order to achieve the Results (Revenues becoming greater than Expenses).

The team realized the rulemaking that a new standard represents always expands, rather than excludes, participation. Proprietary, closed systems of Rules are no longer sustainable for the long term. Brutal, expensive battles had been waged when the Rules themselves were the product: Word™ vs. WordPerfect™; VHS™ vs. Beta™; Apple™ vs. Android™; and currently, eBay™ vs. Alibaba™. RHK had a different objective, enabling T-Info, not the Rules themselves, to become a new product. For RHK and its ecosystems partners, the sustainable competitive advantage to building digital trust would be achieved by being first to bring these new capabilities on line, and then providing the leadership required to bring the new Rules to the table.

That became the team's final recommendation—its strategic plan expressly contemplated sharing the Rules for achieving digital trust with the global, digital marketplace. The plan included the following steps: RHK would begin internally, using its internal operational ecosystems as test beds to improve and refine the Rules and develop its toolkit of Resources into a functional, sustainable TDT for achieving digital trust. Next, RHK would engage with its most vital suppliers and customers, extending the Rules and sharing its knowledge to distribute the benefits within a broader community, creating new wealth upstream and downstream. The team realized that some of those suppliers and customers also

The rulemaking that a new standard represents always expands, rather than excludes, participation.

conducted business with RHK's competitors; they knew that not much time would pass before the innovations became a target for standardization. Rather than resist, RHK would invest in preparing for the collaborative, consensus development, creating the documentation and preparing to meet the demands for transparency.

The press release heralding $110 million in savings had the desired effect. Working in close concert with their key suppliers and customers, only a small chunk of the long-term potential for achieving digital trust had been achieved, but the market immediately understood the implications. Increasing the velocity of digital Information would occupy more than one generation, but being first off the starting line would have long-term, sustainable advantages. Now it was time to begin the globalization of RHK's Rules.

Tucked into the final paragraph of the press release was the announcement that Jung Singh had been promoted internally to the position of Chief Trust Officer. Her first task was to place an important call, one for which she felt it best if she dialed the number from her mobile phone so that the caller ID would be visible. *"After all,"* she thought with a smile, *"the new Rules are all about transparency."*

The CIO at Wise Industries accepted the call.

PART THREE

DISCOVERING AND USING
THE TRUST PRISM

CHAPTER 21

ACHIEVING AND SUSTAINING DIGITAL TRUST

THE STORY OF WISE INDUSTRIES and RHK Enterprises is one, of course, that has no proper ending. Every day we witness how the forces of competition, control, velocity, governance, and wealth creation are doing battle in both ordinary and extraordinary ways. Governments, infrastructure owners, and companies that dominate their markets are installing patches to their versions of Dead Man's Curve. Innovators are boldly building things that are entirely new, leveraging the Net's existing infrastructure to construct solutions to achieve and sustain digital trust. Their work includes creating new digital currencies, new distributed platforms for developing and operating complex software applications, and automated "smart" contracting capabilities that directly confront the power and control of those installing the patches.

Connected into one ecosystem by the Net's capabilities, global companies that ferociously compete in business are becoming collaborators in writing new Rules. In Asia and Europe, governments with long traditions of fierce rivalries are finding powerful, wealth-based motivations to collaborate and author new Rules for achieving greater velocities at all levels of commerce. The EU's commitment to achieving a single digital market is entirely driven by a shared realization that digital trust will create a unified economic ecosystem, overcoming the resistance and inertia once grounded in those historic rivalries. The Europeans not only are focusing on the friction points within the boundaries of Europe; their strategies aim to position Europe as an influential competitor and leader worldwide. One need only reference the influence of Europe's privacy and data protection laws on the global legal landscape to see compelling evidence of the strategy RHK embraced to write the Rules and then globalize them.

As this book is being completed in the early summer of 2015, the world now awaits what comes next from Europe. Responding to the new technologies and innovations, the EU is close to publishing an entirely new rewrite of those privacy and data protection rules, called the General Data Protection Regulation (GDPR). Unlike the prior Directives on privacy and data protection, for which each EU member state had the option to implement with localized variations, the GDPR will apply as mandatory law across all of the member states in nearly all respects, with no optional, local variations. In other words, the EU is unifying the Rules. China is doing the same, with a political force of even greater momentum and attention to granularity, creating Rules for the tagging codes used within accounting software programs (such as XBRL, which stands for Extensible Business Reporting Language) and mandating the security architecture of servers used within financial institutions.

By contrast, the United States continues to exhibit a fundamental misunderstanding of the synergies and interdependencies between the public and private sectors that will be required for its economy to be competitive in a digital global market that is becoming wireless. Companies oppose transparency, resist new regulations that establish Rules for assuring the trustworthiness of their systems (and the Information extracted from them to evaluate compliance), and politicians cut the enforcement budgets of public agencies in order to limit their effectiveness at discovering and proving non-compliant behavior.

In that type of culture, it is no surprise the CIO at Wise Industries struggled so hard to gain the transparency required to assure outsourced services effectively integrated into her own performance and governance models. It also should be no surprise she took the phone call from RHK's Chief Trust Officer, Jung Singh. Merely to have a chance to survive, the time had come to collaborate with Wise's competitors, even if it meant adapting to their Rules. Perhaps, in the globalization initiative, Wise Industries would have a chance to catch up and level the playing field. But in fiction and in real life, what happens next remains to be written. No more honest words were spoken than those from Marc Benioff presented in Chapter 1: "The digital revolution needs a trust revolution."

As each of the tools in this book evolved, so did the overall complexity of the solution as a TDT. Yet, frame by frame, layer by layer, the tools emerged and matured as innovations, building on one another to offer a new way of thinking about making better trust decisions and the persistent, critical role that digital Information will perform for all of society. To make these tools work as a unified TDT, we still need something more, one more innovation built from Rules and Resources that can be trusted to perform the Work of achieving digital trust. In this Part III, you will discover that innovation, called the Trust Prism. You will be introduced to how IT architects, manufacturers, operators, and others can use the Trust Prism to achieve increased velocity and digital trust.

You also will learn how two other vital constituencies—public authorities and malicious actors—will use the Trust Prism. Sadly, as in any war, all sides usually have access to the same weapons. Rather than avoid the obvious, this book confronts it, providing examples of how the bad guys might find alternative uses for the tools presented here.

You should have already figured out that those achieving victories in the war on trust are doing so because they have a superior understanding of many of the key principles and insights offered in these pages. The bad guys know that companies are not investing in rules-based design and governance; their strategies are actually fairly simple—find the points where Rules do not exist, are not being enforced, or for which Data is not being properly analyzed—and gain entry. Each of their victories is not very different than how the Orcs in *Lord of the Rings* gained entry to the fortress through a neglected back sewer gate—someone forgot to place a guard under the bridge.

The final chapter closes this book by offering you the challenge to enter the war on trust, acquire the weapons required, and begin to shift the momentum. The next steps are waiting to be taken.

CHAPTER 22

ACHIEVING THE OUTCOMES

TO UNDERSTAND THE STRENGTH and power of the Trust Prism, it is best to begin by explaining the problems the Trust Prism solves in managing the complexity and volatility of making decisions and, in doing so, achieving trust in those decisions. Recall that complexity and opacity are hostile weapons used by those waging war on trust. To be useful and to succeed, the Trust Prism must deliver transparency and the capabilities to navigate and govern the complexity.

THE RULES AND RESULTS FOR THE TRUST PRISM

The following are the Rules against which I evaluated the Trust Prism during its evolution. Some have been presented earlier in this book; their repetition here is intentional. As Results to be achieved, they gain greater weight when viewed within this larger inventory.

To succeed as an innovation, and to be trusted as a TDT, the Trust Prism must:

≥ Formalize the Trust Decision Model into a visual structure that is consistent, integrated, and scalable for any TDT, regardless of its complexity.

≥ Visually express the varied layers that characterize and give structure to the Trust Decision Model, the Unified Rules Model, and the Unified Information Model.

≥ Visually organize and establish the pairings and functional relationships among Resources, including TDC_{RES} and TDT_{RES}, in order to express and integrate the Descriptive Specifications and Functional Specifications into working descriptions of the TDC, TDT, Work, and individual Tasks.

≥ Provide mechanisms through which Compliance Rulebases can be visually mapped and paired to specific Resources (including Data), and compliance with their requirements can be accurately measured and calculated.

≥ Visually organize the Resources and Rules (as the Assets with which a TDT is constructed) into functional, discrete objects that we can recognize and access for auditing performance and supporting dynamic adaptation and governance.

≥ Visually represent the Results and Risks (as the Attributes by which a TDT is defined) as functional, discrete pairings to the Assets that we can recognize and access for auditing performance and supporting dynamic adaptation and governance.

> Visually express the movement and transformation of Data and Information within TDTs in order to more effectively assure that applicable Rules are properly executed at exchange points between and among internal TDT_{RES} and other TDTs.

> Visually expose how Data moving through TDTs (and specific TDT_{RES}) executes Work (and specific Tasks) and enables the accurate calculation of the Attributes and Costs for any TDT.

> Synthesize and integrate the Data required to calculate properly the Functional Calculation, Value Calculation, and Process Calculation inherent in each trust decision.

> Provide mechanisms through which we can track with greater consistency and precision the Data expressing Attributes and Costs to specific Resources and Tasks.

> Expose the Rules for which responsive Execution Layer Rules have not been authored into a suitable Rulebase.

> Create exposure of the Rules for which Execution Layer Resources have not been effectively assigned to assure the proper execution of the corresponding Compliance Rulebase.

≳ Create exposure of those TDT_{RES} that are not generating Internal Performance Metrics with which to govern their effectiveness at achieving the intended Results and avoiding known Risks.

≳ Create exposure of those TDT_{RUL} for which Data is not being generated in order to measure Costs in support of Value Calculations.

Recall that every decision begins with the alternatives of doing nothing, performing Work alone, or identifying and evaluating a TDT to perform Work with greater efficiency. Of course, if more than one TDT is available, we must calculate comparisons. Whether within the Rules applicable within a TDC or as a result of new boundaries changing the TDC, if TDC_{RUL} changes occur, those changes alter the pairings among the Assets and Attributes of a TDT and also require comparative analysis. Therefore, the Trust Prism has to achieve another layer of Results, which emphasizes something nearly all business decisions require—continual comparisons, choices, and adaptations.

THE TRUST PRISM ENABLES CONTINUAL DECISIONS AMONG OPTIONS

While all of the preceding Results are invaluable in designing, building, and managing a singular TDT, to succeed *fully* as an innovation, the Trust Prism must enable a DM to navigate continually within the larger Context and the shifting TDCs in which decisions need to be made. Any DM constantly must evaluate and choose among existing options and, when needed, innovate new options. It is comparable to wanting to compare apples to apples, but the complexity and opacity that confront any of us in our daily decisions make implementation of comparisons so very difficult. As explained at the outset of this book, those battling to achieve control and waging war fully intend that result. The Trust Prism is the weapon with which we can achieve the transparency required to make consistent, effective decisions.

There are certainly Risks in successfully achieving transparency— mistakes in execution become visible; inadequate surveillance and enforcement controls are more rapidly exposed; and responsibilities for the economic impacts of deciding to "take the risk" are nearly inescapable. When used to calculate trust in a TDT, the Trust Prism is like a clear crystal through which a white light refracts into its component color wavelengths—the strengths and weaknesses of the TDT become visible; Decisional Information Risks are illuminated; and the all-in Costs of choosing to proceed without affirmatively calculating trust are far more meaningful. Those are the favorable Results the Trust Prism achieves, not reasons to reject it. Exposing "fail" creates the opportunity to build and sustain trust.

ACHIEVING VELOCITY

The Trust Prism should do one more thing: continually accelerate the velocity of Information toward achieving the speed of light. At 299,792,458 meters per second, that is really, really fast. There should be no doubt at this point of the importance of velocity to business. But now the reason for the fiber-optic imagery on the cover of this book becomes clear. Achieving trust—and, especially, achieving *digital* trust—is what organizations and individuals require merely to survive in the current global economy. Those who win will have achieved digital trust that was affirmatively calculated at the speed of light.

The Trust Prism is the weapon with which we can achieve the transparency required to make consistent, effective decisions.

In the weeks before finalizing the manuscript for this book, LinkedIn™ published an interview by its Executive Editor with the legendary Jack Welch. Welch made the case for digital trust best of all:

> "When they trust you, you'll get truth. And if you get truth, you get speed. If you get speed, you're going to act. That's how it works. . . . That's why all these leadership books and stuff about leadership, it's all crap."*

*http://linkd.in/1GhYqOy

VISUALIZING TRUST IN FOUR DIMENSIONS

When Zachman first defined the mission of information architecture in 1987 (referenced in Chapter 18), his metaphorical reliance on building architecture emphasized the need to visualize complexity. His manifesto challenged IT professionals to mimic the value of blueprints used by building architects to create and express new types of visualizations describing the computing solutions and systems the engineers were creating. Achieving effective dialogue and understanding among all of the stakeholders in their work simply required a new way of communicating.

As this book and the tools it presents evolved, there was no doubt that the signature innovation had to be visual. I conceived, tested, and discarded endless sketches, diagrams, trial drawings, and many dinner napkins and Post-It™ notes on the wall. Ultimately, the Trust Prism emerged by breaking through the limitations of thinking in two dimensions. Instead, in the same manner that powerful software programs now enable building architects to create full three-dimensional images of rooms, floors, buildings, blocks, and towns, the Trust Prism enables us to view and assess the trust decision process in 3-D.

Every system, of any size, is constructed in layers. So, too, is the Trust Prism. The concept of layers is critical, it is shared with so many of the prevailing IT design tools: the OSI Model, the Semantic Web, Object-Oriented Programming, SOAP, and the like. The layering of the Trust Decision Model, the Unified Rules Model, and the Unified Information Model are entirely intentional, positioning those tools, along with the Trust Prism, to work with and expand the existing and future capabilities of agile design, distributed computing, and open source code development that are the backbone of our 21st Century world.

But the Trust Prism goes further than architectural renderings of buildings. It embeds time as a critical, necessary dimension across which it executes the Work of building and sustaining trust. That is right—calculating trust can be visualized in four dimensions. With each measure of time, any of the Circumstances, Rules, Resources, Results, Risks, or Costs on which a prior trust decision was calculated can change. There is no steady state in how trust is calculated; each change becomes a moment in which trust may be calculated again. New Decisional Information requires new calculations. Trust is never certain nor absolute; trust decisions always are eligible to be recalculated.

So, as you study the structure and design of the Trust Prism, hold in your imagination an image approximating an Egyptian pyramid, its top capstone missing, standing in a driving rainstorm of Data. With each moment, the Trust Prism is infused with new Data, providing fuel for new trust decisions about the TDT that the Trust Prism represents, powering Rewinds & Recalculations of the trust you hold in the TDT, and enabling adaptation. You instantly replace and strengthen blocks and their connecting Information mortar, improving the Assets that construct the TDT, dynamically shifting the Attributes of the TDT toward continuously improved performance, creating Revenues greater than Expenses—all with velocity, moving at the speed of light. New Data flows outbound from the Prism, serving as a Resource to you or to other TDTs. Choose your preferred measure of time, allow that measure to pass, and, once again, calculate trust—the 21st Century's new coin of the realm.

That's how it works.

THE TRUST VOCABULARY

In this chapter, you will learn the following words:

Block

Layer

Risk Inventory

Stack

Trust Prism

Weighting Information

CHAPTER 23

THE TRUST PRISM

THE TRUST PRISM is a visual expression of a TDT. More precisely, when focused on a specific TDT, the Trust Prism integrates and displays a coherent illustration of all of the moving parts involved in calculating trust in a TDT at any moment in time. The Trust Prism works exactly like the visual display of any complex network or system; it is a tool for assembling, processing, and interpreting complex Rules, Resources, and Decisional Information required for making trust decisions. However, unlike 2-D blueprints and systems maps, the Trust Prism is three-dimensional. Even when drawn on a dinner napkin, the Trust Prism enables different views of a TDT and the moving parts involved in calculating trust.

The Trust Prism resembles an Egyptian pyramid. It is constructed of layers, with each layer including one or more blocks. There are no limits on how many layers or blocks can be visualized using the Prism; the size, volume, and dimensionality of a Prism for a specific TDT is a function of the Assets, Attributes, and Costs for

When a TDT
is another
DM, such as a
leader, the Trust
Prism magnifies
and evaluates
that person's
decision
process and
the resulting
decisions with
new objectivity
and precision.

that TDT, as well as the changes that occur with the passage of Time. The Prism works the same, whether a trust decision involves selecting a hammer, a system for controlling rocket launches, or a Cloud service provider. But a Prism is not intended to "look like" the TDT; instead, it is a visual expression of the dynamics of trust in the TDT.

The Prism also helps us decide to trust the decisions of others! Using the Prism, a person can better expose the calculations and decision processes that precede our evaluation, no differently than a border immigrations officer inspects each new arrival. When a TDT is another DM, such as a leader, the Trust Prism magnifies and evaluates that person's decision process and the resulting decisions with new objectivity and precision. In other words, for any person asked to trust the decisions of others, the Prism is an auditing tool that allows the same process calculation that occurs at T Minus and Holding. The resulting transparency that becomes possible with the Prism, with exceptional new granularity and velocity, can overcome the complexity and opacity those waging war on trust use as weapons.

The Trust Prism is both scalable and extensible in its design, capable of supporting trust decisions for the smallest nanotechnology devices to the most complex information networks and eco-systems of the world's largest companies and communities. Perhaps most important to the mission of this book, the Trust Prism enables the alignment of trust decisions in digital devices and digital Information to have continuity with the values and trust decision processes of human beings. In other words, the Trust Prism is a platform and structure that allows us to forge computational trust and human trust into a coherent, unified decision process. The results for each person, organization, and digital asset are a transformative capability to define, govern, and improve our trust in the digital infrastructure and information assets with which we execute our lives.

THE LAYERS CONSTRUCT

The layers construct introduced and used by the Trust Decision Model, the URM, and the UIM is essential to the Trust Prism. That construct aligns the Prism structure generally to the layer-based tools used globally in designing information technology and the Net. For many technologists, the use of layer models to identify, classify, and engineer networks, systems, devices, applications, interfaces, and digital content is nearly instinctive. The Open Systems Interconnection (OSI) standard approved by the International Standards Organization and the service-oriented architecture (SOA) are fundamental backbones of our wired world; the Semantic Web model and the more recent innovations for Hadoop® (a globally adopted mechanism for big data analytics) follow the same structure.

In nearly every one of these technology models, the layer closest to the user is represented visually on top and, like a pyramid, each layer moving upward is smaller in its dimensions than the layer below. That design makes a great deal of sense; as a pyramid rises into the sky, it conveys growth and dimensionality, moving toward an apex at the top that is visually powerful. The Trust Prism adopts these same visual cues, with one exception.

THE MISSING CAPSTONE

In designing the Prism, it seemed instinctive to assume that achieving trust should be like installing the capstone on a pyramid—a capstone is the final piece that crowns the structure (and

> The Trust Prism enables the alignment of trust decisions in digital devices and digital Information to have continuity with the values and trust decision processes of human beings.

was often adorned with precious metals). It made sense that the user interface (i.e., the top) should visually express the notion that all of the other layers come together to a point of perfection. But, as we have learned, in making trust decisions, perfection is never the actual outcome; the Risk of the Unknown Risk is always present. That truth is reflected in the design of the Prism—there is no ultimate apex. However small the uncertainty, the missing capstone in the Prism conveys the inherent limits on achieving perfect trust.

THE CONSTRUCT OF EACH LAYER

In the trust vocabulary, each *layer* represents a functional level of a TDT. There are no Rules for the boundaries of a specific layer; the OSI model is a representative expression of how we might present layers in the Prism, focusing on the functions performed.

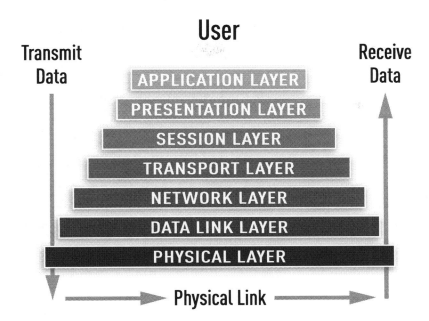

User

Transmit Data

Receive Data

APPLICATION LAYER
PRESENTATION LAYER
SESSION LAYER
TRANSPORT LAYER
NETWORK LAYER
DATA LINK LAYER
PHYSICAL LAYER

Physical Link

Extensive detailed educational resources on the OSI model, SOA, Hadoop®, and other similar references can be accessed via any search engine.

For each layer, the Trust Prism adopts design concepts similar to the OSI model. The layer for each function is assigned specific Tasks (as sub-components of the Work a TDT is to perform). Like the OSI model, each layer of the Trust Prism can be described as reasonably self-contained, in that Tasks in each layer can be implemented and updated independently without adversely affecting the other layers. Each layer can have more than one Resource performing those Tasks; to do so, we must have in place and enforce Rules to enable those Resources to interact within the same layer. In this manner, the Tasks enable each layer (n) to interact with the layer immediately beneath ($n-1$) or above ($n+1$).

Internally within a TDT, those interactions involve the movement of Information and Data between layers. That point is worth emphasizing: within a TDT, Resources connect and perform Work through the movement of Information. The result is that each internal movement involves continuous, internal trust decisions to accept and rely on the Information generated by the Work of

Within a TDT, Resources connect and perform Work through the movement of Information.

the layers below. In visualizing a TDT as a Prism, each of those decisions can be identified and evaluated more conspicuously.

Each layer is constructed of *blocks* similar to the stones from which pyramids are built. Each block has a separate, unique identifier that tags how the Work for that block is described (in other words, naming conventions typical to IT engineering can be used here to label and identify each block). The Work may be one or more Tasks. Resources that manage and perform the related Work are assigned to each block. Resources within a block can perform the Work independently or in combination with other blocks (and related Resources) within that layer.

Parallel processing is an example of having multiple blocks within a layer capable of performing the same Work. If one or more blocks currently are working at full capacity, Data can be routed for processing to another available block. Now, some of the utility of the UIM vocabulary becomes clearer. Assigning Content (such as Data) among parallel blocks does not require direct access to the Content; instead, we consider the relevant Descriptive Layer Information ("What is this Content?"), and use Evaluation Layer Information from the blocks ("Working at 98% utilization" is an Internal Performance Metric) to locate and select available Resources for the Content to perform the Work.

The Prism structure visually uses and adopts component-based design. Rather than viewing a system as a fully integrated, singular structure, a component-based approach (of which SOA is an example) enables adjustments to individual components within a system (thereby adjusting the related services), without modifying the overall system. With the Prism, the same function becomes possible; Resources assigned to a block (or the Rules governing their performance) may be adjusted without affecting other blocks or other layers.

SOA also contemplates Data moving across and among components through reliance on metadata bundled with the primary content. The Prism leverages and integrates the same concepts. The Data is a Resource. Each block represents the Resources used to perform a Task. The boundaries of a block are defined by the Rules those Resources can execute. The Tasks are defined by Descriptive Specifications and Functional Specifications. The Resources use the Data to perform the Tasks pursuant to the Rules paired to the Resources. Data moves into and among blocks according to Rules governing their communication and transfer. Each movement requires validation at the exchange points between the blocks. The validations may require Evaluation Layer Information from the prior block. The additional metadata (based on its use) may be in the Descriptive Layer, Evaluation Layer, and/or Navigational Layer Information. The primary content is Content/Fact.

Much as mortar is used between bricks, the Prism visualizes these movements of Information among blocks and layers. Information can move up, down, or sideways, depending on how the layers and blocks are configured.

While Information often moves as a full bundle (think of an e-mail that also contains multiple metadata fields), the Prism incorporates an important design Rule: blocks (and certain Tasks within a block) may only perform Work using one Information layer (as presented in the UIM). In computers, the Descriptive Layer, Evaluation Layer, and Navigation Layer Information associated with each Content asset enable the applications to navigate, select, and use the correct Information assets required by the Execution Layer Rules.

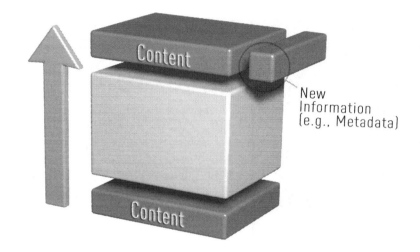

New Information (e.g., Metadata)

Similarly, once a block completes the Work, the Descriptive Layer/ Activity Description (such as a transaction execution log related to a customer's account) is created as new metadata; the Prism enables us to better visualize where that record goes (and its subsequent availability to the next Tasks). We also can visualize how Information enters and leaves a TDT, connecting to other TDC$_{RES}$ that provide or rely on that Information (such as a brokerage's systems connecting to NASDAQ). Viewed within the Trust Prism, all of this occurs with a functional transparency that exceeds what we achieve using two-dimensional blueprints and maps. If architects now design in 3-D, why can't we visualize the flow of Information with the same perspectives?

THE 3-D CONSTRUCTION OF A BLOCK

While a block is the visual expression of a unit of Work, it is also a visual expression of the Assets (Resources, Rules) used to perform the Work. In Chapter 6, this image introduced the concept that a TDT is composed of Rules and Resources:

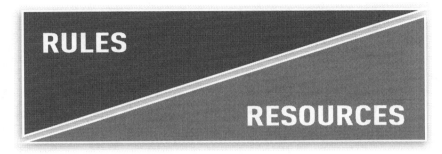

SYSTEM

As a 3-D block, the same concept is expressed as follows:

Notice that the Resources are stacked onto the Rules. In using the Prism, the dividing line between Resources and Rules visually indicates the degree to which the Rules have been automated into the functionality of the Resources. A high level of automation is shown on the left, and on the right is a low level of automation (which logically means that there is a heavy reliance on Human Resources to perform the Rules required by the Work).

The layers of the Unified Rules Model introduce further visual detail inside a block. A block displays Rules from two of the URM layers: the Implementation Layer and the Execution Layer. As we have learned, a corporate system (as a TDT) has many sources of Implementation Layer Rules (policies, procedures, contracts, standards); using the Prism, we abandon the existing structure of those Rules as we extract, deconstruct, and assemble the Rules into Rulebases. So, when visualizing those Rules in a Trust Prism, the Implementation Layer Rules serve as an internal base for the performance of Tasks and Work. As illustrated, Implementation Layer Rules may support more than one set of Execution Layer Rules (and the related Results).

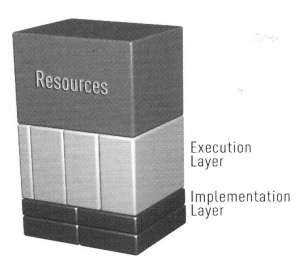

That places the Execution Layer Rules visually adjacent to the Resources. This is useful for mapping and pairing Resources precisely to the Execution Layer Rules governing them. Remember, the actual pairing is occurring in the supporting Rulebases that document how the Resources will execute Rules, but the visualization helps recognize gaps created when specific Resources are not paired to the Rules. The same is true if no Execution Layer Rules exist for specific Work (as is often the case when SIAM Words appear in parent Rules that are not paired to specific Resources). Those situations show up as void spaces in a block.

THE PUBLIC LAYER AS A FOUNDATION

Where do Public Layer Rules go in the Trust Prism? Recall that Rules are part of the TDC; they are not integrated into any TDT, however, as with any other TDC element (Circumstances, such as the weather, or Resources, such as a power supply), a trust decision takes their presence into account. But, unlike other TDC_{CIR} and TDC_{RES}, TDC_{RUL} directly influence how a DM decides to trust a TDT. For example, if Public Layer Rules such as Federal rules for aircraft safety design have been ignored, you may have less trust (or even none at all) in the plane you are scheduled to take to Chicago. So, while external to a TDT, Public Layer Rules that are relevant (i.e., above the line drawn to illustrate a calculated indifference) are visually represented as the foundation for the TDT itself, inherently to be taken into account.

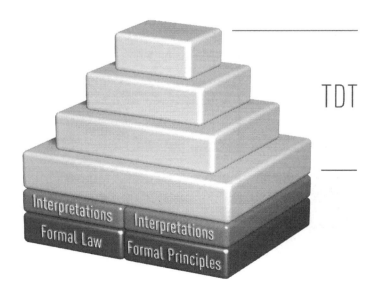

The visual and geometric placement of the Public Layer as the foundation (rather than incorporated into any layer or block) invites three intriguing perspectives.

First, in many ways, both corporate and individual citizens rely upon public law to serve precisely that role—establishing the structural foundation for activities in commerce, education, and government. If the Public Layer is not providing a strong foundation, then a TDT is, quite literally, unstable. This is a condition we have always confronted; the Trust Prism exposes the variations and, in turn, exposes the Rules required to provide stability to the technology solution a TDT represents.

Public laws simply may not address or impose Rules on the type of Work a TDT performs (or control the Risks experienced using a TDT), a common condition with new digital technologies. There may be statutes in place, but no regulations or interpretations, again, very common with evolving digital technologies. A third possibility is the existence of public laws that may seem complete, but are not being executed by the operators of related TDTs (i.e., there are no paired Execution Layer Rules or related Resources), or regularly being enforced by the regulatory agencies (TDC_{RES}). All of these outcomes can be visualized as voids within the Prism, visually expressing the related instability.

In any of these cases, if the Public Layer is unstable or incomplete, a DM may need to author and integrate additional Rules into the TDT at the Implementation Layer and Execution Layer in order to calculate affirmative trust. That is exactly how much of the success

In the absence of any substantive, specific Public Layer Rules, new Rules are authored that enable customers to adopt and use the innovations.

of Net-based innovations has occurred so far. In the absence of any substantive, specific Public Layer Rules, new Rules are authored that enable customers to adopt and use the innovations. This is why subscriptions, licenses, and terms of use for innovations often are so complex—as Implementation Layer Rules, these enable the customers to calculate whether the innovation can be trusted.

In many instances, public regulations follow along in a similar fashion. Whether they mimic the Rules adopted for the innovations or impose new Rules that control Risks experienced by users and other stakeholders, the content of new Public Layer Rules is a function of how well the initial TDT Rules effectively advanced favorable trust calculations. If stakeholders, trading partners, or customers experience adverse Risk events, it is likely that the new Public Layer Rules will be substantive, either as mandatory requirements or prohibitions. Using the Prism, these interactions can be visually organized and examined with greater transparency.

Second, placing the Public Layer as the foundation allows us to examine an entire market as a single TDT. Health, financial services, transportation, and education—core service industries—are outstanding candidates. Each is a functioning, integrated system, composed of Resources governed by Rules intended to create certain Results and avoid Risks, each operating to create new wealth. At this large scale, the relationships between the Rules and the TDT are no different than within an individual block, just larger in number and complexity. Using this methodology, we can examine the overall market, recognize structural weaknesses, and calculate the need for new Rules. These may be new regulations, amendments to existing Rules, new Interpretations, or new mandates for new Rules created at the Implementation Layer or Execution Layer (such as requiring corporate privacy policies and two-factor authentication to access personal information), all serving to advance social and economic trust in the regulated assets, actors, and markets.

Third, if a Public Layer Rule in the foundation is not effectively paired to the Resources and Rules of a market system, then the Rule is not contributing to building trust in that system. So often, corporations lament the abundance of Rules that constrict their behavior. The Trust Prism creates visibility into those Circumstances. Official authorities lose trust when they insist on compliance with Rules that do not have demonstrable positive impact; the Trust Prism enables regulated entities to challenge whether a specific Public Layer Rule advances the public interest. Conversely, the transparency the Trust Prism imposes also allows the regulating authorities to more effectively calculate the impact of Public Layer Rules on the system and its stakeholders.

STACKS WITHIN BLOCKS

As mentioned earlier, the Work assigned to a block may consist of one or more Tasks. To visually illustrate that, a block can be composed of multiple *stacks*, with each stack representing a specific Task constructed of the appropriate Rules and Resources. In other words, a stack is a block within a block.

Just as with a block, stacks may have differing levels of automation, with some Tasks relying more on manual performance of the related Rules. In migrating that concept into the Trust Prism, one or more Rules or Resources may be duplicated and included in more than one stack. This makes logical sense; within many complex systems, a Resource may perform multiple Tasks and do so according to a Rulebase unique to each Task. The Trust Prism is useful to visually map and display the magnification that makes these pairings and alignments more explicit as trust calculations for the full TDT that are occurring.

VISUALIZING RESULTS AND RISKS

The Attributes of a TDT include both Results and Risks. The Design Principles emphasize that an affirmative calculation of trust requires the Results be more likely than the known Risks; by extension, if the Results and Risks are evenly balanced, there is no affirmative trust. Those concepts are reflected in the Trust Prism by introducing the Risks into each Block.

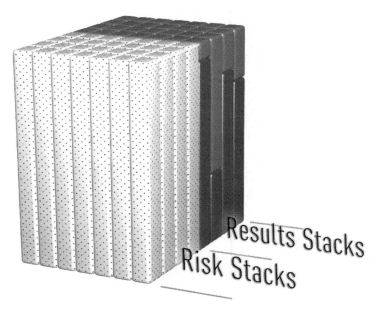

Results Stacks

Risk Stacks

The occurrence of an adverse event based on a known Risk often disrupts complex processes and can damage other assets outside the TDT's boundaries. Identifying those assets and calculating the waterfall effects of a "fail" require some of the best probability mathematics possible, but only if the affected assets are identified first. So often, senior management (or others) will overlook those assets and related collateral Expenses when deciding to take the Risk; the consequences are losses far more substantial than contemplated.

To assure these assets are considered in trust decisions, a Risk stack includes a third element, called *Risk Inventory*. The Risk Inventory consists of the Resources (both TDT_{RES} and TDC_{RES}) affected by a known Risk-based adverse event. By fully accounting for the affected Resources in the Risk Inventory, trust decisions are more effective in executing the required calculations.

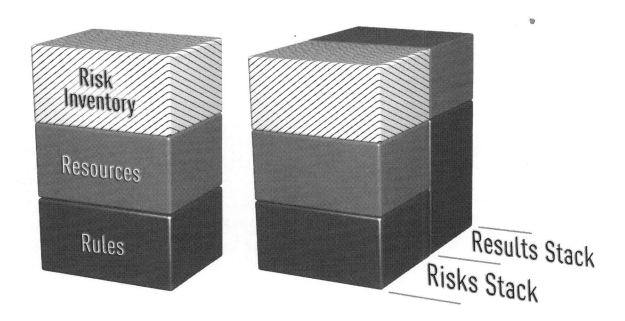

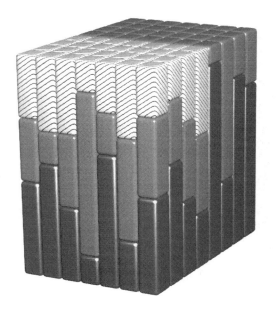

Rather than being paired to Tasks, a Risk stack is paired to the outcomes of Risks. In other words, a Risk stack is defined by the consequences of adverse events. The Rules describe what is required for those outcomes to occur; the Resources in a Risk stack are the TDT_{RES} that are paired with those outcomes (i.e., the controls). The same visual techniques are used to illustrate various balances among Rules, Resources, and Risk Inventories in Risk stacks.

If there are no Resources in place to control against the related Risks, the Risk Inventory is appropriately larger. The Trust Prism allows graphical visualization of this gap. If the controls are absent, the Decisional Information they might produce will also be missing, creating Decisional Information Risk. In other words, shortcomings in the presence of controls visually exposes the Decisional Information Risks.

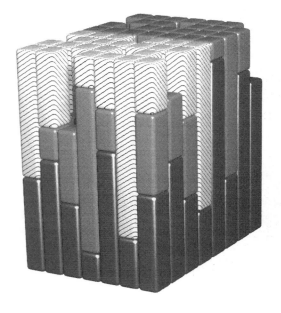

As a result, the Trust Prism can represent a *trusted* block (in which Results outweigh Risks) visually without sacrificing awareness of the calculations the Risks require. Notice how the Results substantially outweigh the visualized Risks.

One final tweak is required to adjust to the complexity with which stacks, blocks, and layers are assembled. In the preceding images, within each block each stack is equal in size, suggesting that a DM considers the values of each Result and each Risk are equal in weight. That, of course, is not reality—different Results and Risks have different influences on our trust decisions in every frame. Figuring out how to present those variations visually was challenging, but the solution is fairly simple to explain.

The Trust Prism assigns a value of 1.00 as the full weight of a block and begins with the assumption that Results and Risks have an equal value of 0.50. In this scenario, no presumption of trust is possible because Results and Risks are equal. As Decisional Information and Rules interact, the DM will adjust those values, with the totals of all Results and Risks "forced" to add to 1.00. In other words, a DM must rank and prioritize the stacks within each block as part of calculating trust. Key to those calculations are the same values discussed in Chapter 17 (notably frequency, causality, and probability) that mathematics can generate. As a result, the DM can see the weight of each Result and Risk independently and in an overall view of the related block (see image on next page).

Weighting Information is largely Decisional Information based on historic performance. As new performances occur with each measure of time, their performance Data (as Evaluation Layer Information) is inputted into the ongoing calculations. High performing Blocks and Stacks gain weight; those experiencing Risks shift in how they are weighed, so that even a single adverse event can dramatically alter the levels of trust placed in a TDT because of the ensuing Expenses and failures to achieve desired Results; all this can be visualized with the Trust Prism.

Similar aggregations occur for all of the blocks in a layer, and for all of a TDT's layers.

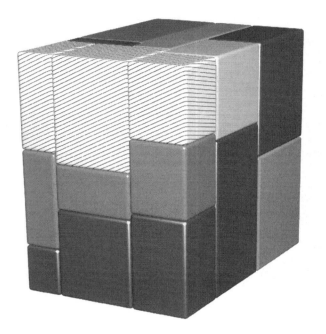

A suitable question is, "Does affirmative trust require Results to outweigh Risks in every block and layer?" While the Trust Prism does not require that outcome, it becomes difficult to imagine a block for which a DM calculates Risks to be more likely than positive Results! Since a final trust calculation ("Trust or No Trust") takes into account all of the blocks and levels within a Trust Prism representation of a TDT, it certainly is possible to have some blocks (and even layers), negatively weighed by the Risks, offset by strong affirmative weights for Results in other blocks and for the TDT as a whole.

TOURING THE TRUST PRISM SO FAR

At this point, we have explored the structure of the Trust Prism; visualized its levels, blocks, stacks, and the Information "mortar" among them; and learned how to express the Assets and Attributes of any TDT visually. The rules-based nature of trust decisions is emphasized by the stacking that begins with the foundation of the Public Layer and the pairing of Resources onto Rules. All of these line up nicely with the Rules for the Trust Prism introduced in Chapter 22. Remember, the Trust Prism is a visualization of very complex Information and expresses all the moving parts of any trust decision. As mentioned earlier, the flexibility of the Trust Prism is that even complex TDTs can be presented in multiple layers; there is no rule that limits the number of layers involved. The layers represent both the manner in which a TDT processes Information (based on the UIM Layers) and the enforcement boundaries of the Rules for the related Resources.

Even working on a whiteboard (i.e., without technology), you can construct a visual model of any TDT using the Trust Prism. By focusing on the components of a TDT, identifying TDC_{RES} that you cannot control and capturing the movements of all of the related Information, you transform your capabilities to evaluate the suitability of a TDT. Now, before exploring the varied ways you can use the Trust Prism, it is time to take one further step in understanding how the Prism can help create wealth.

VISUALIZING REVENUES AND EXPENSES

Since each Descriptive Specification and each Functional Specification, composed correctly, must include measures of Time, viewing them in the Trust Prism allows us to visualize the Costs (Revenues and Expenses) of a TDT. The required Data is already being captured behind the scenes; with each measure of Time, the Decisional Information required to calculate Costs can and should be collected (remember, the RCRs require both measurement and reporting). A DM merely turns the switch to begin.

Calculating Costs begins by tracking Time, identifying the Expenses of Assets (Rules, Resources) and Attributes (Results, Risks), and then allocating the Revenues generated by proper performance of Work. These Costs are accumulated, beginning at the stack and block level, and netted. Incremental Costs can be very small and, particularly

> With each measure of time, the Decisional Information required to calculate Costs can and should be collected . . . A DM merely turns the switch to begin.

for digital TDTs, the Revenues and Expenses of a specific Resource may be allocated across all of the Work performed or supported by that Resource. For Risks (including, of course, the full, related Risk Inventory), the Expenses must include the related charges for repair, replacement, recovery, and corrective action, their calculations based on probabilities and projected net present values (just as insurance companies calculate coverages).

The economic success or failure of any Resource can be added into any visual display of the stacks, blocks, and layers within the Prism. While shown in gray scale here, the capability of doing so in color (green for Revenues, red for Expenses, for example) increases the ease of visual navigation and analysis.

Imagine using this capability to focus a Value Calculation on Resources in order to expose those that are *not* showing success at producing Results and Revenues pursuant to the Rules. The Trust Prism isolates the related layers, blocks, and stacks, and a DM gains greater transparency to analyze the non-conforming performance. Similarly, when Costs are turned on, the weights and trust calculations can shift; once Costs are considered, a single Risk with enormous potential economic adversity can mathematically shift the probability of a TDT being trusted.

None of this is new to probability mathematics or the utility of existing risk management methodologies. What the Trust Prism and its related tools achieve is a significant shift in management's point of view: instead of focusing from the beginning on Risk, first calculate whether there is affirmative trust. The Trust Prism does so visually, allowing full consideration of the depth and complexity of TDTs.

INTEGRATING THE DESIGN PRINCIPLES

Like the laws of gravity, in which mass attracts mass, trust also has force. Trust attracts trust. TDTs, Resources, and Information that perform properly pursuant to the Rules by which a DM calculates trust attract other TDTs, Resources, and Information. This is how TDTs become more complex and interdependent as they develop functional, interactive trust. This is how systems achieve velocity. Just as atoms achieve cohesion, so too can TDTs aggregate and become more complex. They do so by communicating Information between the Resources that serves as Decisional Information that fuels the continuing flow of trust decisions.

The Statement of Need and the Design Principles connect powerfully to this dynamic truth. The Trust Prism provides a means to do so visually. When TDTs can be trusted, they can be assembled into larger, more complex systems. The Risks normally associated with complexity can be seen more clearly because of the understanding

Like the laws of gravity, in which mass attracts mass, trust also has force. Trust attracts trust.

that emerges of the pairings (and gaps) in the flow of Decisional Information. Using the Trust Prism, we can achieve transparency in the design and governance of the TDTs and, with that, accelerate velocity at every frame, in every layer, and in each decision chain linked together into each trust decision.

What can a fully functional, digitally enabled Trust Prism look like? This illustration is just one effort to show all of the preceding working simultaneously.

As hinted at the beginning of Part II of this book, the full potential of the Trust Prism can be imagined thinking of science-fiction action films in which the hero, such as Tony Stark in *Iron Man*, is investigating a data crime involving the breach of a system. Imagine he waves his hand and brings up a 3-D hologram of a Trust Prism visualizing the system that was breached. He expands his hands and is able to look at individual layers; he points a finger and pulls out individual blocks and examines the information mortar to see where the leaks occurred; and he points and selects individual stacks to expose the Rules not executed and the gaps in compliance that the bad actors exploited. A flick of the wrist and he can now see the underlying Decisional Information the system had been generating. Another flick and he pulls in an integrated object built of Rules and Resources and plugs it into a block that was the root cause of the leaks. The new object is activated, the functional and economic outcomes update, and the system, as a TDT, has been restored. That is just how the Trust Prism can work.

The Trust Prism is a map, a blueprint, and a dynamic reporting tool that creates visibility into complex assemblies of Information. It is powerful for evaluating existing TDTs to decide whether to trust them to perform Work. It is invaluable for designing, building, and implementing new TDTs. It is a magnifying glass that brings into focus when Rulebases can be improved. The Trust Prism can also be dangerous, when used by those challenging or seeking to compromise TDTs that are vulnerable or unstable. In the next chapter we survey those capabilities and their utility for different stakeholders in any ecosystem.

CHAPTER 24

USING THE TRUST PRISM

AT EVERY MOMENT IN BUSINESS, trust decisions are being made. Within every company, those decisions are made by professionals—IT architects, developers, security managers, chief executives, traders, sales representatives, accountants, and lawyers—and by machines—networks, systems, devices, and applications. Nothing in this book has suggested that a DM must be a human being. The Trust Prism and the tools presented here will be most valuable to improving how we build and achieve trust in the decisions made by the digital TDTs in which we place our trust.

As you learned in Part I, each trust decision includes a Functional Calculation, a Value Calculation, and a Process Calculation. The Trust Prism supports each of these. What is astounding is that all DMs—human or machine—are calculating their trust in each other simultaneously. Trust is never stable. Trust is dynamic and entirely reciprocal, mutual, and interactive within every ecosystem and with every trading partner. It is not enough to make a trust decision and be done; the selection and use of a TDT creates an

> Trust is dynamic and entirely reciprocal, mutual, and interactive within every ecosystem and with every trading partner.

> The Information required to calculate trust is in a constant state of change, with Decisional Information itself subject to validation at each exchange point through which it passes.

appetite for an ongoing flow of Decisional Information required to confirm the validity and durability of that trust decision. The Information required to calculate trust is in a constant state of change, with Decisional Information itself subject to validation at each exchange point through which it passes.

This chapter presents some examples of how you can use the Trust Prism to make better trust decisions and overcome the complexity and opacity that challenges us in achieving digital trust. As you review these, begin to think of the Trust Prism as a management dashboard that enables continual trust decisions across the full portfolio of responsibilities you must execute.

FUNCTIONAL CALCULATIONS WITH THE TRUST PRISM

Using the Trust Prism, a DM can evaluate an existing TDT to calculate its suitability to perform Work and produce the Results required by the Rules (the Functional Calculation). Those evaluations are nearly continuous from the first frame of any decision process—identifying, organizing, aligning, and calculating the fit of Circumstances, Rules, and Resources, measured against Descriptive Specifications and Functional Specifications, and accounting for the adverse weight of Risks.

As a practical matter, the Trust Prism enables significant improvement of design processes. The rules-based design concept is not new in IT engineering, for example. But the Trust Prism demands that we expose the SIAM Words in any Rule and construct suitable bridges to enable proper composition and alignment of the Execution Layer Rules with the Resources. When overlooked or ignored by applying the Rhett Butler Rule, the outcome will always be new Risks that degrade whatever level of trust was otherwise presumed.

The Trust Prism can be used to improve confidence by a DM when selecting among alternative TDTs to perform Work. For each option, using the Trust Prism creates transparency and accountability. Here the Velocity Principle is particularly useful—a vendor that offers the Decisional Information required by a customer (acting as a DM) will always achieve a competitive advantage, provided its Decisional Information can be trusted and it can be trusted as a Decisional Information Source.

Similarly, the Trust Prism can be used to visualize and structure more efficiently the complex decisions made at any exchange point to qualify and validate the Information that moves among the Resources within complex TDTs. Recall that there is much redundancy in many systems; with the Trust Prism, we can synchronize the Rules so that an earlier, affirmative calculation can be recorded and communicated among exchange points. This only works, of course, if the Rulebases for the exchange points align; the Trust Prism (and the URM) helps those calculations of equivalence accelerate.

Perhaps the management dashboard value of the Trust Prism with the greatest economic value is found in its utility allowing a DM to visualize the continuing operations of a TDT. No different than the radar system tracking aircraft or a railroad network map, the Trust Prism can be used as a visual expression of how Data confirms or contradicts the performance of any Resource against the Rules. Decisional Information can be mapped immediately against both Descriptive Specifications and Functional Specifications to confirm the suitability of performance. The 3-D quality of the Trust Prism goes beyond the single color displays of so many current digital management tools; the scaling of colors and weights introduces precision, granularity, and the dimensionality that allows different perspectives, exposing otherwise hidden Resources, Results, Risks, and Costs, all tied to Rules seeking Information and metric-based Results.

Companies and regulators share a mutual interest in achieving transparency; doing so allows automatic, continual measurement of compliance with Public Layer Rules. With government as the largest external consumer of corporate Information, reducing the Expenses that both sides incur in creating, accessing, and validating such Information ultimately creates greater wealth. Regulators want to know that systems, as TDTs, are functioning according to the Rules. Companies want to devote minimal amounts of capital to non-wealth producing activities. The Trust Prism delivers with greater efficiency the visibility that guarantees those results, while both sides also can detect and address much earlier any non-conforming Resources and institute corrective actions and remediation.

VALUE CALCULATIONS WITH THE TRUST PRISM

Recall that Value Calculations follow Functional Calculations. So, with each example of how to use the Trust Prism for Functional Calculations, a DM then can turn on the switch to measure and produce Value Calculations. With that second calculation, budgets and returns on investment can be defined with greater precision. Once selected and used to perform Work, a TDT's economic value can be measured continually, with a new visibility into the activity-based costs and the value of Time. When presented with optional TDTs, the Trust Prism allows DMs greater control in their analyses of the related economic consequences of their decisions.

Here is where consideration of Risks can be integrated more effectively into the trust decision process. Because Risk-based adverse events can impact operations, Risks are weighed and ranked in

Because Risk-based adverse events can impact operations, Risks are weighed and ranked in trust decisions by their economic consequences.

trust decisions by their economic consequences. Using the Trust Prism, we can better calculate the full impact of Risks because of the emphasis placed on connecting Resources to control of Risks beyond the TDT and addressing all of the Resources listed in the Risk Inventory.

When jointly conducting trust decisions with trading partners and across ecosystems, addressing Risks as part of any trust calculation changes the dialogue, as well as the flow of Decisional Information, among the stakeholders. In the discussion of mergers and acquisitions (in Chapter 14), you may recall that the transactions often involve the brokering of Information so that we can calculate accurately the value of the target company in negotiating the purchase price. The same is true in every trust decision—Information is the Resource required to calculate the economic impact of both Results and Risks. The Trust Prism enables greater visibility into understanding what Decisional Information is required for that purpose and creates earlier availability of the Information indicative of disruptions or failures in performance tied to identified, known Risks.

PROCESS CALCULATIONS WITH THE TRUST PRISM

At T Minus and Holding, a trust decision evaluates the integrity of the decision process itself. Here is where the Trust Prism has its greatest value. The visual display of a TDT's trustworthiness in the consistent structure of the Trust Prism (organizing all of the moving parts into layers, blocks, and stacks) requires that the process have structure and integrity. Exclusions pursuant to the Rhett Butler Rule, patches that do not truly pair to or control Risks, presumed values for calculating compliance with Rules—all of these weaknesses in trust decisions become immediately visible, earlier in time, using the Trust Prism. As a result, the Prism enables better trust decisions by making it more difficult for a DM to act without

At T Minus and Holding, a trust decision evaluates the integrity of the decision process itself.

calculating trust properly. Instabilities in the process result in voids within the Prism.

For official authorities, a productive use of the Trust Prism will be to supervise, monitor, and examine the regulated entities under their jurisdictions. Recall that regulators proceed generally with a presumption of *distrust* for corporate Information assets. As the largest external consumers of corporate Information assets, governments incur substantial Expenses to calculate whether to trust the Decisional Information and Decisional Information Sources they must evaluate to serve the public interest.

The Trust Prism introduces an opportunity for transparency and Rules-based execution in IT systems that can shift the emphases and Expenses associated with overcoming the presumption of distrust. Putting aside the political questions, there is little doubt that China and Europe have recognized the importance of creating integrated trust within their respective economies. Doing so begins with developing trust in the related systems that are the sources of Information used to enforce Public Layer Rules. For that purpose, the Trust Prism becomes invaluable.

Unfortunately, as mentioned in Chapter 21, the Trust Prism is also powerful when used by malicious actors seeking to exploit Resources not within their control. Indeed, it is likely true that the Trust Prism's structure reflects some of the best practices of the bad actors at finding the vulnerabilities and gaps to be exploited within systems. In other words, their tools work the same as the Trust Prism to expose the TDT_{RISKS} that exist! Their tools locate the gaps where Rules have not been composed, where Resources have not been paired to Rules, and where ongoing performance Data is not being properly supervised to identify non-conforming behavior. They achieve entry when the Rules are not being governed.

In modern curricula for IT and software security engineering students, debates are actively underway as to whether to teach how bad actors succeed in exploiting vulnerabilities in systems and gaining improper access to Information. Those favoring teaching the way bad actors succeed argue that, unless an engineer understands how the bank robbers succeed, the engineer will not know how to design safe banks. The Trust Prism introduces a level of transparency that ends the debate, empowering all within an ecosystem, including the bad actors, with equivalent capabilities.

THE RULES FROM DIFFERENT PERSPECTIVES

Imagine a Trust Prism offered in a negotiation between seller and buyer, service provider and client, or company and regulator. The Prism delivers a basis for dialogue that is different, jumping past the inertia inherent to the exchanges that require us first to validate the trustworthiness of the seller, service provider, or company as a Decisional Information Source operating a TDT that delivers Information. Visibility at the design phase into the Rules-based architecture of the TDT (and, in turn, the Information), focuses the participants on their respective Rules. We can identify differences in the Rules and, in turn, evaluate the suitability of Resources for performing under those Rules.

The practical exercise is similar to taking the Trust Prism and, when the Compliance Rulebases used by both sides of the negotiation do not align, replacing the conflicting Rules in the same manner as performing an R & R. Rules are revised, Resources are aligned (or adapted), weights and Costs are inputted, and trust is recalculated. Decisional Information Risks are more visible and the dialogue focuses now on achieving mutual trust, rather than pressuring one side or the other to take the risks of not doing so.

It also is interesting to contemplate how the Trust Prism may be used in negotiations to select a TDT from among competing vendors. A buyer using the Prism can identify more objectively the variances in vendors' service offerings (which are Functional Calculations) and more precisely calculate the competing Costs (both Expenses and Revenues) each optional TDT may produce (Value Calculations). This is exactly what the CIO at Wise Industries and her team were unable to do—they could not compare apples to apples effectively. As competitive pressures push ecosystems toward unified adoption of standards (and the development of Execution Layer Rules that automate compliance), a buyer can identify the similarities and isolate the differentiations more quickly. The R & R process allows those to be recalculated and the results visually displayed in a Prism presentation in order to evaluate whether the differences in pricing align to the differences in the actual Rules and their implementations within the respective TDTs of the vendors.

Once again, that analysis is focusing on the Rules and their implementation. The logical implication is to accelerate the conformity within ecosystems and, in turn, the transparency of the competitive differentiations. Across nearly four decades of IT innovation, the winner in competitive battles often has prevailed only because of small differences in the Rulebases on which their TDTs were designed. The Trust Prism delivers opportunity to those who can demonstrate those differences to their customers. Historically, those vendors have prevailed for two reasons. First, the customers recognize the differences and, in selecting the vendor's offering, adopt the same Rules as their decision criteria. Second, the vendors consistently demonstrate proven performance against those Rules, creating interdependency with their customers that endures, with both customer and vendor achieving sustained Results.

Thus, in all of its potential applications, the Trust Prism represents a new Resource for the Work of creating wealth. What Jack Welch thought, but did not say, is, "When there is trust, there is wealth!" That, however, is *just* how it works!

In all of its potential applications, the Trust Prism represents a new Resource for the Work of creating wealth.

CHAPTER 25

ENTERING THE WAR AND WINNING THE REVOLUTION

ACHIEVING DIGITAL TRUST will require building something new, not merely patching Dead Man's Curve. It will require, as Marc Benioff proclaimed, a revolution. Revolutions usually begin wars, insurrections fueled by frustration that boils over from conspiracy to action. However, in this case, the war is already underway. The revolution requires entering battles already in progress. I believe the Net will survive and prosper as the infrastructure for human society only if those who embrace and prioritize the values and consequences of building and sustaining digital trust can prevail. The revolution must win.

Even now, victories and defeats are being tallied by counting who controls how the new Rules will be composed, who defeats those trying to compose new Rules, and, if new Rules emerge, who is first to perform under those Rules. Nations, regions, industries, and malicious actors are all engaged, battling to control the outcomes.

Enormous capital is being invested, and more is to follow as we shift the world from valuing turf, to valuing control of Information. It is not an understatement to suggest that achieving digital trust is one of the grand challenges that this, and future generations, will face.

Just as the CIO at Wise Industries realized taking the call meant entering into an entirely new mode—collaborating with the competition to write the Rules—you will have to make a decision as to how you, your team, your company, and the ecosystems in which you engage must confront the same challenges. Your decisions will be critical. Your decisions must be trusted by those you lead, by those within your ecosystems, by regulators, and even by those against whom you compete.

THE TOOLS AND THE WEAPONS TO WIN

This book has delivered many new tools and weapons for shifting momentum in the war on trust and beginning to win. The strategy is, of course, to author the Rules required to make decisions and execute transactions with velocity. Microseconds and nanoseconds are now the measure of success. The Velocity Principle means everything. In closing, this chapter identifies what it means to enter the battle, and offers suggestions on the first steps to prepare. Like many wars underway when entering the battlefield, you have very little time to prepare.

A "MAGIC" TRUST ALGORITHM?

I have been often asked: "Is there a magic algorithm we can use to execute the trust calculations?" No, there is not. There is, however, tremendous energy being invested toward closing in on that outcome. Within academic communities, building and maturing trust models is underway, with various mathematical expressions being formulated and tested. The References and Additional Sources identify various conferences addressing digital trust and selected papers and monographs I have evaluated in my research (new ones will be published on the website supporting this book). The conferences, and the energy invested in all of the presentations and papers that are considered and chosen for these venues, confirm that nations, institutions, and individuals perceive enormous economic value in improving the execution of digital trust. That is terrific news.

The Glossary for the Trust Vocabulary includes various examples of basic notations with which to represent some of the key design principles visually. These are intended to help accelerate connecting the content presented here to the need to develop the algorithms. The website supporting this book will also evolve to reference additional work toward the algorithms. However, my own research to try to find a magic algorithm shaped the direction of this book in two ways.

First, there did not seem to be any overall framework or model of the trust decision process; many projects and studies seemed to have emphasized small, incremental, individual steps in building digital trust. Sensor networks, detection of leaks in oil pipes, reliable data packet delivery, context-aware sensors, mobile ad-hoc networks—these are the technology focal points for this area of research. They are very focused, very granular, but lacked an overall context. So, in response, the Trust Decision Model evolved into being.

Second, without any exception I was able to locate, all of the work on computational trust seemed to *presume* the existence of trust in a specific Net element (such as a sensor node), and then focus on how we calculate the threshold of distrust in that element. Yet, as presented earlier in this book, an affirmative decision to trust is how we select and use TDTs; the trust decision is occurring, but in doing so, DMs are selecting the option to presume "Yes, insert '1'" without the objective Decisional Information, and otherwise incur Decisional Information Risk. By creating the business case for transparency regarding how we govern Information, the Velocity Principle confronts the continued viability of presuming trust. By contrast, the Velocity Principle provokes us to strive to reduce our trust in any digital TDT asset, not merely Information, for which we cannot access the Decisional Information with which to evaluate its governance.

The astounding innovations of BitCoin™ and cipher block chaining now underway are captivating. They use mathematics to automate the contracting, distribute the control of the related Information (contracts, transaction records, files), and create trust without centralization. Their work stands as the first evidence that some have already entered the revolution—to see the passion of warriors in the faces of the 20-somethings that are leading those initiatives is thrilling.

NEGOTIATING TRUST

About a year before completing the manuscript for publication, I attended a conference of law professors who teach contracts. I could not help but chuckle when one professor suggested during a floor discussion, "Well, using technology to help draft contracts is helpful, but technology will never eliminate the need for lawyers to draft the agreements."

To the contrary, the Net has become nothing less than a magnificent, functioning, vibrant contract engine. A single packet may cross dozens of exchange points moving from sender to receiver within milliseconds. Each interaction is a negotiation and validation against known Rules. Automated trading in securities and driverless automobiles are merely two examples of how Rules are being automated into Resources and, in turn, how we are trusting Resources to evaluate Circumstances, apply those Rules, and make decisions that will be trusted. On-demand networking and dynamic Cloud-based computing services are digital TDTs pursuing the same design strategies.

One paper, "Establishing Agreements in Dynamic Virtual Organizations" (included in the References and Additional Sources) is worth a look.

The research in computational negotiation now must connect directly to the substantive Public Layer Rules through which contracts can be finalized and become enforceable across the broad dimensions of global commerce. The Velocity Principle simply does not align with the continued presence of SIAM Words in the Rules expressed in Implementation Layer contracts, policies, and procedures. Instead, relying on the RCRs (and future innovations) will help migrate the rule of law into comprehensible automated expressions that will assure certainty, predictability, and trust in the transaction parties' shared understandings. Automated enforcement becomes possible.

The Unified Rules Model is a starting point for how to architect Rulebases that can support automated negotiations as substantive, enforceable agreements. The predicates necessary to gain functionality and impact for those Rulebases must be prioritized. At the same time, we must create enforcement mechanisms that are automated from the inception of transactions, assuring continuing execution against the Rules and removing responsibility for resolving disagreements or conflicts regarding the truth from the control of lawyers and others who leverage and manipulate SIAM Words to preserve their wealth.

THE VOCABULARY OF TRUST

Shared vocabularies are essential to conducting business. International trade, computing, finance, education—virtually any sector of society gains velocity when there is shared vocabulary with known meanings. Digital trust is no different. There is no finality in the trust vocabulary presented here; consensus on a shared vocabulary is like any standard—there must be a first draft with which to begin.

As others join the trust revolution, a shared vocabulary becomes a tool for velocity and certainty; evolutions and adaptations of the trust vocabulary, and even the development of entirely new semantics, are encouraged. To achieve digital trust, we must speak with shared understanding. Therefore, the Glossary here begins by directing you to the website for this book, where you are invited to challenge, edit, compose, and evolve the vocabulary itself. To ignore the opportunity to do so is to remain off the battlefield and wait to be conquered.

See Huang and Nicol, 2010, "A well-defined semantics of trust," in the References and Additional Sources.

IMPLEMENTING THE UNIFIED INFORMATION MODEL

The global information management community continues to invest enormous resources toward developing unified mechanisms and tools for enabling the effective management of the digital knowledge of the human race. Only a few have been mentioned in these pages, but uniformity and standardization are essential to the vibrancy of the Net and each new thing we build to enrich the functions, speed, and reliability with which Work can be performed.

In my own research across this broad field, as with the Trust Decision Model, there did not seem to be a unified understanding of the layers of Information required to calculate trust and improve the governance of information. The Unified Information Model was not developed to be in conflict with existing projects. Instead, it seeks to accelerate our shared understanding of how to compose and adopt connections between the works underway (and their related models, profiles, vocabularies, and rules) and how to make rules-based calculations of digital trust in Information.

BUILDING DATABASE ARCHITECTURES TO CALCULATE TRUST

There is no question that effective calculations of trust will require navigating and processing considerable Data and Decisional Information, far more than can be presented on a dinner napkin. Those writing the new Rules must go beyond and design and build Rulebases from which we can extract and compose Rulebases for specific TDTs and ecosystems. Storage networks must be designed with suitable function and resilience to present and use those Resources in the collaborative, consensus-based mechanisms that digital trust will require. In many respects, the Data already is being gathered; what is not occurring is aligning that Data to serve as Decisional Information for rules-based trust calculations.

One of the first places to start is to create appropriate database architectures that can scale to the requirements of supporting any trust decision for any TDT. The structures must allow the pairings among the Assets, Attributes, and Costs that trust requires and that empower the continual calculations any TDT will demand. Researchers I have met are working to transfer the understandings presented in these pages into their own initiatives—another marker that the revolution is already underway.

TRUST IN THE RULE OF LAW

Achieving digital trust must be made a priority of governments; those that have not already done so are at considerable risk of downward spiraling their economies' into second class status. As ubiquitous computing is achieved (the image of everyday citizens in India, carrying three cell phones, is evidence of how close we are to that reality), digital trust will become the single most important competitive differential within human society. Nation-states that position their Rules to stimulate the private sector to build global digital trust will generate genuine advantage across both the public and private sectors—there is ample reason for why the European Union has committed to achieving a Single Digital Market for their member nations. Doing so is required to compete, and to survive. They understand the war is already underway.

The consequences of neglecting digital trust are now visible. Spending on information security is nothing less than an overwhelming Expense, consistent with the Dilemma of Dead Man's Curve, to patch an infrastructure that was neither designed to support the velocity and volumes of the global demand, nor to protect and safely enable the creation, transit, and storage of valued digital property. The costs are becoming staggering; in March 2014, an authoritative study by PwC concluded that the digital theft of trade secrets was having an adverse economic impact equal to three percent of a nation's annual gross domestic product. For the United States, that damage nears an annual cost of $500 billion.

To shift toward building digital trust, nation-states must acknowledge that existing sanctions are increasingly difficult to enforce, and move toward a regulatory scheme that favors, and provides incentives for, stakeholders that commit to trust-based business methods. Already, both in the United States and other nations, companies that can certify their compliance with third-party standards are receiving direct benefits from government agencies. For example, the United States Environmental Protection Agency allows companies that do so for certain environmental management standards to receive expedited processing of certain types of licenses. Why would the agency do so? Because the certified compliance with the standard demonstrates that the company is aligned to the public interests sufficiently, and that further regulatory scrutiny is not required and, in fact, can be reduced. As the Project Innovate team realized, achieving digital trust will make many accumulative contributions toward greater wealth.

Similar reformations of public sector rules could greatly improve the motivations for corporate stakeholders. This is not a call for reduced public regulation; instead, it is an advocacy for a different kind of regulation in which the nation-state acknowledges the global competitiveness its constituents must navigate and moves away from localized, non-standardized Public Layer Rules and toward international standards that help position companies to demonstrate the metrics that global ecosystems are now demanding. In doing so, governments can shift their orientation from sanctions-based rules dressed in SIAM Words toward standards-based, measurable requirements that provide incentives for companies to embrace delivering trust as a means to create and sustain new wealth.

CONCLUSION

I began to think about digital trust at the earliest stages of my professional career. The simplest question began the journey: "How will the rule of law enforce purchase contracts that are not written?" It has taken that long to work through the complexities, continuously striving to reduce my own ignorance, tolerating the distractions and challenges of making a living, and, in the final analysis, trying to compose a coherent expression of what will be required to achieve digital trust. This book is that expression.

It is fundamental to our human nature to make trust decisions. The Net has become essential to our existence. Whether or not this book prescribes the right direction, we will not survive as a global community unless we commit to establishing and maintaining a new architecture that enables trust in the digital assets of our world. The solution, I believe, is found in understanding that trust is the essential predicate to the creation of new wealth. Working collaboratively, the world's population can achieve both trust and wealth.

Perhaps the greatest power of the Net is its ability to enable trade and commerce for anyone, from micro-farmer to global enterprises. The curious thing about trade is that, when it proceeds properly, enriching all stakeholders, it is the ultimate disincentive for war. We are most reluctant to do battle against those with whom we do business. If achieving digital trust can expand our capacities to trade and connect us effectively into a broader trade network, the strongest possible incentives for sustaining peace emerge. That is my fondest hope for the Net, that it will be the infrastructure for enabling peaceful, global coexistence and not become a perpetual, bloody battlefield. To realize that dream, we *must* achieve digital trust!

In the eyes of my students today, in the passion of those already engaged in the revolution, and in the energy of professionals I have trained and mentored in prior decades who now are engaging with the cause, I see the enthusiasm, resolve and daring to move ahead, build something new, shift the momentum in the war, and win

The curious thing about trade is that . . . it is the ultimate disincentive for war.

the revolution. Their sense of the global challenges is mature, and they are proceeding forward with a respect and sensitivity for all humankind that I find inspiring.

May this book be a meaningful contribution toward empowering their success at doing so for the benefit of their generations and the generations that follow. May this book be the fuel that ignites you to enter the war and join them in winning the revolution.

TRUST DECISION TOOLS

FOR THE CONVENIENCE of readers, the key tools presented in this book are reproduced in this Appendix as full-page images that can be copied directly from the book.

RESOURCES

RULES

INFORMATION

TIME

THE RULES FOR COMPOSING RULES

- WHEN DOES THE RULE APPLY?

- WHO IS THE ACTOR TO PERFORM WHAT THE RULE REQUIRES?

- WHAT IS THE ACTION THE ACTOR IS TO PERFORM?

- WHAT IS THE OBJECT OF THE ACTION?

- HOW WILL PERFORMANCE BE MEASURED?

- HOW WILL PERFORMANCE BE REPORTED?

- TO WHOM WILL PERFORMANCE BE REPORTED?

- WHAT ARE THE INCENTIVES AND SANCTIONS FOR PERFORMANCE?

— UNIFIED RULES MODEL —

PUBLIC LAYER

FORMAL LAW	FORMAL PRINCIPLES
INTERPRETATIONS	INTERPRETATIONS

IMPLEMENTATION LAYER

BUSINESS RULES	TECHNOLOGY RULES
INTERPRETATIONS	INTERPRETATIONS

EXECUTION LAYER RULES

HUMAN RESOURCES	TECHNOLOGY & PHYSICAL RESOURCES	PROCESS	INFORMATION

— UNIFIED INFORMATION MODEL —

DESCRIPTIVE LAYER

DESCRIPTIVE ELEMENTS	CONTENT ELEMENTS	ACTIVITY DESCRIPTION

EVALUATION LAYER

INTERNAL PERFORMANCE METRICS	EXTERNAL PERFORMANCE METRICS	EXTERNAL EVALUATIONS

NAVIGATION LAYER

CONTENT LAYER

CODE/RULES	FACT	FICTION

TRUST VOCABULARY TERMS

THIS BOOK ASSEMBLES and uses a vocabulary of terms with which stakeholders can begin to have conversations toward achieving digital trust. This Glossary organizes those terms into a single location and provides a *working* definition for each term, a reference to the initial chapter in which the term is introduced and, if appropriate, a symbolic notation that may be useful.

The website for this book located at www.jeffreyritter.com/DigitalTrust includes this Glossary and invites you, the reader, to ask questions, suggest revisions, improvements, or introduce new terms useful to the work ahead. As in the story told in this book, now is the time to collaborate on developing a shared vocabulary.

Activity Description is a part of the Descriptive Layer of the Unified Information Model (Chapter 19).

Activity Description Information is Information presented in the Activity Description Sector of the Descriptive Layer (Chapter 19).

Anticipated Causality means a DM possesses (and can directly access) Information that enables a probability to be calculated that the Work can be accomplished through the use of, or reliance on, one or more Resources (Chapter 4).

Assets are the Resources and Rules of a TDT (Chapter 16).

Attributes are the Results and Risks associated with a TDT (Chapter 16).

Block is the building component of the Trust Prism, representing a unit of Work (whether composed of one or more Tasks) and the related Result and Risk Stacks from which it is composed (Chapter 23).

Chaining is the process of how the decisions within a trust decision connect together (Chapter 3).

Chasm of SIAM is the functional gap between the ambiguity of SIAM Words and the precision required by IT systems, devices, and applications (Chapter 15).

Circumstances are those Context elements that have a known causality on how the Work will be performed. If part of a TDC, they are designated TDC_{CIR} (Chapter 4).

Code is a Resource that includes any type of software, whether source code or object code, which instructs computers how to perform specific processes, Tasks, or Work (Chapter 6).

Compliance Rulebase is a Rulebase for a TDT which is designed to align a TDT to the requirements of any TDC_{RUL} such as a Public Layer Rule, corporate policy, or commercial agreement (Chapter 15).

Content Elements are a part of the Descriptive Layer of the Unified Information Model (Chapter 19).

Content Layer is a layer of the Unified Information Model in which the primary content of Information is classified into one of three sectors: Fiction, Fact, or Code/Rules (Chapter 19).

Context is the surrounding environment in which Work is to be performed, described by known Circumstances and Resources (Chapter 4).

Costs include both Revenues and Expenses (Chapter 16). In the Trust Prism, Costs are visually presented in color gradations on a net basis for a specific stack, block, layer, or TDT.

Data is a Resource which is Information required by systems to perform Work or produced by systems as output (Chapter 6). Various Information-related classifications can also be assigned to Data, including Decisional Information and any classification within the Unified Information Model.

Decision Maker (DM) is the entity making a trust decision. A DM may be either an organization of human beings, a single individual, or any digital device executing Rules governing the trust decision (Chapter 3).

Decisional Information is the Information required by the Rules within a TDC (or specific to a TDT) to execute a trust decision (Chapter 5).

Decisional Information Risk exists when Decisional Information required by the Rules for a trust decision is not present, or the Information or Decisional Information Source for that Information has not been separately calculated to be trusted (Chapter 8).

Decisional Information Source is a Resource from which a DM acquires Decisional Information (Chapter 8).

Descriptive Elements are a part of the Descriptive Layer of the Unified Information Model (Chapter 19).

Descriptive Layer is a layer of the Unified Information Model that contains sectors for Descriptive Elements, Content Elements, and Activity Description, each relating to a primary Information asset (Chapter 19).

Descriptive Specification ($_{SP}$) is a complete factual description of the dimensions, features, and characteristics of a TDC_{CIR}, TDC_{RES}, TDT, or TDT_{RES} (Chapter 5).

Execution Layer is a layer of the Unified Rules Model that contains Rules for Human Resources, Technology & Physical Resources, Processes, and Information (Chapter 18).

Expenses are the expenses incurred to secure the production of Revenues and the performance of the Work (Chapter 10). Expenses are also a measurement of the costs incurred by Risk-based adverse events.

Evaluation Layer is a layer of the Unified Information Model includes sectors for Internal Performance Metrics, External Performance Metrics, and External Evaluations, each relating to a primary Information asset (Chapter 19).

External Performance Metrics are a part of the Evaluation Layer of the Unified Information Model (Chapter 19).

External Evaluations are a part of the Evaluation Layer of the Unified Information Model (Chapter 19).

Formal Law Rules are a part of the Public Layer of the Unified Rules Model (Chapter 18).

Formal Principles are a part of the Public Layer of the Unified Rules Model (Chapter 18).

Functional Calculation is the calculation within a trust decision in which a DM determines whether a TDT is functionally capable of performing the Work (Chapter 9).

Functional Specification ($_f$SP) is a complete description of how to measure the performance of a TDC$_{CIR}$, TDC$_{RES}$, TDT, or TDT$_{RES}$. Examples include measuring velocity, volume, units per time, watts per kilogram, purity, etc. (Chapter 5).

Human Resources are Resources consisting of human beings capable of performing Work or specific Tasks (Chapter 6). A DM may be a Human Resource.

Human Resource Rules are a Rules classification within the Execution Layer of the Unified Rules Model (Chapter 18).

Implementation Layer is a layer of the Unified Rules Model that contains Business Rules and Technology Rules and Interpretations for each (Chapter 18).

Information is factual information required to author, execute, follow, apply, or make trust decisions based on Rules (Chapter 3).

Information Rules are Rules within the Execution Layer of the Unified Rules Model (Chapter 18).

Internal Performance Metrics are a part of the Evaluation Layer of the Unified Information Model (Chapter 19).

Interpretations are Rules which interpret one or more Rules located with sectors or layers of the Unified Rules Model that are higher 'parents' of an Interpretation (Chapter 18).

Known Causality means that a DM possesses (and can directly access) Information that a Circumstance can cause different outcomes in the success or failure of the Work (Chapter 4).

Layer is a layer within the Trust Prism composed of Blocks (Chapter 23). Layer also is used to describe layers within the Unified Rules Model, the Unified Information Model, and elements of the trust decision process.

Mandatory Pairing is when Work cannot be completed properly unless a specific Rule, Resource, or Circumstance is included in the manner in which the TDC, Work, or TDT is described. (Chapter 5).

Mobile Rules are Rules designed to be performed by any actor responsible for its execution (Chapter 12). When paired with Information, Mobile Rules enable consistent governance of the Information by travelling with the Information.

Navigation Layer is a layer of the Unified Information Model representing Information used to navigate a primary Information asset (Chapter 19).

Pairing is the action of creating relationships, based on Rules, among the variables taken into account by a trust decision. Pairings may reflect Anticipated Causality, Known Causality, or the requirements of specific Rules (Chapter 5).

Physical Assets are Resources which are tangible, physical assets of any size or dimension, and include any computing device or technology (Chapter 6).

Principle of Indifference, in trust decisions, is the basis on which a DM excludes from consideration certain Circumstances or Resources whose potential for Anticipated Causality or Known Causality is measured to be so insignificant as to have no consequence in the calculations of the trust decision (Chapter 3).

Process Calculation is the calculation within a trust decision in which a DM determines whether Rules governing a trust decision process have been followed (Chapter 11).

Process Rules are Resources that describe how a system's components work together to accomplish Work (Chapter 6). They are what make a system perform as a system, and activate how Physical Assets and Human Resources connect. Process Rules are also a classification within the Execution Layer of the Unified Rules Model (Chapter 18).

Public Layer is a layer of the Unified Rules Model that contains Formal Law Rules, Formal Principles, and Interpretations for each (Chapter 18).

Resources are the assets within a TDC from which TDTs may be assembled or selected. Resources are distinguished from Circumstances by the capability of Resources to be controlled (Chapter 3). Resources may be Physical Assets, Human Resources, Process Rules, Code, or Data. If part of a TDC, they are designated TDC_{RES} and, if part of a TDT, they are designated TDT_{RES}.

Results are the affirmative outcome of a Task to be performed, defined by both a Descriptive Specification and a Functional Specification (Chapter 8).

Revenues are the positive income and contributions to value that a TDT is calculated to produce when used to perform Work (Chapter 10).

Rewind and Recalculate (R & R) is the process within a trust decision in which a DM pauses the decision, rewinds the process to an earlier point in the decision chain, and recalculates the variables to take account of new Information regarding any of the moving parts within the decision (Chapter 3).

Rhett Butler Rule is the basis on which a DM knowingly excludes from the TDC Circumstances or Resources that are appropriate candidates for inclusion within the TDC. The Rule also describes any decision by a DM to otherwise knowingly exclude Rules or Information that are otherwise available for the calculation of a trust decision (Chapter 4).

Risks are the adverse outcomes and consequences that may occur when using a TDT to perform Work or a Specific Task. A Risk is defined by both a Descriptive Specification and a Functional Specification (Chapter 8). Risks are represented in the Trust Prism by Risk Stacks. By example, Risks may be described in notation form as TDC_{RISK} or TDT_{RISK}.

Risk Reserve is that amount reserved from income to pay for possible Expenses of Risk-based adverse events (Chapter 10).

Risk of the Unknown Risk is the Risk within any trust decision in which Circumstances within the Context exist and their impact on a TDT or the performance of Work is not included in a trust decision (Chapter 11). It is another means of expressing the inherent gap between trust that is capable of calculation and perfect trust.

Risk Inventory is a part of any Stack or Block, identifying the Resources at risk if a Risk-based adverse event relating to same occurs (Chapter 23).

Rulebase is a database of Rules relied upon to calculate a trust decision for a specific TDT within a specific TDC (Chapter 15).

Rules are the basis on which a trust decision proceeds. Rules do one of three things: they express what is required, what is permitted, or what is prohibited. If part of a TDC, they are designated TDC_{RUL}. If part of a TDT, they are designated TDT_{RUL} (Chapter 4).

Rules for Composing Rules (RCRs) are a set of Rules relied upon to compose the Rules with which to calculate trust decisions (Chapter 16).

SIAM Words are those words or phrases used in Rules that exhibit semantically intentionally ambiguous meaning (Chapter 15). Examples includes, but are not limited to, "reasonable; appropriate; suitable; material; as necessary; properly responsive to; and commercially acceptable."

Stack is a component of a Block, classified either as a Results Stack or a Risks Stack, within a Trust Prism (Chapter 23).

Tasks are units of Work, usually a single action, event, or decision that contributes to the final outcome of the Work (Chapter 8). A Task is defined by a Descriptive Specification and a Functional Specification. In the Trust Prism, a Task is represented by a Stack within a Block.

Technology & Physical Resources Rules are a Rules classification within the Execution Layer of the Unified Rules Model (Chapter 18).

Trust Decision Context (TDC) is a subset of the Context; the boundary of a TDC defines Circumstances and Resources taken into account by a trust decision (Chapter 4).

Trust Decision Model is a visual model for structurally expressing the layers and moving parts of a trust decision as a consistent, dynamic process (Chapter 3).

Trust Decision Target (TDT) is the target of a trust decision—a tool, a system, a device, data, or other Resource—evaluated to determine whether it can be trusted in performing Work. Generally, for digital trust, a TDT is a system or Information in digital form (Chapter 3).

Trust Discount is the amount that a buyer withholds from payment for a TDT as a possible offset against Risk-based adverse events occurring with the use of a TDT (Chapter 10).

Trusted Information (T-Info) is Information in digital format that has been affirmatively calculated to be trustworthy based on identifiable and accessible Rulebases for which the records of that calculation are also identifiable and accessible (Chapter 17).

Trust Prism is a visual, 3-D expression of a TDT and its Assets, Attributes, and Costs, presented in layers, blocks, and stacks (Chapter 23).

Unified Information Model (UIM) is a visual, interactive tool for organizing, identifying, and classifying Information assets in order to better design and execute trust decisions (Chapter 19).

Unified Rules Model (URM) is a visual, interactive tool for organizing, identifying, and classifying all of the Rules to be considered in structuring a trust decision (Chapter 18).

Value Calculation is the calculation in which a DM determines whether a TDT will produce the intended Costs, measuring expected Revenues and Expenses (Chapter 10).

Velocity Principle is a design principle for achieving digital trust which provides that, "The Velocity of Information is proportional to the transparency of its governance" (Chapter 12).

Weighting Information is Information required by Rules and used to measure and evaluate a TDT and its respective Assets, Attributes, and Costs (Chapter 23).

Work is the description of the Results to be accomplished by a DM, either acting alone or by using one or more TDTs, within a defined TDC (Chapter 3).

REFERENCES AND ADDITIONAL SOURCES

THIS LISTING OF REFERENCES and additional sources is merely an abbreviated accounting of the increasing volume and diversity of research, scholarship, and creative thought on the topics and issues that define the boundaries and substance of digital trust.

The website for this book located at www.jeffreyritter.com/DigitalTrust includes these References and Additional Sources and invites you, the reader, to ask questions, suggest revisions, improvements, or introduce new references and resources useful to the work ahead to build and achieve digital trust. As in the story told in this book, now is the time to collaborate on developing a shared awareness of the building blocks and knowledge on which further work can advance.

Books

Alberts, Christopher, and Dorofee, Audrey. *Managing Information Security Risks: the OCTAVE approach*. 2003. Boston: Addison-Wesley.

Bachmann, Reinhard, and Zaheer, Akbar, ed. *Handbook of Trust Research*. 2006. Cheltenham, UK: Edward Elgar Publishing Limited.

Bayuk, Jennifer L. et al. *Cyber Security Policy Guidebook*. 2012. Hoboken, NJ: John Wiley & Sons, Inc.

Boss, Amy and Ritter, Jeffrey. *Electronic Data Interchange Agreements: A Guide and Sourcebook*. 1994. Paris, France. International Chamber of Commerce.

Bosworth, Seymour, and Kabay, M.E. *Computer Security Handbook Fourth Edition*. 2002. Hoboken, NJ: John Wiley & Sons, Inc.

Boulding, Kenneth E. *The World as a Total System*. 1985. Beverly Hills, CA. Sage Publications.

Buthe, Tim, and Mattli, Walter. *The New Global Rulers: The Privatization of Regulation in the World Economy*. 2011. Princeton, NJ: Princeton University Press.

Covey, Stephen M. R. *The Speed of Trust: The One Thing that Changes Everything*. 2006. New York: Free Press.

Deming, W. Edwards. *Quality, Productivity, and Competitive Position*. 1982. Boston: Massachusetts Institute of Technology.

Gladwell, Malcolm. *Blink: The Power of Thinking Without Thinking*. 2005. New York: Little, Brown & Company.

Harvey, Miles. *The Island of Lost Maps: A True Story of Cartographic Crime*. 2000. New York: Random House, Inc.

Lessig, Lawrence. 1999. *Code and Other Laws of Cyberspace*. New York: Basic Books.

Lidwell, William, Holden, Kritina, and Butler, Jill. *Universal Principles of Design*. 2003. Gloucester, MA: Rockport Publishers, Inc.

Marris, Marie-Helen. *Computer Forensics: cybercriminals, laws, and evidence*. 2012. Sudbury, MA: Jones & Bartlett Learning, LLC.

Mitchell, David. *Cloud Atlas: A Novel*. 2004. New York: Random House.

Morville, Peter. *Ambient Findability: What We Find Changes Who We Become*. 2006. Sebastopol, CA: O'Reilly Media, Inc.

Pande, Peter S. et. al. *The Six Sigma Way: How GE, Motorola, and Other Top Companies are Honing Their Performance*. 2000. New York: The McGraw-Hill Companies, Inc.

Ritter, Jeffrey. *Defending Electronic Mail as Evidence—The Critical E-Discovery Questions*. 2008. Reston, VA: Waters Edge Consulting, LLC.

Ritter, Jeffrey, and Worstell, Karen. *Evaluating the Electronic Discovery Capabilities of Outside Law Firms*. 2006. Silver Spring, MD: Pike & Fischer.

Schneier, Bruce. *Liars & Outliers: Enabling the Trust that Society Needs to Thrive*. 2012. Indianapolis, IN: John Wiley & Sons, Inc.

Usselman, Steven. *Regulating Railroad Innovation: Business, Technology, and Politics in America*. 2002. New York: Cambridge University Press.

Wood, Denis, with Fels, John. *The Power of Maps*. 1992. New York: The Guilford Press.

Reports

Internet Security Alliance. *Contracting for Information Security in Commercial Transactions: An Introductory Guide.* 2005. Arlington, VA: Internet Security Alliance.

Internet Security Alliance. *Navigating Compliance and Security for Unified Communications.* 2009. Arlington, VA: Internet Security Alliance.

NORDIPRO, The Trade Facilitation Committee of the Nordic Council. *Special Paper No. 3: Legal Acceptance of International Trade Data Transmitted by Electronic Means.* 1983. Oslo: Uiversitetsforlaget.

Articles and Papers

Alexander, Carol. "Bayesian Methods for Measuring Operational Risk." Discussion Papers in Finance 2000-02. 2000. Reading, UK: ISMA Centre. http://www.icmacentre.ac.uk/pdf/discussion/DP2000-02.pdf.

Huang, Jingwei and Nicol, David. "A Formal-Sematics-Based Calculus of Trust". 2010. 14 Internet Computing, IEEE 38.

Kaplan, Robert S. and Anderson, Steven R. "Time-Driven Activity-Based Costing". Harvard Business Review. November 2004. https://hbr.org/2004/11/time-driven-activity-based-costing.

Ryutov, Tatyana, Neuman, Clifford, et al. "Establishing Agreements in Dynamic Virtual Organizations". http://www.isi.edu/~tryutov/papers/SECOVAL2005.pdf.

Zachman, J.A. "A Framework for Information Systems Architecture. 1987. Available at: www.cesames.net/wp-content/uploads/2010/04/ibmsj2603e.pdf.

Additional Web Resources

Greico, Anthony. "Trust and Transparency". http://blogs.cisco.com/security/trust-and-transparency#more-170659.

Kennedy, John. "The digital revolution needs a trust revolution, tech leaders tell Davos." 22 January 2015. https://www.siliconrepublic.com/companies/2015/01/22/the-digital-revolution-needs-a-trust-revolution-tech-leaders-tell-davos.

McConnell, Ryan, Ralston, Dianne, and Simon, Charlotte. "Can Computer Models Form Risk Compliance Programs?" 2013. Law Technology News. ALM Media Properties, LLC. www.AmericanLawyer.com.

Neutze, Jan. "Trust and Transparency: Building Blocks for a Single Digital Market". http://blogs.microsoft.com/eupolicy/2015/06/03/trust-and-transparency-building-blocks-for-the-digital-single-market.

Papers, 2014 IEEE 13th International Conference on Trust, Security and Privacy in Computing and Communications (TrustCom), 24-26 September, 2014. http://ieeexplore.ieee.org/xpl/mostRecentIssue.jsp?punumber=7008824.

Roth, Daniel. "Jack Welch Says Only Two Words Matter for Leaders Today: Truth and Trust". April 21, 2015. http://linkd.in/1GhYqOy.

Schneier, Bruce. "Our New Regimes of Trust". Available at: https://www.schneier.com/blog/archives/2013/02/our_new_regimes.html.

The Center for Responsible Enterprise and Trade and PwC. "Economic Impact of Trade Secret Theft: A framework for companies to safeguard trade secrets and mitigate potential threats". 2014. https://www.pwc.com/en_US/us/forensic-services/publications/assets/economic-impact.pdf.

The White House Summit on Cybersecurity and Consumer Protection. February 2015. https://www.whitehouse.gov/issues/foreign-policy/cybersecurity/summit.

Organizations

Cloud Security Alliance. www.cloudsecurityalliance.org.

Dublin Core Metadata Initiative. www.dublincore.org.

Global Legal Information Network Foundation. www.glinf.org.

Trusted Computing and Trusted Infrastructure Research at Oxford, July, 2015. http://www.cs.ox.ac.uk/people/andrew.martin/trust.html.

United Nations Commission on International Trade Law. www.uncitral. org.

Uniform Law Commission (also known as the National Conference of Commissioners on Uniform State Laws). www.uniformlaws.org.

World Wide Web Consortium. www.w3.org.

Other Public Law Materials

General Data Protection Regulation of the Council of the European Union (as of 11 June 2015). http://data.consilium.europa.eu/doc/document/ ST-9565-2015-INIT/en/pdf.

Regulation Systems Compliance and Integrity ("Regulation SCI"), 2014. Securities and Exchange Commission. http://www.sec.gov/rules/ final/2014/34-73639.pdf.

United Nations Commission on International Trade Law. *United Nations Conventions on the Use of Electronic Communications in International Contracts.* 2007. New York: United Nations.

ACKNOWLEDGEMENTS

ON AUGUST 1, 2014, while training for a 400 mile bicycle race, I crashed. Badly. We will never know what happened precisely, but I and my bike went over the edge of a bridge at full speed into a gulley, falling nearly 25 feet. The bike was fine. This book's progress toward publication, however, was delayed a bit.

Unlike Humpty Dumpty, I was put back together again by an amazing team of medical professionals with remarkable success. Now, days away from the first anniversary, with virtually no permanent disabilities, five vertebrae of my neck are held together by titanium rods and screws and I am otherwise completely fine. When you read this, I will be riding again, teaching my courses, and actively preaching the gospel of digital trust.

There is one person who has made this book possible—above all others, she deserves recognition for which no words will ever be enough. Jane Kuhar is my wife, my best friend, my rock, my soulmate, and one outstanding, kick-ass editor. She truly did save my life, climbing into the gulley to find me, nursing me to health, refusing to say "No" in opposition to my rather stubborn tenacity, and loving me unconditionally. In creating this book, she has imagined with me, inspired me, challenged me, fed me when I forgot to eat, provoked me to think harder, and constructively made every page better. In return, she has my heart. Forever.

Before Jane came into my life, three other women gave me what no man deserves, their unconditional belief that my work was important, in which they invested amazing sacrifices, generosity, and patience. Rita Soronen, my friend for life since the day I met her walking home from high school, my wife of nearly 25 years, and the incomparable mother of our daughters, stood beside me through what were both the brightest and darkest parts of this journey with unquestionable love and loyalty. Patricia Ritter, my mother and a soul of great courage and love whose spirit lives on, cheered for me to reach whatever unreachable star I chose to pursue. Amy Boss, an incomparable leader, patient coach, and role model against which to model my professional development, gave me loving friendship, tutoring in the art of making good rules, and unwavering tolerance for my enthusiasm to always want to do more.

The final production of this book was achieved with the invaluable contributions of five additional people. Peter Higgins was the first (and only) person to read the full, complete working draft of this book (70,000+ words longer) and recognize the book was not just about digital trust but trust decisions. David Hazard has been a tremendous literary coach, whose gentle hand provoked many long, hard hours re-shaping the book to be what appears on the preceding pages. Paul McTaggart is the graphic artist who produced the crisp, sharp images that visualize the tools presented here; he is a "best practice" in digital trust since Paul and I have never met and we worked entirely digitally. Peter Gloege, of Look Design Studio, created the design for the book and its cover.

Lee McIntyre did an exceptional job proof-reading the manuscript. Don't let any author ever suggest a book is theirs alone; it takes a team and I am fortunate to have the support of a small, effective group that worked in the same direction.

It is impossible to allow the balance of these acknowledgements to suggest any priority or preference. Each of these people have made contributions that have inspired me to do more, to embrace and demand excellence from myself, and, when pushed down, to rise again. To each I am grateful.

Other first readers of this book's contents provided comments and encouragement that were the early fuel to keep going—my son-in-law David Tucker, Leslie Wharton, David Mortman, David Briglia, and my brother by choice, Russell Nomer. Alex Santos, who taught me so much about visualization, learning, and instructional design, convinced me to press on. Sam Horn, a brilliant coach to authors and speakers, contributed so much direction; all of the members of the writer's workshop retreat in which she included me made the adventure so much less lonely, particularly my sister by choice, Trish Whynot, and Sue Jacques, the CivilityCEO©, whose wise counsel was the "tipping point" for discovering the visual trust prism structure. Brandon Lichtenwalner, a graduate student at Johns Hopkins University, was courageous enough to not only read the manuscript but undertake to build a prototype of the relational database architecture required to implement a Trust Prism.

The Devil's Advocate in Chapter 10 is Walt Whalen, a renaissance man skilled in technology, accounting, and product development who has been a loyal friend for nearly 15 years. Dr. David King, with whom a single dinner conversation created the most enduring friendship, one distinctively colored by our capacity to talk deep theory about digital trust with equal enthusiasm for comparing the qualities of our bicycles, has often given the most important encouragement. Chuck Csuri, considered the father of computer animation, taught me the beauty of visual objects and the potential of computing to make them. Jim Scheeler, one of America's most important global leaders in architecture, taught me and inspired me to see structure and layers differently.

But this book is, in many respects, a chronicle of discovery that unfolded across a career of nearly 30 years, a learning experience influenced by literally hundreds of partners, adversaries, clients, colleagues, protégés, executive assistants and friends. Perhaps the most courageous was the late Dr. Charlie Bender who said early in my international legal work, "Well, if you want to change the world, you are going to have to reduce your ignorance." He was right, and his decision to bet on me made all the difference. Others are gone as well, retired, or out of touch, but not forgotten: Bernard Wheble, Anne Troye, Ray Walker, Anne de la Presle, Paola Palmerini, Renaud Sorieul, Hal Burman, Jim Johnson, Marusa Damjan--each of whom helped me view the world and its complexity with greater honesty and humility.

Bruce Nielson, Hank Judy, David Cohen, Peter Kalis, Lee McCorkle, Ken Warren, Stanley Schwartz, Bob Schwartz, Rich Rubenstein, Jack Levey, Robert Ellis, Alan Solomon, Paul Alagia, Dick Trautwein—each were partners that helped me learn the skills of lawyering and advocacy with patience that few could imagine. David Gaston, Ben Hayes, Nuala O'Connor, Russell Austin, Jon Talotta—five examples of many young lawyers for whom it is my good fortune to be considered as a mentor, each of whom have achieved high levels of excellence as digital lawyers. David Whitaker, Pat Fry, Tom Vartanian, Vince Polley, Michael Baum,

Candace Jones, Corinne Cooper, Sue Daly Tobias—each an ABA colleague that taught me many invaluable lessons in leadership and were so infinitely patient with my "learning curve". Ken Gilman, Verna Gibson, Howard Gross, Don Cohn, Richard Jackson, Simone Seth, Steve Katz, Jon Thurlow, David Cullinane—a small list of the human beings who trusted me to deliver legal services for their companies that enabled me to have a career of service that was so enormously rewarding.

Over three decades, their titles evolved—secretary, administrative assistant, executive assistant—but anyone who worked with them knows that Janice Yohman, Cheryl Stevens, Lori Smith and other exceptional professionals who sat in a chair outside my office made me look and perform far better than I was capable. And to each, whether in heaven or on Earth, I confess I still am often delinquent with my travel expenses!

Finally, unrelated to the book, a word of recognition for the many, many friends that have cheered for me, rode beside me on my bike, sent encouragements through Facebook, and made this life so much richer because they have considered me as their friend. To name any is not to omit the importance of any of them, but these friends have meant so much: Craig Clark, John Chamberlain, Turtle Wilson, Art Tapera, Pete McIntyre, Jamie McIntyre, Sarah Gerould, Lesley Smith, Carol Brooks, Liz Delfs, Bob West, Kim Esteran, Eric Esteran, and "my bestest friend ever" Patrick Bowles, who really was Mickey Mouse at Walt Disney World.

Jeffrey Ritter
Reston, Virginia
July 12, 2015

JEFFREY RITTER  has pursued the challenge of figuring out how to achieve digital trust since 1982, when he was first asked to give a legal opinion on the validity of a purchase order to be sent by fax to China in substitution for a "wet ink" signature on paper. Since then, his career has been shaped by the demands for new bridges to be built across the chasms between law and each new generation of information technology. His passion for doing so has taken him around the world and throughout cyberspace.

Jeffrey has pushed the envelope in nearly every dimension of his education and career. He was recognized as the first student at The Ohio State University to receive his B.A. and M.A. degrees concurrently with a perfect "A" average. He attended Duke University School of Law and actively practiced law for nearly three decades in Louisville, Columbus, and Washington, DC, representing some of the world's finest companies and most adventurous start-ups. But he also left the practice of law more than once to conduct academic research, work for a dot.com, and ultimately pursue the challenge of achieving digital trust.

Jeffrey was the Founding Chair of the American Bar Association Section of Business Law Committee on Cyberspace Law. He served the United Nations Working Party on International Trade Facilitation Procedures as a Co-rapporteur on Legal Questions for nearly a decade and actively contributed to the global legal framework through which online electronic commerce and international trade now occurs. At the Ohio Supercomputer Center at The Ohio State University, he started one of the world's first academic research programs on the law of cyberspace. His previous books and professional publications have addressed electronic commerce, automated contracting, electronic discovery, and information security best practices.

Today, Jeffrey serves as an external lecturer at two of the world's great universities, teaching professionals pursuing graduate degrees in software systems security and engineering. At Johns Hopkins University, he teaches courses he has built on information security policy management and privacy engineering. At the University of Oxford, in the top-ranked Department of Computer Science, he teaches Building Information Governance. He has also taught at Georgetown University Law School.

Jeffrey is an active contributing author on the Internet, including on YouTube, BrightTalk, SearchCIO and SearchCompliance.com, a frequent public speaker, and an advisor to c-level executives. He maintains a website at www.jeffreyritter.com.